* Volumes with an asterisk following the title are a part of the NCRLL set: Approaches to Language and Literacy Research, edited by JoBeth Allen and Donna Alvermann.

(Continued)

The Administration and Supervision of Reading Programs

Fourth Edition

EDITED BY

Shelley B. Wepner
Dorothy S. Strickland

FOREWORD BY Jack Cassidy

TEACHERS
COLLEGE
PRESS

Teachers College, Columbia University
New York and London

Published by Teachers College Press, 1234 Amsterdam Avenue, New York, NY 10027

Copyright © 2008 by Teachers College, Columbia University

Library of Congress Cataloging-in-Publication Data

The administration and supervision of reading programs / edited by Shelley B. Wepner and Dorothy S. Strickland. — 4th ed.
    p. cm. — (Language and literacy series)
  Includes bibliographical references and index.
  ISBN 978-0-8077-4849-7 (pbk. : alk. paper)
  1. Reading—United States.   2. School management and organization—United States.
3. School supervision—United States.   I. Wepner, Shelley B., 1951–
II. Strickland, Dorothy S.
  LB1050.2.A36 2008
  428.4'071—dc22

                                    2007032085

ISBN 978-0-8077-4849-7 (paper)

Printed on acid-free paper
Manufactured in the United States of America

15 14 13 12 11 10 09 08   8 7 6 5 4 3 2 1

A teacher affects eternity; he can never tell where his influence stops.
—Henry B. Adams, 1906, The Education of Henry Adams

Again, to our parents, our first role models and supervisors:
Carole and Bernard Markovitz
Evelyn and Leroy Salley, Sr.

To our families for giving us the opportunity to continue the legacy of our parents:
Husband, Roy Wepner; and daughters and sons-in-law, Meredith and Judd, Leslie and Marc

In memory of husband, Maurice Strickland; to sons, Mark, Randy, and Michael, and
grandchildren, Chelsea, Rebecca, Cooper, Paige, Hannah, Neala, and Michaela

And to our friend and colleague James Flood, one of the chapter authors, who passed away
before this edition was printed, for his significant contributions as a leader of literacy.

Contents

Foreword

Many years ago I was an external evaluator for a graduate reading program at a university in New Jersey. While there, I observed a class in the administration and supervision of reading programs taught by a young, intelligent, and diligent scholar named Shelley Wepner. Since I was a former reading supervisor and also taught a graduate course on the same subject, I was particularly attentive. Needless to say, I was impressed. In a conversation at the conclusion of the class, Shelley and I both bemoaned the fact that there was not a good basic text dealing with the supervision of reading programs. We challenged each other to write one. Over the next few years, I forgot our conversation. Luckily for reading educators nationwide, Shelley Wepner did not! She and her colleague, Dorothy S. Strickland, were two of the editors of the first edition of *The Administration and Supervision of Reading Programs* in 1989. Two subsequent editions of this volume have since appeared. For all of these volumes I have had the honor of writing the foreword. More important, I have had a wonderful text to use in my graduate classes. The text formed the basis on which my whole course was organized, and my graduate students extolled the virtues of the text on a weekly basis.

Shelley and I have both moved on to other universities and other roles. Recently, I have been an associate dean in charge of graduate programs in a college of education. In that role, I developed a doctoral program in reading. Once again, *The Administration and Supervision of Reading Programs* provided the framework for one of the required courses. Although this latest edition should be a required text in all graduate programs in literacy, it will also be a valuable resource for school administrators and all literacy specialists who, in some way, serve in a leadership role.

Like the previous editions, this text is organized into four major sections: overview, program development, program implementation and evaluation, and interconnections. Each of the sections is completely updated. Particularly impressive is the list of authors of the various chapters—a veritable Who's Who in reading education.

The first section of the book gives an overview of the components of an effective reading program as well as the roles of reading personnel. It is noteworthy that Rita Bean of the University of Pittsburgh is the author of the first chapter. For over a quarter of a century, she has been studying the role of the reading professional in schools. Diana Quatroche, coauthor of the second chapter (with Shelly Wepner), is one of her former students. The last chapter of this section, coauthored by Sharon Walpole and Michael McKenna, provides wonderful insight into the role of the literacy coach. This topic is one of the hottest in the new millennium, and Walpole and McKenna have quickly emerged as two of the leading authorities on this role.

The second section of the book deals with the development of reading programs from the preelementary level through adolescence. With the increased prevalence of pre-K–level programs, the chapter on preelementary programs is particularly relevant. Former International Reading Association (IRA) president Dorothy S. Strickland of Rutgers University gives some excellent and practical insights into what should be included in such programs. Two other IRA presidents, Richard Vacca and Kathryn Au, are also contributors to this section. In an era of standards, the focus on standards-based change at the school level is especially significant in this section.

As in previous editions of this volume, the third section of the book deals with all the necessary components of a school reading program—materials, professional development, observation, and assessment. All of the chapters in this section have been significantly revised with an increased emphasis on media literacy: How should school personnel select videos and software for the literacy program? Also included is information on large-scale assessments that have become reality in most classrooms in the United States. Most important, though, this section provides knowledge about how literacy specialists and school administrators can use information from all assessments to become a school of data-driven classrooms.

The last section of this volume deals with different types of interconnections: interconnections between reading, writing, and technology; and reading interconnections with diverse populations and special needs students. Particularly noteworthy is the expanded discussion of the needs of English language learners and culturally diverse populations. There is also cutting edge information on response to intervention models, a full-scale effort to decrease the number of referrals for special education and to meet the needs of struggling readers in the regular classroom. As in the third section, much new information is also provided about the increased role of technology in all literacy programs.

I concluded my foreword in the last edition of this volume with a paragraph of thanks to the editors for providing my students and countless other graduate students with a valuable reference in helping them organize a school reading program. This edition will also provide relevant information and research to present and future graduate students. Furthermore, school administrators at all levels need to read this volume to better understand exactly how a reading program should be organized at both the district and school levels.

In short, Shelley Wepner and Dorothy Strickland have done it again! They have provided us with a relevant, research-based, and readable reference on the organization of school reading programs, an often neglected area in reading education.

Jack Cassidy
Associate Dean for Graduate Studies and
  Professor of Education
Texas A&M University–Corpus Christi
  President of the International
  Reading Association, 1982–1983
President of the College Reading Association,
  1999–2000

Acknowledgments

Edited books are only as good as the individual and collective efforts of the authors who write the chapters. We were fortunate to find authors who were knowledgeable in their respective fields, able to write a chapter with our formulaic image in mind, and willing to revise their chapters until they blended perfectly with the other chapters. Time and again, as we went through yet another round of sending chapters back and forth to someone for something, however important or trivial, we would remark to each other that we were in the best of company. We found ourselves in awe of and inspired by our authors' dedication to the writing process. Authors need to be able to communicate a message that not only can stand on its own but also adds, with just the right measure, to the overall mission of the book. We acknowledge with great appreciation the contribution of each of our authors for their significant role in helping this fourth edition come together.

We pay tribute to Joan T. Feeley who, while no longer one of the coeditors, was instrumental in developing the purpose and contents of this book. We attribute the inclusion of the chapter on writing to Joan's vested interest and work in this area. We also thank Joan for introducing Shelley to Dorothy more than 25 years ago to begin their writing collaborations.

There also are those people on the sideline who contribute directly or indirectly to a publication. Particularly important to recognize is the work of graduate assistants Kris Sullivan and Laura Sullivan for their remarkably sophisticated ability to help with so many of the parts of the book that needed careful and precise attention. Special thanks also to Laura Sullivan for capturing in a photo one of her special student's enchantment with his favorite book. Also significant was the work of our main photographer, Cindy Tangorra, who took time away from her other life to use her photography skills to capture the magic in classrooms and wonder of those who make these classrooms alive with learning. She worked tirelessly with reading personnel, administrators, teachers, and students to identify the perfect shot for many of the chapters in the book. We also sincerely acknowledge those in the photographs who have allowed us to publish a slice of themselves and their classroom life within the professional community. Special thanks to the students, faculty, administration, and parents of the George Washington Elementary School in White Plains, New York, for allowing us to photograph special learning moments. Appreciation is extended to the principal, Terri Klemm, and fifth-grade teachers, Jonathan Monti and Karen Sullivan, for working with us to secure the photographs. Also important to thank is the incredible research work of graduate assistant Paige Cohen who helped to summarize and synthesize information needed from the outset for this book.

We recognize that this fourth edition would not exist without the kind and sincere support of former Teachers College Press Acquisitions Editor Carol Collins. Without fail, Carol was responsive to our questions, encouraging with our plans, and tactfully helpful with our mission. From the beginning, we knew that Carol was in our court, and quite naturally, we are deeply appreciative of her efforts to get us started. We acknowledge the work of Susan Liddicoat who edited the first draft. The entire book is that much stronger because of Susan's unusually strong editing abilities and precise attention to detail. We also appreciate the support of Carole Saltz, the Director of Teachers College Press, who enabled us to publish this fourth edition. Carole's ongoing belief in this book's mission, even with an ever-increasing competitive market of other books on this topic, inspired us to provide the most current and informative book possible.

On a more personal level, we acknowledge the understanding and support of our families, friends, and colleagues. They continue to have this uncanny ability to look the other way when we are late for a social event, miss a deadline or a meeting, or are simply unavailable for the chitchat that makes life that much more full.

Finally, we thank you, the readership, for letting us know again that a new and expanded edition was needed, and would be read.

Looking Forward, Looking Back

Shelley B. Wepner and Dorothy S. Strickland

The fourth edition of *The Administration and Supervision of Reading Programs* represents dramatic changes in literacy education growing out of new legislation at the national level. Referred to as the No Child Left Behind Act of 2001 (NCLB), which was signed into law on January 8, 2002, this legislative mandate makes high-stakes testing, standards-based instruction, and scientifically proven strategies the responsibility of the teaching community.

As a result of NCLB, we as leaders of literacy are more accountable than ever to develop, maintain, and cultivate pre-K–12 literacy. We have had to reform administrative policies and instructional practices to ensure that our colleague teachers are using assessment-driven instruction and responsive adaptive teaching with all types of students (suburban and urban, rich and poor, monolingual and multilingual) at all different grade levels.

Reading First, one of NCLB's programmatic initiatives, provides funds for high-poverty, low-achieving schools to help close the achievement gap. Literacy coaches have been hired to work with teachers so that those teachers can help their students read on grade level by the end of third grade. In fact, one of the greatest changes since the last edition of this book is the growth of the role of the literacy coach. Literacy coaches are responsible for working with classroom teachers as they implement best practice in relation to the five components of

reading (phonemic awareness, phonics, fluency, comprehension, and vocabulary). Depending on state guidelines, literacy coaches are coming from the classroom or are taken from the traditional reading specialist position. The reading specialist role has also been changing to address higher expectations for reading achievement across the grades. To acknowledge this changing role, standards for the reading specialist have been revised to reflect the need to serve as both leaders of literacy and instructors of literacy.

Given that this book focuses on the oversight of reading programs, the role of reading personnel needs to be addressed. Equally important to address is the impact that NCLB is having on different facets of the reading program at all levels of instruction for different types of learners, for example, on selecting materials, developing students as writers, assessing student learning, determining and improving teacher quality, and providing professional development. While the form and framework of NCLB could change with different federal leaders, basic elements from the law, such as standards-based instruction and accountability, probably will not.

This fourth edition aims to help prospective and current leaders of literacy understand how to organize and supervise reading programs within the context of current federal and state mandates. The 31 authors included here provide new insights as they articulate what leaders of literacy programs should know and be able to do. Examples, observations, and research are used to make this text both practical and readable. As with previous editions, the book is divided into four parts; however, chapters have been added, eliminated, and overhauled to incorporate the many and varied changes in literacy education.

Part I provides an overview of reading supervision by describing effective reading program components and the personnel for program implementation. A new chapter on literacy coaches provides a firsthand look at how literacy coaches function in schools and districts in different states. Part II presents guidelines for developing reading programs at the preelementary, elementary, and middle school/junior high/secondary school levels. Part III describes four critical areas for program implementation and evaluation: reading material selection and use, teacher observation, professional development, and assessment. The essence of these four chapters are more critical than ever for helping teachers to maximize their reading and content-based instruction and assessment. Part IV addresses components connected to the reading program: writing, technology, special student needs, and diverse student populations. There are now two chapters devoted to diverse student populations, one providing a general overview of student diversity and the other focusing specifically on English language learners (ELL) because of the growing challenge in schools to meet the needs of students whose first language is not English. The book concludes with a new chapter that helps with the overall analysis of a literacy program, offering specific guidelines for determining how well a literacy program is functioning in a school or district and ideas for helping a program improve.

What follows is a summary of the themes that recur across the four parts of the book. Related as connections and directions, these themes represent the key ideas presented by the authors. This introductory section serves two purposes: (1) to foreshadow overarching concepts and (2) to reflect back on authors' ideas. We encourage you to use this discussion to frame your thoughts for reading and then to return to it after you complete the book to reframe your thinking.

CONNECTIONS

1. *Reading Personnel, Classroom Teachers, and Administrators Need to Work Together to Use Their State and Local Standards to Create a Comprehensive Schoolwide Reading Program (Pre-K–12) That Addresses the Cultural, Ethnic, Linguistic, and Academic Diversity of Students.* Today's comprehensive reading program must be more inclusive than ever, with a focus on students at all developmental ages and stages. All types of students —those beginning to read, those struggling with reading because of special learning needs or non-English-speaking background, those developing as readers, and those advancing as readers—need to be accounted for in a comprehensive reading program.

Comprehensive reading programs need goals and objectives based on research, theory, current policies, issues, and trends. Comprehensive reading programs also need to incorporate teacher beliefs and knowledge about reading into their framework because of the pivotal role that teachers play in students' reading achievement. At the same time, teachers' instructional and assessment practices need to be in sync with state-regulated standards so that students are given the opportunity to meet standards and succeed, as best as possible, with large-scale assessment instruments.

Those responsible for guiding the development of a comprehensive reading program need to convince both key personnel and the parent community that standards provide a focus for instruction, giving all students access to a rigorous curriculum. Leaders need to work with their colleagues to align the school or district's framework for curriculum, instruction, and assessment with standards. Such a framework needs a sound theoretical base, realistic instructional goals, and benchmarks for students' learning that are based on knowledge of the school and the community.

Embedded within the framework are connections between instruction and assessment for both reading and writing. Materials and resources, both traditional and electronic, must be considered in light of such modifications. Equally significant is the need to maintain congruence between revised instructional/assessment practices and programs for students with special learning and language needs.

Teachers' professional development opportunities must be reviewed for their usefulness and contribution to teachers' competencies with changes in the reading program.

Any meaningful change in schools requires a time-consuming and painstaking, collaborative process of rethinking and retooling. These reform efforts, which are organic and based on the organization, require leaders who have the knowledge, skill, and leadership qualities to guide such changes. This ability requires a deep knowledge and understanding of reading research, reading acquisition, reading development, reading instruction, and assessment. It also requires the ability to convince parents, the community, and policy makers about the importance of a shared vision for reforming a reading program.

2. *Administrators and Reading Personnel are Responsible for Creating the Culture and Ethos for Change.* Administrators and reading personnel cannot expect to be expert in all disciplines, developmental levels, and areas of concern for which they are responsible. However, as successful leaders of literacy, they need to have their own set of competencies to serve as credible leaders. This entails having knowledge about the field, instructional and assessment mandates, methodologies, and materials; and using such knowledge to promote change. Such knowledge about the field comes from reading current research, getting involved with professional associations, attending conferences and workshops, working with vendors to stay informed of new products being developed, and working closely with classroom teachers and faculty from colleges and universities. It also means being aware of the conflicting demands and needs of different constituencies and having sufficient intellectual and emotional stamina to work well with all people to get the most from them. Leaders of literacy also need to know enough about a school or district to establish and communicate realistic expectations and to know when to call on the expertise of others. Still other characteristics are needed to be effective leaders, such as enthusiasm for the job and a thick skin.

A major responsibility of administrators and reading personnel is to guide the change process so that teachers perceive it as supportive rather than burdensome. An ongoing program of professional development helps teachers keep current about reading and writing instruction and understand how assessment can be used to guide instruction so that there is an overlap between what is taught and what is tested. Resources must be provided and teachers' voices must be valued in planning both the process and the content of professional development. Consideration should be given to how observations, observation conferences, and professional portfolios help assess and document accomplishments, and how action research helps develop a problem-solving mind-set for answering questions about instructional practices. Because teachers are an essential component of literacy achievement, administrators and reading personnel need to do all that is humanly possible to promote teachers' investment into changing expectations. Administrators and reading personnel play a pivotal role in the advancement of teachers as professionals, the success of instructional reforms, and the quality of educational opportunities offered to students. Administrators and reading personnel need their own professional development in order to keep abreast of current developments in effective literacy practices and assessment tools and learn new ways to coordinate the complexities of schoolwide literacy interventions.

3. *Administrators and Reading Personnel Need to Remember at All Times That the Teacher is the Key to Students' Reading Achievement.* Teachers are responsible for providing a high-quality literacy program that includes explicit instruction in the major components of reading (phonological awareness, fluency, word recognition, vocabulary, and comprehension), access to varied genres of high-quality text, and instruction in learning strategies for reading and writing (especially those related to expository text). Teachers need to understand how to frame instruction with appropriate materials that are considerate of the reader. They also are responsible for differentiating instruction so that students can become independent text readers.

Even though a simple solution for bringing students to high levels of literacy does not exist, there are different types of programs, models, and instructional practices to help students function in and out of school. Early intervention programs help identify children at risk for literacy failure and provide strategy training, immediate reinforcement, and corrective feedback. New paradigms, including response-to-intervention models, are beginning to emerge to help elementary students with special needs. These programs are especially effective when students have qualified teachers who can offer appropriate intervention, monitor and reinforce students' efforts, and expose students to effective instructional practices. These same teachers are able to work effectively with other reading personnel and special educators to provide supplemental instruction that includes not only additional time within small groups but also intensive instruction with still more time and even smaller groups for students struggling with reading. Futhermore, these teachers are equipped to be culturally responsive to English language learners by using appropriate teaching strategies and assessments.

Teachers at the secondary level need to equip students with the strategies necessary to strengthen their learning within and across specific subjects and courses. Teachers, as decision makers and problem solvers about students' learning, need to know how to use assessment data and take ownership of such data to help plan instruction. They need to be able to make decisions about next steps, based on their own assessment of students' performance results.

Professional development is an important element for helping teachers develop the competence and commitment to implement any desired programmatic changes related to their insights from assessment data. High-quality professional development is long term and, in fact, a way of life. Teachers must have a voice in both the process and content of professional development so that it is tailored to meet their needs. Teacher growth and change is most likely to occur when teachers perceive professional development as relevant to the contexts in which they teach. Peer collaboration, peer coaching, observations in one another's classrooms, and mentoring programs for new teachers are some of the many ways to promote teacher growth. Literacy coaches, as the teacher's teachers, can provide the professional development support that teachers need through coteaching, modeling, and observation with feedback.

4. Communication and Collaboration Among Colleagues and With the Community are Essential.   Dynamic reading programs emanate from strong leadership within the school as well as from sincere efforts by school personnel to reach out and involve the family and the community. Regular communication and collaboration with colleagues help educators better understand and plan for the varied complexities of reading programs. This allows leaders of literacy to take stock of the successes and failures with students, and the conditions surrounding each. It also provides for better coordination within and across grade levels, and between regular and special programs. Communication and collaboration develop communities of practice where there is ongoing reflection, problem solving, and planning. When teachers work together, they can maintain their vision of the literacy they want their students to develop, and make instructional decisions accordingly. They can figure out ways to use data to gain insights about their instruction and their students' learning. When teachers work with reading personnel, administrators, and stakeholders, they learn to respect one another's expertise as they collect, analyze, and use data to improve programs.

Communication with the community helps parents understand the reading program and support changes in the way programs are reframed to meet standards. Collaboration with the community helps bring about important initiatives that extend a school's resources. Forming Professional Development Schools and other types of partnership networks between the pre-K–12 and higher education community helps bridge the gap between theory and practice as higher education faculty and students work directly with pre-K–12 faculty and students.

In sum, these four themes communicate that leaders of literacy help determine the quality of a reading program. Leaders administer with care and competence when they possess the necessary knowledge and skill to help schools set appropriate and realistic goals, when they create a culture that values teachers' professionalism and parents' contributions in support of students' literacy, and when they do everything in their power to provide a balanced yet meaningful literacy program. Just as there is no best program for all learners at every level, nor at any level, there is no best way to supervise under all circumstances. A key to administering a program is to create a balance with one's goals, one's abilities, and one's realities.

DIRECTIONS

This fourth edition of *The Administration and Supervision of Reading Programs*, written 6 years after the publication of the third edition, contains 14 directions that speak to major shifts in thinking about educating our youth. These directions account for areas of both rapid change and steady state. They are, in fact, a set of hypotheses about the next steps needed to build on existing opportunities and discoveries. Implicit in these directions is the recognition that leaders of literacy definitely will need to know more, be more, and help more as schools change their expectations for teachers and students.

1. Continued recognition of the need for increased literacy performance of all student calls for the study and *development of comprehensive schoolwide reading programs* that reflect current research and theories about instruction and assessment, incorporate state and local standards, address all types of student needs, and focus on teachers as the lynchpin for student achievement. Rita M. Bean (Chapter 1) describes the elements that leaders of literacy must consider as they collaboratively develop effective reading programs.
2. *The roles and responsibilities of different types of reading personnel* need to be sorted so that both teachers and students are well served. Among the areas to be studied are statewide licensing requirements, educational preparation, and the types of leadership skills that are most effective in those hired to work with and oversee literacy programs. Shelley B. Wepner and Diana J. Quatroche (Chapter 2) look at ways in which the reading specialist role is changing in light of new legislation, added job description standards, and increased accountability of teachers.
3. *The effectiveness of literacy coaches' professional development* on teachers' ability to promote reading achievement needs to be studied rigorously, as Sharon Walpole and Michael C. McKenna

(Chapter 3) explain. Literacy coaching is an evolving concept that will flourish or flounder, based on its ability to improve school-level teaching and learning and its link to growth in reading.
4. Given that teachers are an unmistakable influence on students' achievement in the classroom, we need to determine *how to best help teachers develop professionally*. Bill Harp (Chapter 8) offers guidelines for observing, assisting, and collaborating with teachers so that they are equipped to create instructionally viable classroom environments. Maryann Mraz, JoAnne L. Vacca, and Jean Payne Vintinner (Chapter 9) provide guidelines for creating formal professional development programs that include school-based initiatives, university-school collaborations through Professional Development Schools and action research, and professional portfolio preparation. Critically important to teachers' growth is the development of professional development programs that are perceived as relevant and useful to teachers' instructional situations.
5. Different schoolwide and districtwide models for changing instructional paradigms in the classroom will be tried and researched with teachers so that they truly know *how to differentiate literacy instruction* using the latest methodologies. Kathryn H. Au, Taffy E. Raphael, and Kathleen C. Mooney (Chapter 5) demonstrate how to do this for elementary programs by describing the Standards-Based Change Process that already has been used in over 100 schools.
6. Increased demands to make every child a reader by the end of the primary grades will continue to impact literacy instruction and assessment at the preelementary level. Dorothy S. Strickland (Chapter 4) discusses *what administrators and supervisors need to know to promote literacy in prekindergarten and kindergarten* so that they can take a true leadership role in an area where change and controversy are likely to remain for years to come.
7. There will continue to be a renewed commitment to *develop adolescent literacy for middle and high school students* so that they are prepared to enter the adult world of the twenty-first century. Christine A. McKeon and Richard T. Vacca

(Chapter 6) explain how a new role for reading specialists and literacy coaches is evolving to help content area teachers use effective literacy strategies, appropriate textbooks, and meaningful activities in their teaching.

8. Large-scale assessment for accountability will continue to be a way of life, as Barbara A. Kapinus (Chapter 10) explains, and we will need to use *both large-scale and classroom assessments as tools for data-driven decision making* to support effective teaching and learning. However, we can anticipate that there will be a trend toward broader standards and the involvement of knowledgeable teachers in the development of such assessment tools.

9. There will be a growing use of *early intervention and prevention programs that become part of regular classroom practice* as success rates for preventing reading failure continue to become more evident. Jennifer L. Goeke and Kristen D. Ritchey (Chapter 14) describe the response-to-intervention (RtI) model, a multitiered, individualized assessment and intervention process, which is emerging as a paradigm for promoting effective teaching. How such RtI models can be implemented for students at all developmental levels will need to be researched in the coming decade.

10. The increased cultural, ethnic, and linguistic diversity in the classroom will continue to require teachers, leaders of literacy, and administrators to think differently about *instruction and assessment to meet students' varying needs*. Junko Yokota, William H. Teale, and Ruth E. Quiroa (Chapter 12) advocate for a social constructivist model with/for diverse students to help create a classroom climate that is responsive to diverse student needs. Mary Elizabeth Curran (Chapter 13), in focusing on English language learners, calls for teachers to engage in culturally responsive teaching by drawing upon students' first language and culture as a resource and by using appropriate teaching strategies and assessments to inform teaching.

11. *Instructional materials and assessment instruments* will continue to get more sophisticated, complicated, and precise. Diane Lapp, Douglas Fisher, and James Flood (Chapter 7) explain the importance of a collaborative effort among ad-

ministrators, reading personnel, teachers, and the community to make informed decisions about the best materials to select according to their local literacy guidelines, standards, and instructional beliefs.

12. *Ways to teach and assess writing effectively* will become better understood as more is known about the art and science of writing, sound instructional practices that promote writing, and research that reveals the connection between writing and literacy development. Julie K. Kidd and Karen Bromley (Chapter 11) explain that leaders of literacy need to stay current with both policies and issues related to writing instruction as well as ways to promote the reading-writing-learning connection in the classroom.

13. Literacy programs must *develop students' multi-literacies* so that they can use both the traditional texts and communication technologies that are utilized in all sectors of life. Shelley B. Wepner, Liqing Tao, and Linda D. Labbo (Chapter 15) describe what leaders of literacy can do to stay up-to-date with advances in technology so that they can help their teachers use technology effectively for instruction and assessment.

14. Reading specialists will become increasingly focused on *schoolwide evaluation of literacy programs* to help teachers change their instructional and assessment practices. James V. Hoffman and Misty Sailors (Chapter 16) use ten principles to guide reading specialists on ways to conduct evaluations that create a culture of change within a school that is ongoing and sustainable.

In looking back to look ahead, we recognize that the components for administering and supervising a reading program are essentially the same; however, the research, issues, and policies surrounding these components continue to change. Consequently, the way in which we as leaders of literacy develop and revise school and district literacy programs depends on both what has been discovered and what has been mandated. A critical factor for responding effectively to changing expectations is our collaborative leadership with teachers, other reading personnel, administrators, school districts, the community, colleges and universities, social agencies, and businesses. This collaborative leadership will continue to evolve as each constituent recognizes the value and importance of the other. Collaborative leadership is referenced throughout the book as the hallmark for identifying and implementing special programs, projects, and processes to support specific goals.

As the saying goes, "We've come a long way, baby," in knowing how to use our leadership skills to negotiate effectively in our environments to best support students' literacy development. We also recognize that many of our efforts simply are just the beginning and will continue to change as we study the impact of our individual and collective instructional, assessment, and leadership decisions on students' learning. We invite you, the reader, to join us in using and reusing our authors' insights and ideas to reach for our next developmental milestone in striving to develop literacy for all types of learners.

OVERVIEW OF PROGRAM COMPONENTS AND PERSONNEL

Part I sets the stage for this book by providing an overview of the components and personnel needed to administer an effective reading program. In Chapter 1, Rita M. Bean offers a framework for thinking about a reading program and guidelines for developing the three elements of that framework: curriculum, instruction, and assessment. She addresses how change can occur to develop, implement, and evaluate a comprehensive pre-K–12 reading program and discusses ways to promote cooperation and collaboration of all constituents in using current standards and research to develop a reading program.

In Chapter 2, Shelley B. Wepner and Diana J. Quatroche define the term *reading specialist* and describe reading specialists' roles and responsibilities in relation to instruction, assessment, and leadership. They discuss how other personnel such as classroom teachers and principals work together with reading specialists to promote literacy. They include a description of the special skills and characteristics that reading specialists should possess along four leadership dimensions, and present ideas for preparing reading specialists to assume their job responsibilities. Future directions for reading specialists are provided to help in documenting achievements and getting recognized.

Chapter 3, written by Sharon Walpole and Michael C. McKenna, defines the term *literacy coach* and explains what literacy coaches must know and be able to do. This chapter reviews the qualifications that professional organizations have established for literacy coaches. Different models for conceptualizing the role of the literacy coach are provided along with examples of the real work of coaches in various settings.

These three chapters together illustrate the necessity of having the right systems and people in place for successful reading program development.

CHAPTER 1

Developing an Effective Reading Program

Rita M. Bean

Developing a comprehensive schoolwide reading program (pre-K–2) is an important, complex, and often controversial task. During the past decade, reading education has been the focus not only of teachers, parents, and students, but of legislators, politicians, citizens' groups, and the media. The cry for additional expectations of teachers and increased literacy performance of students has never been louder. Although all schools must address the need for an effective, comprehensive reading program, criticism about the inability of schools across the nation to deal with the achievement gap between majority and poor and minority students has led to legislation such as No Child Left Behind (2001) and its programmatic initiative, Reading First, that provides funds for high-poverty, low-achieving schools. Reading First puts many demands on schools that receive grants, requiring that they adopt programs that are research-based, use assessment data for planning instruction, provide a specific number of minutes of uninterrupted reading instruction, and implement sustained, coherent professional development programs for teachers.

Concerns about the achievement gap, although extremely important, are only part of the picture, however. The need for increased attention to the development of higher level literacy skills, in order for high school graduates to compete in this technology-based, global economy, is a major issue for schools. Such concerns highlight the need for increased attention to literacy development in all content areas and across the grades. These issues have led to more interest in funding programs for adolescent students and to professional development programs for teachers in the content areas. Indeed, the recent document, *Standards for Middle and High School Literacy Coaches* (International Reading Association [IRA], 2006), addresses the need for coaches who can provide job-embedded professional development for teachers across the curriculum in these upper grades.

All schools (pre-K–12) in all communities, therefore, need to think seriously about their reading program—what it includes, how reading is taught and assessed, and the ways by which teachers are provided with the knowledge and understandings they need to implement the program. Guiding the development of a comprehensive reading program is an important role for those in leadership positions. It requires a deep knowledge and understanding of reading acquisition, reading research, reading instruction, and assessment, and an understanding of how the broader concept, *literacy*, affects and influences the reading program. It also requires an ability to create an atmosphere that encourages and rewards continual learning and change, and

thus an understanding of the dynamics of leadership and the change process. In this chapter, I present the following:

- A framework for thinking about reading program development
- A discussion of the elements of that framework
- A process for change

FRAMEWORK OF A SCHOOL READING PROGRAM

Although individual teachers may work effectively in the classroom with students, their individual efforts do not constitute an overall reading program, nor do they provide an assurance that students will receive pre-K–12 instruction that has been thoughtfully considered and orchestrated. A comprehensive school reading program must be based upon a well-developed and articulated vision of what reading is from its early stages on; it demands a concerted effort that involves all professionals in the school working toward that shared vision. These professionals include teachers, administrators, and support personnel such as reading specialists, counselors, and librarians. The development of a reading program also requires knowledge of the community in which the school or district is located and communication with parents.

Researchers who have studied effective schools and teachers indicate that a number of factors, external and internal, are present in such schools. Taylor, Pearson, Clark, and Walpole (2000), for example, in their study of primary-grade reading indicated that school factors such as parental involvement, systematic use of data and student progress, and strong buildingwide communication and collaboration were found to be important. Teacher factors included time spent in small-group instruction and independent reading, and high levels of student on-task behavior. Highly accomplished teachers used higher level questions in their book discussions and tended to ask students to write in response to reading. Explicit teaching of phonics was supplemented with coaching, in which students were taught how to apply what they were learning. Other researchers have identified similar characteristics of successful school literacy programs (Johnson, 2002; Taylor, Pressley, & Pearson, 2002).

The work of these researchers lends credence to the notion that the comprehensive reading program is a composite of many different factors; it is more than the selection of a core reading program, provision of supplemental materials, or the administration of frequent assessment measures. The goal of this chapter is to set the stage for thinking about these various elements and the need to orchestrate a process by which each is taken into consideration. The framework described in the following sections provides a model for developing a comprehensive reading program. It includes three essential elements of any school reading program: curriculum (what is taught), instruction (how something is taught), and assessment (has it been learned?). Al-though educational writers often combine curriculum and instruction when describing a school reading program, I discuss each as a separate entity for clarification and elaboration purposes. The framework is graphically portrayed in Figure 1.1.

Curriculum

1. *Establish Goals and Standards for Reading Based on Theory and Research.* The reading curriculum is the plan for guiding learning in the school; it provides the ideas for making decisions about classroom instruction. When teachers are asked to rethink the curriculum for their school, among the essential elements that they must consider is the identification of a vision with accompanying goals or outcomes for students; for example, what do we

Figure 1.1. Essential Elements of an Effective School Reading Program Pre-K–12

Curriculum

1. Establish goals and standards for reading based on theory and research.
2. Select materials that facilitate accomplishment of school goals.
3. Organize a usable curriculum framework.
4. Relate teacher beliefs and knowledge about reading instruction to research.

Instruction

1. Develop an organizational structure that highlights individual needs of students.
2. Plan instruction to make effective use of time, including additional instruction for those who need it.
3. Provide for coordination among all reading programs offered in the school.
4. Extend teachers' understandings so that they are able to differentiate instruction.

Assessment

1. Use assessment to guide instruction.
2. Develop scoring guides or rubrics.
3. Seek alignment among various layers of assessment.

want the graduates of our elementary school to know and be able to do? Our fourth graders? Our twelfth graders? In other words, the school reading program should address the need for a developmental continuum that considers the reader at all stages: emergent, beginning, transitional, intermediate, and skilled reading and writing (Bear, Invernizzi, Templeton, & Johnston, 2003).

These goals should reflect and address the standards provided by the state and the district, but other useful resources are available from current literature provided by various organizations and educational sources. Some examples include Learning First Alliance (2000); New Standards Project of the National Center on Education and the Economy and the University of Pittsburgh (New Standards, 1999); Snow, Burns, and Griffin (1998); and Standards of the National Council of Teachers of English and the International Reading Association (NCTE/IRA, 1996). Standards provide statements that indicate what students should know and be able to do at various levels, but they vary in the level of specificity and approach toward reading instruction. Educators must, of course, consider what is required by their states and districts; however, they may wish to compare their state standards with others by reading various analyses conducted by researchers (Joftus & Berman, 1998; Schenck, Walker, Nagel, & Webb, 2005; Stotsky, 2000).

Wixson and Dutro (1999) analyzed state standards for primary-grade reading/language arts and drew some telling conclusions. First, standards too often did not provide detailed information and therefore lacked the content that is unique to these levels. Second, many different arrangements were used to conceptualize and organize the field of reading, thus creating challenges for districts in developing their own standards and assessments. Third, benchmarks established by states varied from general to very specific, thus either being of little help or, at the other end, lacking flexibility. Fourth, too many documents did not provide a logical developmental sequence. Finally, in some documents there was inappropriate content or content was ignored. One of Wixson and Dutro's recommendations is that districts develop standards that provide the basis for a coherent K–12 curriculum, standards that "provide a progression of

knowledge and skills from kindergarten to grade 3 and from grade 3 through grade 12" (p. 107).

The need for standards from grades pre-K–12 is an important one. Although there will be differences in goals and implementation at the various levels, instructing students in how to become effective readers is a responsibility from the early grades through high school. Teachers in the middle and secondary schools must also address and meet the standards set for reading in their state or district. Therefore, throughout this chapter, specific ideas are discussed as they apply to middle and secondary levels.

Although standards aligned with appropriate assessments can be helpful in raising expectations for all students and help educators set appropriate goals, there are cautions to consider. Standards themselves may be confusing and exhaustive (Schmoker & Marzano, 1999). Further, unintended consequences of standards for students, including greater pressure and a lack of attention to what is known about student learning, need to be addressed (Gratz, 2000). These concerns must be considered in developing standards for the reading program. Schmoker and Marzano (1999) stress the importance of developing "a clear, manageable, grade-by-grade set of standards and learning benchmarks that make sense and allow a reasonable measure of autonomy" (p. 21).

Discussions about articulation among teachers at various grade levels and across grade levels can enlighten all teachers about the needs of students and how they can be met. Such discussions can help upper grade teachers better understand what students are learning in the early grades; likewise, teachers at the lower grades can become more cognizant of the expectations of teachers who work with intermediate and adolescent students. Given that all teachers, including those responsible for teaching content subjects, assist in the development of literacy performance, these conversations are essential. Questions relating to how curriculum needs to be structured so that students learn how to read, write, and think effectively in the various disciplines must be asked—and answered.

Moreover, discussions between elementary school educators and preschool providers can lead to a much better transition for young children into the kindergarten program. Language and literacy experiences at the preschool level provide the basis for successful reading and writing. The importance of oral language, including vocabulary development, to proficient reading is certainly a well-established notion (Snow et al., 1998), and therefore, the home and preschool experiences of students need to be considered when developing a comprehensive reading program.

The need for evidence-based reading instruction is one that has been addressed by many in the field (IRA, 2000; National Institute of Child Health and Development [NICHD], 2000; Snow et al., 1998). There is general consensus that many children need early instruction that explicitly teaches them to use the code-based nature of written language within a broader context of a meaning-based, language-rich curriculum, with rich exposure to various genres of text. Such a program should also include writing instruction to support and reinforce reading instruction, as well as the development of speaking and listening vocabularies (Snow et al., 1998). This approach makes great sense because it emphasizes the need for a balanced curriculum, one that highlights the need for students to "break the code," and at the same time acknowledges that reading ultimately requires meaning making. Unfortunately, balance is too often misunderstood; and indeed, constructs that redefine and lead to a misunderstanding of balance become part of the definition. For example, a focus on the code is sometimes believed to require direct instruction or ability grouping; likewise, a focus on meaning is sometimes thought to be synonymous with a whole-language approach. Pearson and Raphael (2003), in a discussion about balance, indicate that "we must shift the debates about balance *away* from single-dimension discussions of what to teach and what not to teach, and *toward* the notion that achieving a balanced literacy curriculum is a logical goal of all literacy educators" (p. 34).

At the secondary level, sources such as *Reading Next: A Vision for Action and Research in Middle and High School Literacy* (Biancarosa & Snow, 2004) and *Creating a Culture of Literacy: A Guide for Middle and High School Principals* (National Associated Secondary School Principals [NASSP], 2005) provide the background and specific ideas that those working on curriculum development can consult to build

knowledge and understanding of the necessary components of an effective literacy program. These documents also call for a new way of thinking about how literacy is taught and practiced in secondary schools, one that calls for attention to literacy and its requirements in the various disciplines (e.g., social studies, science, and mathematics).

Certainly, reading instruction should be based on research and the literature so that it reflects what is known in the field. Important documents such as *Preventing Reading Difficulties in Young Children*, The Report of the National Research Council (Snow et al., 1998) and *Handbook of Early Literacy Research* (Neuman & Dickinson, 2001) provide up-to-date information for those interested in early reading instruction. Likewise, the *Report of the National Reading Panel* (NICHD, 2000) provides syntheses of research on various aspects of reading. *Developing Literacy in Second-Language Learners: Report of the National Literacy Panel on Language Minority Children and Youth* (August & Shanahan, 2006) is an important resource for information about English language learners. The *Handbook of Reading Research*, edited by Kamil, Mosenthal, Pearson, and Barr (2000), is also an excellent source of information, and position statements developed by the International Reading Association can be helpful in informing teachers and in generating support for program development (e.g., *What Is Evidence-Based Reading Instruction?*, 2002).

The present emphasis in the field relative to the essential components of all reading programs in the elementary grades is that they incorporate the five elements discussed in the *Report of the National Reading Panel* (NICHD, 2000): phonemic awareness, phonics, fluency, vocabulary, and text comprehension. Although these are critical components, there are other essential aspects of reading that need to be considered in developing a comprehensive plan. In Figure 1.2 I identify 10 essential components that need to be considered in reading curriculum development, at levels prekindergarten through Grade 12, and highlight the levels at which each is emphasized. The building blocks or foundations for reading, which need to be addressed at *all* levels, include oral language, vocabulary, comprehension (beginning with listening comprehension), writing, and motivation to participate in literacy activities. All

Figure 1.2. Components of Reading Program (Pre-K–12)

Pre-K	*K*	*1*	*2*	*3*	*4*	*5*	*6*	*7*	*8*	*9*	*10*	*11*	*12*

Motivation (Independent Reading)

Writing

Comprehension of Text

Meaning Vocabulary

Oral Language/Concept Development

Concepts of Print

Phonemic Awareness

Phonics

Fluency of Words and Text

Other Decoding Skills: Structural Analysis, Latin Roots, Greek Combining Forms.

teachers at all grade levels will focus on these essentials, although the nature and difficulty of the understandings, the skills, and the materials will become more complex.

Although schools at early grade levels tend to focus on what Paris (2005) calls the "constrained" skills—those that can be mastered in a relatively short amount of time—attention to oral language development, meaning vocabulary, and comprehension builds the knowledge that enables young students to make sense of what they hear and read. In addition, however, the curriculum in Grades pre-K through 2 must address the early reading skills identified in Figure 1.2. So, although many students come to kindergarten with a good understanding of print concepts (e.g., how to hold and read a book, knowing that one reads from left to right), there is often a need to reinforce these notions. Likewise, phonemic awareness, an auditory skill that requires students to blend, segment, and manipulate phonemes in spoken words, is an essential component in any early literacy program, with instruction beginning quite early, often in pre-K or kindergarten. Phonics instruction must be included in any comprehensive plan, and as suggested by the National Reading Panel (NICHD, 2000), such instruction should begin early and be terminated near the end of second grade. But other means of analyzing words should also be part of the decoding continuum: students need learning experiences that enable them to analyze multisyllabic words, understanding how to use syllabication, prefixes, suffixes, Latin roots, and Greek combining forms. These skills can be introduced as early as Grade 1

(e. g., in compound words) and become much more sophisticated in the middle grades when students are taught to identify and use various Latin roots and Greek combining forms, found frequently in various content texts, to identify the meaning of words. Fluency, the ability to read words and text accurately and with expression, is especially important for developing readers as a means of helping them apply and practice the skills that they are learning. Fluency practice occurs early, that is, as soon as students begin reading text and should continue through the primary and intermediate grades for some readers. Specific information about each of these components is addressed in other chapters in this text. However, the graphic provides curriculum developers with an overall picture of what needs to be included in a comprehensive plan. With a pre-K–12 framework, a school can develop a broad plan that illustrates where in the curriculum various understandings, skills, and attitudes are addressed. Otherwise, students may receive little or no experience with various aspects of reading (e.g., no introduction to any study strategy), or they may receive the same experiences again and again.

2. Select Materials that Facilitate Accomplishment of School Goals. The identification of school goals and objectives is the first task to be considered in curriculum development; too often, the specific materials purchased determine and drive the curriculum. They influence both activities and the content that students learn (Duffy, Roehler, & Mason, 1984). However, without the initial discussions and efforts that help teachers understand what they want students to achieve, the selection of materials can be problematic. The vision and goals should assist educators in determining the criteria and guidelines for materials selection and development. Although the basal reader or anthology is still used extensively in schools as the core reading program, it cannot and should not be used as the sole determinant of the comprehensive reading program. Selection of a core program must be done thoughtfully, using an inclusive process. Schools can develop their own checklists or can choose from those that are available to them. Although most schools select an anthology or basal reader as the core program, some districts choose to develop what is commonly called a "homegrown" program. What is essential

is that there is a sequential, commonly agreed-upon set of standards or goals. Some districts have used the development of a homegrown program as a means of professional development and have developed a very sophisticated curricular map. Such a task is a formidable one, but if done well, can lead to a comprehensive program that meets the needs of the specific students in that district.

In addition to the materials provided by the core program, however, teachers will need extensive classroom libraries that provide easy-to-read and challenging books. Various genres of books should be made available, both to provide choice for students and to extend opportunities to read text related to what is taught in the various content areas. Books that extend students' knowledge about their own culture and that of others should be found in classrooms and in the school library.

Current research has emphasized the need for more exposure to expository texts; indeed, Duke's research (2000) on the lack of informational text in the primary grades has led to an increased awareness of the need for children to have more exposure to such text in the early grades. Obviously, students in the intermediate and upper grades should also have easy access to such texts. Classrooms should contain a wide variety of text—print and nonprint (for example, software, DVDs, and games). Providing a print-rich environment encourages students to view reading as an important communication and learning tool. (See Chapter 7 of this volume for further discussion about material selection.)

Likewise, materials to aid the teacher in differentiating instruction will need to be selected. For example, schools may want to select easy to read or decodable books that students can use for fluency practice. Various software or gamelike materials can be used to help students practice and apply strategies or skills that they are learning. Some schools may select specific materials that have been identified as useful for helping the struggling reader.

3. Organize a Usable Curriculum Framework. Another issue is how a specific school will organize its curriculum framework for reading so that essential components of reading are included. Although reading is a complex process that requires integrated use of multiple skills and strategies, there is still a need to identify the components of reading so that specific goals and instructional activities can be selected. The framework should have a sound theoretical base and at the same time be one that classroom teachers can use effectively. As mentioned previously, standards developed by organizations or by one's state can be used as a guide for a discussion and as a basis for program development. Frameworks can be modified, of course, to meet the specific characteristics of a school district. Personnel in an individual school district must think through for themselves how they conceptualize the framework for the reading curriculum. In other words, they must decide what works best for them and their students and at the same time reflects what is known about effective reading instruction.

4. Relate Teacher Beliefs and Knowledge About Reading Instruction to Research. In addition to reviewing the research that is available about reading curriculum and instruction, teachers will need to think carefully about their own beliefs and values as they formulate goals and select curricula for students in their school. Research tells us that the teacher is an important variable in determining whether students will be successful (Goldhaber & Anthony, 2004; Rice, 2003; Sanders & Rivers, 1996).

Teachers' own life and school experiences as well as their cultural backgrounds influence their beliefs and actions. Further, beliefs are often resistant to change unless individuals are willing to think and reflect on what they already believe, read new information, and relate that information to what they already know. Working with other teachers in developing an effective reading program provides much opportunity for discussion of beliefs and knowledge and is a critical part of the curriculum development process.

Instruction

Any discussion of instruction needs to include a description of the learning activities, strategies, and grouping arrangements that help teachers meet the needs of individual learners. Resources such as time and personnel need to be carefully used if a reading program is to be effective. Although a teacher working with an individual student must have an excellent understanding of the reading

process and reading methodology, this task is simple compared to the responsibility of providing instruction for 20 or more students whose range in reading performance may vary tremendously. Any reading program must provide experiences that enable each student to grow and learn in an environment that promotes risk taking and guarantees success. This means that students who are performing at accelerated rates are challenged and encouraged to continue their learning. At the same time, students who are experiencing difficulties with grade-level curriculum need to receive specialized reading instruction that will help them to succeed and progress. One of the important tasks of the professionals responsible for developing a total reading program is to promote communication and congruence between the special programs in schools and the classroom reading program. In this section, four major guidelines are discussed.

1. Develop an Organizational Structure that Highlights Individual Needs of Students. In the 1990s, there was much emphasis on whole-class grouping in reading programs (Reutzel & Cooter, 1996). There were several reasons for such an approach. First, whole-class teaching negated the problems associated with ability grouping in which groups, once formed, tended to become permanent arrangements. Previous research indicated that such arrangements were not beneficial for students placed in low groups (Allington, 1983; Gambrell, Wilson, & Gantt, 1981; Hiebert, 1983). Second, whole-class instruction promoted the important notion that becoming literate was a social endeavor: all the children were engaged in meaningful literacy activities, such as telling stories, reading big books together, creating language experience charts, sharing student-written stories.

However, recent research (Foorman & Torgesen, 2001; Taylor et al., 2000) and the emphasis on helping all students to become successful readers has led to an increased interest in small-group, differentiated instruction. Several alternative strategies are often used by schools to provide this differentiation. Teachers are encouraged to use *flexible grouping*, in which students are placed into temporary groups on the basis of interest, learning styles, social, or instructional needs. *Cooperative learning*, another grouping strategy, is based on heterogeneous grouping, in which two to five children of varying abilities, work together. Teachers using literature circles may choose to use such a procedure. *Guided reading*, an approach in which the teacher works with a small group of children who use similar reading processes and are able to read similar levels of text with teacher support, enables students to learn how to use reading strategies successfully (Fountas & Pinnell, 1996). Teachers can also establish *learning centers* or stations in their classrooms to which children can be assigned as a means of providing reinforcement activities or personalizing instruction. Managing a classroom in which students are assigned or choose to do different tasks is not easy for teachers, especially for a novice teacher. School leaders can serve an important role in helping teachers understand the importance of providing for individual differences and, more specifically, assist teachers in implementing grouping procedures in their classrooms. They provide such support by developing schedules that assist such differentiation and by promoting small-group instruction as a critical element in the program. Other personnel, such as teacher aides, reading specialists, or special educators may also be scheduled to work in the classroom during specific periods to assist the teacher in differentiating instruction.

2. *Plan Instruction to Make Effective Use of Time, Including Additional Instruction for Those Who Need It.* Each school district will need to decide, based upon state requirements, the amount of time to be allocated to reading instruction, especially at the primary and intermediate levels. They will also need to decide whether such a block of time will include other language arts, or whether reading is to be the sole focus of a specific period of time.

Further, struggling readers, who benefit from more intensive instruction (Borman, Wong, Hedges, & D'Agostino, 2001; Foorman & Torgesen, 2001), may need additional time and support to master the skills and strategies of classroom curriculum. Such intensive instruction may call for the support of other specialized personnel in the school.

3. *Provide for Coordination Among All Reading Programs in the School.* There has been a great deal of criticism about separate systems of education for students who experience difficulties in learning,

especially those who are Title I or special education students (Allington & McGill-Franzen, 1988; Borman et al., 2001; Ysseldyke, Thurlow, Mecklenburg, & Graden, 1984). Much of this criticism has revolved around the pull-out arrangements that were the prevalent model for compensatory education. Although there are many concerns about pull-out models—including scheduling, less instructional time because of student movement, and possible stigmatizing of participants—one of the major concerns has been the nature of the instruction, specifically that the two programs received by the students were not congruent (Borman et al., 2001; Johnston, Allington, & Afflerbach, 1985). Low-achieving students have had to handle the demands of two different classroom settings, approaches, and teachers. Borman et al. (2001) indicate in their large-scale study that setting was not the critical variable: "What matters is that Title I and regular classroom teachers use the same curriculum and assessments for all students. If the Title I coursework is not the same, there must be some articulation of how it will reinforce and complement the students' learning of the regular classroom curriculum" (p. 113). Although quality "first-line" teaching is critical (Allington & Baker, 1999; IRA, 2000), teachers may need support in meeting the needs of struggling readers. Reading specialists can have several roles, each of which necessitates communication and collaboration with classroom teachers. First, the reading specialist may provide direct instruction for struggling readers, but that instruction must be intensive and personalized, taking into consideration the instruction being received in the classroom (Allington & Baker, 1999; Borman et al., 2001). Second, the reading specialist can assist the classroom teacher by providing advice, materials, and staff development, all focused on improving classroom instruction (Allington & Baker, 1999; Bean, 2004b; Bean, Swan, & Knaub, 2003). The climate in the school must be one that encourages communication and collaboration among all responsible for reading instruction. Teachers, whether specialists or classroom, can no longer work in isolation. All professionals need to work as members of a team to plan for student needs.

One of the current approaches to differentiating instruction, the Three-Tier Model, developed at the University of Texas–Austin (2003), seems to have some potential for helping teachers and schools think about how to organize instruction. The model as proposed calls for the following:

Tier 1: High-quality comprehensive classroom reading instruction

Tier 2: Supplemental instruction, which includes additional time and more small-group instruction

Tier 3: Intensive instruction, which includes more time and very-small-group (2–3) or one-on-one tutorial instruction

Unfortunately, as stated by Allington (2006), some districts interpret this model as calling for three different curricula and/or sets of instructional strategies. It is his contention that such an interpretation flies in the face of what we know about congruent instruction. He proposes that Tiers 2 and 3 include additional time and/or more personalized instruction that improves upon or extends classroom reading instruction. Such an approach in his view calls for instruction provided by experts who can "identify just where the reader has gotten off-track and then . . . design instruction that moves the reader back onto an accelerated track of development" (p. 20). This makes eminent sense; at the same time, there may be a few students who do need an approach that is different from that provided in the classroom. I see the possibility that those working with Tier 3 students may need to use instructional practices that are more explicit, more multisensory, and more intensive so that they provide the additional support needed by these students. Certainly, this type of intervention is supported by the IRA position statement *Making a Difference Means Making It Different* (IRA, 2000). Such a decision, however, needs to be made thoughtfully, and collaboration with the classroom teachers would be essential so that there is clear articulation about how such an approach complements or reinforces what is being taught in the classroom.

4. *Extend Teachers' Understandings So That They Are Able to Differentiate Instruction.* Described below are six critical points from research and theory that school personnel need to consider as they think about the instructional aspects of their reading program.

First, the core program or curriculum serves as a guide. Although the core curriculum will include instructional strategies that are appropriate for many or even most of the students in the classroom, the notion that some children may need additional scaffolding, supplemental support, or additional practice is an important one. Teachers in the classroom need to have the expertise to make decisions about whether the core program is meeting the needs of their students and how they may need to modify the program. In the previous section, I identified several documents that provide current information about what is known about effective reading curriculum and instruction. Again, these documents can serve as the starting place for those involved in designing a schoolwide reading program.

Second, those involved in designing or selecting instructional activities need to consider the variables that contribute to success in reading, given its interactive, constructive nature. These variables include the reader, the text, and the context. Readers approach reading with varying experiences and knowledge; they will handle some assignments better than others and will need more assistance with some than with others. Moreover, all readers need to read material that relates to their own experiences and culture; at the same time, there is a need for them to read about cultures other than their own.

Text material will affect students' ability to be successful. There must be a match between the reading levels of students and the materials used for instruction if students are to be successful in learning to read (Allington, 2006; O'Connor et al., 2002). Certainly, this reinforces the need for small-group instruction in which students are reading materials at their instructional level. In addition, regardless of the designated reading level of the material, there will be variability in readability of these materials. Anderson and Armbruster (1984) discuss what they call inconsiderate text, that material that necessitates more teacher direction and intervention. There is a need, for example, at the primary level, for both decodable text (text which includes a large number of phonetically regular words that students can successfully decode) and high-quality literature that appeals to and interests children. Decodable text may give students opportunities to develop fluency, but may not provide the "hook" that is needed to develop the motivation to read. As mentioned previously, at all levels students also need exposure to informational text (Duke, 2000) that develops the knowledge essential for reading and understanding more difficult text.

Guthrie and Humenick (2004), in a meta-analysis of studies of reading motivation and achievement, found that the opportunity for choice was one of the key variables related to student achievement. Although this is true for all levels, it is especially important for students at the middle and secondary levels.

The context for reading also influences students' performance. Context includes many factors, such as establishing a purpose for reading, classroom climate, reading group composition, and interactions with the teachers. For example, the struggling reader may respond positively to one-to-one instruction yet not be able to work constructively in a whole-classroom setting. Moreover, collaboration with peers can increase motivation and self-directed learning among students; such experiences build on the notion that one of the lenses of successful reading is that it is socially constructed.

Those developing reading programs need to help teachers think about these three variables—reader, text, and context—in deciding how much and what kinds of instruction are necessary, for example, the amount of prereading preparation, which vocabulary words to teach and how extensively, the degree of guided reading, the approach to group work, and the types of follow up to text reading. In order to do this, teachers must have an excellent understanding of the reading process and how it affects instruction.

Third, as part of the instructional framework, students must be given opportunities to read independently or in small groups. Research points to the importance of oral reading in the early grades and for struggling readers as a means of developing fluency (NICHD, 2000). At the same time, the amount of independent reading, both in and out of school, correlates highly with reading performance (National Center for Education Statistics [NCES], 1999). Thus, at all levels time for students to read—both orally or silently—must be provided on a regular basis.

Fourth, composing should be an integral part of the reading program. As mentioned previously, research evidence supports the connection between these two formal language skills. The notion of comprehension and composition as "two sides of the same

basic process" (Squire, 1983) is an important concept for the curriculum developer. Students should participate in experiences that help them see the relationship between the reading and writing process (e.g., being an audience for someone else's writing, writing for an audience, responding to the reading they do, and keeping a journal about the materials they have read).

Fifth, developing opportunities for students to become independent learners and to self-monitor their literacy progress is an essential. From kindergarten on, students need experiences that help them realize that the task of reading relies on what readers bring to it and their purposes for reading, as well as on the type of materials or text. Lessons can be planned to help students monitor their reading and to reflect upon what they may have learned.

Sixth, the climate in a school must be conducive to the development of students as readers and writers. Not only should classrooms contain all sorts of reading material, but there should be an atmosphere in the school that promotes reading as an enjoyable and necessary part of life. There should be opportunities for teachers to read to their students, even in the upper grades. Teachers can select challenging books—perhaps ones that students cannot read themselves as a means of developing conceptual knowledge and creating an interest in reading. Motivational programs that encourage student reading should be part of the mix. Those involved in developing a comprehensive reading program must think about how motivation to read is incorporated into the overall plan.

Assessment

Schools use assessment results for many purposes: accountability or outcome, decision making for teachers, feedback to students, classification and certification, and reform (Asp, 2000). During the past decade, we have witnessed much change in educational assessment practices, both with large-scale, standardized tests and classroom-level practices. Some of this has been driven by the standards-based education movement, which calls for a clearer identification of what students should know and be able to do—and for evidence that students have met those standards. Federal legislation has also created a focus on assessment, with the passage of the No Child Left Behind Act (2001). This legislation calls for accountability at the state, district, and school levels. Often testing programs are "high stake," that is, decisions about resources, sanctions, and rewards may be based upon the results (Popham, 2005).

When developing or selecting the assessment measures for accountability, it would be wise to take into consideration the recommendation of Suzanne Lane (2004) in her Presidential Address to the National Council on Measurement in Education: High-quality challenging standards that require complex thinking are essentials, and they must be aligned with cognitively rich assessments. She makes the point that assessment measures signal goals, and therefore, a measure that focuses on low-level, basic skills may have a negative impact on classroom instruction. Lane calls for a "balanced, coordinated assessment and instructional system" (p. 13). Such a system, therefore, should include classroom assessment tools, designed for screening, diagnostic, and monitoring purposes. In the section below I identify several specific guidelines related to assessment.

1. *Use Assessment to Guide Instruction.* Currently, results of school reform studies indicate that successful schools do use data to support and guide instruction (Reeves, 2005; Taylor et al., 2000). This information has led to an emphasis on assessing students several times a year to determine their progress and to make decisions about modifying and adapting instruction. Unfortunately, too often, time is provided for testing, but little emphasis is placed on helping teachers understand how to interpret and use the data. What is important is that teachers understand what the assessment measure can tell them and how it can be helpful in guiding instruction; otherwise, it is likely that they will not be able to use these measures in a purposeful and meaningful manner. Often, teachers become frustrated by what they view as an overemphasis on assessment and rightfully so, if assessment data are not used effectively. Much of this frustration can be alleviated if teachers are involved in the decision-making process, if they have opportunities to administer the tasks themselves as a means of developing ownership, and if they are able to see that the results are helpful in planning instruction.

What is essential is that the assessment measures used for determining instruction be ones that can help teachers make instructional decisions and are easy to administer so that they will be used. DIBELS, or the Dynamic Indicators of Basic Educational Skills (Good & Kaminski, 2002), has been selected by many schools, especially Reading First schools, as a tool for initial screening and progress monitoring. These one-minute measures do not take much time to use; at the same time, they are screening measures, and teachers may need to use other more authentic measures to make specific determinations of how to modify instruction. In Goodman's edited volume (2006), cautions and criticisms about this specific measure are discussed; such information can help school districts think more carefully about what such an instrument can and cannot tell them.

Classroom measures, in my view, ought to do more than assess what is learned; they should provide information *for* learning (Stiggins, 2002). Such assessment "refers to a variety of tasks and situations in which students are given opportunities to demonstrate their understanding and to thoughtfully apply knowledge, skills, and habits of mind in a variety of contexts" (Marzano, Pickering, & McTighe, 1993, p. 13); in other words, they should be performance based or authentic. Many different assessment measures for the various elements of reading can be developed, adapted, or purchased. Assessment tools such as retellings, in which students listen to or read a story and then tell or write all that they remember, may be used as an indication that students have a sense of story and can identify relevant elements (characters, plot, setting, and resolution). By listening to a child read orally, a teacher can identify the accuracy, rate, and fluency of that reader. The number and type of books that a student reads in one year can be monitored to determine students' interests and desire to read. What is essential is that students and their parents are given feedback and suggestions on how to improve students' learning, and that teachers use the results to modify and adapt classroom instruction.

2. *Develop Scoring Guides or Rubrics.* Classroom assessments, especially those that are performance based, can be problematic in terms of subjectivity in scoring. Rubrics, plans for assessing the quality of student work, can be helpful to teachers and

can serve as a tool for involving students in self-assessing their own learning. Arter and McTighe (2001) suggest four criteria for assessing the quality of rubrics: (1) content/coverage, (2) clarity, (3) practicality, and (4) technical soundness or fairness. They also discuss the importance of teaching students how to self-assess using rubrics. Teachers who teach a specific subject or at a particular grade level can work collaboratively, using student work samples, to develop rubrics that will assist them in scoring and interpreting students' performance more objectively.

3. Seek Alignment Among Various Layers of Assessment. As mentioned previously, there is a need for a congruent, well-articulated assessment program. School districts generally select their own standardized assessments, which include large-scale testing, and classroom assessment measures. At the same time, students may be required to take state-mandated tests that reflect state content standards. At times, there is little comparability among those tests: students may do well on one assessment measure and less well on another. Teachers may become frustrated and confused about what really matters. As Asp (2000) states, "Assessment at all levels needed to be linked together to support and reinforce a set of clearly articulated goals" (p. 151). To the degree possible, there should be overlap between what is taught and what is tested or the tests are not a fair and valid measure of what students know, or what teachers have taught.

In sum, assessment is a critical piece of reading program development. The development of standards and curriculum, instruction, and assessment must be carefully thought through so that there is an appropriate fit of all elements. Yet these elements do not occur instantaneously, nor are they easily achieved. Sizer (1985) states it well: "A good school does not emerge like a prepackaged frozen dinner stuck for 15 seconds in a radar range; it develops from the slow simmering of carefully blended ingredients" (p. 22).

PROCESS FOR CHANGE

Those interested in improving instruction in schools should read educational literature about school reform, school restructuring, scale-up initiatives, and school change. Most of this literature and research speaks to the importance of school leadership, establishing a process for change, teacher learning, high expectations for all learners, as well as other factors. No Child Left Behind has increased efforts to improve schools as a whole since accountability is based on school improvement, not only overall achievement but achievement of various subgroups such as minority, high-poverty, English language learners (ELL), and special education groups. Various initiatives have been developed at the school, district, and state levels to meet these improvement demands. Literacy is at the heart of many of these reforms, given its importance as a foundation for all learning and the fact that accountability is most often measured by scores on a reading test. Thus, developing a reading program is no trivial task, and the process for development is as important as the end result. Too many curriculum development efforts start with much enthusiasm and excitement but fall short of reaching their mark. We have learned that the change process is a complex one that is "rolling" rather than linear. Specifically, changing behaviors involves collective, innovative action, and constant assessment of this action (Joyce, Wolf, & Calhoun, 1993). In Figure 1.3 I provide a set of questions that can be used by those involved in developing reading programs as a means of self-analysis before starting a process for change; these questions can also be used at any time as a basis for discussion among school staff, teachers, and/or administrators. In the sections below I discuss principles that may be useful to those involved in making changes in school reading programs.

Involve All Constituents by Building a Community of Learners

Change is systemic; therefore the process for change must involve all constituents. Fullan and Miles (1992) indicate that working systemically means focusing on "the development and interrelationships of all the main components of the system simultaneously—curriculum, teaching and teacher development, community support systems, and so on," as well as on "the deeper issues of the culture of the system" (p. 751). In other words, even

Figure 1.3. Developing a Comprehensive Reading Program: Questions To Consider

---

Curriculum

1. Has the school established goals and standards (pre-K–12)?
   - Amount of time for reading instruction at the primary and intermediate levels?
   - Relationship between reading and the other language arts?
   - Role of subject matter teachers at all levels, but especially at the middle school/high school levels in helping students handle the literacy demands of their classroom?
2. Do standards address the need for a developmental continuum that considers the reader at all stages: emergent, beginning, transitional, intermediate, and skilled reading and writing? Do they recognize the needs of learners at the middle school and secondary levels?
3. Are the standards based on what is known about effective reading instruction and assessment; that is, are they evidence-based?
4. Do they address the essential elements of effective reading instruction (see Figure 1.2)?
5. Have materials been selected that enable teachers to address the goals? Do these materials address the needs of all learners (e.g., struggling readers, ELL students)? Do they provide for the varying reading levels of students? Is a variety of materials available (e.g., narrative, informational, poetry)? Do they provide students with opportunities to understand their own backgrounds and that of others?
6. Has the school decided on a "framework" that makes the curriculum visible and usable?

Instruction

1. Has consideration been given to how reading instruction will be organized? How will the differing needs of students be met? Grouping options? Materials? Additional time? Additional support of specialized professionals?
2. Is there coordination and coherence among all the reading programs in the school (the core, the programs for struggling readers, ELL students, and so on)?
3. Are teachers given opportunities to gain knowledge and understanding of the current research and literature about effective reading instruction? Is there coherence between the written curriculum of the school and actual classroom practices?

Assessment

1. Is the assessment balanced and coordinated? Is there provision for outcome measures? Screening measures? Diagnostic measures? Progress monitoring measures?
2. Is there alignment between the standards of the district and the assessment system (i.e., is the assessment system measuring what is being taught)?
3. Do the assessment measures address the need for high-level cognitive thinking?
4. Do the classroom assessment measures assist teachers in instructional decision making? Do they assist teachers in identifying the needs of the struggling readers, ELL students, high achievers?

Process for Change

1. Are teachers involved in the curriculum development process? Have they had opportunities to discuss their beliefs and understandings and learn more about how reading can be taught effectively?
2. Have they been provided with the professional development they need to implement the program effectively? Does this include opportunity for support and feedback (e.g., literacy coaching)?
3. Does professional development provide teachers with opportunities to learn from each other, to collaborate? In other words, are teachers working together so that change can occur at the school level?
4. Are administrators supportive and involved in the change effort? Do they understand what is required of their teachers so that they can provide support?

changing only one aspect of the school—its reading program—involves a host of different issues. Individuals involved in the process will come to it with differing perceptions of how reading should be taught. Anyone involved in a leadership position must be sensitive to the complexity of bringing about long-lasting change.

There are many different ideas about how to apply knowledge about change processes to curriculum development. The definitions of curriculum in *The Literacy Dictionary* (Harris & Hodges, 1995) illustrate its complexity:

> Curriculum: Definitions of curriculum vary widely because of alternative perceptions held by theorists about the nature and organization of formal schooling. 1. an overall plan or design of institutionalized education. 2. the actual opportunities for learning provided at a particular place and time. (p. 51)

In other words, developing a reading program requires educators to think about what will be taught, when, by whom, how, and in what sequence or order. Oliva and Pawkas (2001) identify three components in their simplified model of curriculum development: planning, implementation, and evaluation. Ideas that may be helpful in thinking about these components for developing a reading curriculum follow.

Stage 1: Planning. As part of any process for curricular change, an initial step is reviewing the current program to determine where there is a need for change. Information should come from school sources such as test data, teacher interviews, and observations in classrooms; it can also come from published information about curriculum trends or research findings. Teachers who agree to work with curriculum development can select or be given articles to read that can then be discussed and debated. School districts can also identify an expert who might make a presentation to teachers on the "state of the art" in reading instruction.

It is imperative that teachers discuss the current status of reading instruction in their school. Often a set of guidelines that help the leaders of such an initiative can be helpful. For example, Learning Point Associates (Levesque & Carnahan, 2005) has developed an instrument that elementary schools can use to evaluate their own school literacy programs. At the secondary levels, reports such as the one written by Biancarosa & Snow (2004) can help schools think about the essentials.

Another useful activity is for teachers to "map" their curriculum. According to Jacobs (1997), "curriculum mapping is a procedure for collecting data about the actual curriculum in a school district using the school calendar as an organizer" (p. 62). Such a process helps teachers think about the various types of curricula: the written, the taught, and the assessed (English, 1993). At least three types of data need to be collected to develop such a map: content, description of processes and skills emphasized, and the assessments produced by students. Such a procedure enables teachers to analyze the "operational curriculum," to compare what they are doing, and to notice gaps as well as redundancies.

At this stage, teachers and others (consultants, parents, administrators) can investigate various ideas, materials, and approaches that may be useful for a particular school. Fullan (1999) states it succinctly: "There is no single solution. . . . The change process is too intricate and organic, organization by organization, to be captured in any single model" (p. 28). Again, outside consultants may be invited to work with teachers; however, the process needs to center around the teachers who must work together with a common goal to develop standards, instructional activities, and congruent assessment measures.

Stage 2: Implementation. In order that curricular changes are actually implemented in the school, there must be staff development for all those involved. Too often, good ideas that are placed in curriculum guides or district manuals are not implemented appropriately or at all by classroom teachers. Often this is caused by inadequate staff development for teachers, who must have a solid understanding and acceptance of the proposed changes. According to Joyce et al. (1993), "a curriculum change in a major area probably requires ten to fifteen days of training rather than the one or two that are often provided now" (p. 32). Curriculum implementation may also create a need for staff development beyond building knowledge and understanding; in other words, there may be a need for coaching to assist teachers in the actual implementation effort. Joyce and Showers (2002) emphasize the importance of such coaching as a means of enhancing teachers' ability to actually implement the curriculum as expected.

Stage 3: Evaluation. There should be formative evaluation that documents how well the change process is progressing. Such evaluation can come from classroom assessment measures used frequently, from interviews with teachers, and from visits to classrooms. In addition, a process for determining the effect of the changes should be identified. This stage calls for specific attention to assessing the success of the change (Does it make a difference?) and the degree to which the changes have become institutionalized (Are teachers using the programmatic approaches?).

Encourage Professional Development

As mentioned previously, recent research has emphasized the importance of the teacher in student success (Goldhaber & Anthony, 2004; Rice, 2003; Sanders & Rivers, 1996). Professional development, therefore, must be ongoing in any school, especially when teachers are being asked to make changes in how they are teaching. As stated previously, too often good ideas never become a reality in classroom practice. There are too many examples of one-shot, in-service programs that provide initial enthusiasm but no more. One very important finding from the Huberman and Miles (1984) studies is that commitment follows competence. Individuals are more willing to maintain and practice certain innovations if they have the competence to do them well; in other words, behavior changes before beliefs. Thus professional development must be ongoing and intensive in order to provide continuing support and feedback to teachers. At the present time, many schools at all levels are employing literacy coaches whose responsibility is to provide that support. Although literacy coaches may indeed be helpful, they are not miracle workers. Schools interested in literacy coaching should become informed about what literacy coaching is and the necessary qualifications for such support personnel. Books such as those by Toll (2005), Walpole and McKenna (2004), or Bean (2004b) or articles about the role of the literacy coach (Bean, 2004a; Dole,

2004) can serve as resources for those interested in such job-embedded professional development. Bean and Carroll (2006) provide administrators with a set of guidelines for thinking about literacy coaching, its characteristics, and qualifications for selecting such coaches.

There is consistency in the many reports of research about the essential ingredients of any effective professional development program (Anders, Hoffman, & Duffy, 2000; National Staff Development Council, 2001). In a recent publication of the American Educational Research Association (2005), four points were identified: the need for focus on subject matter or content knowledge; the importance of job-embedded professional development that is based on the "real" work of teachers and provides them with support in their efforts; the need for time to enable teachers to develop an understanding of the topic being discussed; and the importance of evaluation to determine whether the professional development has had an effect. Teachers themselves indicate that they value collaborative models of professional development, including book clubs, peer coaching, study groups, action research, and shared teaching experiences (Teberg, 1999).

The principles described above illustrate the need for involvement of the classroom teacher in both generating ideas for change and implementing change in the classroom. They acknowledge the importance of the teacher as a decision maker in creating excellent learning experiences for students. The cyclical nature of the change process is also evident. As stated by Fullan and Miles (1992), "change is a journey, not a blueprint. . . . One should not plan, then do, but do, then plan . . . and do and plan some more" (p. 749).

CONCLUSION

The development, implementation, and evaluation of a comprehensive pre-K–12 reading program is an exciting and challenging task that requires the cooperation and collaboration of all concerned. Such a process is ongoing and cyclical, and it must include teachers and other constituents as part of the process if understanding and ownership are to occur. When developing a school reading program, the first task is to address the vision and accompanying goals that form the basis for curriculum, instruction, and assessment. Developing such a vision calls for a deep understanding of the research and literature to assist schools in making decisions about reading instruction. It also calls for professional development that enables teachers to increase their knowledge and understanding of reading instruction. The development of a comprehensive reading program can and should be a professional development experience itself. When teachers are involved in the development of the program, there is more likelihood that they will also have an investment in implementing it in their classrooms.

REFERENCES

Allington, R. L. (1983). The reading instruction provided readers of differing ability. *The Elementary School Journal, 83*(5), 548–559.

Allington, R. L. (2006). *What really matters for struggling readers: Designing research-based programs.* New York: Pearson.

Allington, R. L., & Baker, K. (1999). Best practices in literacy instruction for children with special needs. In L. B. Gambrell, L. M. Morrow, S. B. Neuman, & M. Pressley (Eds.), *Best practices in literacy instruction* (pp. 292–310). New York: Guilford Press.

Allington, R. L., & McGill-Franzen, A. (1988). *Coherence or chaos? Qualitative dimensions of the literacy instruction provided low-achievement children.* Albany: State University of New York at Albany. (ERIC Document Reproduction Service No. ED292060)

American Educational Research Association. (2005). *Teaching teachers: Professional development to improve student achievement. Research Points, 3*(1).

Anders, P., Hoffman, J., & Duffy, G. (2000). Teaching teachers to teach reading: Paradigm shifts, persistent problems, and challenges. In M. Kamil, P. Mosenthal, P. D. Pearson, & R. Barr (Eds.), *Handbook of reading research:* (Vol. 3, pp. 719–742). Mahwah, NJ: Erlbaum.

Anderson, R. H., & Armbruster, B. B. (1984). Content area textbooks. In R. C. Anderson, J. Osborn, & R. J. Tierney (Eds.), *Learning to read in American schools* (pp. 193–224). Hillsdale, NJ: Erlbaum.

Arter, J., & McTighe, J. (2001). *Scoring rubrics in the classroom: Using performance criteria for assessing and improving student performance.* Thousand Oaks, CA: Corwin Press.

Asp, E. (2000). Assessment in education: Where have we been? Where are we headed? In R. S. Brandt (Ed.), *Education in a new era* (pp. 123–157). Washington, DC: Association for Supervision and Curriculum Development.

August, D., & Shanahan, T. (2006). *Developing literacy in second-language learners: Report of the National Literacy Panel on Language Minority Children and Youth.* Mahwah, NJ: Erlbaum.

Bean, R. M. (2004a). Promoting effective literacy instruction: The challenge for literacy coaches. *The California Reader, 37*(3), 58–63.

Bean, R. M. (2004b). *The reading specialist: Leadership for the classroom, school, and community.* New York: Guilford Press.

Bean, R. M., & Carroll, K. (2006). The literacy coach as a catalyst for change. In C. Cummins (Ed.), *Understanding and implementing Reading First initiatives: The changing role of administrators.* Newark, DE: International Reading Association.

Bean, R. M., Swan, A. L., & Knaub, R. (2003). Reading specialists in schools with exemplary reading programs: Functional, versatile, and prepared. *The Reading Teacher, 56*(5), 446–455.

Bear, D. R., Invernizzi, M., Templeton, S., & Johnston, F. (2004). *Words their way: Word study for phonics, vocabulary, and spelling instruction.* Upper Saddle River, NJ: Prentice-Hall.

Biancarosa, G., & Snow, C. (2004). *Reading next: A vision for action and research in middle and high school literacy.* Washington, DC: Alliance for Education.

Borman, G. D., Wong, K. K., Hedges, L. V., & D'Agostino, J. V. (2001). Coordinating categorical and regular programs: Effects on Title I students' educational opportunities and outcomes. In G. D. Borman, S. C. Stringfield, & R. E. Slavin (Eds.), *Title I: Compensatory education at the crossroad* (pp. 79–116). Mahwah, NJ: Erlbaum.

Dole, J. A. (2004). The changing role of the reading specialist in school reform. *The Reading Teacher, 57*(5), 462–471.

Duffy, G. G., Roehler, R. L., & Mason, J. (1984). *Comprehension instruction: Perspectives and suggestions.* New York: Longman.

Duke, N. (2000). 3.6 minutes per day: The scarcity of informational texts in first grade. *Reading Research Quarterly, 35,* 202–224.

English, F. (1993). *Deciding what to teach and test.* Newbury Park, CA: Corwin Press.

Foorman, B. R., & Torgesen, J. (2001). Critical elements of classroom and small-group instruction promote reading success in all children. *Learning Disabilities Research & Practice, 16*(4), 203–212.

Fountas, I. C., & Pinnell, G. S. (1996). *Guided reading: Good first teaching for all children.* Portsmouth, NH: Heinemann.

Fullan, M. (1999). *Change forces: The sequel.* Philadelphia, PA: Falmer Press.

Fullan, M. G., & Miles, M. B. (1992). Getting reform right: What works and what doesn't. *Phi Delta Kappan, 73*(10), 745–752.

Gambrell, L., Wilson, R., & Gantt, W. M. (1981). Classroom observations of task-attending behaviors of good and poor readers. *Journal of Educational Research, 74*(6), 400–404.

Goldhaber, D., & Anthony, E. (2004). *Can teacher quality be effectively assessed?* Retrieved May 16, 2007, from the Urban Institute Web site at http://www.urban.org/url.cfm?ID=410958.html

Good, R. H., & Kaminski, R. A. (Eds.). (2002). *Dynamic indicators of basic early literacy* (Rev. 6th ed.). Eugene, OR: Institute for the Development of Educational Achievement. Available from DIBELS Web site at http://dibels.uoregon.edu

Goodman, K. (Ed.). (2006). *The truth about DIBELS: What it is, What it does.* Portsmouth, NH: Heinemann.

Gratz, D. B. (2000). High standards for whom? *Phi Delta Kappan, 81*(9), 681–687.

Guthrie, J. T., & Humenick, N. M. (2004). Motivating students to read: Evidence for classroom practices that increase motivation and achievement. In P. McCardle & V. Chabra (Eds.), *The voice of evidence in reading research* (pp. 329–354). Baltimore: Brookes.

Harris, T., & Hodges, R. E. (1995). *The literacy dictionary.* Newark, DE: International Reading Association.

Hiebert, E. H. (1983). An examination of ability grouping for reading instruction. *Reading Research Quarterly, 18*, 231–255.

Huberman, A. M., & Miles, M. (1984*). Innovation up close: How school improvement works.* New York: Plenum Press.

International Reading Association (IRA). (2000). *Making a difference means making it different: Honoring children's rights to excellent reading instruction.* Newark, DE: Author.

International Reading Association (IRA). (2002). *What is evidence-based reading instruction?* [Brochure]. Newark, DE: Author.

International Reading Association (IRA). (2006). *Standards for middle and high school literacy coaches.* Newark, DE: Author.

Jacobs, H. H. (1997). *Mapping the big picture: Integrating curriculum and assessment, K–12.* Alexandria, VA: Association for Supervision and Curriculum Development.

Joftus, S., & Berman, I. (1998). *Great expectations? Defining and assessing rigor in state standards for mathematics and English language arts.* Washington, DC: Council for Basic Education.

Johnson, J. F., Jr. (2002). High-performing, high-poverty, urban elementary schools. In B. S. Taylor & P. D. Pearson (Eds.), *Teaching reading: Effective schools, accomplished teachers* (pp. 89–114). Mahwah, NJ: Erlbaum.

Johnston, P., Allington, R., & Afflerbach, P. (1985). The congruence of classroom and remedial reading instruction. *Elementary School Journal, 85*(4), 465–477.

Joyce, B., & Showers, B. (2002). *Student achievement through staff development* (3rd ed.). Washington, DC: Association for Supervision and Curriculum Development.

Joyce, B., Wolf, J., & Calhoun, E. (1993). *The self-renewing school.* Alexandria, VA: Association for Supervision and Curriculum Development.

Kamil, M. L., Mosenthal, P. B., Pearson, P. D., & Barr, R. (Eds.). (2000). *Handbook of Reading Research* (Vol. 3). Mahwah, NJ: Erlbaum.

Lane, S. (2004). Validity of high-stakes assessment: Are students engaged in complex thinking? *Educational Measurement: Issues and Practice, 23*(3), 6–14.

Learning First Alliance. (2000). *Every child reading: A professional development guide.* Retrieved May 16, 2007, from http://www.learningfirst.org/lfa-web/rp?pa=doc&docId=48

Levesque, J., & Carnahan, D. (2005). *Stepping stones to evaluating your own school literacy program.* Naperville, IL: Learning Point Associates.

Marzano, R. J., Pickering, D., & McTighe, J. (1993). *Assessing student outcomes: Performance assessment using the dimensions of learning model.* Washington, DC: Association for Supervision and Curriculum Development.

National Association of Secondary School Principals (NASSP). (2005). *Creating a culture of literacy: A guide for middle and high school principals.* Reston, VA: Author.

National Center for Education Statistics (NCES). (1999). *Reading report card for the nation and the states.* Washington, DC: U.S. Department of Education.

National Council of Teachers of English (NCTE) & International Reading Association (IRA). (1996). *Standards for the English Language Arts.* Newark, DE, and Urbana, IL: Authors. Retrieved May 16, 2007, from http://www.ncte.org/about/over/standards/110846.htm or http://www.ncte.org/store/books/standards/105977.htm

National Institute of Child Health and Human Development (NICHD). (2000). *Report of the National Reading Panel. Teaching children to read: An evidence-based assessment of the scientific research literature on reading and its implications for reading instruction* (NIH Publication No. 00-4769). Washington, DC: U.S. Government Printing Office.

National Staff Development Council. (2001). *Standards for staff development* (Rev. ed.). Retrieved May 16, 2007, from http://www.nsdc.org/standards/index.cfm

Neuman, S. B., & Dickinson, D. K. (Eds.) (2001). *Handbook of early literacy research.* New York: Guilford Press.

New Standards. (1999). *Reading and writing grade by grade.* Washington, DC: National Center on Education and the Economy and the University of Pittsburgh.

No Child Left Behind Act of 2001 (NCLB). Pub. L. No. 107-110, 115 Stat. 1425 (2002).

O'Connor, R. E., Bell, K. M., Harty, K. R., Larkin, L. K., Sackor, S. M., & Zigmond, N. (2002). Teaching reading to poor readers in the intermediate grades: A comparison of text difficulty. *Journal of Educational Psychology, 94,* 474–485.

Oliva, P. F., & Pawlas, G. E. (2001). *Supervision for today's schools.* New York: Wiley.

Paris, S. G. (2005). Reinterpreting the development of reading skills. *Reading Research Quarterly, 40*(2), 184–202.

Pearson, P. D., & Raphael, T. E. (2003). Toward an ecologically balanced literacy curriculum. In L. B. Gambrell, L. M. Morrow, S. B. Neuman, & M. Pressley (Eds.), *Best practices in literacy instruction* (pp. 23–39). New York: Guilford Press.

Popham, W. J. (2005). *America's "failing" schools: How parents and teachers can cope with No Child Left Behind.* New York: Routledge.

Reeves, D. B. (2005). High performance in high-poverty schools: 90/90/90 and beyond. In Flood, J., & Anders, P. (Eds.), *Literacy development of students in urban schools* (pp. 362–388). Newark, DE: International Reading Association.

Reutzel, D. R., & Cooter, R. B., Jr. (1996) *Teaching children to read: From basals to books* (2nd ed.). Englewood Cliffs, NJ: Merrill.

Rice, J. K. (2003). *Teacher quality: Understanding the effectiveness of teacher attributes.* Washington, DC: Economic Policy Institute. Retrieved May 16, 2007, from Economic Policy Institute Web site at http://www.epinet.org/content.cfm?id=1500

Sanders, W. L., & Rivers, J. C. (1996). *Cumulative and residual effects of teachers on future student academic achievement.* Knoxville, TN: University of Tennessee, Value-Added Research and Assessment Center.

Schenck, E. A., Walker, D. R., Nagel, C. R., & Webb, L. C. (2005). *Analysis of state K–3 reading standards and assessments.* Retrieved May 16, 2007, from the U.S. Department of Education Web site at http://www.ed.gov/rschstat/eval/other/reading/state-K3-reading.pdf

Schmoker, M., & Marzano, R. J. (1999). Realizing the promise of standards-based education. *Educational Leadership, 56*(6), 17–21.

Sizer, T. R. (1985). Common sense. *Educational Leadership, 42*(6), 21–22.

Snow, C. E., Burns, M. S., & Griffin, P. (Eds.). (1998). *Preventing reading difficulties in young children* (Report of the National Research Council, Committee on the Prevention of Reading Difficulties in Young Children). Washington, DC: National Academy Press.

Squire, J. (1983). Composing and comprehending: Two sides of the same basic process. *Language Arts, 60*(5), 627–643.

Stiggins, R. J. (2002). Assessment crisis: The absence of assessment for learning. *Phi Delta Kappan, 83*(10), 758–765.

Stotsky, S. (2000). *The state of the state standards in English language arts/reading.* Washington, DC: Fordham Foundation. Retrieved May 16, 2007, from http://www.edexcellence.net/foundation/publication/publication.cfm?id=24&pubsubid=187#187

Taylor, B. M., Pearson, P. D., Clark, K., & Walpole, S. (2000). Effective schools and accomplished teachers: Lessons about primary-grade reading instruction in low-income schools. *The Elementary School Journal, 101*(2), 121–166.

Taylor, B. M., Pressley, M., & Pearson, P. D. (2002). Research-supported characteristics of teachers and schools that promote reading achievement. In B. M. Taylor & P. D. Pearson (Eds.), *Teaching reading: Effective schools, accomplished teachers* (pp. 361–374). Mahwah, NJ: Erlbaum.

Teberg, A. (1999, April). *Identified professional development needs of teachers in curriculum reform.* Paper presented at the meeting of the American Educational Research Association, Montreal, Canada.

Toll, C. A. (2005). *The literacy coach's survival guide: Essential questions and practical answers.* Newark, DE: International Reading Association.

Walpole, S., & McKenna, M. (2004). *The literacy coach's handbook.* New York: Guilford Press.

Wixson, K. K., & Dutro, E. (1999). Standards for primary-grade reading: An analysis of state frameworks. *The Elementary School Journal, 100*(2), 89–110.

University of Texas–Austin. (2003). *Preventing reading difficulties: A three-tiered intervention model.* Retrieved May 16, 2007, from http://www.texasreading.org/3tier/

Ysseldyke, J. E., Thurlow, M. L., Mecklenburg, C., & Graden, J. (1984). Opportunity to learn for regular and special education students during reading instruction. *Remedial and Special Education, 5,* 29–37.

CHAPTER 2

Reading Specialists

On Becoming Leaders of Literacy

Shelley B. Wepner and Diana J. Quatroche

Lara Parent is a reading specialist for a Grades 4–8 school in Holland, Michigan (30 miles from Grand Rapids). The principal chose her for this position because of her master's degree in reading and her reading specialist certification. Previously, she was the reading specialist for Grades 4 and 5 in a different elementary school building within the same district that had Reading First coaches for

Grades 1–3. Lara wanted to become a reading specialist so that she could work directly with hard-to-reach students. She feels committed to getting the right books into their hands and helping them understand that reading is for meaning. Lara follows the principal's request that she support classroom teachers, and she believes in supporting them in any way they want. This includes doing a lesson in the teacher's classroom or providing ideas for the teacher's own lessons. In addition, she does "push-in" work with students in the classroom or works individually with students, as needed. She sees her role mainly as supporting classroom teachers by modeling strategies, providing materials, and being generally helpful. Even though the building has class periods, her time spent with teachers and students is fluid, depending on the needs. She has worked hard to develop partnerships with the principal, the teachers, and the parents, and attributes her success to the vision that she shares with them.

Sue Tosti is a high school reading specialist in Cinnaminson, New Jersey (10 miles east of Philadelphia, Pennsylvania), where she has evolved into serving as a leader of literacy. In addition to teaching classes to students in need of additional reading instruction, Sue coaches classroom teachers on how to help their students process content material from textbooks. She refers to her method as "collaborative consultation," in which she sees the classroom teacher as the expert with students and the curriculum, and sees herself as the expert on how to teach reading. Sue believes that her success with teachers stems from her fervent belief about collaborating with teachers as equals with full appreciation of their knowledge and professionalism. It does not hurt that her high school's test scores on the state-wide language arts assessment have been first in the county. This fact has simply strengthened her position about the importance of involving the entire school community in support of students' reading achievement. Sue attributes her ability to penetrate as a "coach" to the full support of her administration and the Board of Education. Recently, she also became the half-time reading coordinator for the district, which allows her to work with teachers across the district.

Lara and Sue are licensed by their states to serve as reading specialists. Lara has a master's degree in reading and reading specialist certification in Wisconsin and Michigan. Sue has a master's and doctorate in reading, and is certified in special education and reading in Pennsylvania and New Jersey. Sue also has a supervisory certificate in New Jersey. While both have been formally prepared to serve as reading specialists, they have different roles and responsibilities that are shaped by their school culture and themselves. Nevertheless, they share a common purpose in promoting students' literacy development and, according to their colleagues, have been successful in their respective positions. The purpose of this chapter is to examine the reading specialist position by means of the following:

- Describing roles and responsibilities of reading specialists
- Examining reading specialists as leaders
- Discussing how other personnel serve as partners with reading specialists to promote literacy
- Identifying ways to help reading specialists succeed in their positions

WHAT IS A READING SPECIALIST?

A *reading specialist* is a professional with advanced preparation and experience in teaching reading who has responsibility for the literacy performance of readers in general and of struggling readers in particular (International Reading Association [IRA], 2000). Today's reading specialist is expected to be a leader of literacy for teachers, schools, and the community. Depending on the school system, a reading specialist can be referred to as a *reading teacher, literacy coach, reading coach, reading consultant, reading supervisor,* or *reading coordinator* (Quatroche & Wepner, 2007).

Advanced preparation and experience in teaching reading typically means that a reading specialist has a minimum of 2 years of classroom teaching experience along with a master's degree in reading that leads to statewide certification. The master's degree usually includes at least 24 graduate credits in reading/language arts and related courses as well as 6 hours of a supervised practicum experience. Reading specialist candidates are expected to graduate from such programs with an understanding of the following: the reading process; the psychological, sociological, and linguistic foundations of reading; language development and reading acquisition; the major components of reading; grouping options for instruction; and varied instructional practices, approaches, and methods (IRA, 2000,

2004). (Additional information about reading specialist preparation is provided later in the chapter.)

Reading specialists work with early childhood, elementary, adolescent, and/or adult learners. They help preschoolers to emerge as readers, elementary children to develop as readers, adolescents to use reading to learn across content areas, and adults to continue to read or develop as readers, depending on their previous experiences and abilities. While most reading specialists work at the elementary level, many serve an important role at the middle and high school levels (IRA, 2000), especially with a recent focus on the importance of adolescent literacy (see Chapter 6). There now are separate statewide certificates for reading specialists, Grades 5–12. Reading specialists work in public and private schools, reading resource centers, and reading clinics.

WHAT ARE THE ROLES OF READING SPECIALISTS?

Reading specialists have three primary roles: instruction, assessment, and leadership (IRA, 2000). Each role, as described below, contributes to the others in order to promote student learning.

Instruction

Reading specialists work with students to support, supplement, and extend classroom teaching (IRA, 2000). They provide instruction for individuals or small groups of students, especially those identified as struggling readers. However, as one of us experienced firsthand, reading specialists also work with students who are advanced readers to help them read strategically above grade-level texts. Such instruction, whether for struggling readers or advanced readers, tends to go beyond what is provided by classroom teachers. Reading specialists typically use a combination of models, both pull-out and push-in, to accommodate the needs of the students, the instructional context, and the school culture (Bean, Swan, & Knaub, 2003).

Reading specialists' work as instructors is becoming increasingly important as schools begin to recognize the significance of students' literacy development at all grade levels. Reading specialists

help teachers in the upper grades focus on vocabulary, comprehension, and critical reading skills, and provide guidance to content teachers on ways to help students succeed with content-specific texts (Farstrup, 2005/2006).

Reading specialists use specific programs supported by research (e.g., Reading Recovery) or a combination of programs they developed to address students' needs. Reading specialists use a variety of materials for instruction, sometimes offered with a specific program and sometimes selected or developed by the reading specialists. Sue Tosti uses materials that come from her high school classroom teachers so that she can help students read and comprehend specific content material. She also uses test preparation books and authentic literature to supplement content-based instruction. Like Sue, Lara Parent uses a variety of texts and books, including magazines, picture books, fiction, and nonfiction. The materials used depend on student and teacher needs. She also works with teachers to develop special materials that will help students pass the Michigan writing exam. These materials include cross-text writing pieces so that students have opportunities to work with the reading, thinking, and writing framework necessary for success on the exam. She has been working with the classroom teachers and another reading specialist in the building to build a special collection of leveled books. For example, they collected 1,000 fiction and nonfiction books that relate to Michigan's social studies content standards.

Materials used by reading specialists include publisher-designed books, children's literature with a variety of genres, manipulatives, audiotapes, videotapes, computer software, and Web sites. Lara Parent developed a Web site for summer reading so that students would be engaged all summer. The Web site includes titles and pictures of books at all levels, prereading and up. She has found her blogs (or Web logs) with teachers and students about the books to be time-consuming, yet rewarding.

As with other supplementary specialists such as resource room teachers, school counselors, and speech therapists, the reading specialists' goal is to help students acquire enough skills and strategies so that they no longer need the additional assistance. Sue Tosti is particularly excited when her students' newfound skills and strategies enable them to pass the statewide test.

The instructional role is important because it allows reading specialists to have a direct impact on students' reading achievement. This role also enables reading specialists to serve as role models for classroom teachers since reading specialists teach directly in the classroom or report to classroom teachers what they are doing during pull-out sessions. Critically important for students' reading development is the coordinated instructional effort of the reading specialist and the classroom teacher so that their objectives, strategies, assignments, and materials are aligned to maximize students' learning.

The instructional role helps to establish credibility with classroom teachers because reading specialists can communicate their understanding of students' needs and their knowledge of ways to help with such needs. By having access to teachers to discuss both students and the reading program, reading specialists have a pathway to serving as a leader (Bean et al., 2003).

Assessment

Reading specialists evaluate the literacy program in general, assess the reading strengths and needs of students, and communicate findings to classroom teachers, parents, and specialized personnel such as psychologists, special educators, or speech therapists (IRA, 2000). Reading specialists understand the purpose of assessment in relation to instruction, and know the types of assessment instruments (or tests) and what they measure, how to use such assessment instruments, test-preparation strategies, and ways to interpret and report test results. They assist in the development and selection of assessment instruments and activities (retelling protocols, running records, sight word lists, informal reading inventories, interviews, and fluency activities). They understand how to use all types of assessment information to inform instruction (IRA, 2000, 2004).

Reading specialists conduct assessments for individuals or groups of students. For example, they can assess the reading skills of all entering first graders (Bean et al., 2003), test all those who failed a specific test, or test those recommended by classroom teachers. Sue Tosti tests all those who receive below-basic scores on the eighth-grade statewide test and those recommended by teachers the

first few weeks of the school year. She uses the *Gray Oral Reading Tests*, 4th ed. (Wiederholt & Bryant, 2000), the *Gray Silent Reading Tests* (Wiederholt & Blalock, 2000), the *Qualitative Reading Inventory–4* (Leslie & Caldwell, 2005), and the *Critical Reading Inventory: Assessing Student's Reading and Thinking* (Applegate, Quinn, & Applegate, 2004) to determine whether a student is in need of a basic skills reading class. She informally assesses during the year to determine students' progress and at the end of the year to determine students' placements for the next school year.

Reading specialists also use and help teachers to use test preparation strategies. Some of the strategies include using testlike material to help students receive feedback on the skills needed to be successful with the test; familiarizing students with a specific test format; modeling test taking so that students can listen to a respected person respond to test questions; and simulating testing conditions (McCabe, 2003). Sue Tosti goes into every 11th-grade English class to help teach students test preparation strategies for the 11th-grade statewide test. She helps them understand what to expect from the test, and gives them strategies for working with both expository and narrative text. Lara Parent works with the teachers to develop supplemental lessons that will help students, including those who are English language learners, pass the statewide writing assessment.

Leadership

As leaders, reading specialists serve as a resource to other educators, parents, and the community (IRA, 2000). Leadership activities include planning lessons with teachers, working with teachers and administrators to select reading material, coordinating the reading program, developing curriculum and special initiatives, coteaching, providing professional development activities, participating in school-based study teams, and working with allied professionals.

Lara Parent spends 80% of her time working with teachers to support their work. As part of her leadership role, she trains and supports adult tutors in the school to help them understand the need to balance skill support with strategy support so that students recognize the importance of reading for meaning.

Lara has initiated a number of projects across the school. For example, she has invited authors of children's books to the school for an assembly. Before the assembly she introduces the author to students via the author's Web site. She gives teachers information about the author to share with students and provides teachers with the author's books for read-alouds. Other initiatives she has undertaken include the following:

- *The Super-Cool After-School Reading Club:* This club is intended to help students develop the habit of reading independently for sustained amounts of time. Students voluntarily meet in the media center after school to read. She listens to each student read and helps each student practice comprehension strategies. Some of her former students, who are now in middle school, help as student assistants.
- *The Small-Group Differentiated Reading Instruction:* This action research project is being piloted as a teaching model in several classrooms as Lara does push-in work with students. The purpose of this project is to determine whether a teaching model of using book study, discussion groups, and video promotes student growth in fluency, word study, and comprehension. Lara and her teachers will meet to share ideas and data about student growth.

Lara also works with parents during the parent nights that take place twice a year. She models strategies for parents, gives parents books for their children, and shares her Web site to provide additional ideas and get parent feedback on ways to improve the site for home use. The Read-at-Home project that she initiated enables students to choose books at their level of independent reading to take home to practice with their families. Her reward comes when parents share with her that they have seen a difference in their child's reading, often for the first time since attending school.

Sue Tosti, who spends 75% of her time in the beginning of the year working with teachers, also has developed a number of initiatives for her high school as well as the other schools. She arranged to have the district's reading specialists and most of the district's elementary teachers participate in a book club using Gerald Duffy's *Explaining Reading:*

A Resource for Teaching Concepts, Skills, and Strategies (2003). She gave a book to each teacher, and they all met every month for 10 months. As a culminating learning experience, Duffy came to the district to provide a full-day in-service about his techniques.

Intent on promoting her high school students' reading, Sue implemented with her teachers and students various ways to celebrate reading, some of which are described below:

- *Read Across America:* High school students (basic-skills reading students who have remedial instruction with Sue) go to the district's K–2 building to perform Reader's Theater for the younger students to celebrate Dr. Seuss' birthday.
- *Storybook TIME (To Improve Motivation and Enthusiasm):* Basic-skills reading students create storybooks for second-grade students in the K–2 building and go to the school to read the books. Each second grader has his or her name in one of the books about a created character that has his or her same hair color and characteristics. The books are then donated to the classroom library.
- *CARE (Cross-Aged Reading Experience):* Each Monday a group of basic-skills reading students go the Grades 3–5 building and teach reading strategies to the third- and fourth-grade basic-skills reading students.
- *Battle of the Books:* Sue Tosti and the librarian are the advisers for an after-school club. All students and staff are welcome to participate. Teams of students and staff compete by reading 10 books and answering questions about the books.

Both reading specialists have spent a great deal of their time developing a leadership role in their schools and creating a culture that responds positively and enthusiastically to initiatives that promote literacy. Lara Parent believes that, to develop as a leader, one must observe other leaders, talk to them about what works, attend conferences, join professional organizations, and have a support group.

While there is not yet enough research on the way in which the leadership role should be executed in schools, there is feedback from principals and reading specialists that the leadership role contributes to classroom teachers' ability to provide high-quality literacy instruction (Bean et al., 2003; Klein, Monti,

Mulcahy-Ernt, & Speck, 1997). In many schools, reading specialist activities have shifted away from direct teaching of students to serving as a resource to classroom teachers (IRA, 2004).

Serving as a resource to teachers actually supports student learning by making classroom teachers aware of the connection between their dispositions regarding reading and student achievement. Lara Parent sees her role as one of helping all teachers become specialists of reading and writing. Cobb (2005) describes how one reading specialist provided professional development for a team of teachers to improve Annual Yearly Progress. This reading specialist used her role as a leader to assist the school in managing professional development services provided by the district.

The leadership role is important because it helps build teachers' capacity for serving students. Put another way, the best way to serve students is to serve teachers. Providing professional development to teachers helps to build capacity. One type of professional development that shows promise is coaching.

Coaching is a form of instruction where there is an ongoing relationship between an experienced and a less experienced person in which the coach provides training, guidance, advice, support, and feedback to the protégé. Coaching helps teachers learn to use new ideas, tools, and strategies, and practice what they learn within their own contexts. Practicing within their own contexts allows teachers to see the whether such ideas and techniques are relevant for their unique teaching situations. For example, a reading specialist who knew that her teachers were not confident with their ability to do read-alouds would go into classrooms to demonstrate how to read narrative text and ask questions before, during, and after the read-aloud. Another reading specialist, who knew that some of her teachers were overwhelmed by the large numbers of students with special reading needs, would team teach with the classroom teacher to serve as both a role model and an assistant.

Sue Tosti, who is a push-in "coach" for her high school teachers, demonstrates the use of think-alouds in an advanced placement physics class so that the students can visualize the concepts presented in the textbook. She works with the teacher to help him understand how to incorporate other strategies into his instruction (for example, rereading and working with text structure). She intends to survey all students to determine if such coaching is increasing students' knowledge of which strategies they should use or are using when reading science text.

Collaborative coaching that impacts teacher practice comes from a shared vision, commitment, and positive interactions (Brownell, Yeager, Rennells, & Riley, 1997). Teachers have a heightened sense of self-efficacy, an improved knowledge base, and a better understanding of how to improve learning for students. Specific suggestions on ways to promote collaboration include clear guidelines, discussion of such guidelines, and the reading specialist's maintenance of a flexible schedule to be available for such collaborative work with teachers (Guth & Pettengill, 2005).

HISTORICAL CONTEXT AND CURRENT STANDARDS FOR READING SPECIALISTS AS LEADERS

The role of reading specialists as leaders is not new. In the 1960s and 1970s, when the role developed to address post-Sputnik concerns about literacy in the United States, reading specialists served as resource persons, advisors, and in-service leaders (Robinson & Rauch, 1965; Vogt & Shearer, 2003). A shift in the reading specialist position occurred in the early 1980s with the advent of changes in Title I when the role evolved into functioning primarily as a remedial reading teacher with the primary function of assessing and instructing students. A downward trend in the use of reading specialists as leaders continued until the late 1990s and early 2000s. Studies that were conducted during this period found that reading specialists needed to have responsibility for schoolwide literacy improvement for all students (Allington & Walmsley, 1995; Bean, Cassidy, Grumet, Shelton, & Wallis, 2002; Long, 1995; Quatroche, Bean, & Hamilton, 2001).

Current standards for reading specialists call for the leadership role because, as Pipes (2004) reports, work with classroom teachers ensures that there is quality "first" teaching. Widespread recognition of the leadership role has occurred recently because of the emergence of the literacy coach who is not necessarily a licensed reading specialist. While the role of the literacy coach varies from venue to venue, it is generally used for the improvement of the instructional capacity of teachers (Hall, 2004). Reading First, one of the many outgrowths of No Child Left Behind, requires the hiring of literacy coaches to work with classroom teachers as they implement best practice in relation to the five components of reading: phonemic awareness, phonics, fluency, comprehension, and vocabulary.

Literacy Coach

The role of the literacy coach appears in the current standards for reading professionals (IRA, 2004), where one of the categories is designated as "reading specialist/literacy coach." The description of the category lists the following responsibilities for this role: be a resource to teachers, paraprofessionals, administrators, and the community; collaborate and work cooperatively with other professionals; provide professional development; and advocate for students.

Literacy coaches (or reading coaches) are full-time, site-based professionals responsible for leading change (Walpole & Blamey, 2006). Literacy coaches often are reading specialists who are called upon to work with teachers; however, some literacy coaches are not certified as reading specialists. Sometimes, reading specialists are given the title of reading or literacy coach, and sometimes they are not. The roles of reading specialist and literacy coach can be quite distinct or overlap, depending on school and district needs. In some schools, there are both reading specialists who work with children and coaches who work with teachers and reading specialists. Generally, reading specialists spend most of their day with children, and literacy coaches spend most of their day with teachers. However, these roles can become blurred and meshed, depending on school or district needs. The different types of roles of literacy coaches will be described in depth in Chapter 3. However, for purposes of this chapter, we are looking at those who have been prepared to serve as reading specialists who have added leadership responsibilities as literacy coaches (Bean, 2004; Dole, 2004; IRA, 2004).

Reading Supervisor/Coordinator

Reading supervisors or *reading coordinators* possess the skills of reading specialists plus the supervisory skills and certification to officially observe teachers. They are responsible for teacher supervision, which requires skill in observing, conferring, and evaluating teachers across the district. They also might have responsibility for evaluating the district reading program and its outcomes, providing professional development for other specialists in the district, putting into place formal and informal assessment tools, administering the Title I program, and facilitating the work of other reading specialists in the district (IRA, 2000). Sue Tosti, with her supervisory certification, was appointed half-time for the new district reading coordinator position so that she could help the entire district move forward with its literacy program. See Table 2.1 for a brief overview of general similarities and differences among reading specialists, literacy coaches, and reading supervisors/coordinators.

WHAT SPECIAL SKILLS AND CHARACTERISTICS SHOULD A READING SPECIALIST POSSESS?

Charged with the responsibility of improving reading achievement and responding to the literacy needs of the students in a school, reading specialists should possess the skills and characteristics that are reflective of good leaders. They need to have the expertise to deliver exemplary instruction (Allington, 2006). They also need to be able to get their teacher colleagues to work with them to deliver high-quality instruction that meets students' needs.

Reading specialists who have credibility as leaders are able to do what they are charged to do, usually have advanced preparation in reading, and have experience as a classroom teacher. Their teaching experience enables them to understand and assist teachers with the challenges that they face in addressing students' needs.

In addition to the necessary educational and professional background, reading specialists have certain leadership skills that enable them to succeed in their roles. Borrowing from a conceptual frame-

Table 2.1. Comparison of the Positions of Reading Specialist, Literacy Coach, and Reading Supervisor/Coordinator

	Reading Specialist	*Literacy Coach*	*Reading Supervisor/Coordinator*
Qualifications	Master's degree	At least some graduate coursework that may or may not lead to a master's degree	Master's degree
	Reading specialist certificate		Reading specialist certificate
			Supervisory certificate
	Prior teaching experience	Prior teaching experience	Prior teaching experience
Roles and responsibilities	Instruct students	Sometimes instruct students	Work with and supervise teachers
	Assess students and reading program	Sometimes analyze student test results	Facilitate the work of other reading specialists and/or literacy coaches
	Work with teachers	Primarily work with teachers	Oversee reading program in the district
Level of responsibility	School-based	School-based	District-based

work about the leadership of education deans (Wepner, D'Onofrio, & Wilhite, 2003, 2006), it appears that reading specialists who are successful as leaders possess characteristics that enable them to function in four dimensions: intellectual, emotional, social, and moral (see Figure 2.1).

The *intellectual* dimension refers to reading specialists' knowledge of the various facets of their job, and their ability to juggle each responsibility within their own contexts. The assumption with this dimension is that reading specialists have the necessary knowledge about the field of literacy and about their own reading program. They know how their reading program addresses state and national standards and assessment mandates, and how to modify accordingly. They know how to administer and interpret multiple assessment instruments. They are aware of trends, research, and alternative methodologies. They have their own sense of automaticity in using specific content area reading strategies. As leaders, reading specialists know when, where, and how to use this information within their own schools and districts to promote change. For example, Sue Tosti is confident with her knowledge of reading and her school culture, is aware of her administrators' support, and knows how to work with her teacher colleagues so that they are receptive to her

professional development offerings. She is aware of teachers' often conflicting demands and needs, and uses this knowledge as well as her own understanding of students' needs to assist both groups.

The *emotional* dimension refers to feelings and sensibilities that include an ability to acknowledge inner conflict and an ability to express feelings vividly and convincingly. Successful reading personnel are confident in overseeing their job and have a balanced perspective about their roles as leaders. They recognize their own strengths and weaknesses, and know when they can help and when they can't. They are honest with themselves about people, policies, and practices that are bothersome, yet can set them aside as appropriate. They also are comfortable in expressing their thoughts when people, policies, and practices inhibit learning or stifle teaching. For instance, Sue Tosti has had to be patient with her teachers until they allowed her to come into their classrooms. As she said, "Every year, people get more comfortable." She also knows that she has to deal with union issues (cannot use lunch or prep time) and continues to figure out ways to work around this policy. Sue is convinced about the importance of her role as a leader of literacy and believes that she will eventually get most of her teachers involved with her in some capacity. She

Figure 2.1. Four Dimensions of Leadership of Reading Personnel

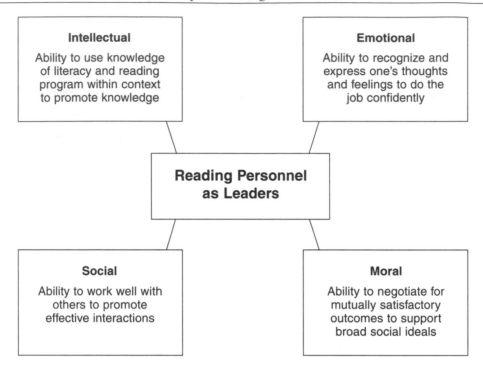

believes that her flexibility, positive attitude, and good communication skills will help to get her into classrooms. She also knows that, once there, she will work hard to convince teachers that she is helping them to help their students succeed. She is secure enough in her role to be focused on her pursuit of promoting literacy across the school and district. Lara Parent also sees flexibility as a huge dimension of her role. She knows that teachers must be supported in the way they want and that she must meet the teachers where they "are." She also knows that she must demonstrate patience with her teachers.

The *social* dimension is about transactions with others, including societal and organizational relationships. Successful reading personnel cope with conflict rather than ignore it, are tolerant and empathetic toward others, and respect individual differences. They listen, cooperate, collaborate, and encourage others to try new things. They work effectively with teachers, administrators, students, and parents on an individual and on a group basis. Their interactions with their constituencies promote positive responses to themselves and to their ideas. Lara Parent has worked particularly hard with this

dimension in developing a partnership with the teachers in her building. She demonstrates that she cares about them and interacts with them nonjudgmentally. She partners with them by engaging in action research activities together and writing grants to benefit the whole school. These grants have provided books for teachers and professional development for the science and social studies teachers. She is constantly encouraging her teachers to identify ways that they can use her ideas in their own classrooms.

The *moral* dimension has to do with a sense of conscience and accountability, and the desire to negotiate energetically for mutually satisfactory solutions to problems and broad social ideals. Reading personnel who are successful know to maintain confidentiality and believe strongly in working together with others to get the best possible outcome for both parties. They do what they say they are going to do. They are committed to doing the right thing as much as doing the thing right. In other words, short-term losses are seen as opportunities for long-term gains. Both Sue and Lara are aware of colleagues in other school districts who engage in questionable practices with their respective state-wide assessments. As with their colleagues, they know that some students will have great difficulty passing the test, no matter what is tried. Unlike them, they do not condone some of the practices that exist such as encouraging high absenteeism on testing days or withholding the tests of certain low-achieving students.

Both Lara and Sue know that when they work with their teachers to help them align instruction with state standards, and guide students with test preparation strategies, they are doing their best to help as many students as possible pass their respective statewide tests. While they feel accountable for students' performance and know that they and their administrators want as many students as possible to succeed, they will not compromise their values for a few better scores.

In summary, reading specialists with characteristics in these four dimensions are able to meet the demands of their roles. Committed to the ideal of developing students' literacy, they have the intellectual and emotional stamina to work well with all constituencies to get the most from them. They know enough about their school or district to establish and communicate realistic expectations. They are able to suggest ideas and materials, conduct professional development workshops, model strategies or techniques, and conduct demonstration lessons (IRA, 2000) that fit with their teachers' needs. Their steadfast belief in the purpose of their role gives them emotional license to find ways to be heard, to be humored, and eventually to be respected. This is especially important as they work with all other stakeholders connected directly or indirectly to a school or district literacy program.

OTHER PERSONNEL AS PARTNERS WITH READING SPECIALISTS IN A LITERACY PROGRAM

The Principal

Principals, as instructional leaders, are in a unique position to support the schoolwide literacy program. They are responsible for ensuring that the literacy program is being implemented through teacher observations, teacher conferences, and professional development opportunities in the form of workshops, demonstration lessons, and coaching. As a supporter of the reading specialist, the school principal can make sure that teachers regard the reading specialist as the primary person for developing the literacy program. The principal can also help teachers understand the importance of collaborating with the reading specialist.

If a principal has a reading background, a powerful partnership can be created. For example, one of us was a liaison to an elementary Professional Development School where the principal had been a reading specialist. As the teachers in this school planned for the implementation of a Title I schoolwide program, this principal was especially supportive and knowledgeable about the process. She attended the planning meetings, provided time for teachers to research current practices in literacy, and encouraged teachers to consider ways to make literacy a high priority in this school. This principal is indeed involved in every facet of the program. Lara Parent's former principal was very committed to the reading program and actually modeled reading strategies in classrooms. The principal in her current building understands the importance of the reading specialist role and intentionally selected Lara because she could work effectively with classroom teachers in a supportive role.

If the principal does not have a reading background, it is even more essential that a reading specialist be available to guide teachers with the implementation of the schoolwide literacy program. The reading specialist can inform the principal about current research and best practice for reading programs, and involve the principal in professional development along with the classroom teachers. When principals become knowledgeable about reading, they become even more supportive of the reading specialist and the total school literacy program.

The Classroom Teacher

Now, more than ever, classroom teachers are seen as partners with reading specialists in helping with students' literacy development. Classroom teachers have consistent, long-term experience with their students in all areas of the curriculum (Jaeger, 1996) and can work with reading specialists to strengthen their own teaching and help individual students. Content teachers, in particular, benefit from their work with reading specialists in teaching students how to use strategies that will help them make their way through their texts (Henwood, 1999/2000).

Whereas the classroom teacher has knowledge about students and specific content areas, the reading specialist has knowledge of reading and students' reading behaviors. The reading specialist can note the reading strategies that students use or do not use effectively for different types of texts and content areas. Together, the classroom teacher and reading specialist can develop a plan that reinforces students' strengths and expands their repertoire of strategies that help with learning (Jaeger, 1996).

To facilitate such collaborative work, classroom teachers need to understand the psychology of reading and reading development, the structure of the English language, best practices in reading and content area instruction, and assessment strategies that will inform classroom teaching of reading and specific content areas (American Federation of Teachers, 1999). It is their responsibility to avail themselves of professional development opportunities when necessary. And the reading specialist can provide much of this professional development in a way that meets the needs of the classroom teacher, the students, and the school.

Other Partners

Parents. The reading specialist can build positive home-school relationships, and help classroom teachers do the same. They can also take on the role of advocate for students (Hamilton, 1993). Reading specialists can provide workshops for parents so that children can receive positive support at home in their efforts to become or develop as readers. Parents should keep in close contact with their child's teachers and be supportive of the school literacy program. They can spend time listening to their children read or discuss learning events from school, take children to the library, read aloud to children, talk about and review homework assignments, limit the amount of television and unsuitable video/computer games in the home, and provide a positive role model for their children. Lara Parent's parent nights are just one way that she

helps parents see how their children are being taught so that they can support their children at home. The demonstrations to parents help them to understand how reading to children is important, and provides them with activities related to books that can be easily used at home.

Local School Boards. Local school boards should be informed of all facets of the district's literacy program. It is their responsibility to endorse exemplary practice of school personnel. Local school boards should be knowledgeable of what teachers, principals, and reading specialists are doing to further the district's goals for the literacy program. They should support the literacy program by making informed decisions regarding budget, personnel, and curriculum.

State Departments of Education. The International Reading Association (2000, 2004), in its position statements about the roles of and standards for reading specialists, believes that state departments of education should consider six major requirements or performance standards when approving graduate teacher education programs for prospective reading specialists. Graduate programs need to ensure that graduates (1) are proficient in knowledge and beliefs about reading; (2) have a broad and deep knowledge of literacy instruction and assessment; (3) have skills to organize and enhance reading programs; (4) can communicate and collaborate with others; (5) complete a practicum where they have experience working with students experiencing reading difficulties and with adult learners; and (6) have experiences that enable them to develop leadership skills. The need for state departments of education to look closely at IRA standards is confirmed by a study conducted by Dole, Liang, Watkins, and Wiggins (2006).

State Boards of Education. Reading specialists should have a role in determining their state's educational policy by being active participants in statewide professional organizations and volunteering to participate in statewide committees or task forces. State boards create standards and policy that affect the curriculum and assessment that impact local school districts. As a result of the No Child Left Behind Act of 2001, many states have implemented high-stakes statewide assessment systems that affect school funding and school classifications. These assessments reflect statewide curriculum standards for students. It is therefore important for school personnel to understand how and where these types of decisions are made, and to determine ways to help their school and district adjust accordingly.

HOW SHOULD A READING SPECIALIST BE PREPARED TO ASSUME THIS POSITION?

Reading specialists need to be knowledgeable about their three major roles (instruction, assessment, and leadership), and have experiences that enable them to develop in these three roles. Graduate programs that prepare reading specialists need to provide experiences that focus on these three roles. Practicum experiences should take place in classrooms and schools, and not just in clinical settings, so that reading specialist candidates can apply their college/university classroom understandings to real classroom and school situations. Of particular importance in recent years is the need for graduate programs to prepare reading specialist candidates for the leadership role, especially given coaching responsibilities.

Increasingly aware of the lack of research on what college and university graduate programs for reading specialists are actually doing, we surveyed reading professors across the United States to find out their perceptions about the way they prepare or want to prepare reading specialists to serve as leaders of literacy (Quatroche & Wepner, 2007). We developed a 19-question survey to seek answers to two major questions: What aspects of leadership are currently in place to develop reading specialists? What content and experiences should be included in programs to develop reading specialists?

As for the aspects of leadership that currently are in place, we found that only slightly more than half of the programs had a course in the organization, administration, and/or supervision of reading programs, and less than half required some type of practicum for developing leadership skills. When a practicum requirement existed, reading specialist candidates had to analyze a reading program, perform a needs assessment, prepare staff develop-

ment for classroom teachers, provide in-class demonstration lessons, and develop and present an improvement plan.

As for the content and experiences that should be in place, most respondents indicated that a course in the organization, administration, and/or supervision of reading programs should be offered so that reading specialist candidates could learn how to serve as a resource to classroom teachers, administrators, and parents; how to provide staff development; and how to develop and coordinate a literacy program. They also indicated the need to have a leadership practicum in a school setting. A majority of the respondents also indicated that reading specialists need to demonstrate leadership competencies in the three aforementioned areas before they are eligible for certification. They believe that reading specialists should focus on helping teachers become more knowledgeable about the teaching of reading by assisting them with ideas, strategies, and materials; modeling strategies and techniques; and providing professional development workshops.

As Bean et al. (2003) believe, and we agree, standards at the state level for reading specialist certification may need to be more explicit in their call for leadership skills, thus requiring colleges and universities to modify their programs for reading specialist certification. To better understand what states require, we worked with a colleague to collect information about different state's certification requirements. We found that, while some states do require a master's degree in reading and 2 years teaching experience, many still do not. One state, in fact, only requires a bachelor's degree in reading and one year of employment as a teacher. In addition to the lack of consistency about qualifications to serve as a reading specialist, there is a lack of evidence of the inclusion of leadership as a requirement for licensure as a reading specialist (K. Sullivan, personal communication, October 2, 2006). Our findings were confirmed by a study conducted by Dole et al. (2006), who also found variability with licensure requirements for reading specialists among the states.

To help promote the leadership role, we should look to our professional organizations such as the International Reading Association to bring national attention to the issue and enforce its standards for the preparation of reading specialists. The standards developed by the IRA (2004) require that graduate programs prepare reading specialists for the leadership role. Preparation for the leadership role should come from coursework and field experiences (Shaw, Smith, Chesler, & Romeo, 2005). Although changes in the curriculum for reading specialists at many colleges and universities have not yet caught up with the most recent standards, it is anticipated that if graduate literacy programs want national recognition, they will eventually change their programs to include at least one course on administering a reading program.

We should also learn how to work with our legislators to promote statewide changes in the licensure requirements for reading specialists. When working with legislators, we should have the latest information available, and give concise information that can be easily understood (Fox, 2004; Lewis, 2004; Mraz, 2004). D. Ray Reutzel (2006) and the Honorable Fred Hunsaker, a member of the Utah House of Representatives (2006), believe that we should work within our own organizations, become familiar with the legislative process, develop potential solutions and ideas for changing standards, and establish credibility and trust as we lobby for our needs.

A good example is the work of reading specialists through the Keystone State Reading Association in Pennsylvania. This group was successful in changing the state policy for credentialing reading specialists. The Pennsylvania Department of Education (PDE) had determined that teachers with an initial teaching license could add "reading specialist" to their license by passing the PRAXIS exam without any further training. This particular association convinced the PDE of the importance of completing a reading specialist program at a college or university ("Persistence pays," 2006).

WHAT ARE FUTURE DIRECTIONS FOR READING SPECIALISTS?

Reading specialists are poised to document their achievements and get recognized for their accomplishments because of a recent appreciation of the role that they play in promoting pre-K–12 student achievement. Four types of documentation include the following:

- Accomplishments with students and students' test scores through pre/post informal and formal assessments
- Evidence of teachers' growth as a result of collaboration with the reading specialist/literacy coach through pre/post assessment data
- Records of changes in teachers' classrooms and the school environment with pre/post assessment instruments such as surveys, observations, and visual representations
- Records of interactions and initiatives with parents such as workshops in study skills or meetings about tests through printed programs, attendance lists, and evaluation forms.

These types of documentation help the local school district and educational community become aware of accomplishments that might not otherwise be evident. Of critical importance is the need for comparative achievement data of schools and school districts with and without reading specialists to further document the importance of the role.

Also essential is the need to bring recognition to the role of the reading specialist by, for example, conducting case studies of exemplary reading specialists, developing and presenting awards for outstanding reading specialists, conducting special institutes about reading specialists, and publishing separate sections in journals and thematic issues about ways that reading specialists are effecting teacher growth and student achievement (Wepner, 2005).

Documenting and highlighting the significance of the role of the reading specialist will help to ensure the position's solvency across schools, promote high standards for reading specialist licensure across states, and recognize the value of cultivating reading specialists as leaders who encourage literacy across grades and disciplines.

CONCLUSION

As the roles and responsibilities of reading specialists continue to evolve, the leadership characteristics that contribute to creating a community of literacy advocates will be better understood. Every success story about the impact of reading specialists on the literacy achievement of students helps others to acknowledge the need to have academically and professionally qualified reading educators in such positions. Reading specialists should be expected to have the necessary credentials (graduate coursework and field experiences with a focus on leadership) and should be able to help define their roles and responsibilities. If placed in leadership positions where much of their work focuses on teachers, administrators, and the community, they should be expected to function effectively in the four dimensions (intellectual, emotional, social, and moral) described above. They also should look for ways to highlight their accomplishments. As more schools and districts realize the importance of using qualified reading specialists who can put into place the critical elements of literacy programs (see chapters that follow), students' potential for learning will be realized.

REFERENCES

Allington, R. L. (2006, February/March). Reading specialists, reading teachers, reading coaches: A question of credentials. *Reading Today, 23*(4), 16.

Allington, R. L., & Walmsley, S. (Eds). (1995). *No quick fix: Rethinking literacy programs in America's elementary schools.* New York: Teachers College Press; Newark, DE: International Reading Association.

American Federation of Teachers. (1999). *Teaching reading is rocket science: What expert teachers of reading should know and be able to do.* Washington, DC: Author.

Applegate, M. D., Quinn, K. B., & Applegate, A. J. (2004). *The critical reading inventory: Assessing student's reading and thinking.* Upper Saddle River, NJ: Pearson.

Bean, R. M. (2004). *The reading specialist: Leadership for the classroom, school, and community.* New York: Guilford Press.

Bean, R. M., Cassidy, J., Grumet, J. E., Shelton, D. S., & Wallis, S. R. (2002). What do reading specialists do? Results from a national survey. *The Reading Teacher, 55,* 736–745.

Bean, R. M., Swan, A. L., & Knaub, R. (2003). Reading specialists in schools with exemplary reading programs: Functional, versatile, and prepared. *The Reading Teacher, 56,* 446–455.

Brownell, M. T., Yeager, E., Rennells, M. S., & Riley, T. (1997). Teachers working together: What teacher educators and researchers should know. *Teacher Education and Special Education, 20,* 340–359.

Cobb, C. (2005). Professional development for literacy: Who's in charge. *The Reading Teacher, 59,* 388–390.

Dole, J. A. (2004). The changing role of the reading specialist in school reform. *The Reading Teacher, 57,* 462–471.

Dole, J. A., Liang, L. A., Watkins, N. M., & Wiggins, C. M. (2006). The state of reading professionals in the United States. *The Reading Teacher, 60,* 194–199.

Duffy, G. G. (2003). *Explaining reading: A resource for teaching concepts, skills, and strategies.* New York: Guilford Press.

Farstrup, A. E. (2005/2006). Qualified reading specialists: More important than ever. *Reading Today, 23*(3), 18.

Fox, B. J. (2004). Advocacy for the literacy professional: A federal perspective. In P. E. Linder, M. B. Sampson, J. R. Dugan, & B. A. Brancaot (Eds.), *Celebrating the power of literacy: 26th yearbook of the College Reading Association* (pp. 206–208). Corpus Christi, TX: College Reading Association.

Guth, N. D., & Pettengill, S. S. (2005). *Leading a successful reading program: Administrators and reading specialists working together to make it happen.* Newark, DE: International Reading Association.

Hall, B. (2004). Literacy coaches: An evolving role. *Carnegie Reporter, 3*(1). Retrieved May 22, 2006, from http://www.carnegie.org/reporter/09/literacy/index.html

Hamilton, R. (1993). *Chapter I reading instruction: Exemplary reading specialists in an inclass model.* Unpublished doctoral dissertation, University of Pittsburgh, Pittsburgh, PA.

Henwood, G. F. (1999/2000). A new role for the reading specialist: Contributing toward a high school's collaborative educational culture. *Journal of Adolescent & Adult Literacy, 43,* 316–325.

Hunzaker, F. (2006, May). *What do legislators really want to hear?* Paper presented at the annual meeting of the International Reading Association, Chicago, IL.

International Reading Association (IRA). (2000). *Teaching all children to read: The roles of the reading specialist.* Newark, DE: Author.

International Reading Association (IRA). (2004). *The role and qualifications of the reading coach in the United States.* Newark, DE: Author.

Jaeger, E. L. (1996). The reading specialist as collaborative consultant. *The Reading Teacher, 49,* 622–629.

Klein, J., Monti, D., Mulcahy-Ernt, P., & Speck, A. (1997). *Literacy for all: Reading/language arts programs and personnel in Connecticut schools.* Wethersfield: Connecticut Association for Reading Research.

Leslie, L., & Caldwell, J. (2005). *Qualitative reading inventory–4.* Boston: Allyn & Bacon.

Lewis, J. (2004). Working as an education advocate: A state perspective. In P. E. Linder, M. B. Sampson, J. R. Dugan, & B. A. Brancaot (Eds.), *Celebrating the power of literacy: 26th yearbook of the College Reading Association* (pp. 208–211). Corpus Christi, TX: College Reading Association.

Long, R. (1995, April). Preserving the role of the reading specialist. *Reading Today, 12*(5), 6.

McCabe, P. R. (2003). Enhancing self-efficacy for high-stakes reading tests. *The Reading Teacher, 57,* 12–20.

Mraz, M. (2004). Teaching teachers to be politically proactive: A researcher to practice perspective. In P. E. Linder, M. B. Sampson, J. R. Dugan, & B. A. Brancaot (Eds.), *Celebrating the power of literacy: 26th yearbook of the College Reading Association* (pp. 211–212). Corpus Christi, TX: College Reading Association.

No Child Left Behind Act of 2001. (NCLB). Pub. L. No. 107-110, 115 Stat. 1425 (2002).

Persistence pays: KSRA efforts to help bring about policy change. (2006, February/March). *Reading Today, 23*(4), 8.

Pipes, G. (2004). *What are they really doing? A mixed methodology inquiry into the multi-faceted role of the elementary reading specialist.* Unpublished doctoral dissertation, University of Alabama, Tuscaloosa.

Quatroche, D. J., Bean, R. M., & Hamilton, R. L. (2001). The role of the reading specialist: A review of research. *The Reading Teacher, 55,* 282–294.

Quatroche, D., & Wepner, S. B. (2007). *Developing reading specialists as leaders: New directions for program development.* Manuscript submitted for publication.

Reutzel, D. R. (2006, May). *Understanding and advocating for literacy in a climate of political division.* Paper presented at the annual meeting of the International Reading Association, Chicago, IL.

Robinson, H. A., & Rauch, S. J. (1965). *Guiding the reading program: A reading consultant's handbook.* Chicago: Science Research Associates.

Shaw, M. L., Smith, W. E., Chesler, B. J., & Romeo, L. (2005, June/July). Moving forward: The reading specialist as literacy coach. *Reading Today, 22*(6), 6.

Vogt, M. E., & Shearer, B. A. (2003). *Reading specialists in the real world: A sociocultural view.* Boston: Allyn & Bacon.

Walpole, S., & Blamey, K. L. (2006, May). *Building leadership for literacy: Roles of literacy coaches in federally funded reform.* Presentation at the Research Roundtable, International Reading Association, Chicago, IL.

Wepner, S. B. (2005, May). *Top ten celebrations for literacy leaders.* Presentation at the annual meeting of the International Reading Association, San Antonio, TX.

Wepner, S. B., D'Onofrio, A., & Wilhite, S. C. (2003). Understanding four dimensions of leadership as education dean. *Action in Teacher Education, 25*(3), 13–23.

Wepner, S. B., D'Onofrio, A., & Wilhite, S. (2006). *The leadership of education deans.* Manuscript submitted for publication.

Wiederholt, J. L., & Blalock, G. (2000). *Gray silent reading tests.* Austin, TX: ProEd.

Wiederholt, J. L., & Bryant, B. R. (2000). *Gray oral reading tests* (4th ed.). Austin, TX: ProEd.

CHAPTER 3

Literacy Coaches

Their Emerging Leadership Roles

Sharon Walpole and Michael C. McKenna

By one name or another, individual schools or school districts have long used "literacy coaches" as part of their professional devel-opment plans, but the recent focus on coaching has engendered a major shift in thinking about the or-ganization and supervision of reading programs.

The multiple roles and responsibilities of literacy coaches, particularly those who are supporting school-level improvements in teaching and learning, have brought literacy coaching squarely into the spotlight, and we think the movement has great potential. That potential, though, is not yet documented through rigorous research evidence. Such research will be crucial to the long-range policy debate concerning whether to continue funding coaching positions. In the meantime, however, we work directly with practicing coaches who are engaged in the professional support of teachers, and we work with potential coaches in our reading specialist master's degree coursework. In this chapter we will

- Define the literacy coach
- Review the qualifications that professional organizations have established for literacy coaches
- Present models for conceptualizing the role of the literacy coach
- Describe the real work of coaches in various settings.

Reading Today's tenth annual survey of issues in research indicates that literacy coaches are "hot" and "should be hot" (Cassidy & Cassidy, 2005). That is no surprise. Increasingly, state- and district-level leaders are turning to coaches to enact the professional development that teachers need. That professional development is intensive, ongoing, site-based, and firmly nested in day-to-day teaching and learning (Birman, Desimone, Porter, & Garet, 2000; Desimone, 2002; Guskey & Sparks, 1996). Literacy coaches, whom we describe as full-time, site-based staff developers, are especially poised to make that type of professional development a reality.

Last spring, we each taught a course on organization and supervision of the reading program to our candidates for the master's degree in reading in our respective universities—the degree that leads to certification as a reading specialist. We were shocked to discover that our students did not see themselves as future literacy coaches. In fact, they did not really understand what literacy coaches were or how they were similar to and different from reading specialists. Perhaps we should have expected such a reaction, but we did not. By the end of the course, though, most of our students saw

themselves as future coaches and were committed to making coaching work for teachers and for readers of all ages. In fact, those who took positions as reading specialists incorporated part-time coaching into their job description, and many actually sought full-time coaching positions. As in our courses, then, we will begin with definitions.

WHAT IS A LITERACY COACH?

Defining the term *literacy coach* should be an easy task, but it is not. Literacy coach is such a complex concept, and it is surely not unitary. One way to define a complex concept is to provide nonexamples. We'll start there. Literacy coaches are not the same as reading specialists. In the best circumstances, literacy coaches have the same advanced education as reading specialists. In addition, both reading specialists and literacy coaches are charged with improving achievement, but they use different strategies. Reading specialists typically spend the bulk of their day working directly with students. Literacy coaches, on the other hand, spend the bulk of their day working directly with teachers so that those teachers can better meet the needs of their students.

Literacy coaches provide ongoing formative professional support for teachers. That support takes place outside the classroom, in traditional professional development sessions, book studies, and review of work samples and student achievement data. It also takes place inside the classroom—in the complex environment of teaching—in coteaching, modeling, and observation with feedback. In the most intensive coaching programs, the coach is a full-time, site-based professional developer. In less intensive coaching programs, the coach may be shared among several buildings. Coaching, though, is an evolving concept. Because it is so specifically nested in the needs of a particular group of teachers serving a particular group of students, coaching takes many forms. We think this is as it should be.

Although the number of literacy coaches has exploded, the idea is really not a new one and not a concept that is necessarily connected to literacy. In fact, the best-developed conceptualizations of coaching come from the literature of teacher professional development. That literature is filled with references to cycles of professional development that include theory or knowledge-building, demonstration, time for teachers to practice in a safe environment, and feedback (for a comprehensive and accessible review, see Joyce, Showers, & Fullan, 2002). We use that cycle to plan our work with coaches (to coach the coaches, if you can imagine such a thing), and we ask coaches to use it to plan their work with teachers.

This professional development cycle informs the research on the effectiveness of peer coaching (Showers & Joyce, 1996). To us, this model is an important one for conceptualizing the dual "outside-the-classroom" and "inside-the-classroom" focus of literacy coaches. In a well-conceived peer coaching program, a consultant from outside the school works with the administration to define a schoolwide curriculum initiative. That consultant engages the entire staff in study of the concept outside the classroom, and together they define the characteristics of implementation inside the classroom.

The next step is the inside-the-classroom one. In peer coaching programs, it is not the consultant who provides this coaching, it is the entire teaching staff who coach one another. The building principal organizes the staff into coaching teams. Those teams are charged with modeling the implementation of the new strategy inside the classroom. They meet together before modeling, to describe the lesson and to provide a focus for observation. The real inside-the-classroom coaching occurs when members of a peer coaching team observe one another in action; the coach is teaching and the coached are the teachers watching. Peer coaches coach by demonstration. For us, this model is a reminder that coaching must involve access to and reflection on the realities of daily instruction. Coaches might act as collaborative consultants, a model that began in special education (Friend, 1988; Jaeger, 1996). Special educators realized that the demands of inclusive classrooms would create questions about the needs of specific children, and that those questions would be best answered individually and very specifically. Collaborative consultants built their own instructional schedules to facilitate such collaboration; they spend part of their time working directly with children, and part providing what we in the university might call "office hours"—time to support teachers directly and personally as they attempt to solve individual problems they encounter in instruction. In collaborative consultation, the teacher approaches the coach, and the coach provides support and suggestions. The form of that support is open-ended; it might involve observation or demonstration, it might involve analysis of work samples, it might involve professional readings. The focus of the support is improving or adding to the teacher's strategies for serving the needs of particular students and working together to address the questions that the teacher brings to the coaching table.

Serving the needs of adults who are struggling to meet the needs of students takes specialized skills and strategies. Coaches might act as cognitive coaches (Costa & Garmston, 1997), providing metacognitive support to teachers to help them define and solve problems in teaching and learning by increasing their ability to reflect. Cognitive coaches receive specialized training in the use of tools and strategies to enhance teachers' effectiveness. Developers refer to the metaphor of a stagecoach: Cognitive coaches bring teachers from where they are to where they want to be, but their training is not specific to the structure of any one discipline. Again, literacy coaches might benefit from cognitive coaching strategies, but their work involves more than that; it is specialized to address the needs of teachers who are building literacy skills and strategies.

Literacy coaches are not generic professional developers; their mission is specific to issues and strategies in reading and writing instruction across the curriculum. They may be informed by the literature of professional development that informs the peer coaching model and they may use strategies such as those developed for cognitive coaching, but their work is specific to the development of strategic readers and writers in classrooms and schools. They do this work in a hybrid position in schools: They are not teachers (in that they do not have full-time instructional responsibilities) and they are not administrators (in that they do not have evaluation responsibilities). In this section we have done more to tell what a literacy coach is *not* than to define what a coach is. A look at the evolution of standards and policy documents related to coaching bears clear testimony to the evolution of this complex, complicated position and will fine-tune our definition.

WHAT MUST LITERACY COACHES KNOW AND BE ABLE TO DO?

An important question in conceptualizing the role of a literacy coach involves differentiating the job from that of the more traditional one of reading specialist, which is the focus of Chapter 2. The distinction is an elusive one, however. If we lay the International Reading Association's position statements on reading specialists (IRA, 2000) and reading coaches (IRA, 2004) side by side, there are far more similarities than differences. For example, both are expected to work in collaboration with teachers to ensure high-quality instruction aligned with curriculum and standards.

It is perhaps in the area of leadership that the expectations for specialists and coaches overlap the most. In fact, IRA has stated that with respect to leadership, "coaches frequently act as reading specialists" (IRA, 2000) and should seek certification as specialists if they do not already have it (IRA, 2004). This statement may seem odd until one examines all that the association expects of the reading specialist. The 2000 IRA position statement on specialists reveals that many of the functions now connected with coaching have actually been expectations of specialists: The reading specialist should provide advice pertaining to "strategies, ideas, and materials," and should take the lead in helping to select new materials. The reading specialist should play "an essential role in supporting individual teachers—especially new teachers," but also aides and volunteers. Reading specialists are expected to conduct workshops designed to update the expertise of teachers, and they should model instructional techniques. Reading specialists are liaisons between home and school. They should also be knowledgeable about funding sources and write successful grant applications for such funding. They may be assigned to administrative tasks involving federal programs, such as Title I. Reading specialists may assume supervisory responsibilities that include observing and conferring for evaluation purposes. This language is mirrored in the 2004 position statement on coaching.

One is indeed tempted to think that reading specialists have been coaches all along and wonder why the coaching movement got started at all. One

reason is that IRA's description of the reading specialist calls to mind an individual with superhuman powers and unlimited time. Second, there are some important differences in the two job descriptions, some of which are matters of degree. For instance, a clear expectation is that the reading specialist will instruct students, either on a push-in or pull-out basis. Instruction is not an expectation of the coach, however. With respect to assessment, the reading specialist is expected to be able to administer assessments in order to determine the needs of individual students, but functions such as helping classroom teachers "administer and interpret" assessments is clearly not a primary function. It is more integral to the work of a coach.

If the in-class aspects of coaching are to be realized—and IRA (2004) recognizes this aspect as central—then the two jobs must be relegated to more than a single individual. We describe the division of responsibilities, based on the two position statements and our own work with coaches, as involving two principal distinctions:

1. While a specialist may assume an evaluation function and while IRA suggests that coaches may do so, we think it is vital for the coach never to evaluate.
2. While the specialist may instruct children, it is important that the coach's in-class work with teachers be maximized by eliminating this expectation.

HOW ARE COACHES CONCEPTUALIZING THEIR WORK?

Although we have described a fairly comprehensive set of standards to guide coaching initiatives, many very different literacy coaching models are currently being implemented. We think this is a good thing; if literacy coaches are site-based professional developers, they need to conceptualize their work around the specific needs of their site. At the same time, regardless of the specific setting, the work of coaches should fall within some overarching parameters. A fall 2006 brief, composed by the director of the Literacy Coach Clearinghouse,

Nancy Shanklin, identified six characteristics of effective coaching:

1. It involves collaborative dialogue for teachers at all levels of knowledge and expertise.
2. It facilitates development of a school vision about literacy that is linked to district goals.
3. It is characterized by data-oriented student and teacher learning.
4. It is a form of ongoing, job-embedded professional learning that increases teacher capacity to meet students' needs.
5. It involves classroom observations that are cyclical and that build knowledge over time.
6. It is supportive rather than evaluative.

Each of these characteristics is essential to an effective coaching program; each, also, allows for great variation of coaching programs across sites. We think that the effectiveness of any coaching effort is intimately tied to the very specific ways that the coaching work is defined in relation to the needs of that specific site.

We found the work of Neufield and Roper (2003) especially helpful in organizing our thinking about potential coaching models. They identified two categories of coaches: change coaches and content coaches. Change coaches work with the building leadership to build capacity for schoolwide change. They help principals develop their own instructional knowledge and design schoolwide strategies to support instructional improvements. Content coaches work more directly with teachers, and they typically focus on one content area (like literacy). They work in classrooms to support individual teachers, and they work with entire grade levels or teams of teachers. Obviously, the work of a particular coach may involve a combination of these functions.

We have envisioned and described just such a hybrid model of coaching (Walpole & McKenna, 2004). Such a model was essential, given the particular context in which we have been working—whole-school reform funded through the Reading Excellence Act and Reading First. Both of these federally funded initiatives target low-performing, high-poverty schools with a commitment to change; both provide resources for professional development, instructional materials, and assessments. Both are fast-paced, outcomes-oriented, high-stakes endeavors; schools have to enact changes and measure their effects on student achievement. Finally, both typically employ literacy coaches as the main vehicle for professional development.

The coaches whom we have met through these initiatives have been extremely dedicated to their own professional learning. Interestingly, almost none of them met the standards or qualifications that IRA has identified—at least not initially. We have worked with these coaches to build their skills and to evaluate their effectiveness. We have also identified five specific roles that these coaches have undertaken. We see coaches as learners, grant writers, school-level planners, curriculum experts, researchers, and teachers. Our conceptualization of these roles for primary-grade coaches has been well received (Snow, Ippolito, & Schwartz, 2006). We will describe each of them below.

Coaches Are Learners

We always begin with the coach as a learner, because we know that coaches will be faced with many questions that they cannot answer. We know this because coaches ask us many questions that we cannot answer! We turn to the work of our research colleagues to investigate specific answers to specific questions, and we help coaches develop strategies for locating research to inform their work. Those strategies typically incorporate aggressive reading of new professional books, including research reviews and monographs on particular topics.

Equally important to a coach's professional growth are the burgeoning number of resources available online. These include Web-based research and policy documents, research reports, and suggestions for problem solving. Organizations with a stake in coaching maintain sites likely to be helpful to coaches looking for ideas. These organizations include the following:

International Reading Association (IRA) (http://www.reading.org)
National Council of Teachers of English (NCTE) (http://www.ncte.org)
National Staff Development Council (http://www.nsdc.org)

Association for Supervision and Curriculum Development (http://www.ascd.org)

Two of these organizations, IRA and NCTE, jointly launched the Literacy Coaching Clearinghouse in 2006, a Web-based source of support for coaches (http://literacycoachingonline.org/). However, we recommend that the main sites of IRA and NCTE be examined for resources as well.

Coaches Are Grant Writers

Although they do not typically begin with this role in mind, many coaches we know do have responsibilities in applying for and implementing grants. Because we have specifically worked with Reading Excellence Act and Reading First projects, we have evidence that coaches are involved with the initial design and subsequent revision of these grants. We also know, though, that coaches sometimes take on other extensive writing projects: They work with principals and district staff to make Title I schoolwide applications, garner resources through 21st Century Schools, apply for Comprehensive School Reform moneys, and take advantage of local business partnership grant opportunities. Such writing projects stem from the fact that the literacy coach is often the local literacy content expert, and the grants require a review of applicable research. Literacy coaches do this kind of writing by necessity, and they find such tasks both challenging and satisfying but also distracting.

Coaches Are School-Level Planners

School-level planning is a real part of the life of all of the coaches we work with. It is an iterative process: New data about teaching and learning lead to new school-level planning. One of the most important school-level planning responsibilities that literacy coaches assume is scheduling. Some elementary school coaches assist principals in scheduling for every classroom in the school. They do this for several reasons. First, they want to ensure that there is sufficient, uninterrupted time for literacy instruction. Second, they want to create time for teachers to collaborate with them and with one another during the school day. Both of these goals can be met by creative scheduling of what teachers

usually refer to as "specials" (e.g., physical education, art, music, library, and computer lab). If a group of teachers who should work together in professional development, perhaps an entire grade level, is scheduled for specials at the same time, teachers can be free for grade-level team meetings with the coach. Other coaches we know, especially those who work in very large schools, plan for such sessions by bringing in substitutes for a part of the school day each month, again freeing teachers for professional development during their regular school day.

One other reason that many coaches work as school-level planners is that they help match students to services from specialists in the school (e.g., special educators, speech and language pathologists, gifted education specialists, reading specialists). In order to use the resources of these specialists efficiently and to protect instructional time for regular classroom teachers, coaches often schedule intervention blocks at each grade level. In addition, coaches may work with teachers to schedule their literacy block so that students have specified time for whole-group instruction and specified time for small-group instruction. Such school-level scheduling permits specialists to serve groups of children during the reading block. Figure 3.1 presents an example of such a schedule for a second grade. The grade-level team reserves three hours each day for reading and writing instruction. One hour is devoted to whole-class instruction, one hour to small-group instruction, and one hour to writing instruction. Because the teachers organize their small-group instruction so that it does not overlap, a reading specialist is able to spend one hour in each of the three rooms. Because the literacy coach was able to influence the school-level plan for instructional time, the reading specialist was able to support many more students.

Coaches Are Curriculum Experts

In order to make such school-level decisions thoughtfully, literacy coaches have to be curriculum experts. At times, they may guide the process of selecting commercial reading programs or intervention programs that represent the best fit with a school's literacy curriculum and with state standards. When that process is undertaken thoughtfully, coaches use available data to help identify

Figure 3.1. Second-Grade Collaborative Instructional Schedule

Period	Classroom A	Classroom B	Classroom C
8:00–9:00	Small-group rotation with reading specialist	Whole-group lesson	Whole-group lesson
9:00–10:00	Whole-group lesson	Small-group rotation with reading specialist	Writing Instruction
10:00–11:00	Writing Instruction	Writing Instruction	Small-group rotation with reading specialist

the needs of students in achieving curricular goals, characterize the strengths and weaknesses of the professional staff in addressing those needs, and then locate materials likely to support growth in teaching and growth in learning. We have never assumed there to be any one magical set of commercial materials. Rather, we contend that there are better and worse choices for a particular site with respect to selecting materials that are best aligned with curricular goals. Literacy coaches can help to minimize poor choices.

Another aspect of the coach's role as curriculum expert is the selection of appropriate materials and books for classroom libraries. We know that coaches are instrumental in working with media specialists to locate high-quality children's literature for read-alouds; we know that coaches build genre-based and leveled classroom libraries for fluency practice; we know that coaches locate information trade books linked to state social studies and science standards. Such efforts place the coach squarely in the role of curriculum expert, again focused on selection of curriculum materials that are right for a particular school.

Coaches Are Researchers

The next role that we have identified tends to be the one that is scariest at first, but ultimately the favorite among literacy coaches. It is the role of researcher. We are increasingly convinced that coaching is a very intensive form of schoolwide action research. Effective coaching must be informed by data, and those data are of two specific types. The first type is data on student outcomes. Typically, coaches help to select and interpret assessments for each of several categories: screening tools to quickly

identify students who might be at risk, diagnostic assessments to guide differentiated instruction for those students, progress-monitoring assessments to evaluate the effectiveness of differentiated instruction and intervention, and outcome measures to evaluate program effectiveness and plan program improvements (Walpole & McKenna, 2007).

We have learned that the coach—as researcher—must also collect and consider a second type of data—data about teaching. Unfortunately, some interpret this call as a form of evaluation; it is not, and it never should be. However, it does not make sense to evaluate the effectiveness of any aspect of the literacy curriculum through student achievement data without first documenting teacher fidelity to the implementation of that aspect (Walpole & Blamey, 2007). The concept of fidelity can apply to any aspect of a program, and it does not invoke the use of scripted teaching protocols. Rather, it is a more general measure of whether the teachers are actually teaching the program as it has been envisioned by and for the school. We cannot imagine an effective coach who could not describe, very specifically, what teachers are supposed to be doing during reading and writing instruction. We also cannot imagine an effective coach who does not know the extent to which individual teachers are actually able to enact that vision.

Coaches Are Teachers

We present the literacy coach as teacher last because that role is informed by all of the others. The literacy coach is an adult educator—in fact, a teacher's teacher—and he or she accomplishes that role in an ongoing way. The literacy coach as teacher builds trusting relationships with all members of the school's staff. Teaching is informed directly by the coach's own learning, but it is designed to support the particular goals of a particular building. That teaching is aimed at developing the capacity of the entire staff to design and define their curriculum, and then to engage children in effective and engaging literacy learning.

Part of the work of the literacy coach as teacher involves outside-the-classroom professional development. Such sessions may include brief formal presentations and demonstrations of instructional techniques. In these cases, we encourage coaches to become familiar with the standards established by the National Staff Development Council (2001). An important type of formal presentation is one that summarizes achievement data and draws reasonable conclusions about where problems lie and how to address them. We have helped coaches plan these "State of the School" addresses to update the entire staff on the progress of all students toward achieving the goals that the school has set (Walpole & McKenna, 2004). Such presentations typically summarize student achievement data for all students, for specific grade levels, and even for specific groups of students (e.g., English language learners, special education students, students living in poverty) whose achievement may be especially important to track. State of the school addresses keep the staff updated on progress and problems, and they help marshal a sense of creative collective responsibility.

Outside-the-classroom sessions may also include less formal activities. Book studies, for example, are conducted to foster collaborative discussion of texts that have been selected for their match to the goals of the building. Another type of informal outside-the-classroom teaching important to literacy coaches is coplanning. Our experience is that the effectiveness of schoolwide coaching initiatives is directly related to the extent to which such initiatives support organized, flexible, differentiated instruction. Coaches support teachers in the design of such instruction by working with them outside the classroom to interpret student achievement data or work samples and to plan instruction based on that work.

Once that part of the job is underway, coaches can get to the function that makes coaching unique—inside-the-classroom support. Literacy coaches actually help teachers teach their own students with their specific curriculum materials, using the time and groupings that make sense in their program. Literacy coaches model, actually teaching the lesson while the classroom teacher observes. Literacy coaches observe, both through brief walk-throughs and through extended observations. Literacy coaches provide teachers with confidential, supportive, formative feedback. And finally, literacy coaches practice what they preach about meeting individual needs, by providing differentiated support to teachers with different needs.

The best methods of working with teachers, both inside and outside their classrooms, depend in part on whether coaching is done at the elementary, middle, or high school level. Although most of the literature presently available on coaching centers on the elementary context, middle and secondary coaching is an emerging focus, one that has unique considerations (Sturtevant, 2003). For example, working with subject matter specialists (e.g., middle school social studies teachers or high school biology teachers) differs considerably from working with elementary teachers who teach reading during part of the school day and social studies and science at other times. Such differences led IRA, in collaboration with NCTE and the professional organizations associated with key content subjects, to develop coaching standards specific to the middle and secondary school settings (IRA, 2006).

WHAT ARE THE COACHES WE KNOW ACTUALLY DOING WITH THEIR TIME?

It would be fair to say that all of the coaches we know wish there were more hours in the school day! Effective literacy coaches work very hard, but so do effective teachers. Given the multiple definitions we have provided, the rigorous standards and policy documents we have identified, and the roles that coaches must juggle, this comes as no surprise. We also know coaches who are constantly worried about their choices concerning the use of time. We offer this advice: Coaches have used time well during a given day if they have made the complicated work of teaching easier for someone on their staff. That said, we have identified some basic patterns in the choices that coaches make in their use of time. Some gravitate more toward school-level work, consistent with the Neufeld and Roper's (2003) notion of change coaches; others are more squarely focused on direct support of teachers, more like content coaches.

We have termed these coaches *mentors* and *directors*. Mentors work in schools with strong, organized instructional programs. They work with administrators who have been successful in scheduling time for teaching and learning and who have set the agenda for the professional work of the coach. Mentors are able to observe or model in classrooms every single day for the entire reading block; they have regular time for grade-level meetings where they help teachers review data and engage with them in collaborative planning.

Not all coaches start out in such situations, however. Some coaches must work in partnership with the principal to provide more leadership and organization to the building. We call these coaches directors. Directors are more engaged with issues such as grant writing, curriculum selection, and school-level scheduling. In order to accomplish these tasks, they cannot observe or model every day. Good directors, though, keep a very careful schedule so that that the all-important inside-the-classroom work is not neglected. Working in the contexts of real classrooms is what distinguishes coaching from other forms of professional development, and it is what provides the real promise of effective support for effective teaching.

CONCLUSION

The coaching movement, though founded on accepted principles of school reform, is similar to most movements in literacy education in that it has preceded hard evidence of its impact on student achievement (see Stahl, 1998). During the next decade, we predict that literacy coaching will flourish or flounder depending on whether researchers can link it causally to growth in reading. We suspect that the multitude of coaching models will complicate this process and that a few effective approaches to coaching will ultimately emerge as the most likely to enhance achievement. Some may argue that this "horse race" approach to research

is unfair, or even that establishing a causal relationship to student growth is irrelevant. We agree that other approaches to research are important to gaining a better understanding of how coaching can work. Sharon has in fact contributed to such inquiry by conducting a qualitative study contrasting how principals and coaches tend to perceive the coach's role (Walpole & Blamey, 2005). However, coaching's connection to achievement is central to its longevity as a part of literacy instruction. This is simply an economic reality. Funding a position with no demonstrable connection to learning would be impossible to justify, especially when such funds might be used to reduce class size, purchase books, or acquire materials.

What type of coaching, then, is most likely to be validated as an effective means of enhancing literacy achievement? This question is presently the subject of extensive conjecture, and yet that will not prevent us from offering a portrait of a model of coaching we believe possesses the greatest potential. To ensure substantial student growth in reading, a coach must spend as much time as possible in classrooms, both modeling and observing. Conferencing must be focused and frequent. The most effective coach will not have instructional responsibilities and will not be co-opted by administrators for other purposes. On the contrary, we believe the most effective coaches will be shown to operate in tandem with supportive administrators who share a similar vision for the school. In fact, we suspect that the most effective models will be defined not only in terms of a coach's expertise and actions but also in terms of his or her relationship to the principal, for the principal is in a position to magnify or nullify the impact of any coach. We further suspect that the most effective coaches will prove to be those with an infectious enthusiasm for the job, with the courage to confront as well as reassure, and with a necessarily thick skin. The most influential coaches will prove to be active—perhaps insatiable—adult learners, whose expertise as literacy instructors can be easily appreciated but not easily challenged. Such coaches will by no means be gurus but will nevertheless know where to seek answers to practical concerns. They will realize that those answers will not always be certain and that judgments will frequently need to made in the absence of certainty, just as they are in life.

REFERENCES

Birman, B. F., Desimone, L., Porter, A. C., & Garet, M. S. (2000). Designing professional development that works. *Educational Leadership, 57*(8), 28–33.

Cassidy, J., & Cassidy, D. (2005, December). What's hot, what's not for 2006. *Reading Today, 23*(3), 1.

Costa, A., & Garmston, R. (1997). *Cognitive coaching: A foundation for Renaissance Schools* (3rd ed.). Norwood, MA: Christopher-Gordon.

Desimone, L. (2002). How can comprehensive school reform models be successfully implemented? *Review of Educational Research, 72*, 433–479.

Friend, M. (1988). Putting consultation into context: Historical and contemporary perspectives. *Remedial and Special Education, 9*, 7–13.

Guskey, T. R., & Sparks, D. (1996). Exploring the relationship between staff development and improvements in student learning. *Journal of Staff Development, 17*(4), 34–38.

International Reading Association (IRA). (2000). *Teaching all children to read: The roles of the reading specialist.* Newark, DE: Author.

International Reading Association (IRA). (2004). *The role and qualifications of the reading coach in the United States.* Newark, DE: Author.

International Reading Association (IRA). (2006). *Standards for middle and high school literacy coaches.* Newark, DE: Author.

Jaeger, E. L. (1996). The reading specialist as collaborative consultant. *The Reading Teacher, 49*, 622–629.

Joyce, B., Showers, B., & Fullan, M. G. (2002). *Student achievement through staff development* (3rd ed.). Alexandria, VA: Association for Supervision and Curriculum Development.

National Staff Development Council (NSDC). (2001). NSDC's *standards for staff development.* Retrieved January 31, 2006, from http://www.nsdc.org/standards/index.cfm

Neufeld, B., & Roper, D. (2003). *Coaching: A strategy for developing instructional capacity.* Providence, RI: The Annenberg Institute for School Reform.

Shankin, N. L. (2006). *What are the characteristics of effective literacy coaching?* Retrieved October 16, 2006, from http://www.literacycoachingonline.org/briefs/Charof LiteracyCoachingNLS10-04-06.pdf

Showers, B., & Joyce, B. (1996). The evolution of peer coaching. *Educational Leadership, 53*(6), 12–16.

Snow, C. E., Ippolito, J., & Schwartz, R. (2006). *What we know and what we need to know about literacy coaches in middle and high schools: A research synthesis and proposed research agenda.* Newark, DE: International Reading Association.

Stahl, S. A. (1998). Understanding shifts in reading and its instruction. *Peabody Journal of Education, 73*(3&4), 31–67.

Sturtevant, E. G. (2003). *The literacy coach: A key to improving teaching and learning in secondary schools.* Washington, DC: Alliance for Excellent Education.

Walpole, S., & Blamey, K. L. (2005, December). *Defining their roles: Literacy coach perspectives.* Paper presented at the meeting of the National Reading Conference, Miami, FL.

Walpole, S., & Blamey, K. L. (2007). Assessing implementation of literacy curricula. In K. Pence (Ed.), *Assessment in emergent and early literacy.* San Diego, CA: Plural Publishing.

Walpole, S., & McKenna, M. C. (2004). *The literacy coach's handbook: A guide to research-based reform.* New York: Guilford Press.

Walpole, S., & McKenna, M. C. (2007). *Differentiated reading instruction: Strategies for the primary grades.* New York: Guilford Press.

PROGRAM DEVELOPMENT

Literacy development is both similar and different across grade levels and contexts. It is similar in that the basic principles of language and learning hold true throughout. It is different in that the application of these principles differs, depending on what is developmentally appropriate at each level. Part II includes three chapters that focus on the various settings for which reading personnel must plan and carry out reading programs. It offers suggestions for responding to the differing instructional needs of students as they progress through school.

Chapter 4, written by Dorothy S. Strickland, focuses on early childhood education and how standards-based reform is impacting both programs and expectations for early childhood teachers and administrators. It discusses research on young children's literacy development, including the most recent findings on brain research, and ways to develop and implement sound instructional practices for accomplishing literacy learning goals. Also included are strategies for assessing children's language and literacy development and determining the effectiveness of early childhood programs.

A set of comprehensive guidelines for developing a successful elementary reading program is the focus of Chapter 5, written by Kathryn H. Au, Taffy E. Raphael, and Kathleen C. Mooney. This chapter explains how to use the Standards-Based Change (SBC) Process to guide teachers to create coherent, sustainable, high-quality literacy curricula designed to meet the specific needs of diverse learners. The authors describe how a network of schools in Chicago and in Hawaii are using this systematic approach to develop professional learning communities within and across grade levels to create a staircase curriculum that focuses on helping students reach target performance levels.

In Chapter 6, Christine McKeon and Richard T. Vacca focus on adolescent literacy. Historical and contemporary perspectives of adolescent reading and writing are provided as a backdrop for discussing leadership standards for middle and high school literacy coaches. Content area literacy standards and instruction are discussed for English, language arts, mathematics, science, and social studies. Issues to consider in understanding adolescent literacy instruction also are presented.

Broadly interpreted, the principles and guidelines presented in each chapter may be applied to all the others. This is reassuring for reading specialists, literacy coaches, and administrators since it means that the essence of sound, effective reading instruction remains the same for students at any level.

CHAPTER 4

Preelementary Reading Programs

New Challenges for Policy and Practice

Dorothy S. Strickland

In recent years, early childhood education has received increased attention both in the classroom and in the public policy arena. This is largely due to an accumulating body of evidence showing that early learning experiences are linked with later school achievement, emotional and social well-being, fewer grade retentions, and reduced incidences of juvenile delinquency. These outcomes are all factors associated with later adult productivity (National Institute of Child Health and Human Development Early Child Care Research Network, 2005; Storch & Whitehurst, 2002; Strickland & Barnett, 2003). The research pointed to early literacy as an area of particular significance and prompted additional research to identify the key early language and literacy predictors for reading and school success (Strickland & Shanahan, 2004). As a result, much more is known today about what educators can do to promote long-term language and literacy achievement.

As the field of early childhood education has changed, so too has the work of today's curriculum supervisors and school principals. Unfortunately for some, the work has extended into an area where they have little or no expertise. They know that competent leadership is essential. Yet, they may have come to their positions with little background in literacy education at the prekindergarten and kindergarten levels. Today's supervisors and administrators are asked to do more, know more, and produce "results." The following vignette describes the beginning stages of an approach taken by the leaders in one school district.

The usual hectic and hurried school opening in the River Falls Elementary Schools took on new meaning as the staff braced itself for the addition of prekindergarten students for the first time in the history of the district. Although the state mandate to offer education to 4-year-old children was greeted with enthusiasm by faculty and community, few elementary principals and supervisors in the district had either the experience or training to plan and implement such a program. Last spring, Jean Porter, the District Language Arts Supervisor, began planning with the school principals. She sought help from early childhood supervisors in neighboring districts and read all she could about current trends in early childhood education. She also enlisted the help of the reading specialist to work with teachers and parents to solve what seemed to be an endless series of challenges involving space, curriculum, and staffing. Certainly this would have implications for possible changes in the current kindergarten curriculum as well. Staff met during the summer and made plans for ongoing professional development throughout the school year. Although they felt somewhat ready when those prekindergarteners and their parents arrived, as Jean Porter put it, "This is a work in progress."

It seems obvious that in order to make good decisions for the very youngest children in their care, today's administrators and supervisors should be familiar with current issues and practices in the full range of early childhood education. Indeed, much of the information in this chapter could very well apply to children from prekindergarten through Grade 3. However, the content will focus on issues most likely to affect children ages 4 to 6, since this age group is most likely to be enrolled in prekindergarten and kindergarten programs within the public school. The following issues will be discussed:

- Standards-based reform in early childhood education
- Language and literacy development in young children
- Strategies for learning and teaching
- Strategies for accountability and assessment

STANDARDS-BASED REFORM IN EARLY CHILDHOOD EDUCATION

Increased demands to make every child a reader by the end of the primary grades have spurred early intervention efforts at the national, state, and local levels. School reform movements have not only raised expectations for what young learners should know and be able to do, they specify the grade levels at which they should be able to do it. Standards have been raised for all students regardless of who they are, where they live, their linguistic backgrounds, or whether or not they have been classified as having a learning disability. Typically, young children under the age of 5 had not been included in national content area standards, nor in local or statewide curricula. Because access to prekindergarten education is offered by a growing number of school districts and is thus administered by the public schools, these programs are now included in the reform efforts initiated at the state level. Although a latecomer, the field of early education has entered the world of standards and standard setting for programs, teacher preparation, and curriculum (Seefeldt, 2005). These reform efforts have focused particular attention on literacy learning and teaching.

Federal legislation has also added impetus to standards-based reform, particularly in the area of early literacy. In an effort to improve literacy instruction in Head Start programs, the federal government included educational performance standards and performance measures in the Head Start Reauthorization Act and outlined in the Head Start Program Performance Standards (1998). The performance standards include the development of the following:

- Phonemic, print, and numeracy awareness
- Understanding and use of oral language to communicate for different purposes
- Understanding and use of increasingly complex and varied vocabulary
- An appreciation of books
- In the case of non-English-background children, progress toward acquisition of the English language

Performance assessment of these standards includes demonstration that children

- Know that letters of the alphabet are a special category of visual graphics that can be individually named
- Recognize a word as a unit of print
- Identify at least 10 letters of the alphabet
- Associate sounds with written words

Because Head Start is a national effort, these standards have influenced the curriculum for large numbers of children, have had resulting implications for the qualifications of their teachers, and have caused the broader community of early childhood education to rethink their efforts as well.

Many states and districts have established educational standards for the teachers of young children. Establishing teacher standards is in line with the thinking of most systemic reform advocates, who believe that improving teaching is one of the most direct ways to improve students' learning. Efforts such as the National Board for Professional Teaching Standards (2001), the International Reading Association (2003), and the National Association for the Education of Young Children (2002) attempt to outline what early childhood teachers of English language arts should know and be able to do.

Following is a specific example of teacher standards taken from a range of teacher competencies developed by a state department of education in one area of early literacy (Connecticut State Department of Education, 2000). Effective teachers of early literacy understand the relationship between oral language and literacy:

1. They are knowledgeable about a variety of oral language competences (e.g., vocabulary, phonological awareness, listening comprehension) and how these competencies play a role in learning to read.
2. They understand the differences between informal/conversational language and formal/literate language.
3. They recognize the importance of talking with children, and encouraging talk among children, in developing oral language competencies.
4. They recognize the importance of reading to children in developing both oral-language competencies and print-related knowledge (e.g., basic print concepts).
5. They understand the basis for common speech-sound confusions that may affect reading and spelling.
6. They have knowledge about comprehension strategies and apply that knowledge in response to literature during reading aloud.
7. They understand the meaning and importance of children's active construction of meaning.
8. They understand the meaning and importance of "emergent literacy."
9. They have knowledge about learning theory.

Attention to standards will remain a key consideration for early literacy programs. Clearly stated, research-based expectations for the content and desired results of early learning experiences can help focus curriculum and instruction and increase the likelihood of later positive outcomes.

LANGUAGE AND LITERACY DEVELOPMENT IN YOUNG CHILDREN

Early intervention efforts were given impetus by the results of a relatively recent body of research on the literacy development of young children. Often termed *emergent literacy* research, this body of information has had a profound influence on educational policy and curriculum. Sulzby and Teale (1991) describe the unique dimensions of the new research:

- The age range studied has been extended to include children 14 months and younger.
- Literacy is no longer regarded as simply a cognitive skill but as a complex activity with social, linguistic, and psychological aspects.
- Since literacy learning is multidimensional and tied to the child's natural surroundings, it is studied in both home and school environments.
- Literacy learning is studied from the child's point of view.

Results of these studies provide important understandings about the nature of children's literacy learning and the kind of educational environment that best supports it. They suggest that the physical, social, emotional, cognitive, and language development of young children are major factors influencing their early literacy development (Strickland & Schickedanz, 2004). Strickland, Galda, and Cullinan (2004) list six important points to summarize these understandings:

1. *Literacy learning begins early in life and is ongoing.* It is evidenced when children begin to distinguish between their favorite books and records and demonstrate their recognition of environmental print. As children search for patterns and make connections, they bring what they know to each new situation and apply their own childlike logic to make sense of it.
2. *Literacy develops concurrently with oral language.* Fluency in oral language is no longer seen as a precursor to literacy, but as a goal to be accomplished with and through literacy as each language process informs and supports the others. It would seem that each child stores what is learned about language and literacy in a private linguistic database and then draws on what is needed when it is needed.
3. *Learning to read and write are both social and cognitive endeavors.* Children are active participants in the process. Children are not interested merely in learning about literacy; they want to actively engage in it with others.

4. *Learning to read and write is a developmental process.* Extensive observations of children reveal some general developmental patterns in the ways they acquire literacy. It is important to note, however, that these very general patterns reveal themselves in very different ways among individual children.
5. *Storybook reading, particularly family storybook reading, plays a special role in young children's literacy development.* In their accounts of parents sharing books with children, Taylor and Strickland (1986; Strickland & Taylor, 1989) observed that the talk surrounding the words and pictures in books inevitably turns to questions about print. Parents and teachers of young children expand, explain, and elaborate on the text as they help youngsters link the text to their personal knowledge and background experience.
6. *Literacy learning is deeply rooted in the cultural milieu and in the family communications patterns.* While it is safe to say that children growing up in our print-rich society are exposed to an abundance of print, the nature, quality, and amount of those experiences will differ from one family to another and from one community to another. The understandings children gain, largely through their everyday experiences at home, are significant and valuable.

Wolfe and Brandt (1998) present a series of findings from brain research that help support what has already been outlined above regarding emergent literacy. For example, a child's experience and environment have a strong influence on the development of the brain. At birth, humans have limited ability in terms of speech and motor development, and their brains are not fully operational. The brain that eventually takes shape is a result of the interaction between the child's genetic inheritance and everything he or she experiences. This fits well with another important finding, that IQ is not fixed at birth. Again, researchers have demonstrated that early educational intervention can actually raise infants' scores on IQ tests (Ramey & Ramey, 1992).

Research on the brain also suggests that some abilities are acquired more easily during certain sensitive periods, or "windows of opportunity."

Since the earliest years are considered critical for learning language, the importance of stimulating environments for language development at the pre-kindergarten level is stressed. The role of emotion in learning also received attention from the brain researchers. Emotion appears to play a dual role in human learning. "First, it plays a positive role in that the stronger the emotion connected with an experience, the stronger the memory of that experience. In contrast, if the emotion is too strong then learning is decreased" (Wolfe & Brandt, 1998, p. 13). This would imply that teachers who build on what children bring to the learning task and provide a reasonable amount of challenge help children move forward with a feeling of success while avoiding frustration.

STRATEGIES FOR LEARNING AND TEACHING

Learning to read and write is not something that is done in a vacuum. Nor is it something that begins in first grade. Long before formal schooling begins, parents and caregivers help lay the foundation for the development of essential cognitive skills and positive attitudes toward learning. Building on this foundation, preelementary programs should include

- Clear curriculum goals
- Evidence of intentional planning and implementation of developmentally appropriate strategies that correspond with the curriculum goals
- A plan for ongoing student assessment
- A plan for program evaluation

Although not all preelementary language and literacy programs will place emphasis on the same components, there is considerable agreement on the overall nature of the curriculum. We discuss below the literacy curriculum components generally included in literacy programs at the preelementary level. Accompanying a brief description of each topic are representative examples of the kinds of teaching strategies that supervisors and administrators should expect to observe when teachers are implementing the curriculum wisely.

Literacy as a Source of Enjoyment

Early childhood educators are aware that play is an essential element in every aspect of children's learning. It follows that children who have positive attitudes and expectations about reading are more likely to be motivated to learn to read. Strategies that promote a positive view toward reading and other literacy experiences are essential to helping children learn to read and want to read.

Teaching Strategies for Observation. Teachers who are aware of children's capabilities, provide activities such as singing the alphabet song, reorganizing letters to match one's name, and opportunities to write one's own name independently. Each activity is approached in a way that offers a modest challenge and some degree of success for children in a nonthreatening and playful atmosphere. When selecting material to read aloud, teachers include selections that are humorous and invite participation. Throughout, they show their own enthusiasm for reading.

Language Development with a Stress on Vocabulary and Concepts

Extending children's vocabulary and discourse patterns involves both linguistic and cognitive development. Making sense of print requires the use of a combination of strategies, including the use of word meanings, sentence structure, sound/letter relationships (phonics), and background knowledge. All of these strategies help children make good predictions about print. Children who have an abundance of opportunities to expand their language and linguistic repertoires are more apt to decipher words unknown to them as readers and to make sense of what they read (Dickinson & Tabors, 2001; Morrow 2000).

Teaching Strategies for Observation. Sharing and discussing books and stories may be the single most important thing teachers do to foster children's language and literacy development. Full-day programs should offer numerous opportunities throughout the day. For very young children, frequent, brief read-aloud experiences are best. Whenever possible, use volunteers to read to individuals or pairs of children. Volunteers who feel uncomfortable reading aloud may share wordless picture books. Keep in mind that it is both the reading and the talking that help expand children's vocabularies and conceptual understandings. Figure 4.1 offers some tips for sharing literature with children.

Figure 4.1. Some Tips for Sharing Literature with Children

---

1. Vary the material: stories; poems; basic concept books, such as books about colors, numbers, the alphabet; other kinds of informational books.

2. Include some enlarged texts and big books, so that children can see the words as they hear them.

3. Put poetry, as well as recipes and songs, on charts, and point to the words while reading or singing them.

4. Read and discuss a variety of material on the same theme over an extended period of time. For example, for 2 or 3 weeks you may wish to include several books and poems about families, the neighborhood, or ways to travel.

5. Link literature selections to firsthand activities tied to topics of interest, class trips, and current events.

6. Preview books before you read them. Your reading will be more expressive.

7. During a first reading, avoid interrupting the flow of a storybook with too much discussion. Revisit the story after the reading to reflect and respond.

8. When reading informational books, invite generous discussion before, during, and after the reading. They need not be completed in one sitting.

9. Do repeated readings of books, so that children become participants in the process.

10. Place the books you have read in the book center so that children have access to them for independent browsing.

Understandings About the Functions of Print

Knowledge of how print is used for everyday purposes helps children view literacy learning as a meaningful activity. Children who realize the functional relevance of written language are more likely to be motivated to explore its use for their own purposes (Neuman & Roskos, 1989).

Teaching Strategies for Observation. Teachers encourage the *use* of literacy in various interest areas in the classroom and in other purposeful ways throughout the day. Everyday purposes for literacy include: writing notes and letters, reading newspapers and magazines, making and using lists, and using a television guide. Real materials such as labeled food containers, menus, cookbooks, tickets, paper and writing utensils, and sales slips should be included and used in interest centers.

Print Awareness and Concepts About Print

In order to make sense of written language, young learners need to acquire both a general knowledge about reading and writing as representations of ideas, knowledge, and thoughts and also an understanding of how print works. Sensitivity to print in the environment is a significant first step toward developing an understanding of what it means to be a reader and writer. Print concepts are the arbitrary conventions that govern written language, such as spaces between words, directionality, and punctuation (Strickland et al., 2004).

Teaching Strategies for Observation. Opportunities for teaching concepts about print abound in the Framework for Reading/Writing Workshops and in incidental ways throughout the day. When teachers read aloud from big books, children learn that it is the print that evokes the words. When teachers speak as they write, children hear and see the written words. In both cases children begin to develop an awareness of the importance of top to bottom and left to right directionality and the concept of a word as it appears in print. Teachers should deliberately plan to focus on various concepts about print throughout the year, reinforcing them in a variety of ways every day.

Knowledge of Narrative Structure

Children's understanding about the nature of stories and how they are constructed greatly influences their ability to comprehend and compose. Most of the material used to teach reading to young children is written in narrative form. It follows that they are apt to understand material presented in a form with which they are familiar.

Teaching Strategies for Observation. Teachers should use prediction prompts during the reading of a story to elicit what children think might happen next. To keep their answers grounded in the story line, children should be asked: What made you think so? After the reading, children may be asked to retell the story. Teachers might use prompts that follow the elements of story structure, such as these questions: Who were the main characters? What happened to them? What happened next? How did things turn out?

Listening Comprehension

The ability to make predictions and inferences, draw conclusions, and summarize ideas begins with opportunities to engage informally in these kinds of cognitive operations during the early years. Young children need many opportunities to listen and respond to books, stories, and various other types of texts in order to understand their content or to perform a task. Exposure to a variety of kinds of texts expands children's language and concepts and contributes to their understanding of the reading process (Dickinson & Smith, 1994; Robbins & Ehri, 1994).

Teaching Strategies for Observation. Retelling a story, which has already been described in the example above, taps into children's ability to use the structure of texts to recall information. While this is very important, it does little to help children make inferences and draw conclusions about what has been read to them. Teachers need to pose questions that require children to consider why they think a character behaved in a certain way or what they

might have done under similar circumstances. Questions of this type involve the ability to use information from various sources to form an answer.

Knowledge of the Alphabet

Letter recognition is a good predictor of success in early reading. Research in this area suggests that alphabet knowledge is a by-product of extensive early literacy experiences. Thus simply training children on the alphabet in isolation of rich literacy experiences has proven unsuccessful (Ehri, 1983).

Teaching Strategies for Observation. The alphabet should be displayed at eye level and its use should be modeled during group writing experiences. Children's names are excellent vehicles for focusing on letters as components of words. Names should be displayed, read, and used for various purposes, such as taking attendance and identifying ownership of items. Teachers can demonstrate how names are constructed by cutting a child's name into its individual letters and then reconstructing it. Children may be given the opportunity to do the same with their own names. Children should be encouraged to learn the letters in their own names and to find them in print throughout the classroom or at home.

Phonemic Awareness

Research indicates that *phonemic awareness*, the understanding that speech is composed of individual sounds, is a good predictor of reading success (Armbruster, Lehr, & Osborn, 2003). Like knowledge of the alphabet, however, there is reason to believe that phonemic awareness is best learned within a context of a variety of literacy experiences (Moustafa, 2000).

Teaching Strategies for Observation. Phonemic awareness activities should be included as part of the daily read-aloud and writing experiences. Activities should be playful and gamelike. Teachers should include nursery rhymes, poems, and storybooks with patterned rhymes in their daily read-aloud offerings. They should read poetry and stories that contain alliteration and word play, including alphabet books. When reading or chanting a familiar poem or rhyme, teachers might pause before a rhyming word and let children fill in the rhyme. Children can be invited to clap the number of syllables they hear in someone's name. First the name is said, then repeated with the children as they clap along. John gets one clap. Mary gets two, Jonathan gets three, and so on.

Phonics

Learning the code involves the ability to link written symbols and sounds. Knowledge of phonics is a word identification strategy that is important to both reading and spelling (Strickland, 1998).

Teaching Strategies for Observation. Opportunities to point out patterns in the language emerge constantly throughout the day in early childhood classrooms. Attention to sound-letter relationships can be made through shared reading and writing activities. Teachers need to focus children's learning on the alphabetic principle, not simply memorizing sounds that relate to letters. In this way, children will generalize the concepts underlying phonics and be able to apply what they know to reading and writing. As teachers and children begin to informally call attention to letters, sounds, and words of interest to them, the children are helped to make the necessary connections regarding the patterns in our language. Perhaps the best evidence of children's growing awareness of phonics is the invented, phonics-based spelling they produce as they attempt to write. The child who writes "d nt t" for "do not touch" is demonstrating knowledge of at least three sound-symbol relationships. One of these, the letter *t*, is used correctly in both the initial and final positions.

Opportunities to Write

Reading and writing development go hand in hand. Children learn a great deal about the purposes for writing long before they attempt to write on their own. For young children, drawing and writing blend as a way to express what they think and talk about. Children's written expression should not be mistaken as simply handwriting. It may range from scribbling to the use of letters and the beginnings of spelling. Children's attempts at spelling provide opportunities to apply what they

know about written language and develop new understandings about word structure and the relationships between language and print (Schickendanz & Casbergue, 2004; Sulzby, 1992).

Teaching Strategies for Observation. Teachers should demonstrate and invite children to participate in writing every day. This may be done as a group activity before or after a read-aloud session. The Daily Journal outlined in Figure 4.2 offers a structure for shared writing activities. Various opportunities for independent writing adapt easily to children's literacy levels and past experiences with writing. A writing area where all the materials for writing are available to children should be included among the interest centers. Junk mail, clipboards, stickers, alphabet charts at eye level, and alphabet manipulatives may be included. Children should be encouraged to use the center during activity time and to share what they have done at the end of the day. Occasionally, teachers should offer students a prompt for drawing/writing about something relevant to the individual or to the group's activities.

ESTABLISHING AN INSTRUCTIONAL FRAMEWORK

The establishment of an instructional framework within which children develop literacy and learn through literacy is critical. The framework for Reading/Writing Workshops shown in Figure 4.3 is offered as an organizational guide for teachers to plan literacy experiences for children. Teachers are asked to begin each day with a literacy workshop of this type and to adjust the content to the ages and maturity levels of their students. The workshop may last as little as 15 or 20 minutes. Materials are selected to support several areas of the curriculum simultaneously: language and literacy development, social studies and science, mathematics, and basic concept development, such as sequencing, opposites, and so on.

There are three components in the Framework for Reading/Writing Workshops: teacher-directed activities, independent reading and writing, and sharing. Teacher-directed activities generally take place at circle time "on the rug" and include teacher

Figure 4.2. The Daily Journal

The daily journal is a group writing activity in which the teacher demonstrates and children participate in the process of writing. Chart paper or chalkboards may be used. The text may be as brief as one sentence. Simple pictures may be included. Topics may encompass current events, including personal experiences and news; responses to stories; recipes; notes; and lists of things to do or buy.

A typical daily journal entry could include the following activities:

1. Children participate in a hands-on activity, a read aloud experience, or simply share personal news. A discussion follows.

2. Teacher elicits comments to be written down by asking questions such as these: What Ideas do you want to save? What did you like best about the story?

3. Teacher writes what the children suggest and reads it aloud during the writing. Teacher may pause for children to predict the next word or letter.

4. Teacher reads and discusses finished writing with children. They discuss ideas, language patterns, words, and letters. Focus is on what they know at their stage of development.

5. Group rereads with teacher.

6. Children are encouraged to draw/write their own journal entries independently during the day.

7. Children are given an opportunity to share their independent writing.

8. Extensions. Teachers may save daily journal entries and laminate them to make class big books. These are displayed and returned for rereading. Children find or match known words and letters.

demonstration of reading and writing with child participation and response. Independent reading and writing provides time for children to reenact and apply what they learned through direct instruction. Sharing is a time for children to reconvene and report informally to others about what they did independently. At times all activities may be theme related.

STRATEGIES FOR ACCOUNTABILITY AND ASSESSMENT

Monitoring and assessing children's early literacy development is an important part of a comprehensive early childhood program. Assessment has a number of purposes. It is used to monitor children's development and learning, guide planning and decision making, identify children who might benefit from special services, and report to and communicate with others (McAfee, Leong, & Bodrova, 2004). In addition to the ongoing, day-by-day assessments that link closely to the early childhood curriculum, there is a growing trend toward the use of child assessments for program accountability. These assessments, in which early literacy is often a major component, reflect an increasingly high-stakes climate in which programs are required to demonstrate effectiveness (often in terms of standardized measures) in improving school readiness and creating positive child outcomes. Information related to early literacy is sometimes interpreted as being representative of the larger picture involving all aspects of the instructional program. Helpful assessments reveal what children can do as well as what they cannot do.

Assessing Children's Language and Literacy Development

Assessment in early childhood classrooms should reflect what is known about how young children learn to read and write. It should be based on information gathered from a variety of sources and real learning experiences. It should be an ongoing process, integral to instruction, and not take large amounts of time in preparation.

Administrators and supervisors should expect teachers to have a system in place for keeping track of children's literacy development. The system may use checklists, work samples, and anecdotal records. It should be used as an ongoing resource for making curricular decisions about the performance of individual children and about the group relative to the goals of instruction. For example, assessment during shared reading could take the form of an informal observation of the overall progress of the

Figure 4.3. A Framework for Reading/Writing Workshops

---

1. Teacher-Directed Activities

Reading/Writing Aloud involves activities in which the teacher models reading and writing process; students observe, listen, and respond.

MATERIALS: primarily trade books, chart paper, chalkboards, whiteboards

PURPOSES:

- to stretch students' experiential and literary backgrounds; expand vocabulary; concepts
- to expose students to varied forms: fiction, nonfiction, poetry
- to elicit varied forms of response: discussion; drawing/writing; drama, art, music/movement, and so on
- to expose children to various genres, literary devices, writers' and illustrators' craft
- to expose children to various purposes for reading and writing

Shared Reading/Writing involves child participation in acts of reading and writing led by the teacher.

MATERIALS: enlarged texts; may include literature trade books and content materials (books and charts) for reading; whiteboards, chart paper, chalkboards for interactive writing

PURPOSES:

- to demonstrate/support concepts about print
- to support comprehension and interpretation
- to emphasize textual features
- to provide opportunities for children to apply what they know about reading, writing, spelling

Word Study involves activities that call children's attention to the sounds within words (phonemic awareness), letter and word recognition, and sound-letter relationships.

MATERIALS: name cards, lists, charts, enlarged texts, listening activities for phonemic awareness

PURPOSES:

- to develop sight vocabulary through environmental print
- to develop sight vocabulary through the use of students' names
- to promote phonemic awareness
- to foster understanding of the alphabetic principle; phonics

Guided Reading involves small-group instruction with easy materials. Usually starts at the kindergarten level with only those children who demonstrate they are ready.

MATERIALS: primarily core program materials or sets of leveled trade books

PURPOSES:

- to monitor specific strategies/skills—highly focused manner
- to provide instruction as close as possible to students' instructional levels, gradually increasing difficulty

2. Independent Reading and Writing

MATERIALS: for reading—primarily trade books (fiction and nonfiction); for writing—various types of writing utensils and paper

PURPOSES: to provide time for child to reenact or practice book experiences and writing experiences; self-select materials and topics; assume control, independence

3. Sharing

MATERIALS: any materials used during independent reading and writing

PURPOSES: to provide time for children to recall and share information of common interest to the group; oral expression group. The items suggested the Observation Checklist During Shared Reading shown in Figure 4.4 may be helpful in deciding upon a set of observational criteria. At times a teacher might select an individual for special monitoring. For example, a teacher might want to assess the literacy development of a child who rarely participates in the group, or take a closer look at the literacy knowledge of a particularly advanced child.

Children's growing abilities and confidence with literacy can be monitored by saving samples of their drawing/writing over time and analyzing it both for content and for evidence of what they know about sound-letter relationships.

Evidence of oral language competence can also be gathered as teachers listen critically to children's sharing over time. Figure 4.5 contains some criteria to keep in mind regarding oral language development. Emphasis should be placed on praising children when these criteria are evidenced, rather than having specific lessons on their value or the castigation of individual children.

Assessing the Language and Literacy Program

Assessment of the preelementary program requires that administrators and teachers keep up with new developments in the field and adjust their programs accordingly. Professional cooperation among prekindergarten, kindergarten, and primary-grade teachers must be fostered as a critical component of program continuity. All of the professionals involved should work together to design and implement a long-range plan for ongoing self assessment and change. Teachers and administrators might engage in brainstorming activities, during which they work together to set goals for 3 to 5 years. Some possible goals for teachers and administrators are outlined here:

Possible Goals for Teachers

1. Literacy will be made more visible and integral to all activities throughout the day.
   Examples: Dramatic play area will contain signs, environmental print, and materials for children to read and write; lists of children's names will be displayed and used purposefully.

Figure 4.4. Observation Checklist During Shared Reading

Book Handling and Knowledge

Students demonstrate an understanding of the following:

- Right side up of reading material
- Front and back of book
- Front to back directionality
- Title
- Author
- Illustrator

Concepts About Print

Students demonstrate an understanding of the following concepts:

- Print evokes meaning
- Pictures evoke and enhance meaning
- Left to right direction
- Sentence
- Word
- Letter
- Similarities in words and letters

Comprehension and Interpretation

Students demonstrate understanding of familiar books and stories through the following:

- Discuss meanings related to characters and events
- Make and confirm reasonable predictions
- Infer words in cloze-type activities
- Remember sequence of events
- Compare/contrast events within and between books
- State main ideas
- State causes and effects
- Recall details

Interest in Books and Reading

Students demonstrate their interest in books and reading through the following:

- Show interest in listening to stories
- Participate in reading patterned and predictable language
- Engage in talk about books and stories
- Request favorite books to be read aloud
- View themselves as readers

As follow-up to shared reading, students:

- Voluntarily use classroom library
- Show pleasure in "reading" independently

Figure 4.5. Oral Language Checklist

1. Uses language with increasing confidence. (Note that this has nothing to do with the child's home language or dialect; the focus is on self-assurance, regardless of the language in use.)

2. Organizes ideas with some sense of logic

3. Has a sense of audience: looks at audience, speaks loudly enough for all to hear

4. Listens and responds appropriately to others

2. More small-group activities will be provided in which children work together on block building, dramatic play, and literacy.
   Examples: Children will engage in the supermarket play area in which counting and reading environmental print on boxes, cans, and signs are integral; group books patterned after predictable texts will be created on a regular basis.
3. More opportunities will be offered children to select from a variety of literacy-related activities.
   Examples: Throughout the day, including center time, there will be "invitations" for children to engage in literacy events such as handling interesting picture books on display (with covers facing children so that they are appealing) and browsing in a writing center where writing materials are made readily accessible.
4. Opportunities for children to express their imagination and creativity through a variety of literacy experiences will be emphasized.
   Examples: Response to literature will take the form of discussion; telling original stories; acting out parts of the story; moving like people, animals, or other creatures in the story; making collages or engaging with other artistic media. There will be few, if any, times when children are asked to use commercially prepared worksheets or workbooks.
5. Teachers will observe children and document their development, literacy and otherwise, in some systematic manner.
   Examples: Teachers will make use of a checklist for observing children during shared reading, collect samples of children's drawing/writing

over time, and make evaluative comments on their literacy development.

Possible Goals for Administrators

1. Show continued interest in, and support of, the early childhood program.
   Examples: Meet regularly with the early childhood staff alone; support opportunities for external visits to conferences whenever feasible; stress the importance of these activities with the central administration.
2. Place emphasis on the need for continuity of new directions and practices across grade levels.
   Examples: Help teachers find a balance between prescribed similarity of practice and a shared vision from which similar practice evolves.
3. Work with teachers to initiate a parent involvement program and to articulate new practices to parents.
   Examples: Support development of a coordinated reporting system to parents across pre-K through Grade 2.
4. Continue the dialogue in formal and informal ways.
   Examples: Continue to read and bring to the attention of teachers materials relevant to their work, and conversely read and be willing to discuss materials distributed by teachers.
5. Help teachers rethink the current procedures for assessing and reporting children's literacy development.
   Examples: Push at the district level for the elimination of standardized testing before third grade and work with teachers to help them develop informal, systematic assessment strategies and an appropriate instrument for reporting to parents.

CONCLUSION

One of the great dilemmas of school administrators and supervisors is the fact that they can never hope to be expert in all the disciplines, developmental levels, and areas of concern for which they are responsible. Everyone concedes that this is true. It is possible, however, for administrators and supervisors to become well enough acquainted with each area under their supervision to become effective observers and questioners of those who are expected to have the expertise. School administrators and supervisors certainly may not have all the answers. However, they should have well-informed questions.

Literacy at the preelementary level is a highly important, issue-laden topic. It is a topic in which the public is increasingly interested and about which they are likely to have questions and opinions. For these reasons, it is essential that administrators and supervisors have sufficient background to serve as active, informed participants in the discussion. It is our hope that they take a true leadership role in an area in which change and controversy are likely to remain for some years to come.

REFERENCES

Armbruster, B. B., Lehr, F., Osborn, J. (2003). *Put reading first: The research building blocks for teaching children to read, kindergarten through grade 3* (2nd ed). Washington, DC: Partnership for Reading.

Connecticut State Department of Education. (2000). *Connecticut's blueprint for reading achievement.* Hartford, CT: Author.

Dickinson, D., & Smith, M. W. (1994). Long-term effects of preschool teachers' book reading on low-income children's vocabulary and story comprehension. *Reading Research Quarterly, 29,* 104–122.

Dickinson, D. K., & Tabors, P. O. (Eds.). (2001). *Beginning literacy with language.* Baltimore: Brookes.

Ehri, L. (1983). A critique of five studies related to letter-name knowledge and learning to read. In L. M. Gentile, M. L. Kamil, & J. S. Blanchard (Eds.), *Reading research revisited* (pp. 143–153). Columbus, OH: Merrill.

Head Start Program Performance Standards. (1998). Washington, DC: *Congressional Federal Record* 1304, subpart B, 1306 and 1308.

International Reading Association (IRA). (2003). *Standards for reading professionals.* Newark, DE: Author.

McAfee, O., Leong, D. J., & Bodrova, E. (2004). *Basics of assessment: A primer for early childhood educators.* Washington, DC: National Association for the Education of Young Children.

Morrow, L. M. (2000). *Literacy development in the early years: Helping children read and write.* Needham Heights, MA: Allyn & Bacon.

Moustafa, M. (2000). Phonics instruction. In D. Strickland & L. Morrow (Eds.), *Beginning Reading and Writing* (pp. 121–133). New York: Teachers College Press.

National Association for the Education of Young Children (NAEYC) & National Association of Early Childhood Specialists in State Departments of Education (NAECS/SDE). (2002). *Early learning standards: Creating the conditions for success.* Washington, DC: NAEYC.

National Board for Professional Teaching Standards. (2001). *Early childhood generalist standards* (2nd ed.). Arlington, VA: Author.

National Institute of Child Health and Human Development (NICHD) Early Child Care Research Network. (2005). Pathways to reading: The role of oral language in the transition to reading. *Developmental Psychology, 41,* 428–442.

Neuman S., & Roskos, K. (1989). Preschoolers' conceptions of literacy as reflected in their spontaneous play. In S. McCormick & J. Zutell (Eds.), *Cognitive and social perspectives for literacy research and instruction* (pp. 87–94). Chicago: National Reading Conference.

Ramey, C. T., & Ramey, S. L. (1992, February). *At risk does not mean doomed.* National Health/Education Consortium Occasional Paper No. 4. Washington, DC: National Commission to Prevent Infant Mortality.

Robbins, C., & Ehri, L. (1994). Reading storybooks to kindergartners helps them learn new vocabulary words. *Journal of Educational Psychology, 86,* 54–56.

Schickedanz, J. A., & Casbergue, R. M. (2004). *Writing in preschool: Learning to orchestrate meaning and marks.* Newark, DE: International Reading Association.

Seefeldt, C. (2005). *How to work with standards in the early childhood classroom.* New York: Teachers College Press.

Storch, S., & Whitehurst, G. (2002). Oral language and code-related precursors to reading: Evidence from a longitudinal structural model. *Developmental Psychology, 38,* 934–947.

Strickland, D. S. (1998). *Teaching phonics today.* Newark, DE: International Reading Association.

Strickland, D. S., & Barnett, W. S. (2003). Literacy interventions for preschool children considered at risk: Implications for curriculum, professional development, and parent involvement. In C. Fairbanks, J. Worthy, B. Maloch, J. V. Hoffman, & D. Schallert (Eds.), *52nd yearbook of the National Reading Conference* (pp. 104–116). Oak Creek, WI: National Reading Conference.

Strickland, D. S., Galda, L., & Cullinan, B. E. (2004). *Language arts: Learning and teaching.* Belmont, CA: Wadsworth.

Strickland, D. S., & Schickedanz, J. A. (2004). *Learning about print in preschool: Working with letters, words, and beginning links with phonemic awareness.* Newark, DE: International Reading Association.

Strickland, D. S., & Shanahan, T. (2004). Laying the

groundwork for literacy. *Educational Leadership, 61,* 74–77.

Strickland, D. S., & Taylor, D. (1989). Family storybook reading: Implications for children, families, and curriculum. In D. S. Strickland & L. M. Morrow (Eds.), *Emerging literacy: Young children learn to read and write* (pp. 27–34). Newark, DE: International Reading Association.

Sulzby, E. (1992). Writing and reading: Signs of oral and written language organization in the young child. In W. Teale & E. Sulzby (Eds.), *Emergent literacy: Reading and writing* (pp. 50–89). Norwood, NJ: Ablex.

Sulzby, E., & Teale, W. (1991). Emergent literacy. In R. Barr, M. L. Kamil, P. Mosenthal, & P. D. Pearson (Eds.), *Handbook of reading research* (Vol. 2, pp. 727–757). White Plains, NY: Longman.

Taylor, D., & Strickland, D. (1986). *Family storybook reading.* Portsmouth, NH: Heinemann.

Wolfe, P., & Brandt, R. (1998). What do we know from brain research? *Educational Leadership, 56,* 8–13.

CHAPTER 5

Improving Reading Achievement in Elementary Schools

Guiding Change in a Time of Standards

Kathryn H. Au, Taffy E. Raphael, and Kathleen C. Mooney

All schools today face similar demands for a high-quality literacy curriculum aimed at helping children learn to read at the high levels required for purposes of citizenship, economic well-being, and personal growth. In the United States, schools face new challenges in developing and sustaining an effective literacy curriculum that can meet the learning needs of a diverse population of students, with a growing economic disparity among their families. While today's educators accept accountability and standards as part of the landscape, they are often frustrated by unrealistic or even unreasonable demands to improve test scores, in the absence of adequate resources and time to address the underlying problems that led to the low performance levels.

This chapter provides a window into how a network of schools in Chicago and Hawaii have used a systematic approach—the Standards-Based Change (SBC) Process—to guide teachers to create coherent, sustainable, high-quality literacy curricula designed to meet the specific needs of their diverse learners. We begin by introducing the networks with which we have worked, with a focus on two elementary schools, Holomua in Hawaii and South Loop in Chicago.[1] We then introduce the SBC Process and explain how it was used effectively by schools such as Holomua and South Loop to guide literacy improvement efforts.

Key points addressed in this chapter include

- The importance of considering both student achievement and teacher ownership of a change effort
- The necessity of building a strong school infrastructure to support teacher involvement in change efforts in reading
- The difference between developing a literacy curriculum and simply choosing a program

THE SBC PROCESS SCHOOLS AND NETWORKS

The SBC Process was developed by Kathy Au as she worked with schools in Hawaii, beginning with Kipapa Elementary School in 1997. Kipapa's curriculum coordinator, with the support of the principal, had approached Kathy for help with their literacy curriculum. School leaders felt that the school was stagnating. While some elements of the literacy curriculum and instruction were in reasonably good shape, teachers and students were not moving forward as they had hoped. Kathy collaborated with Kipapa's curriculum leaders and teachers to create a process that allowed them to align their instruction with state standards and to analyze the school's strengths and potential challenges for sustainable school improvement. By 2005, Kathy had introduced the SBC Process to almost 100 schools (see Au, 2005, 2006). Approximately 30 of these schools formed the Standards Network of Hawaii (SNOH) in spring 2002, and most of these same schools continued their involvement with the new SchoolRise national network established in 2006.

The Hawaii school featured in this chapter—Holomua Elementary School—was the second school to work with the SBC Process, starting in 1999. Holomua (Hawaiian for to "improve" or "progress") opened in 1996 to serve a rapidly developing suburban community located on lands formerly held by a sugar plantation. Serving over 1,400 students from kindergarten through Grade 6, Holomua is now Hawaii's largest elementary school. The school runs on a year-round multitrack schedule, with three of four tracks in session at any one time. The majority of Holomua's students come from middle-class families, with 20% qualifying for free or reduced-cost lunch. In common with most schools in Hawaii, Holomua enrolls students from a wide variety of cultural and ethnic backgrounds, with about 40% of the students being Filipino, about 13% Hawaiian, and about 7% Japanese.

From the start, the approach taken at Holomua was to use integrated thematic units, including literature-based instruction. However, in the process of creating these units, the teachers discovered two problems: First, they were all doing something different in terms of reading and writing instruction; and second, they needed a systematic assessment system to chart their students' progress (Colleen Hokutan, personal communication, April 1, 2004). After Kathy conducted an introductory workshop, the school's leaders, including principal Norman Pang and language arts curriculum coordinator Colleen Hokutan, believed that the SBC Process could be used to guide the teachers to pull the literacy curriculum together. The teachers developed a writing curriculum and then a reading curriculum, and they applied the principles of the SBC Process to improve their work with math. Development of a science curriculum is next on the agenda at Holomua. Because Holomua's students typically exceed state averages and national norms on large-scale tests, the focus has not been so much on test scores as on high-quality curricula that will further enhance students' learning. By 2002, Holomua and other SNOH schools had shown that the SBC Process was effective in helping to create coherent curricula, promoting both student learning and teacher ownership within the framework of standards-based education.

In 2002, when Taffy Raphael joined the faculty at the University of Illinois at Chicago, she had the opportunity to create a sister project to SNOH, introducing the SBC Process to the Chicago Public Schools (CPS). The Chicago work was part of the Advanced Reading Development Demonstration Project (ARDDP) supported by the Searle Family Funds of the Chicago Community Trust. ARDDP maintained five university projects, each designed to build capacity to improve the quality of literacy teaching and learning within the project schools and ultimately within the CPS system. The project at the University of Illinois at Chicago, led by Taffy, became the core work of Partnership READ (Reading Essentials and Assessment Development), serving a network of 10 schools guided by the SBC Process to improve their students' literacy achievement. Partnership READ provided the opportunity for scaling the SBC Process from Hawaii, the 10th largest district in the United States, to Chicago, the 3rd largest (Raphael, Goldman, Au, & Hirata, 2006), and it provided an important test of the SBC Process in a new, complex urban setting.

South Loop Elementary School joined Partnership READ the year it began in Chicago. South Loop serves a pre-K–8 student population from the local neighborhood that is predominantly African American, where 72% of the students qualify for reduced-cost or free lunch. Its principal, Patrick Baccellieri, became aware of Partnership READ through his contacts within the University of Illinois at Chicago. He had started doctoral work in school leadership, and when he learned of the SBC Process, he asked that South Loop become one of the founding 10 CPS elementary schools. South

Loop had been in turmoil for several years prior to his appointment as principal. For example, he was the seventh person to fill the principal position since 1997. South Loop's test scores on the Illinois Standards Achievement Test (ISAT) had hovered around 34% (only one-third of the students met performance expectations). Teachers, watching the administrators move through a revolving door, did not coalesce as a professional learning community. Instead, they tended to push back against any initiative under the assumption that they could simply wait it out until a new administrator came in and the initiative went away.

Against this backdrop, Patrick could have tried for a quick fix—a test preparation program to boost the students' scores, for instance. He recognized, however, that there was little evidence that after an initial boost, any deep or lasting changes would have taken place. Instead, he opted to become part of the 5-year school-university partnership using the SBC Process. Since fall 2003 he has worked to construct an infrastructure to support the work: a literacy leadership team including Lead Literacy Teachers to guide the work, time for weekly grade-level meetings, and use of restructured and professional development days as well as teacher-paid after-school professional development. Teachers have worked on modifying classroom practices—assessment, curriculum, and instruction—to differentiate instruction to meet the needs of their diverse students. And the result has been improved student outcomes such as consistent improvement on the state achievement test (see Figure 5.1).

Schools like Holomua and South Loop in the SNOH and Partnership READ networks represent a diverse array in terms of grade levels served, student populations in the schools, teacher experience, geographic regions, disparity between current and targeted student performance levels, school subject area foci for the SBC Process, and degree of time and progress in the SBC Process. In the remainder of the chapter, we describe how schools such as Holomua and South Loop used the components of the SBC Process and focused the work of the leadership team and professional learning community, guided by the SBC Process. We then present the SBC Process Seven-Level Developmental Model (Raphael, Goldman, Au, & Hirata, 2006) that can help schools anticipate their path to school improvement.

Figure 5.1. South Loop's Annual State Test Scores

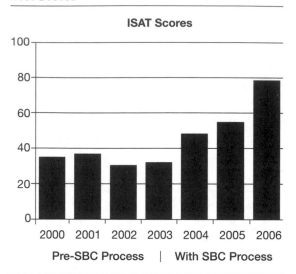

ISAT Scores

Source: Department of Data Management, Office of Research, Evaluation and Accountability, Chicago Public Schools (2006)

THE STANDARDS-BASED CHANGE PROCESS

The SBC Process guides schools such as Holomua and South Loop in implementing a system for improving student achievement through standards. The SBC Process differs from conventional approaches to improving achievement because it focuses on fidelity to a process rather than to a set program. Through professional development, the SBC Process guides educators in creating their own solutions for raising students' literacy achievement. Rather than implementing a solution designed by outsiders, the SBC Process is adapted by insiders to meet the needs of their own school setting.

The SBC Process centers on the nine components illustrated in Figure 5.2, organized within four concepts, starting at the top of the figure and moving clockwise: (1) establishing a philosophy and vision of the excellent reader, (2) establishing grade level end-of-year goals stated both in teachers' professional language and in student-friendly language, (3) collecting, evaluating, and representing assessment evidence of where students are in relation to end-of-year goals, and (4) improving instruction on the basis of this assessment evidence. These con-

cepts form an ongoing, iterative cycle of work in the professional learning community that leads to the construction of a staircase curriculum. We define a staircase curriculum, and then describe how South Loop, Holomua, and other schools in the SchoolRise network have used the SBC Process to guide their school and literacy improvement efforts.

Building a Staircase Curriculum

A staircase curriculum stands in contrast with what is often the case in schools struggling to achieve targeted levels of student performance. First, all schools tend to have desired outcomes of some sort for their students. At SBC Process schools, these outcomes are clearly articulated and defined. In contrast, schools that struggle often have vague or ill-defined goals, generally stated in terms of wanting to "improve" but without specific attention to what such improvements look like for the school as a whole and for each grade level.

Second, a staircase curriculum conveys coherence (Newmann, Smith, Allensworth, & Bryk, 2001), in which each grade-level team consciously builds upon the specific instruction of the prior grade level and works to insure their students are ready for the next grade level. The concept that each grade level is a step toward the desired outcome upon graduation from the school contrasts with the idea underlying a spiral curriculum (Taba, 1962), which inadvertently can convey a sense that if something isn't learned in one year, it will be revisited and can be learned later.

Third, a staircase curriculum contrasts with a fragmented curriculum in which teachers at different grade levels may have good ideas for instruction, but their work is not closely coordinated with what adjacent grade levels are doing. There is no schoolwide vision of their graduates' literacy knowledge and skills. The achievement of struggling learners, in particular, suffers because of gaps in instruction. The possibilities of cumulative learning are greatly reduced in a fragmented curriculum, as opposed to a staircased curriculum.

The staircase metaphor encourages the school staff to develop their curriculum so that students receive strong, well-coordinated instruction as they progress through the grades. Teachers understand how the literacy curriculum flows across all grades

Figure 5.2. Concepts and Components of the SBC Process

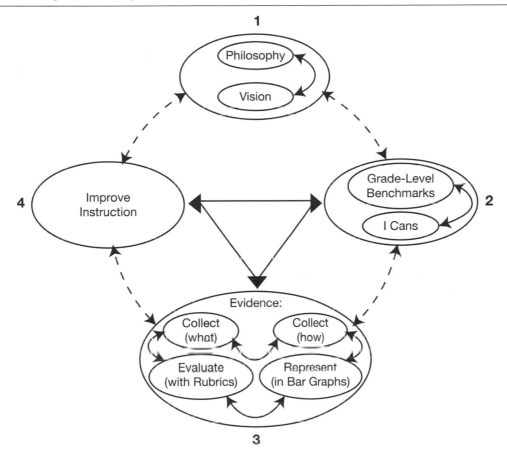

in the school. They can build upon the foundation established in earlier grade levels, as well as prepare students for the challenges in the grade levels that follow. Furthermore, after a school puts a staircase curriculum in place, teachers begin to notice that students enter their classrooms better prepared as readers and writers than in the past. Students' higher levels of performance as they enter a new grade cause teachers to raise their expectations for their performance at the end of the school year. As time passes, teachers' rising expectations result in improved student achievement revealed first in classroom-based assessments and later in large-scale assessments, such as state tests of reading and writing, as South Loop's teachers experienced.

Many educators believe that a staircase curriculum can be achieved by adopting a packaged reading program, such as a basal reading program or a comprehensive reform model like Success for All (Slavin & Madden, 2001) or America's Choice (Supowitz, Poglinco, & Snyder, 2001). Research suggests otherwise. Simply adopting a reading program does not lead to schoolwide curriculum coherence (Newmann et al., 2001) because teachers can choose not to follow the adopted program closely, or they can interpret the program in different ways. Our own research supports these findings (Au, 2005). The vast majority of schools that have worked with the SBC Process started out with some type of packaged reading program already in place. Yet teachers at every one of our schools recognized at the outset that they did not have a staircase curriculum in place. At most schools, teachers were not sure of what was actually being taught at grade levels other than their own. A true staircase curriculum does not just exist on paper, but can be witnessed in classroom instruction on a daily basis. Such a curriculum requires teacher buy-in and detailed planning, discussion, and coordination within and across grade levels. This is the kind of curriculum building we seek to facilitate through the SBC Process.

The SBC Process in Action

Like all schools, when Holomua and South Loop began their work with the SBC Process, the professional learning community within the school first focused on getting the nine components in place. As South Loop teachers and administrators discovered, this took over 2 years of intensive discussion. Schools did not have a visible school philosophy or literacy vision to guide the work, so they engaged in discussions within school staff meetings and professional development days to establish something that represented everyone's voice. They used grade-level meetings to construct end-of-year benchmarks that would be clear to everyone—teachers, administrators, students, and their families. They worked to develop assessment systems that established the evidence they would use to track students' progress toward the end-of-year goals, rubrics to guide instructional decisions related to students' performance levels, and means for sharing with the rest of the school staff their students' status and progress through bar graphs. And they developed instructional plans and related curriculum content to address their students' needs based on the evidence they had collected (Mooney, 2006).

Philosophy and School Literacy Vision. Schools begin by first addressing issues of philosophy. Facilitators such as ourselves typically start the school process by asking teachers to meet by grade levels to come up with two central beliefs they hold about each of the following:

Teaching
Learning
Literacy

This discussion of philosophy, leading to a school's vision of the excellent reader, provides the foundation upon which a sound reading program can be built. Schools that take the time to hold such discussions have spelled out their beliefs and know

what they want a reading program to accomplish. They are in a good position to move forward, because they know where they are heading. They can make decisions in a principled manner. For example, they can decide whether they should develop a reading program unique to their school or whether a commercial program will do the job. Schools that do not take the time to hold these discussions frequently encounter difficulty later on in the process because they have not made explicit the beliefs and vision that should guide their decision making. Often these schools see their task as choosing among commercial programs. This task is difficult and sometimes leads to conflict within the faculty because the school does not have its own, previously agreed-upon criteria for assessing the merits of various programs.

Each grade level prepares a chart with its belief statements and presents these statements to the entire faculty. Typical examples of belief statements include the notions that teaching involves accepting responsibility for every child's learning, that learning is a process of making connections between the known and the new, and that literacy cuts across all content areas. Figure 5.3 displays the notes of two groups of teachers at Drake Elementary School in Chicago, as they discussed within their teams, then shared with the whole school, their beliefs about teaching, learning, and literacy. Following these presentations, the facilitator encourages the teachers to identify themes running across the grade levels.

Next the facilitator asks teachers to discuss what good readers do. Each grade-level or cross-grade-level small group compiles a list of 5 to 10 points, and these are shared with the whole group. Typical examples include the ideas that good readers can critically evaluate what they read, make personal connections to what they read, and decode words quickly and accurately.

Finally, the facilitator asks teachers to come up with a vision of the excellent reader who will graduate from their school. This discussion is held within grade levels, but everyone is asked to think about the vision of the excellent reader at the highest grade in the school (typically Grade 5 in Hawaii and Grade 8 in Chicago). The vision of the excellent reader is based on the expectations teachers hold for a representative student, neither the

Figure 5.3. Teachers' Philosophy Notes

Our Philosophy

Teaching

- Instruction varies depending on level
- Enthusiasm

Learning

- Actively engaged (materials, activity, strategies, etc.)
- Ongoing and Integrated

Literacy

- Read/write for variety of purposes
- Enjoy/value reading/writing

Our School Philosophy

Teaching

- Consistency
- Flexibility

Learning

- Continuous process (lifelong love for reading and learning)
- Ability to solve/resolve problems

Literacy

- Read for meaning (interpreting written materials)
- Express ideas and thoughts

- The graduating students of South Loop Elementary School will be lifelong readers who read for both information and enjoyment. They use reading effectively in their everyday lives.
- The excellent reader who graduates from Laurel Elementary School will find joy in reading and be able to read with understanding for a wide variety of purposes in school and in everyday life.
- A student graduating from Potter Academy will be an enthusiastic lifelong reader, who enjoys reading, connects reading with everyday experiences, and uses reading as an important tool throughout his or her life.

Obviously, time for staff to meet for discussions is a key factor. The approach proposed here is based on the assumption that a school's reading curriculum can only be successful if it is consistent with the faculty's beliefs about teaching, learning, and literacy, and if it reflects their contributions to and ownership of the curriculum. Further, the administration, teachers, parents, students, and community must share a common vision of the excellent reader who is to graduate from the school. The reading curriculum is the means for accomplishing this vision.

Grade-Level Benchmarks and I Can Statements. Once the discussion of philosophy has been completed and the school has a statement describing its vision of the excellent reader, the faculty are ready to begin work on the curriculum. Teachers start by establishing grade-level benchmarks and making them transparent to the students, other grade levels, administrators, parents, and community members through restating them as "I Can" statements. I Can statements are benchmarks reworded in student-friendly language. All of this work is driven by the literacy vision and the staircase curriculum. Each grade level discusses how it will specifically contribute to the vision of the literate graduate— metaphorically, what each grade level's step in the staircase will accomplish. Teachers work collaboratively to capture their thinking in terms of grade-level benchmarks, or goals they would like their students to achieve as readers by the end of the school year; these are high but attainable levels of accomplishment for a representative or typical student. The goals align with the literacy components empha-

highest achieving nor the lowest achieving. Teachers imagine that this representative student has been in the school since kindergarten and has received strong instruction at every grade along the way. Grade levels write their vision statements on chart paper, and these are presented to the whole faculty. Once again, the facilitator encourages teachers to find commonalities shown in the statements. Later, the school's language arts committee, lead literacy team, or another small group takes the drafts and puts together a composite statement describing the whole school's vision of the excellent reader they would like to see graduate. The composite vision statement is brought back to the entire faculty for approval. Vision statements differ across schools, but generally focus on literacy across the life span and the ability to engage in a variety of literate practices. These are some examples:

sized in their particular school or district, but may also expand upon local or state criteria.

For example, teachers at Holomua used three categories—attitudes, comprehension, and strategies and skills—to shape their reading benchmarks, with at least one benchmark for each area, arriving at a total of five to seven benchmarks. In contrast, teachers at South Loop framed their benchmarks using the categories of the Chicago Reading Initiative, a district effort which emphasizes word-level knowledge, comprehension strategies and skills, fluency, and written response to text.

At Shields School in Chicago, grade-level teams began their process of developing benchmarks in the area of reading comprehension. Comprehension had been chosen as the starting point for the SBC Process at Shields by the school's leadership team after analyses of the school's assessment results suggested a schoolwide need for attention to this area. A facilitator led each grade-level team's initial discussion by asking teachers to brainstorm their end-of-year goals in comprehension for students at their grade level. When teachers responded by pulling out their lists of state goals and standards, facilitators requested that these documents be set aside temporarily and that teachers begin by drawing upon their own professional knowledge and experiences to describe their comprehension goals. Most grade-level teams filled several pages of chart paper with comprehension statements, which facilitators helped them collapse into one or two broader end-of-year comprehension benchmarks. Later, grade-level teams worked independently to transfer the professional language of the benchmarks into student- and family-friendly I Can statements.

After these 40-minute sessions, grade-level teams brought their benchmarks back to the full faculty, where each grade level shared their statements. Looking across the statements vertically, the faculty then reflected upon how the benchmarks progressed from grade level to grade level—where there were curricular repetitions, gaps, and so on—and how the benchmarks aligned with their newly developed literacy vision. For the next 2 weeks, the work initiated at this whole-school session continued in weekly grade-level team meetings with further revision and editing to the comprehension benchmarks and "I Cans." Importantly, grade-level teams' follow-up work also included cross checking for alignment between the benchmarks they had developed and local/state criteria for their grade levels. Teams were often surprised to find that their benchmarks encompassed most, if not all, of the state comprehension goals, although their statements usually condensed external standards to make them more accessible.

Schools experience a wide range of responses when grade-level teams meet to share their benchmarks for the first time. Often, teachers spot issues warranting faculty discussion. For example, after seeing the benchmarks proposed for each grade, teachers at one school observed that every grade included story elements in its benchmarks, but that it was unclear how students' knowledge of story elements was expected to differ across the grades. At another school, teachers observed that the benchmarks for the fourth through sixth grades referred to students' comprehension of informative text, but that no mention of informative text appeared in the primary grades.

In most SBC Process schools, teachers describe how challenging this task of developing benchmarks was initially, since they were more accustomed to seeing long lists of reading objectives (particularly in the area of strategies and skills). By thinking in terms of a small number of broadly stated benchmarks, however, they were able to group strategies and skills to be taught in focused, meaningful ways. Over time, they recognized that the "laundry lists" of skills and strategies were not as effective or accessible to their students and families and often interfered with students' learning to use multiple strategies as they read. Figure 5.4 displays the reading comprehension benchmarks and I Can statements developed by the teachers at South Loop for comprehension and at Drake for writing. The South Loop comprehension I Cans are part of a system they have developed for reporting in the areas of comprehension, fluency, writing, and math (2006–07). Thus they were committed to identifying one broad I Can statement that would guide specific instructional activities for each instructional area within each grade level, which we discuss later in the chapter. The writing I Cans from Drake reflect their current (2006–07) focus on writing, building on their work in comprehension of the previous year.

While this process of developing benchmarks does take time, there are two important advantages to the approach of beginning with teachers' own thoughts about benchmarks, rather than with outside sources. First, this approach *requires teachers to think deeply about what is important for learning to read.* The open-ended nature of the task of creating grade-level benchmarks promotes rich, generative thinking and discussion. These professional reflections and conversations are circumvented when teachers are handed a ready-made list. Aurene Pila, a fifth-grade teacher at Holomua, described her experiences in this way:

> I have a really good grasp of the language arts standards and it's not because I memorized the standards. It's because first, I looked at what my students could do and what I thought they needed to do . . . since I did it in my language first and I was teaching first, it gave me a really good grasp of what the standards mean. (quoted in Hokutan, 2005, p. 20)

Second, this approach *shows respect for teachers' professional judgment and promotes their commitment to and ownership of the curriculum development process.* Teachers' deep knowledge of their students and their school setting can be reflected in the benchmarks. Teachers are more likely to feel ownership of the benchmarks since they are the result of their own best thinking and tailored to their own students, rather than external mandates for generic students. Results of a state-administered school-quality survey at Holomua showed that 96% of teachers agreed or strongly agreed with the idea that they have a major role in standards-based curriculum development at their school (Hokutan, 2005).

Beginning, Middle, and End-of-Year Assessments. The time had come to move into the assessment phase of our work. Many teachers have attended workshops on content standards, performance standards, performance indicators, portfolios, rubrics, and other aspects of innovative or standards-based assessment—but without having gained a good framework for fitting these ideas together. Thus they often express confusion and hesitation regarding assessment. Given this context and the constraints on teachers' time, we help teachers develop a classroom-based assessment system that they can implement and maintain; one that ensures they are doing what is needed so their students can achieve the highest levels of performance.

Schools vary in how they begin this part of the process. Some choose one benchmark upon which to assess their students' progress, allowing teachers to gain a deep understanding of how the standards-based assessment process works without feeling overwhelmed. Other schools (in response to external pressures, patterns in schoolwide evidence identified by in-school leadership, or the presence of highly experienced teachers on a school's faculty) select two or three benchmark areas to begin. Regardless of these choices, we recommend keeping the standards-based assessment process highly focused in the initial phases.

Once the benchmark has been chosen, teachers begin by determining the kinds of evidence they will collect to document students' progress toward meeting the benchmark. At this point, many grade-level teams have the tendency to turn to existing tests, rubrics, and other measures to collect data about their students. While external tests and assessment tools may be useful starting points, we encourage teachers to think about evidence that may be available as part of the everyday life of the classroom. Mitzie Higa (2006) describes how she and the other fifth-grade teachers at Holomua worked on benchmarks addressing the quality of students' writing in the areas of meaning, design, and conventions and skills. The I Can statement for design read, "I can organize my thoughts and information in concise paragraphs including an introduction, body, and conclusion on the assigned topic." The teachers wanted students to write to a prompt on their classroom assessment, in order to parallel procedures on the state writing test. Since they also wanted to make connections to the life of the classroom, the teachers developed prompts tied to their existing social studies units.

Next, grade-level teams consider the kinds of data that they are already collecting to meet school and/or district requirements. Since they were conducting one-on-one early literacy screenings to meet district requirements, kindergarten and first-grade teachers in one Chicago school decided to draw largely from this data pool to determine their students' progress toward their benchmarks and I Cans. The teachers then supplemented the assessment, making adjustments and additions as needed (the kindergarten teachers found, for instance, that the screening measured students' progress for "I can

Figure 5.4. A Staircase of I Can Statements: Comprehension and Writing

Grade Level	South Loop Elementary School Comprehension I Can Statements	Drake Elementary School Writing I Can Statements
K	I can listen to a story and tell about the beginning, middle, and end.	*Process:* I can brainstorm. *Product* • I can print and write capital and lowercase letters. • I can put spaces between words. • I can use correct end marks. • I can print from left to right and top to bottom. *Craft:* I can write a response from my drawing.
1	I can understand a story I've read and retell it in order using my own words.	*Process:* I can use written language and illustrations to communicate my ideas. *Product:* I can create different forms of writing: invitations, letters, lists, stories. *Craft:* I can write for a variety of purposes: descriptive, informative, persuasive, narrative.
2	I can understand, make connections to, and summarize stories I read.	*Process* • I can brainstorm and complete a graphic organizer on my own. • I can use my graphic organizer to write a first draft on my own. • I can revise/edit with support from my teacher. *Product* • I can write complete sentences with correct punctuation. • I can write a multiparagraph paper that is well organized and contains a topic and multiple details. *Craft* • I can make my writing interesting to the reader by using descriptive words.
3	I can tell the difference between fiction and nonfiction books, what is important in a text, make inferences, and summarize what I've read.	*Process* • I can create my own graphic organizer to write a draft. • I can edit my own draft. • I can engage in teacher conferencing to make revisions. *Product* • I can write a multiparagraph paper with main ideas which will be supported by details in each paragraph. • I can use transitions between paragraphs. *Craft* • I can understand the purpose for my writing. • I can make my writing more interesting through elaboration and descriptive word choice.
4	I can understand different genres of literature and effectively use sources of information to recall explicit ideas and make inferences.	*Process* • I can edit my own and classmates' writing. • I can offer constructive feedback to my classmates' writing. • I can apply my classmates' suggestions to improve my writing. *Product* • I can understand the difference between topic, main idea, and details, and apply them to my writing. • I can put my main ideas into an order that makes sense to me and my readers. • I can logically express my ideas. *Craft* • I can write with audience in mind. • I can use creative transitions. • I can use simple literary devices.

Figure 5.4. (*continued*)

5	I can explain important information from the author, using examples and details, while connecting them to text that I've read and my own experiences.	*Process* • I can peer-conference with my classmates and apply constructive feedback to my writing. • I can go through the writing process on my own, using a checklist as a guide. *Product* • I can show ownership of the writing prompt and final product. *Craft* • I can write with a broader audience in mind. • I can show excitement for writing through my final product. • I can use descriptive words and creative transitions.
6	I can demonstrate critical thinking about narrative and expository texts through explanations of explicit and implicit key ideas.	*Process* • I can fully complete a graphic organizer in order to have more than enough information to complete a draft. • I can apply a variety of revising techniques while checking for figurative language, powerful transitions, and varied sentence structure and length. • I can select appropriate writing samples to publish and determine the best way to share them with my audiences. *Product* • I can write formal and informal writing depending on the purpose and audience. *Craft* • I can use rhetorical devices (figurative language, repetition, quotes, etc.) in order to engage my audience. • I can use advanced and appropriate vocabulary in order to demonstrate my understanding of words.
7	I can critically analyze a variety of literary works by constructing inferences and by using explicit and implicit ideas from the text to support an argument.	*Process* • I can keep a portfolio to use during teacher-student conferences and peer editing and revision. • I can own the writing process in a way that is an intrinsic process. *Product* • I can be clear, expressive, and concise when writing. • I can express my ideas and support my position with evidence. • I can integrate language and ideas from content areas. *Craft* • I can show pride in my work. • I can use dialogue and apply a variety of literary devices and word choices to express my own voice. • I can demonstrate creativity throughout my writing.
8	I can synthesize across sources of information and construct inferences to develop and defend arguments, using the text for support and my own ideas.	Same as 7th grade.

read a sentence," but was insufficient regarding "I can listen to a story and tell the beginning, middle, and end"). However, they chose not to create or administer an entirely different assessment when they already had the necessary evidence to determine students' instructional needs.

In a related way, teachers at other Chicago and Hawaii schools streamlined the evidence collection process when they developed assessments for their comprehension benchmarks. Although in varying ways, the teachers included vocabulary questions, strategies reflection, and written literature response components along with text reading and comprehension questions—all within a single assessment. This combination of benchmark evidence makes the assessment process less time-consuming while still providing rich data on students. Following the approach of gathering evidence through everyday classroom products and existing assessments makes it more reasonable for teachers to collect evidence, because they do not have to administer additional tests.

Gathering evidence in the second grade and above is made easier by the fact that students are better able to express their thoughts in writing and to maintain their own records. As seen in the example above, teachers in kindergarten and first grade often find that certain kinds of evidence can only be gathered through labor-intensive, individual assessment (e.g., running records or miscue analyses of oral reading) or observation (e.g., anecdotal records of children's behavior during time set aside for sharing and reading books). Administrators can support standards-based assessment by providing the extra help teachers need, such as organizing paraprofessional aides to assist with evidence gathering in the early grades. As the assessment process becomes more comprehensive, it may become unrealistic to expect kindergarten and first-grade teachers, in particular, to gather all the evidence needed while continuing to provide a rich menu of literacy instruction.

Students themselves can and should be involved in the collecting of evidence. We have found this to be especially true beginning in second grade, though in some of our schools, even kindergarten and first-grade students do so. Once students are familiar with the I Can statements, teachers ask students what evidence they have to show that they are making progress toward the I Can statements. These discussions have occurred at the end of the quarter, or at the time evidence is to be collected (e.g., in anticipation of reporting results in schoolwide meetings at the beginning, middle, and end of the year). For example, when Grade 5 students were asked to identify evidence illustrating how they make connections between a novel and their own lives, their ideas included using writing in their literature response journals as well as their book reports.

For convenience, teachers maintain an assessment handbook (usually in both hard copy and electronically) so that they can more easily remember their decisions about how to gather and score evidence for the three times per year whole-school reporting. The handbook includes both the procedures they will follow to collect the evidence and the procedures they will follow to score the evidence (i.e., assessment tools). In their first year of the SBC Pro-

cess, rather than keeping a handbook, each grade level at South Loop created a poster board so that the information could be easily shared with their colleagues and the students' families. While they eventually moved into the assessment handbook, they continue to use the boards as part of their display during the schoolwide reporting sessions.

We have found that teachers at a grade level discover the importance of having set procedures for collecting evidence the first time they sit down together with their samples of student work. In one school, the third-grade teachers discovered that they had inadvertently assessed their students' reading comprehension under two different sets of conditions. They had agreed upon the text their students would read. Three of the four teachers had distributed copies of the text to each student and asked them to read and write a summary. The fourth teacher had held a brief class discussion before students wrote their summary. As a result, her students' summaries were stronger than those from the other classes, making it impossible to aggregate the data for the grade level as a whole. The teachers all simply agreed upon a common procedure to be used the next time, and recorded it in their assessment handbook. Another discovery teachers have made is the importance of being specific about their expectations. For example, in their second year of work with the SBC Process, South Loop's fourth-grade teachers were disappointed to find that few of their students' summaries included discussion of the theme of the novel. Upon reflection, they realized that they had not made it clear to students that discussion of the theme was a necessary part of the summaries (South Loop Mid-Year Gallery Walk, January 2004; gallery walks are explained later in this chapter).

The assessment handbook becomes a place for teachers to record all the decisions they have made about the exact procedures to be followed in collecting evidence and the areas that will be assessed through their scoring tool (e.g., rubric, checklist). Further, the handbook serves as a valuable means for orienting teachers new to the school or the grade level to the assessment procedures established.

After teachers at a grade level have identified the evidence for their chosen benchmark, they discuss how they will score the evidence. In other words, they develop a rubric, checklist, rating scale, or similar assessment tool. Some teachers' previous experience has led them to believe that such tools must involve seven-point scales with elaborate criteria. We strongly encourage teachers to think of the process of scoring evidence in a much simpler way. In standards-based assessment, a straightforward approach is to arrive at a scoring tool that allows student evidence to be placed in one of three categories: above grade level, at grade level, or below grade level with respect to performance on that particular benchmark. Teachers often prefer to use terms with a more developmental tone, such as *exceeding*, *meeting*, or *working on* the benchmark. As with the benchmarks, assessment tools are geared toward end-of-year performance. Teachers work in grade levels to test their assessment tool on actual samples of evidence, and this reality check usually results in some revisions.

Here is an example of a rubric developed by third-grade teachers for the I Can statement, "I can summarize what I've read by retelling the main ideas." Students were required to read a text appropriate for the end of third grade and write a summary of it.

1. Above grade level
   a. The response shows a clear understanding of the story and includes the elements of setting, character, problem, solution, and theme.
   b. The response provides accurate and relevant information and shows sound reasoning about the story.
2. At grade level
   a. The response shows an adequate understanding of the story and includes the story elements of setting, character, problem, and solution.
   b. The response provides accurate information although not all of this information may be central to the story.
3. Below grade level
   a. The response is incomplete and shows little understanding, or an inaccurate understanding, of the story.
   b. The response may include random details and unimportant information.

Developing and using the rubric required teachers to exercise considerable professional judgment.

They had to arrive at a common understanding of exactly what they hoped to see in a summary written by their students at the end of the year, contributing to building coherence in their literacy curriculum and instruction within the grade level. Working together across several grade-level meetings helped them arrive at consensus. And, having reached consensus on the assessment evidence and procedures, they more easily developed criteria for identifying above-grade-level and below-grade-level performance.

We have noted that when teachers select anchor pieces, it generally reduces the need for elaborate scoring criteria. An *anchor piece* is a student product used to represent a certain level of performance. For example, the third-grade teachers who created the rubric presented above chose a student summary that represented the performance they wanted to see in students rated at grade level. Some teachers find it valuable as well to select anchor pieces representing performance below and above grade level. The process of selecting anchor pieces often helps teachers to clarify their thinking about scoring criteria. Having anchor pieces helps teachers to become confident in their decisions about rating students' work.

Some teachers introduce students to the teacher-developed rubric (with appropriate changes in wording). Other teachers prefer to have students discuss what should go into the rubric, and if necessary, they add to the students' criteria. The rubric is visible through a chart posted in the classroom, and copies of the chart may be placed in students' portfolios as well. These charts may include anchor pieces that are not actual student products but teacher-made samples that illustrate the features of grade-level, below-grade-level, or above-grade-level performance. On a regular basis, students can be guided through the process of evaluating their own work by referring to the rubric. At the end of the quarter—or whenever the period for evidence-gathering has been set—the students can select the piece of evidence that shows their best effort toward meeting the I Can statements. Students have the opportunity to assess their own performance, as well as to receive feedback from the teacher. Some teachers believe students should be aware that their reading performance is above, at, or below grade level. Many primary-grade teachers, however, prefer to use terms such as "developing" or "working toward the benchmark" and do not make explicit for children the level of their performance relative to grade-level standards.

Evidence-Based Instruction. The standards movement has important implications for the way administrators and curriculum leaders ask teachers to conceptualize instruction. The focus on benchmarks and assessment evidence allows instruction to be clearly defined as the means teachers use to improve student achievement. Once grade-level teams have established clear goals for student learning and collected evidence about students' progress toward these goals, their next step is to examine the evidence for what it can tell them about how to improve instruction—about how to bring students closer to the goals set for their learning.

At South Loop, each grade level has identified strategies that students would need to be successful on the grade-level I Cans. For example, to successfully achieve the I Can for comprehension in fourth grade, teachers know that students will need to learn to

- Connect author's ideas to their own ideas
- Explain main ideas from the text
- Explain important information from the text
- Include examples and details to support their answer
- Include details to support
- Discuss and interpret author's ideas
- Discuss personal ideas
- Identify literary genres
- Identify literary elements
- Summarize parts and entire pieces of text

Comprehension strategies overlap considerably with one another, so another group of fourth-grade teachers might arrive at a list with wordings quite different from this one.

As teachers analyze students' evidence, they look for patterns within the assessment evidence of areas of strengths and areas of needs. They may see trends demonstrated by the whole class or subsets of students. From these patterns, teachers (with the support of their grade-level teams) craft instructional plans for the whole class, small groups, and individual students. Assessment evidence often

indicates a need to differentiate instruction—by establishing flexible groups to meet students' varied needs in achieving a particular end-of-year goal or by reorganizing existing small-group arrangements.

Most important, the identification of these patterns in assessment evidence makes the selection of particular instructional strategies by teachers and grade-level teams purposeful. After identifying a need to develop students' interest in and awareness of unknown vocabulary words, one kindergarten grade-level team agreed upon three instructional strategies to address this need. In the following weeks and months, the teachers included attention to specific vocabulary words during whole-class read-aloud time, highlighted on a poster interesting words that the children identified (with student-drawn pictures to represent word meanings), and communicated with family members about word-learning strategies. A third-grade team used evidence from their three-times-per-year assessment to craft quarterly goals for each leveled, guided reading group. Drawing upon their I Can statements to frame the construction of these short-term goals, the teachers identified particular instructional strategies for each group to support their unique paths toward end-of-year goals.

At a recent whole-school mid-year reporting session, third-grade teachers at South Loop discussed concerns that had emerged when they analyzed students' extended response to text they had read. The extended response was supposed to reflect a balance between ideas students had taken from the text and their response to those ideas. The teachers reported that they were concerned about students' slow progress in referencing the prompt to which they were responding, remembering what they had been asked to address. Students also had trouble striking a good balance between their own ideas and ideas from the text. Two instructional strategies they were planning to use were to have students underline key words in the question so that they would "have a better understanding of what is being asked of them" and use two different color highlighters, one to highlight text information and one to highlight their own experiences so they can "visually see the balance." Further, they plan to explicitly talk about and model the difference between creating a viable summary and simply listing details from the text (South Loop Mid-Year Gallery Walk, January 2007).

As often as possible (and in ways that are appropriate to the grade and age levels of the students), we encourage teachers to share what they have learned from the assessments with their students. This establishes clarity of purpose in upcoming instruction for students as well as teachers, and includes students in this reflective learning process.

THE SBC PROCESS JOURNEY: A PROCESS OF DEVELOPMENT

As the school's professional learning community works with the SBC Process, its focus shifts over time. First, as described above, the focus is solely on getting the nine elements of the process in place. Second, when the elements are in place, the community focuses on institutionalizing the systematic reporting and schoolwide sharing of classroom-based assessment results by each grade at the beginning, middle, and end of the school year. Teachers may present their results electronically through PowerPoints, or they may post their results on display boards. (In Chicago, posting results on display boards are known as Gallery Walks.) During sharing sessions, each grade level receives feedback and responds to questions about its work. At the end of the session, all grade levels reflect upon and discuss the progress that their whole school is making with the SBC Process.

At the beginning of the year, teachers at each grade level present what they have learned from the evidence gathered about students' entering performance levels and share their plans for differentiating instruction to best meet their students' needs. Midyear presentations focus on discussing how students in each grade level are progressing and sharing any changes to plans based on this midterm checkpoint. Teachers sometimes include steps they will be taking to prepare students for state testing scheduled for later in the spring. The end of the year presentations focus on what the students have accomplished and where they will begin in the subsequent year, celebrating successes and engaging in important analyses of changes that will be needed

based on end-of-year evidence. For example, teachers may decide they can raise the bar on their grade-level benchmarks because students have shown the potential to reach higher levels of achievement. Or, teachers may decide to revise assessments that were not as useful as predicted in pointing the direction to needed instruction.

Third, when the process is understood and the schoolwide reporting institutionalized, the community focuses on creating its curriculum guides for reading or for writing. As products, the guides are thick three-ring binders that contain the grade-level goals, classroom assessments, instructional materials, and instructional strategies that all the teachers have agreed to address or include. Each grade level maintains a master copy of its guide, and each teacher has a personal copy as well. Teachers often customize their personal curriculum guides, for example, by adding lesson ideas they find useful (which are not used by all the other teachers at the grade level). The reading and writing curriculum guides serve to insure that as school staff turns over, there will be continuity as new teachers have access to the guide for their grade level. Many SBC Process schools have access to curriculum mapping software, but teachers have not found this type of software to be an adequate substitute for curriculum guides in hard copy.

These teacher-developed reading and writing guides also serve to underscore the difference between a school's curriculum and the particular programs and materials it uses to support the implementation of that curriculum. When teachers have developed their own curriculum guides, the school has reached the point where strong teacher ownership exists and is visible to those outside the school. Norman Pang, principal at Holomua, made the decision when opening the school that teachers would develop the curriculum. He saw teachers' commitment to curriculum development as crucial: "You have the people believing in what they're doing and it becomes more powerful because the teachers start taking ownership. They started with their beliefs and they made the curriculum" (quoted in Hokutan, 2005, p. 20). Ownership is reflected in the words of the teachers at Holomua as well. Teacher Aurene Pila stated: "I have no fear when it comes to curriculum. I've been through the process.

I created a curriculum from scratch. It's not just that we went through the process but what we ended up with was such a good product that we could really use and that we could really see growth in our students" (quoted in Hokutan, 2005, p. 24).

Fourth, the community focuses on student ownership and community involvement through the construction of student portfolios that are shared in situations such as parent-teacher-student (three-way) conferences (Davies, Cameron, Politano, & Gregory, 1992) and school open houses. Teachers at Holomua agreed that all grades would begin by developing individual, composite student portfolios (Valencia, 1998), combining evaluation and progress components. The evaluation component was based on the assessment evidence they were already collecting for their three-times-per-year reporting of results. The teachers used this evidence to back up the grades they entered for students on the state's new standards-based report cards. The progress component included additional evidence of students' growth as readers and writers, especially important in documenting the achievement of struggling learners and special education students whose work might remain well below grade-level standards.

Student portfolios and three-way conferences are just one component of Holomua's efforts to make parents full-fledged members of the school's learning community. During literacy coffee hours, Colleen Hokutan, the language arts curriculum coordinator, introduced parents to the SBC Process and gave them an overview of how the teachers had developed the reading and writing curricula. She then guided parents through the writing process. Rubrics for different grade levels were posted in the room, and parents assessed their completed writing against the rubrics. Colleen observed that parents were surprised at the rigor of the rubrics, often making remarks such as, "My piece doesn't have voice." Parents learned that aspects of writing such as meaning and voice were as important as conventions and skills, such as spelling and punctuation. Time was also scheduled for interested parents to visit their children's classrooms during the language arts period (C. Hokutan, personal communication, April 1, 2004).

The Seven-Level Model

As our description implies, schools undertake a complex journey as they work with the SBC Process to build the staircase curriculum and grow as professional learning communities, eventually encompassing students and parents as well as educators. Using design research that examined data from almost 100 schools from Hawaii and Chicago, we and our colleagues (Raphael et al., 2006) constructed the Seven-Level Model that could be used to describe the progress of successful schools over time. Here is a listing of the seven levels:

1. Recognizing a need
2. Organizing for change
3. Working on the building blocks
4. Moving as a whole school
5. Establishing the system
6. Implementing the staircase curriculum
7. Fully engaging students and families

This research has provided us with the knowledge base needed to customize support for schools that adopt the SBC Process, by addressing issues with more precision than was previously possible. No two schools are exactly alike, even when the demographics of the students appear similar. Thus, before introducing the SBC Process at a school, we now conduct a needs assessment to determine where the school falls on the Seven-Level Model in dimensions related to infrastructure, classroom practices, and student outcomes. We know from our experience that such a needs assessment helps educators at the school gain insights about their present situation and make evidence-guided plans for the future. Our goal is to help schools push forward to Levels 6 and 7, because we know it is at these levels that schools see increases in reading achievement on large-scale tests (Au, 2005), an especially important consideration for schools in low-income communities. Further, in schools at these advanced levels, teachers have ownership over the process and a deep understanding of how it works to support curriculum development and improve student achievement. Although some schools have seen test scores rise at Level 5, our observations indicate that the SBC Process often has not spread widely enough, or been ingrained deeply enough, among the educators at these schools to ensure sustained improvement. In the SBC Process, our goal is sustained excellence in teacher and student performance, not just a short-term change in test scores. Holomua principal Norman Pang, who was nearing retirement when we were drafting this chapter, expressed confidence that the SBC Process would continue after his tenure at the school "because the staff has bought in and it's a school belief" (quoted in Hokutan, 2005, p. 20).

Critical Lessons

Imagine that you have invited us to come to your school to discuss the SBC Process and how it might further your school's efforts to improve students' literacy achievement. As we familiarized you with the SBC Process, became better acquainted with your school, and made recommendations to you based on our research, we would share with you three critical lessons learned from our combined work with hundreds of teachers in dozens of schools.

A Literacy Program Is Not a Literacy Curriculum. In the SBC Process, we differentiate between a school's reading curriculum and its reading program. We define a *reading curriculum* as all the planned experiences, such as instruction, assessment, and other learning activities, that educators have designed and/or implemented to foster students' growth as readers (Marsh, 1997). A reading curriculum starts with goals for student learning (Tyler, 1950), usually tied to state and district standards. It includes instructional strategies designed to help students reach these goals, as well as the instructional materials (such as trade books, textbooks, and Web pages) that teachers will use in lessons and activities. Finally, a curriculum incorporates assessment to determine how students are progressing toward meeting the goals established for their learning (Tyler, 1950).

Every school is unique, serving a somewhat different community and students, and having teachers with different kinds of knowledge and experience. Because no school is exactly like another, we think each school must develop its own reading curriculum, informed by research, tailored to the needs of its students in learning to read, and drawing upon the strengths and interests of its faculty. In addition, through the process of developing the curriculum, teachers gain a deeper understanding of literacy, instruction, and assessment and take ownership of the curriculum and the improvement process. The *reading program*—whether it is a basal reading program or a reform model such as Success for All—is a set of materials and resources that teachers use to implement the school's reading curriculum.

Deep and Lasting Change Takes Time and Requires a Stable Infrastructure and Strong School Leadership to Help Teachers Stay the Course. When we first begin work with a school, we know that we must look carefully at its infrastructure. This is especially true in Title I schools, in both urban and rural areas, that serve a high proportion of students from low-income families, who are often of diverse cultural and linguistic backgrounds. Many of the Title I schools where we have introduced the SBC Process have had significant weaknesses in infrastructure. For example, some had a high rate of turnover of both administrators and teachers, while others suffered from being "Christmas tree schools" (Newmann et al., 2001), decorated with so many shiny new initiatives that teachers never had adequate time and support to do anything well.

We have learned that we must guide a school to build a strong infrastructure before we can start in earnest to work with the teachers on building the staircase curriculum. If we undertake curriculum improvement efforts before the infrastructure is in place, we know from experience that those efforts will either stall or take hold only temporarily. For example, in both Hawaii and Chicago we have worked in schools where principals expressed an interest in having teachers engage in SBC Process activities, but then did not provide adequate time for teachers to work together within and across grades. We now know that we must consult with the school's leadership to solve infrastructure problems, such as by creating a schedule that includes ample time for teachers to work within grade levels as well as to share their ideas across grade levels. In both locations, we have encountered schools with either a weak curriculum leader or no curriculum leader at all. We know that we must help the school see the importance of finding a strong curriculum leader, both knowledgeable and respected by the teachers, in order to serve in this critical role. Putting a solid infrastructure in place is essential for long-term success with the SBC Process.

Engagement Is An Important Step Toward Ownership. The SBC Process is a new way of thinking for many teachers as individuals, and certainly for a school staff as a whole. This way of thinking can be challenging to teachers who must work collaboratively as they create their school's literacy curriculum. This means that principals who are beginning this work in their schools may find that they have to convince teachers of its value before they can expect teachers to have the ownership needed to sustain the effort. In her analysis of the successful SBC Process schools in Chicago, Cosner (2006) differentiates between teacher engagement and teacher ownership. She notes that schools began to see increases in their school's achievement level with high teacher *engagement* in the SBC Process, while at the same time cautioning that engagement alone is not enough to sustain the work over time. Only teacher *ownership* of the curriculum will overcome the power of competing mandates from the district and/or turnovers in leadership and school staff.

Schools like Holomua and Kipapa that have sustained the SBC Process for several years are characterized by shared leadership of the process and a "deep bench," to use a sports metaphor. With shared leadership and a deep bench, current work can continue effectively, led by members of an active school leadership team that includes administrators and teachers. With a deep bench, or numerous individuals capable of stepping into leadership roles, there is sufficient expertise within the school to build on existing work, even in the face of turnover.

CONCLUSION

The SBC Process is a model that creates lasting school improvement by providing teachers with the opportunity to apply standards-based assessment and instruction. The process works by systematically engaging teachers in within-grade-level and across-grade-level conversations about teaching and

learning. As they work through the process, participants learn why there are no shortcuts. While many teachers describe the process as overwhelming in the beginning, they also describe how much they have learned: how the process has created a permanent change in the way they think about teaching, and how they have shifted to teaching based on evidence of their students' needs. This contrasts distinctly with teaching based on what external sources have proposed for a generic set of students. This intensive, problem-solving experience, which may extend over several years, gives participants a solid working knowledge of standards-based teaching, learning, and assessment. As one teacher wrote, a key insight she gained was that the process of standards-based assessment and school improvement was ongoing and "never really finished" (Kawaguchi & Au, 2001).

Because the literacy curriculum is built by the teachers within each school rather than outsiders, the teachers see themselves and are seen by others (e.g., parents, community members, colleagues) as professionals. In turn, they feel trusted to make decisions about how evidence-based teaching that aligns with high standards will be implemented in their schools. This contributes to teachers' ownership over the change process. They can tailor their vision statement, grade-level benchmarks, evidence, and rubrics to fit their own students. The constructivist nature of this process parallels the expectations for personal meaning making and higher level thinking that teachers should expect of their students (Kawaguchi & Au, 2001). A teacher at Holomua stated:

> It's a long process and sometimes you think it's tedious, but you only understand all that you've accomplished after you go through the whole process and you see the outcome. Then you'll understand why we had to take ownership from the beginning and why we had to make our own benchmarks before looking at the standards. (Hokutan, 2005, p. 26)

Finally, this process brings student achievement to center stage in a way that makes a practical contribution to teachers' professional development, as well as to new forms of collaboration with students and parents. Collecting and graphing their own standards-based achievement data gives teachers a greater awareness of their students' accomplishments and needs as readers and writers. They come to understand how assessment can be a tool for improving their teaching. In many cases, because teachers help students become aware of the standards through I Can statements and rubrics, students gain a much clearer picture of the kind of learning expected of them. When evidence is shared with parents, they can see where their children stand with respect to the rubrics. Because parents have a clear idea of what students are expected to do, they are in a better position to provide assistance at home.

Meeting high standards is currently the predominant concern in most efforts to improve reading achievement in elementary schools. In this context, a major challenge faced by school leaders who seek to facilitate standards-based reform is guiding the change process so that it can be perceived by teachers as supportive, rather than burdensome. Meaningful change in schools requires a time-consuming and painstaking process of rethinking. Teachers are more likely to undertake this process if they can see that changes are built on their contributions and reflect their own best thinking about what will help their students become better readers. This is why we believe that standards-based reform in reading must be a process of change from the inside out.

Acknowledgment. The Chicago work was funded in part by a grant from the Searle Funds of the Chicago Community Trust.

NOTES

1. Actual school names were used for Holomua, Kipapa, South Loop, Drake, and Shields, while pseudonyms were used for all others, based on the schools' preference. Persons' names for the actual schools are real.

REFERENCES

Au, K. H. (2005). Negotiating the slippery slope: School change and literacy achievement. *Journal of Literacy Research*, 37(3), 267–286.

Au, K. H. (2006). *Multicultural issues and literacy achievement.* Mahwah, NJ: Lawrence Erlbaum.

Cosner, S. (2006, November). *Elementary principals and standards-based change.* Paper presented at the annual meeting of the National Reading Conference, Los Angeles, CA.

Davies, A., Cameron, C., Politano, C., & Gregory, K. (1992). *Together is better: Collaborative assessment, evaluation and reporting.* Winnipeg, Canada: Peguis.

Higa, M. (2006). *The standards-based change process: The real scoop from a classroom teacher.* Paper presented at the meeting of the International Reading Association, Chicago, IL.

Hokutan, C. (2005). *The effects of the Standards Based Change Process on Teachers.* Unpublished master's thesis, College of Education, University of Hawaii, Honolulu.

Kawaguchi, K., & Au, K. (2001). Addressing standards through a complex-wide change process. *Educational Perspectives*, 34(1), 11–14.

Marsh, C. J. (1997). *Planning, management and ideology: Key concepts for understanding curriculum 2.* London: Routledge.

Mooney, K., & Raphael, T. (2006, November). *Turning points in school reform: One school's journey through the Standards-Based Change Process.* Paper presented at the annual meeting of the National Reading Conference, Los Angeles, CA.

Newmann, F. M., Smith, B., Allensworth, E., & Bryk, A. S. (2001). Instructional program coherence: What it is and why it should guide school improvement policy. *Educational Evaluation and Policy Analysis*, 23(4), 297–321.

Raphael, T., Goldman, S., Au, K., & Hirata, S. (2006, April). *A developmental model of the Standards-Based Change Process: A case study of school literacy reform.* Paper presented at the American Educational Research Association, San Francisco, CA.

Slavin, R. E., & Madden, N. (2001). *One million children: Success for all.* Thousand Oaks, CA: Corwin Press.

Supowitz, J. A., Poglinco, S., & Snyder, B. A. (2001). Moving mountains: Successes and challenges of the America's Choice comprehensive school reform design. Philadelphia, Consortium for Policy Research in Education.

Taba, H. (1962). *Curriculum development: Theory and practice.* New York: Harcourt, Brace & World.

Tyler, R. (1950). *Basic principles of curriculum and instruction.* Chicago: University of Chicago Press.

Valencia, S. W. (1998). *Literacy portfolios in action.* Fort Worth, TX: Harcourt Brace.

CHAPTER 6

Adolescent Literacy

Bird's-Eye Views

Christine A. McKeon and Richard T. Vacca

"Maynard Gull, you have the freedom to be yourself, your true self, here and now, and nothing can stand in your way." . . . "Are you saying I can fly?" "I say you are free." As simply and as quickly as that, Kirk Maynard

Gull spread his wings, effortlessly, and lifted into the dark of the night air. The Flock was roused from sleep by his cry, as loud as he could scream it, from five hundred feet up: "I can fly! Listen! I CAN FLY!" (Bach, 1970, p. 112)

And so, Richard Bach, in his best-selling book, *Jonathan Livingston Seagull* (1970), shares the essence of Jonathan's teaching, coaching, and encouragement that lead to the joy that Maynard, another seagull, experiences when he aspires to new heights. The book captures the essence of leadership, growth, change, and freedom through the eyes of seagulls in search of meaning. In the spirit of metaphors (Alvermann & Reinking, 2003), we thread the analogy of Jonathan Livingston Seagull as student, coach, and teacher throughout this chapter because the story's messages of urgent needs, frustration, and burning desires relate to the situations of adolescents and content area teachers today, but the story also connects to a renewed commitment to new perspectives on adolescent literacy.

In this chapter we synthesize the following topics:

- Historical and contemporary overviews of adolescent reading and writing
- Leadership standards for middle and high school literacy coaches
- Content area literacy standards for middle and high school literacy coaches
- Thoughts about adolescent literacy instruction

HISTORICAL AND CONTEMPORARY OVERVIEW OF ADOLESCENT READING AND WRITING

Historical Perspectives

> Most gulls don't bother to learn more than the simplest facts of flight—how to get from shore to food and back again. For most gulls, it is not flying that matters, but eating. For this gull, though, it was not eating that mattered, but flight. More than anything else, Jonathan Livingston Seagull loved to fly. (Bach, 1970, p. 12)

Jonathan was initially rejected by the Flock. He was advised to be an ordinary seagull with the elementary goal of survival, not the freedom of soaring high above the horizon. Much like Jonathan, most middle school and high school readers in the past were typically characterized with labels similar to elementary students; they received traditional instruction based on the notions of developmental, corrective, or remedial reading. Developmental readers were those who were near or above grade level in reading, and instruction took place in the regular classroom setting. Corrective readers fell below grade level and required additional help from the classroom teacher. Remedial readers needed some sort of specialized assistance from a reading teacher.

Remedial reading and writing in middle and secondary schools focused around a medical metaphor. Thus students who had a language illness (who were deficient in reading and writing), went to the laboratory for intervention and treatment. By looking at the students' symptoms (slow reading, poor comprehension, error-laden writing), the specialist could diagnose the problem, prescribe a treatment (usually worksheets or drill on isolated reading or writing skills), and effect a cure (Pemberton, 1992). The middle and secondary writing program often consisted of compositions assigned in English class without much instruction; these were often returned to the adolescents bleeding with red ink where punctuation was missed, spelling was incorrect, or words were used that didn't fit the teacher's expectations for school writing.

In the 1960s and 1970s content area reading—the idea that reading could not be approached separately from the content material of the subjects requiring reading—was touted as the way to reach all students who needed instructional support in using reading to learn. The phrase "every teacher a teacher of reading" was well known. It was believed that content area teachers could best help students master vocabulary, comprehension strategies, and study skills necessary to learn that particular discipline. However, most content area teachers misunderstood what it meant to be a "teacher of reading," believing that the skills for reading were best taught by reading teachers. Content area teachers did not feel prepared to undertake the kinds of teaching that would enable students to be proficient readers in their disciplines. This belief prevailed through the 1980s and 1990s as preservice and in-service teachers continued to resist content area reading coursework (Maimon, 1997) and reading intervention programs for remediation continued to prevail (Alvermann & Rush, 2004).

Even if content area reading and writing were part of the school's curriculum, the institutional practices worked against teachers of adolescents. The numbers of students that a teacher saw each day, the organization of subject matter specialties into departments, and the segregation of reading and writing to English classes, all contributed to teachers' beliefs that their job was to teach content only. Although literacy activities may have existed in the planned curriculum, they were realized in practice in only a very few classrooms (Sturtevant & Linek, 2003).

What were adolescents' actual experiences with the reading and writing curriculum? For the most part, teens were assigned pages in a content area textbook, answered questions that were narrowly focused, and took quizzes to "prove" that they read the book. Often the students did not read the assignments because they found them boring and irrelevant or because the material would be covered in a lecture the following day. School reading for many adolescents became purposeless and passive.

Writing instruction was laborious and tended to focus on the form of the text. Students were either assigned a topic or given a limited number of choices about which to write. A composition was judged as much by the number of errors the teacher found as by the meaning it conveyed. Although teachers meant well, the literacy experiences that adolescents underwent unfortunately seemed focused more on the product than the process.

An extraordinary amount of funding for the research and development of early childhood programs, though necessary, has not been balanced by research funding for adolescents (Moje, Young, Readance, & Moore, 2000; Vacca, 1998). The goals of preventing difficulties in young children consumed a national agenda that focused on early reading during the 1990s (Snow, Burns, & Griffin, 1998). Up until the late 1990s, the needs of adolescent literacy learners had gone largely unnoticed (Ivey & Broaddus, 2000; Moje et al., 2000; Moore, Bean, Birdyshaw, & Rycik, 1999) to the point of being "marginalized" (Vacca, 1998).

Contemporary Perspectives

His thought was triumph. . . . A seagull at two hundred fourteen miles per hour! It was a breakthrough,

the greatest single moment in the history of the Flock, and in that moment a new age opened for Jonathan Gull. Flying out to his lonely practice area, folding his wings for a dive from eight thousand feet, he set himself at once to discover how to turn. (Bach, 1970, p. 29)

Although adolescent readers today may still suffer from old teaching habits and curricular decisions that no longer make sense in terms of their changing needs in the twenty-first century, much like Jonathan Gull's triumph, a substantial shift in the way adolescent literacy learning is approached and a strong commitment on the part of teachers, administrators, and policy makers to rethink traditional notions of literacy for adolescents emerged in the late 1990s (Stevens, 2002). Recognizing the needs of adolescent learners, the International Reading Association's Commission on Adolescent Literacy issued a strong position statement that called for renewed commitment to adolescent reading and outlined beliefs and guidelines for instructional practices at the adolescent level. Literacy professionals realized that "adolescents entering the adult world in the twenty-first century will read and write more than at any other time in human history . . . [and that] continual instruction beyond the early grades is needed" (Moore et al., 1999, p. 99). The commission proposed a significant shift in viewpoints from content area literacy to adolescent literacy. Whereas content literacy recognizes the importance of prior knowledge, reading, and writing related to subject area disciplines (Sturtevant & Linek, 2004; Vacca & Vacca, 2005), as outlined by the commission (Moore et al., 1999, pp. 101–106), effective programs for adolescents should provide them with the following:

1. *Access to a wide variety of reading material that they can and want to read.* This means that students must be given the opportunity to read text every day that taps their interests and expands their knowledge of the world in a meaningful way. Adolescents need access to trade books, magazines, reference materials, and technology resources from which they can choose to read and write about topics in the content areas that not only pique their interests but also stretch their abilities.

2. *Instruction that builds both the skill and desire to read increasingly complex materials.* It is essential that middle and secondary school teachers provide

adolescents with explicit instruction in how to question, analyze, evaluate, and synthesize—in other words, how to think critically as they read.

3. *Assessment that shows them their strengths as well as their needs and that guides their teachers to design instruction that will best help them grow as readers.* Adolescents need a variety of ways to demonstrate what they know and alternative forms of assessment in which they have a choice and voice in evaluating their progress.

4. *Expert teachers who model and provide explicit instruction in reading comprehension and study strategies across the curriculum.* Adolescents need effective strategies that will lay the groundwork for their ability to maneuver print to meet their personal, social, cognitive, and emotional needs as adults.

5. *Reading specialists who assist individual students having difficulty learning how to read.* Literacy specialists and coaches who have a thorough knowledge about the processes of learning to read and write are in a good position to offer these teens appropriate intervention strategies that are meaningful, challenging, and relevant.

6. *Teachers who understand the complexities of individual adolescent readers, respect their differences, and respond to their characteristics.* Adolescents need teachers who listen, watch, observe, and notice the diversity that adolescents bring to the classrooms as individuals and as readers and writers. Teachers need to create literacy environments that are responsive to those differences.

7. *Homes, communities, and a nation that will support their efforts to achieve advanced levels of literacy.* Adolescents need the support of parents, community institutions such as libraries, businesses, and colleges; policy makers; and law makers to attain the literacy skills necessary to live productive lives and the critical thinking skills needed to make responsible decisions as they become adults.

The commission's recommendations are broad guidelines that play out differently in classrooms, schools, and programs. In the past, however, the visible organizational structure of reading instruction for adolescents was reserved for those students identified as deficient in reading and often took place in a laboratory setting. The position statement suggests that the visible organization ought not to be restricted to a reading lab for struggling readers. Not only does the commission emphasize the importance of recognizing the needs of struggling adolescent readers, but it also stresses the importance of addressing the developmental literacy needs of *all* adolescents in *all* areas of the curriculum in a variety of meaningful settings (Vacca, 2002).

Shortly after the establishment of the Commission on Adolescent Literacy, several position statements directed attention to the importance of adolescent reading with a major focus on professional development for content area teachers. The role of the reading specialist in middle and high schools shifted from that of remedial teacher to one of leadership in which literacy or reading coaches serve as mentors for classroom teachers as they model strategies in content classrooms, assist teachers in implementing strategies, and foster reflective teaching. In *Teaching All Children to Read: The Roles of the Reading Specialist* (2000), the International Reading Association (IRA) emphasizes that reading specialists need to work with middle and secondary content area teachers in order to ensure that effective literacy strategies, textbooks, and meaningful activities are implemented in content area teaching. The International Reading Association's publication *Supporting Young Adolescents' Literacy Learning* (2002) clarifies that middle school students deserve instruction that helps them refine their literacy skills. In *The Role and Qualifications of the Reading Coach in the United States* (IRA, 2004), the importance of successful teaching experiences for middle and high school reading coaches stresses a significant emphasis on the new role of reading specialists as individuals who provide support for classroom teachers in the content areas. In 2006 the International Reading Association in collaboration with the National Council of Teachers of English, National Council of Teachers of Mathematics, National Science Teachers Association, and National Council for the Social Studies completed the comprehensive document *Standards for Middle and High School Literacy Coaches*. The standards specify "what literacy coaches must know and be able to do to function effectively to train [content area] faculty in literacy techniques" (p. 3).

In tandem with position statements and standards that highlight the needed attention to adolescent literacy and the role of literacy coaches, a plethora of articles, books, and initiatives now pervade the literature. *Reading Today*, the bimonthly newspaper of the International Reading Association, for example, has consistently published articles that reiterate the renewed focus on reading coaches and adolescent literacy (Allington, 2006; "IRA, Others Develop Standards," 2005; "IRA Surveys Coaches," 2006; "Spotlight on Reading Coaches," 2004; Vogt, 2004). In summary, the shift toward adolescent literacy and middle and high school literacy coaches characterizes approaches to reading and writing instruction that go beyond remedial strategies delivered in pull-out programs. Instead, contemporary adolescent literacy instruction needs to be expertly orchestrated for all students by teachers who have in-depth knowledge of adolescents and strategies to enhance independent reading and writing.

Literacy coaches can begin helping teachers develop professional expertise by assisting them in identifying their core beliefs, selecting a professional development model, determining the content, providing time for reflection, and deciding how any new effort will be evaluated (Santa, 2006). In addition, "among the most important kinds of reading coaches' activities are teaching demonstrations and modeling of lessons" (Dole, 2004, p. 466). Other critical characteristics of effective literacy coaches include the ability to foster caring, trustworthy relationships with teachers, stress-free learning environments, and positive conversations (Lyons, 2002). Successful professional development programs are ongoing rather than isolated workshops where teachers are "given" new ideas, and their strategies are based on research (Greenleaf, Jimenez, & Roller, 2002; Rodgers, 2002).

There are many federal, state, and local literacy professional development programs for teachers of adolescents that are being initiated nationwide (Biancarosa & Snow, 2004; National Association of Secondary School Principals, 2005; National Association of State Boards of Education, 2005; National Governors Association Center for Best Practices, 2005). Although research that demonstrates the effectiveness of professional development plans is needed but challenging to carry out (Anders, Hoffman, & Duffy, 2000), there are elements that consistently emerge as key components of effective programs. These components include follow-up support for teachers and hands-on opportunities for practicing practical strategies (Hughes, Cash, Ahwee, & Klinger, 2002). In the next section we synthesize the critical leadership elements of the *Standards for Middle and High School Literacy Coaches* (IRA, 2006).

LEADERSHIP STANDARDS FOR LITERACY COACHES

Not long after he perfected soaring higher and higher, Jonathan had students.

> Every hour Jonathan was there at the side of his students, demonstrating, suggesting, pressuring, guiding. He flew with them through night and cloud and storm. . . . When the flying was done, the students relaxed in the sand, and in time they listened more closely to Jonathan. He had some crazy ideas they couldn't understand, but then he had some good ones that they could. (Bach, 1970, pp. 110–111)

Just as Jonathan was determined to share his expertise with his students through leadership, the first set of standards for adolescent literacy coaches emphasizes the common leadership roles that are recommended (IRA, 2006). Table 6.1 captures the elements within each leadership standard.

In meeting the first standard of skillful collaboration, middle and high school literacy coaches should begin by developing a schoolwide literacy team to conduct a literacy needs assessment. That task essentially focuses the team's efforts toward goals for each content area. Literacy coaches facilitate discussions based on needs, goals, and concerns; they are good listeners who respect and value the team's input. Since literacy coaches primarily work with teachers, they need to consider adult learning strategies such as utilizing collaborative groups, engaging presentation formats, and appropriate settings. It is important that literacy coaches have excellent communication and interpersonal skills (Bean, Swan, & Knaub, 2003). As part of their own professional development, literacy coaches keep up-to-date on current research about teaching, learning, best practices, and curriculum materials. In the following fictional vignette, consider how

Table 6.1. Leadership Standards for Adolescent Literacy Coaches

Standard	Elements
1. Skillful collaborators	1.1. Conduct needs assessment
	1.2. Promote productive relationships
	1.3. Work on professional knowledge, skills, strategies
2. Job-embedded coaches	2.1. Provide practical support to individuals/teams
	2.2. Observe teachers/provide feedback
3. Evaluators of literacy needs	3.1. Lead faculty in use of assessment tools
	3.2. Conduct regular meetings with content teachers

Adapted from *Standards for Middle and High School Literacy Coaches* (2006) with permission of the International Reading Association (www.reading.org). Copyright 2006 by the Carnegie Corporation of New York. All rights reserved. A full-text PDF of this document is available at www.reading.org/resources/issues/reports/coaching.html

Jim, a new literacy coach, approaches the task of keeping up-to-date.

Jim has 6 years teaching experience in social studies at the middle level in Ohio, is currently working on a master's degree in reading, and has recently taken on the part-time responsibility of literacy coach for the social studies teachers in his school. Although somewhat overwhelmed by this new role, Jim has volunteered to participate in Ohio's Core Curriculum for Teaching Adolescent Literacy (Ohio Department of Education, 2004). He participates in monthly professional development sessions that enhance his ability to coach, and he communicates weekly with a field faculty member who observes him coach and provides Jim with constructive feedback. Joe also keeps up regularly through Ohio's online resource (www.ohiorc.org/adlit) for middle and high school teachers.

In fulfilling the second standard, literacy coaches work with individual teachers and content area teams to observe teachers teach, provide constructive feedback, and model instructional strategies that address the content, as well as the literacy needs of the students. They assist teachers in evaluating text-based materials that are interesting and are written for multiple ability levels, and they guide teachers in using evidence-based reading, writing, vocabulary, and comprehension strategies. In the following fictional vignette, consider how literacy coach Beth provides feedback after observing Joe teaching his ninth-grade algebra class.

Beth: Joe, your lesson seemed to go smoothly. What do you think?

Joe: I think that I accomplished the goals of my lesson.

Beth: I think so, too. How do you think you accomplished your goals?

Joe: Well, I took time to think about the idea of problem solving and decided that I'd give the kids the chance to think about their own problems and solving them before we started problem solving in this algebra chapter. It seemed to get them interested. Gee, all kids seem to have problems they are trying to solve.

Beth: Great point, Joe. Can you reflect on how you made the transition between the students' problem solving and the chapter?

Joe: Well, do you remember when we talked about graphic organizers in our last session together?

Beth: Sure.

Joe: Well, I drew a graphic organizer on the board that focused on one of the kids' problems and sketched a web in which we brainstormed the solutions to that problem. It was pretty cool.

Beth: And then what happened?

Joe: Well, you saw it! All of a sudden, problem solving made sense to the kids, and we worked out problems by graphically organizing them using math examples from the book!

Beth: Yes, Joe. You provided the students with the opportunity to connect the idea of problem solving to their own lives by first activating prior knowledge and then making the transition to the examples in the book by using their experiences as a framework for understanding mathematics problems. Excellent work!

Joe: Thanks, Beth.

As skilled evaluators (the third standard), coaches collaborate with content faculty in developing and selecting formal and informal assessments as tools for making instructional decisions. Assessments might include portfolios, pre- and post-tests, anecdotal records, checklists, and reading inventories, as well as more formal measures of learning. Regular meetings help content teachers reflect on the effectiveness of strategies they use, analyze assessment results, and plan additional goals. Literacy coaches assist teachers in setting assessment schedules so that the assessments will inform instruction. In the following fictional vignette, José helps Marta construct a literacy assessment in her eighth-grade science class.

It is the first week of school and José, the newly appointed literacy coach at Middlebury High School, is trying to help the subject area teachers develop preliminary assessment tools that will capture the reading strengths and weaknesses of the adolescents in their content area classes. Marta, a first-year science teacher, is rather lost. She knows the science content of her biology course, but that's about it. Although José has had extensive experience as a middle school science teacher, this is his first year as a literacy coach. Consider the dialogue that occurs between José and Marta.

José: Marta, welcome! We are pleased to have you join our staff! I'm José, and I am here to assist you with teaching your students how to "read" science.

Marta: Oh, gosh, José! I don't know anything about teaching reading.

José: Not to worry. Teaching adolescents to read science texts is something we'll work on together.

Marta: OK, José, if you say so, but I'll need "big time" help with this!

José: Let's start with one class of students and figure out what they know about science books.

Marta: Sounds OK to me.

José: Great, let's give it a whirl! In your BIO 101 class do you have a textbook?

Marta: Sure. It's a required one.

José: OK. Let's start with the book, and see how much your students know about its organization, and design an informal assessment to see about their knowledge. We could distribute the biology books to your students and develop a performance survey. Your students might be asked to locate steps in a procedure, a scientific notation, a table, or a definition. In essence, the survey would give you a synthesis of your students' ability to *use* your textbook. That might be a starting point.

Marta: Oh, José. I'm willing to give it a try, although all of this reading assessment is so new to me.

José: That's okay. We'll work as a team.

In the next section, we summarize what literacy coaches should know and be able to perform in content area literacy instruction (IRA, 2006), and we share several examples and references to ideas in which teachers have implemented approaches to ensuring that middle and secondary students grasp, understand, and relate to content area instruction.

CONTENT AREA LITERACY STANDARDS

One of Jonathan's students was Fletcher.

Fletcher Seagull, who loved aerobatics like no one else, conquered his sixteen-point vertical slow roll and the next day topped it off with a triple cartwheel, his feathers flashing white sunlight to a beach from which more than one furtive eye watched. (Bach, 1970, p. 110)

Just as Fletcher Seagull perfected his skilled flight performances, the content area literacy standards for middle and high school literacy coaches indicate skillful performances for each of four content areas: English language arts, mathematics, science, and social studies. Members of the national professional associations affiliated with each content area developed the respective literacy-coach standards as guidelines that reflect reading skills as well as content area knowledge and skills (IRA, 2006). Although each content area section identifies specific literacy performances appropriate for the subject area, guidelines overlap and reinforce each other. Table 6.2 synthesizes the underlying principles of content area literacy coaching across all disciplines.

It is essential that middle and secondary literacy coaches know the subject matter (English language arts, mathematics, science, social studies) in which they are going to coach as well as the professional state and local standards of the discipline. They also should be experienced teachers at the middle or secondary levels who understand adolescent development (IRA, 2006). Coaches need to have an expert repertoire of reading strategies for the content area in which they will coach, and they need to know effective ways of demonstrating those strategies for teachers in their classrooms.

Turning to the specific content areas, Table 6.3 presents several performances English language arts coaches should be able to do. Grisham and Wolsey (2006) provide a practical example of a teacher and university professor collaboration that encouraged middle school language arts students to voice opinions about literature they read using electronic threaded discussion groups. Using a data projector, Wolsey, the classroom teacher, demonstrated how to reply to messages appropriately. As a result of the teamwork between the teacher and

Table 6.3. Performances and Examples for Literacy Coaches of English Language Arts Teachers

Performance	Examples
Help teachers understand text structures	Narrative, description/main idea, comparison/contrast, chronological/sequential, cause and effect, argument/evidence
Model effective reading strategies	Think-alouds, visual aids—charts, Venn diagrams—analyzing author's purpose, character analysis, retelling, summarizing
Demonstrate ways to engage students	Expressing points of view, role playing, think-pair-share, imaginative writing

Adapted from *Standards for Middle and High School Literacy Coaches* (2006) with permission of the International Reading Association (www.reading.org). Copyright 2006 by the Carnegie Corporation of New York. All rights reserved. A full-text PDF of this document is available at www.reading.org/resources/issues/reports/coaching.html

professor, the "students found voice, developed perspectives, made meaningful predictions, connected the literature with other media, and [were motivated] to read" (p. 654).

In middle and high school mathematics, students need to go beyond numerical skills "to master the higher order skills of reading, interpreting, and representing life situations in mathematical settings . . . and [yet] students do not necessarily talk or write about mathematics naturally, especially as it becomes more complex and abstract" (IRA, 2006, p. 23). Mathematics literacy coaches, for example, can model how to interpret diagrams, graphs, or tables through think-pair-share activities in which students are encouraged to evaluate information, discuss the process with a partner, then share with a larger group. The standards for middle and secondary literacy coaches outline guidelines that will enhance content area teachers' understanding of the literacy of mathematics. Table 6.4 synthesizes the performance standards for mathematics literacy coaches.

Draper (2002) offers specific suggestions for incorporating reading strategies such as DR-TA

Table 6.2. Content Area Literacy Standards

Standard	Elements
Skillful Instructional Strategists	1. Are accomplished content area teachers Know the content area subject matter Know the reading and writing processes associated with the content 2. Know and can demonstrate appropriate reading strategies for the content area

Adapted from *Standards for Middle and High School Literacy Coaches* (2006) with permission of the International Reading Association (www.reading.org). Copyright 2006 by the Carnegie Corporation of New York. All rights reserved. A full-text PDF of this document is available at www.reading.org/resources/issues/reports/coaching.html

Table 6.4. Performances and Examples for Literacy Coaches of Mathematics Teachers

Performance	Examples
Help teachers understand the structure of mathematics textbooks	Density of ideas; concepts built across chapters; technical vocabulary; use of symbols; diagrams, graphs, tables; culturally different number systems
Model the way logic and reasoning are used in mathematical contexts	Making and testing validity, reasoning inductively, making deductive arguments, evaluating and producing proofs
Demonstrate ways to engage students in active learning	Dialogue, discussions, group projects, think-pair-share, jigsaw, pair problem solving

Adapted from *Standards for Middle and High School Literacy Coaches* (2006) with permission of the International Reading Association (www.reading.org). Copyright 2006 by the Carnegie Corporation of New York. All rights reserved. A full-text PDF of this document is available at www.reading.org/resources/issues/reports/coaching.html

Table 6.5. Performances and Examples for Literacy Coaches of Science Teachers

Performance	Examples
Help teachers understand the specific demands of reading science textbooks	Importance of prior knowledge; density of ideas, concepts built across chapters; technical concepts; facts, opinions, inferences; cause and effect; diagrams, symbols
Model strategies that use logic and reasoning in scientific contexts	Making and testing the validity of hypotheses, reasoning inductively, making deductive arguments, describing laboratory procedures, recording observations
Demonstrate ways to engage students in active learning	Design and describe laboratory procedures, think-pair-share, jigsaw, pair problem solving

Adapted from *Standards for Middle and High School Literacy Coaches* (2006) with permission of the International Reading Association (www.reading.org). Copyright 2006 by the Carnegie Corporation of New York. All rights reserved. A full-text PDF of this document is available at www.reading.org/resources/issues/reports/coaching.html

(Direct Reading-Thinking Activity) and K-W-L (What I *Know*, What I *Want* to learn and What I have *Learned*) in mathematics classrooms. The importance of teaching middle and secondary students how to "read" math is reflected in the following. According to Yoakum (1945, p. 462), as cited in Draper, "'When asked, 'If I teach reading, what will happen to [mathematics]?' Yoakum replied, 'The more important question is, what will happen if you don't.'"

For science literacy coaches, the challenges of meeting the literacy needs of middle and secondary science teachers and students are equally critical. Not only do science textbooks require intense, critical reading, but special skills are necessary in order to interpret complex issues (IRA, 2006). Science literacy coaches, for example, can model for teachers how to design graphic organizers that visually synthesize the nature of complex issues. Table 6.5 captures performances for science literacy coaches.

Kane and Rule (2004) describe strategies in which they used poetry with preservice teachers who were enrolled in a content literacy course with the intention that the preservice teachers would learn how to use the strategies in their future classrooms. Poetry was incorporated into several disciplines including science. As cited in Kane and Rule, Abisdris and Casuga (2001) explain the value of using poetry in the science classroom to clarify complex issues:

> The language of science is metaphorical in nature. Due to the nature of certain abstract concepts, metaphors are used constantly by scientists to help them understand and conceptualize knowledge. . . . Scientific models are essentially equivalent to the metaphorical language used in poetry. (p. 59)

Needless to say, the *Standards for Middle and High School Literacy Coaches* (IRA, 2006) also address the challenges that students meet when reading and learning social studies—economics, government, history, geography, and civics, to name a few topics. Table 6.6 summarizes the performances of literacy coaches of social studies teachers. Massey and Heafner (2004) provide before, during, and after

Table 6.6. Performances and Examples for Literacy Coaches of Social Studies Teachers

Performance	Examples
Help teachers understand the specific demands of social studies texts	Fact and opinion; distinguishing between primary and secondary sources; thinking critically by analyzing point of view; detecting bias; navigating factual information; using maps, globes, glossaries, indexes
Model strategies that assist teachers in identifying social studies text structures	Sequence of events, cause and effect, comparison/contrast, concepts and definitions, main idea and detail, description
Demonstrate ways to engage students in active learning	Expressing informed viewpoints, visual discovery, experiential exercises, problem solving, group work, Web quests

Adapted from *Standards for Middle and High School Literacy Coaches* (2006) with permission of the International Reading Association (www.reading.org). Copyright 2006 by the Carnegie Corporation of New York. All rights reserved. A full-text PDF of this document is available at www.reading.org/resources/issues/reports/coaching.html

reading strategies for teaching social studies. In their example of lessons about the American Revolution, a prereading activity facilitates students' background knowledge when they group a list of concepts they have generated about the topic and subsequently label each list. During reading, the students are taught how to construct an outline in which they predict what they will read; the purpose for reading is to revise the outlines based on what is read. An activity following the reading is reciprocal questioning. Massey and Heafner suggest that these strategies and others can assist teachers as they strive to teach reading comprehension in the social studies classroom.

In this section we highlighted specific performances that middle school and high school coaches need to consider within the content areas (IRA, 2006). In the next section, we pose additional considerations for policy makers, administrators, literacy coaches, and middle and secondary classroom teachers.

THOUGHTS ABOUT ADOLESCENT LITERACY INSTRUCTION

[Jonathan] spoke of very simple things—that it is right for a gull to fly, that freedom is the very nature of his being, that whatever stands against that freedom must be set aside. "The only difference [between these seagulls and others], the very only one, is that they have begun to understand what they really are and have begun to practice it." (Bach, 1970, p. 114)

And so it is with those whose goal is to improve adolescent literacy—understanding is critical. Policy makers, administrators, coaches, and content area teachers need to *understand* their roles in the overall scheme of adolescent literacy instruction and implement those roles. More specifically, policy makers and administrators need be knowledgeable about and respect the literacy educational needs of *all* adolescent learners. They need to understand that literacy learning does not end in the primary grades, that in fact it becomes more complex as students enter the upper grades. In addition, policy makers and administrators need to be committed to adolescent literacy by hiring highly qualified teachers as literacy coaches who have expert knowledge about literacy, have teaching experience in middle or high school classrooms, and have demonstrated outstanding mentoring and communication skills with other teachers. In essence, policy makers and administrators need to embrace a philosophy of "leave no teacher behind." Although there is a growing body of literature that reflects a wide variety of approaches to adolescent literacy and guidelines for coaching secondary-level content area teachers (Dole, 2004; Donahue, 2003; Faulkner, 2005; Hinchman, Alvermann, Boyd, Brozo, & Vacca, 2004; Jetton & Dole, 2004; Ohio Department of Education, 2004; Rycik & Irvin, 2001), what is recommended consistently is that literacy coaches and subject area teachers balance their leadership efforts and develop realistic and reasonable goals based on the specific needs of their students. Literacy coaches need to maintain expertise and share with content area teachers in an open, caring atmosphere.

Although school reform, teacher professional development, and the implementation of effective literacy strategies are critical components of new reforms regarding adolescent literacy, it is just as important to include the learners themselves in the process. Student choice, time to read, issues of identity, and self-efficacy should be at the center of decisions regarding adolescent literacy initiatives (Alvermann, 2002; Franzak, 2004; Ivey, 2001; Rycik & Irvin, 2001; Strauss & Irvin, 2001; Sturtevant, 2001; Vacca & Vacca, 2005). This point was aptly made by Baker (2002) in an interview with her middle school son. In response to her question regarding his thoughts on reading, he replied, "I wish I didn't have to do it so much. I don't like having to read for school [but] when I get to choose it's all right" (p. 365). Similarly, when asked by Brozo (2006) about the new school improvement plan at his high school, a 10th grader replied, "[I go] 'cause I can't read . . . well, I can read, but not good. Man, I hate reading, and that class is stupid" (p. 413). Comments such as these confirm that we need to listen to the voices of adolescents as we strive to rethink adolescent literacy and design effective programs. Moje (2002) argues that the "future of adolescent and secondary literacy research . . . is in research that examines the connections between everyday discourses of adolescents and the academic discourses they navigate each day" (p. 211). How might this occur? Involving students is critical. It seems logical that enlisting the input of students who hold leadership roles makes sense (i.e., Student Council, Honor Society). On the other hand, inviting students who hold average and below-average grades and who have a potentially vested interest in programs that will assist their notions of learning also makes sense. Voluntary input from the latter groups could be orchestrated so that classroom and practical learning are the issues at stake. Discussion questions such as the following would be helpful in starting to work with such groups:

- Why do you need to take these classes? (i.e., history, biology, and so on)
- Can you share any links to your lives that these classes have?
- If you have some "links," what could your teacher do to make those links more relevant in those classes?
- Do you have a textbook for most of your classes? Do you read your textbooks? How or why not?

- Do you have to learn for tests based on the textbook? Why does your teacher test you? Do you study for those tests? How? What could your teacher do to help you know what will be tested? If you didn't take a test, how could you show the teacher that you understand the information in the course?

Needless to say, there are countless questions that can engage middle and high school students in discussions that serve as input for initiating literacy coach and teacher collaboratives that are student-centered. The key to success on any level is partnership.

CONCLUSION

Fletcher Gull [Jonathan's student] turned to his instructor, and there was a moment of fright in his eye.
"Me leading? What do you mean, *me* leading? You're the instructor here. You couldn't leave!"
"Couldn't I? Don't you think that there might be other flocks, other Fletchers, that need an instructor more than [you]. . . ."
"Me? Jon, I'm just a plain seagull, and you're . . ."
Jonathan sighed and looked out to the sea. "You don't need me any longer. You need to keep finding yourself, a little more each day, that real, unlimited Fletcher Seagull. He's your instructor." (Bach, 1970, pp. 124–125)

And so, his coaching complete, Jonathan Livingston Seagull disappeared. And Fletcher faced a new group of young gulls eager to learn. He would mentor, coach, and guide them, much like Jonathan did for him.

In this chapter we have attempted to capture the historical and contemporary viewpoints that reflect the evolving nature of adolescent literacy instruction and roles of literacy coaches. Much like Jonathan and Fletcher, literacy coaches are reflective leaders. A primary focus of this chapter was to synthesize the role of adolescent literacy coaches as leaders and to spotlight the content area performances they should address when working collaboratively with teachers. We also highlighted several issues to consider regarding adolescent literacy, including taking into account the voices of the adolescents.

In closing, we suggest that just as the sky provided no limits for Jonathan Livingston Seagull, and he in turn encouraged other gulls to reach beyond the horizon, the time is ripe to approach adolescent literacy from new perspectives—perhaps bird's-eye views.

REFERENCES

Abisdris, G., & Casuga, A. (2001). Atomic poetry: Using poetry to teach Rutherford's discovery of the nucleus. *The Science Teacher, 68,* 58–62.

Allington, R. L. (2006). Reading specialists, reading teachers, reading coaches: A question of credentials. *Reading Today, 23*(4), 16–17.

Alvermann, D. E. (2002). Effective literacy instruction for adolescents. *Journal of Literacy Research, 34,* 189–208.

Alvermann, D. E., & Reinking, D. (2003). On metaphors and editing. *Reading Research Quarterly, 38,* 8–11.

Alvermann, D. E., & Rush, L. (2004). Literacy intervention programs at the middle and high school levels. In T. L. Jetton & J. A. Dole (Eds.), *Adolescent literacy research and practice* (pp. 210–227). New York: Guilford Press.

Anders, P. L., Hoffman, J. V., & Duffy, G. G. (2000). Teaching teachers to teach reading: Paradigm shifts, persistent problems, and challenges. In M. Kamil, P. B. Mosenthal, P. D. Pearson, & R. Barr (Eds.), *Handbook of Reading Research* (Vol. 3, pp. 719–742). Mahwah, NJ: Erlbaum.

Bach, R. (1970). *Jonathan Livingston Seagull: A story.* New York: Avon Books.

Baker, M. I. (2002). Reading resistance in middle school: What can be done? *Journal of Adolescent & Adult Literacy, 45,* 364–366.

Bean, R. M., Swan, A. L., & Knaub, R. (2003). Reading specialists in schools with exemplary reading programs: Functional, versatile, and prepared. *The Reading Teacher, 56,* 446–454.

Biancarosa, G., & Snow, C. E. (2004). *Reading next: A vision for action and research in middle and high school literacy.* Washington, DC: Alliance for Excellent Education.

Brozo, W. (2006). Tales out of school: Accounting for adolescents in a literacy reform community. *Journal of Adolescent & Adult Literacy, 49,* 410–418.

Dole, J. A. (2004). The changing role of the reading specialist in school reform. *The Reading Teacher, 57,* 462–470.

Donahue, D. (2003). Reading across the great divide: English and math teachers apprentice one another as readers and disciplinary insiders. *Journal of Adolescent & Adult Literacy, 47,* 24–37.

Draper, R. J. (2002). School mathematics reform, constructivism, and literacy: A case for literacy instruction in the reform-oriented math classroom. *Journal of Adolescent & Adult Literacy, 45,* 520–529.

Faulkner, V. (2005). Adolescent literacies within the middle years of schooling: A case study of a year 8 homeroom. *Journal of Adolescent & Adult Literacy, 49,* 108–117.

Franzak, J. K. (2004). Constructing struggling readers: Policy and the experiences of eighth-grade readers. In J. Worthy, B. Maloch, J. V. Hoffman, D. L. Schallert, & C. M. Fairbanks (Eds.), *53rd yearbook of the National Reading Conference* (pp. 189–205). Oak Creek, WI: National Reading Conference.

Greenleaf, C. L., Jimenez, R. T., & Roller, C. M. (2002). Reclaiming secondary reading interventions: From limited to rich conceptions, from narrow to broad conversations, *Reading Research Quarterly, 37,* 484–496.

Grisham, D. L., & Wolsey, T. D. (2006). Recentering the middle school classroom as a vibrant learning community: Students, literacy, and technology intersect. *Journal of Adolescent & Adult Literacy, 49,* 648–660.

Hinchman, K. A, Alvermann, D. E., Boyd, F. B., Brozo, W. G., & Vacca, R. T. (2004). Supporting older students' in- and out-of-school literacies. *Journal of Adolescent & Adult Literacy, 47,* 304–310.

Hughes, M. T., Cash, M. M., Ahwee, S., & Klinger, J. (2002). A national overview of professional development programs in reading. In E. M. Rodgers & G. S. Pinnell (Eds.), *Learning from teaching in literacy education: New perspectives on professional development* (pp. 9–28). Portsmouth, NH: Heinemann.

International Reading Association (IRA). (2000). *Teaching all children to read: The roles of the reading specialist.* Newark, DE: Author.

International Reading Association (IRA). (2002). *Supporting young adolescents' literacy learning.* Newark, DE: Author.

International Reading Association. (2004). *The role and qualifications of the reading coach in the United States.* Newark, DE: Author.

International Reading Association (IRA). (2006). *Standards for middle and high school literacy coaches.* Newark, DE: Author.

IRA, others develop middle, high school literacy coaching standards. (2005, December). *Reading Today, 23*(3), 1–3.

IRA surveys coaches. (2006, April). *Reading Today, 23*(5), 1–3.

Ivey, G. (2001). Discovering readers in the middle level school: A few helpful clues. In J. A. Rycik & J. L. Irvin (Eds), *What adolescents deserve: A commitment to stu-*

dents' literacy learning (pp. 63–71). Newark, DE: International Reading Association.

Ivey, G., & Broaddus, K. (2000). Tailoring the fit: Reading instruction and middle school readers. *The Reading Teacher, 54,* 68–78.

Jetton, T. L., & Dole, J. A. (Eds.). (2004). *Adolescent literacy research and practice.* New York: Guilford Press.

Kane, S., & Rule, A. C. (2004). Poetry connections can enhance content area learning. *Journal of Adolescent & Adult Literacy, 47,* 658–669.

Lyons, C. A. (2002). Becoming an effective literacy coach. In E. M. Rodgers & G. S. Pinnell (Eds.), *Learning from teaching in literacy education: New perspectives on professional development* (pp. 93–118). Portsmouth, NH: Heinemann.

Maimon, L. (1997). Reducing resistance to content area literacy courses. In W. M. Linek & E. G. Sturtevant (Eds.), *Exploring literacy. 19th yearbook of the College Reading Association* (pp. 267–281). College Reading Association.

Massey, D. D., & Heafner, T. L. (2004). Promoting reading comprehension in social studies. *Journal of Adolescent & Adult Literacy, 48,* 28–40.

Moje, E. B. (2002). Re-framing adolescent literacy research for new times: Studying youth as a resource. *Reading Research and Instruction, 41,* 211–228.

Moje, E. B., Young, J. P., Readance, J. E., & Moore, D. W. (2000). Reinventing adolescent literacy for new times: Perennial and millennial issues. *Journal of Adolescent & Adult Literacy, 43,* 400–410.

Moore, D. W., Bean, T. W., Birdyshaw, D., & Rycik, J. A. (1999). Adolescent literacy: A position statement. *Journal of Adolescent & Adult Literacy, 43,* 97–112.

National Association of Secondary School Principals. (2005). *Creating a culture of literacy: A guide for middle and high school principals.* Reston, VA: Author.

National Association of State Boards of Education. (2005). *Reading at risk: How states can respond to the crisis in adolescent literacy.* Alexandria, VA: Author.

National Governors Association Center for Best Practices. (2005). *Reading to achieve: A governor's guide to adolescent literacy.* Washington, DC: Author.

Ohio Department of Education. (2004). *Teaching adolescent literacy: A core curriculum for educators (Grades 4–12).* Columbus, OH: Author.

Pemberton, M. (1992). The prison, the hospital, the madhouse: Redefining metaphors for the writing center. *Writing Lab Newsletter, 17*(1), 11–16.

Rodgers, A. (2002). Old roads and new paths: What happens when two teachers attempt an alternative teaching strategy within a peer collaborative relationship. In E. M. Rodgers & G. S. Pinnell (Eds.), *Learning from teaching in literacy education: New perspectives on professional development* (pp. 135–157). Portsmouth, NH: Heinemann.

Rycik, J. A., & Irvin, J. L (Eds.). (2001). *What adolescents deserve: A commitment to students' literacy learning.* Newark, DE: International Reading Association.

Santa, C. M. (2006). A vision for adolescent literacy: Ours or theirs? *Journal of Adolescent & Adult Literacy, 49,* 466–476.

Snow, C. E., Burns, M. S., & Griffin, P. (Eds.). (1998). *Preventing reading difficulties in young children.* Washington, DC: National Academy Press.

Spotlight on reading coaches. (2004, June/July). *Reading Today, 21*(6), 1–3.

Stevens, L. P. (2002). Making the road by walking: The transition from content area literacy to adolescent literacy. *Reading Research and Instruction, 41,* 267–278.

Strauss, S. E., & Irvin, J. L. (2001). Exemplary literacy learning programs. In J. A. Rycik & J. L. Irvin (Eds.), *What adolescents' deserve: A commitment to students' literacy learning* (pp. 114–119). Newark, DE: International Reading Association.

Sturtevant, E. G. (2001). What middle and high school educators need to know about language minority students. In J. A. Rycik & J. L. Irvin (Eds.), *What adolescents deserve: A commitment to students' literacy learning* (pp. 40–44). Newark, DE: International Reading Association.

Sturtevant, E. G., & Linek, W. M. (2003). The instructional beliefs and decisions of middle and secondary teachers who successfully blend literacy and content. *Reading Research and Instruction, 43*(1), 74–90.

Sturtevant, E. G., & Linek, W. M. (2004). *Content literacy: An inquiry-based case approach.* Saddle River, NJ: Pearson.

Vacca, R. T. (1998). Let's not marginalize adolescent literacy. *Journal of Adolescent & Adult Literacy, 41,* 604–609.

Vacca, R. T. (2002). Making a difference in adolescents' school lives: Visible and invisible aspects of content area reading. In A. E. Farstrup & S. J. Samuels (Eds.), *What research has to say about reading instruction* (pp. 184–204). Newark, DE: International Reading Association.

Vacca, R. T., & Vacca, J. L. (2005). *Content area reading: Literacy and learning across the curriculum* (8th ed.). New York: Allyn & Bacon.

Vogt, M. E. (2004, December). President's message: Fitful nights. *Reading Today, 22*(3), 6.

Yoakum, G. A. (1945). Essential relationships between reading and the subject fields or areas of the curriculum. *Journal of Educational Research, 38,* 462–469.

PROGRAM IMPLEMENTATION AND EVALUATION

Part III includes four chapters about program implementation and evaluation. Many factors contribute to effective reading program development; the collaborative efforts of administrators and teachers to select and use appropriate materials, evaluate teacher's instructional practices, participate in professional development, and assess students' progress with instruction are examined in this part.

Chapter 7, written by Diane Lapp, Douglas Fisher, and James Flood, presents ideas for selecting materials and resources. Issues surrounding material selection to support content standards are addressed as different types of instructional and assessment materials and resources are described. Guidelines for organizing the selection of materials, such as textbooks, newspapers, magazines, audiotapes, videotapes, and other supplemental tools, are also included in this chapter.

In Chapter 8 Bill Harp offers ideas and guidelines for teacher observation by both reading coaches and reading supervisors. This chapter compares and contrasts coaching and evaluation and explains how both can be done to support the development of teachers of reading. Choice, activity, and authenticity are explained as essential elements to observe when focusing on the interactions between the teacher and students. A Reading Lesson Observation Framework is presented as a guidepost for evaluating teachers' growth as instructional leaders. A five-step process also is outlined for teachers' professional growth using

a portfolio, environmental scan, written self-assessment, the observation framework, and observation conference.

Chapter 9, written by Maryann Mraz, JoAnne L. Vacca, and Jean Payne Vintinner, addresses professional development and its impact on the practices of those involved in literacy instruction. Characteristics of high-quality professional development and the role of administrators in promoting professional development are discussed. Examples of strategies to support change, such as school-based professional development and teacher research, are described. The chapter closes with a set of guidelines to consider for professional development programs.

In Chapter 10, Barbara A. Kapinus discusses assessment as a tool for gaining insights into the goals of education. She addresses the issues and impact of the current role of large-scale assessment for accountability. Ways in which data-driven decision making can be used at the school and classroom level to inform instruction are described. The chapter closes with a call for a collaborative undertaking of classroom teachers, reading personnel, and administrators to use assessment data wisely so that sound educational decisions are made.

This part of the book helps leaders of literacy provide the best possible instructional reading programs by focusing on four critical areas of implementation and evaluation: selection of materials, teacher observations, professional development, and assessment.

CHAPTER 7

Selecting Instructional Materials for the Literacy Program

Diane Lapp, Douglas Fisher, and James Flood

Selecting instructional materials is a complex task that should be viewed as a significantly important process by every member of the educational community. Classroom teachers have the daunting job of providing students with access to the formal curriculum information and ideas deemed important by state committees in ways that support the operational instructional curriculum

(Posner, 2004). The instructional materials that are selected can limit or expand the role of the teacher and can directly impact student learning (Meyer, 2002). For these reasons, the selection of instructional materials is highly charged and political. From debates about evolution in science texts to the role of scripted reading programs, to the inclusion of contributions of gays and lesbians in history books, to banned books at all grade levels, the selection of instructional materials deserves the attention of the administrator and literacy leadership team at all grade levels.

This chapter examines the key factors that need to be addressed as literacy materials are selected:

- The key role played by administrators and other literacy leaders in selecting instructional materials
- The importance of matching instructional materials with content standards and instructional uses and having them represent a variety of genres, topics, and reading difficulty levels
- The criteria to be used for the selection of basals and textbooks, children's magazines, videos, software programs, and assessments

THE PRINCIPAL'S ROLE IN SELECTING MATERIALS

We begin this discussion by sharing the findings from a survey that we administered in 2006 to 65 elementary, middle, and high school principals from nine states. We asked them two questions: (1) What do you believe are your primary responsibilities? (2) What role do you believe you should play in selecting instructional materials at your school site? After the surveys were completed, we interviewed 35 of the principals.

The first question on the survey asked principals to rank order their responsibilities. They answered with the following list:

1. Overseeing student learning as the instructional leader
2. Improving test scores
3. Evaluating teacher performance
4. Administering student discipline
5. Providing teachers with professional development

6. Developing public relations with parents and community leaders
7. Selecting curriculum materials
8. Working with budgets
9. Implementing state standards
10. Conferencing with teachers

While the ordered list created enough conversation among literacy leaders to fill a chapter, if not a book, we will be concentrating on "7. Selecting curriculum materials."

It is interesting to note that selecting curriculum materials was listed as number 7 in terms of importance out of the top 10 perceived responsibilities, especially given the political and economic issues raised by a community when schools buy materials. The only items that were scored lower were "working with budgets," "implementing state standards," and "conferencing with teachers." One administrator stated:

> While this is low on my list of current responsibilities, it is critical. When we are selecting reading materials, I have to support my teachers to make sure they select the best materials—materials that will give our students a chance to master the standards. Once the materials are selected, my job really begins—making sure that the materials are used effectively. This successfully happens by working with the publisher to design effective staff development.

Since we had designed the survey to collect information about the principal's role in materials selection, we asked a specific question about the responsibility the principal felt he or she played in material selection. Their answers overwhelmingly indicated that their role was to provide informational support to teachers who worked as a team to make the selections. Given the geographic diversity represented in our sample, we were not surprised by the discussions administrators had about the role of the state or district in approving instructional materials. In some states, materials must be adopted by the board of education before being used in schools. In other states, the local school board approves choices or makes the selection for all schools within the district. In addition, high schools are often allowed to select their own materials, even in places where the state approves K–8 textbooks.

The administrators who worked in systems where they had some influence over the decisions were clear that this was a critical decision and one that they would have to live with for several years. As one principal, who voiced the sentiment of many, said: "We're going to have the materials we select for several years, and I want to know that they are the best for our students. I'm not sure that I have enough current knowledge about each curriculum area to make the decision alone, but my teachers know a lot and are very clear about what materials they need to be effective." Another noted the role that the district plays in selecting instructional materials and said, "I want to get at least one teacher from my school on the district adoption team so that our ideas are represented. Our district narrows the choice and then we get to pick from the list approved by the district."

What Procedures Are Used to Select Materials?

We asked the principals how they identified effective literacy materials. Across all grade levels their most common responses were: (1) they checked with other instructional leaders about the effectiveness of the materials they used, (2) they asked their teachers and literacy specialists for suggestions, and (3) they invited publishers to present their materials to the teachers at the school site. During our interviews, 94% of those interviewed stated that they also get insights about materials when they attend professional conferences. For principals who lived in states where textbooks were adopted by the state, they acknowledged that their choices were confined to the state-approved lists.

Based on survey and interview responses, we believe that principals rely heavily on their teachers, department heads, curriculum specialists, reading specialists, and peer coaches to select the materials. We wondered if this philosophy might be altered by the amount of funding that was available for the task, so in the survey we asked who would have the primary decision-making authority for selecting materials if the school were given $10,000, $20,000, and $100,000. Regardless of the increase in amount of funding, their answers remained consistent: The teachers, department heads, curriculum specialists, reading specialists, and peer coaches should make the decisions on the materials for the literacy program, as long as they meet the content standards.

What Factors Will Aid the Selection?

In addition to the procedures and responsibilities questions, we were also interested in identifying the types of materials that would be purchased. In response to the question "What type of materials would you like to purchase?" the principals identified, in rank order, the following:

1. Quality literature selections
2. A wide array of information articles, books, and magazines that would address language and knowledge differences
3. Materials containing a strong emphasis on decoding at the early grades
4. Materials containing explicit directions for teachers on how to use the materials
5. Materials having a strong assessment component that was correlated with the proposed instruction
6. Materials with useful suggestions for teachers about grouping and management
7. Materials with effective workbooks and practice materials to accompany the texts

All principals were interested in the support that the selected materials would provide to the teachers who used them. As one administrator noted, "If I'm going to spend money, I want a package. I want to know that everything a teacher needs to use the materials is included. I don't want to have to secure additional money for staff development and then more money for assessments and then more money for supplemental readings."

What Materials Should be Purchased?

When asked if they were given money, in addition to the dollars specified for basal materials, what would be purchased, the number one priority noted by all principals was quality fiction and nonfiction literature that would support the multiple instructional reading levels of students in a classroom. One administrator wrote,

We would spend all our money on books. We get textbook adoption money from the state but hardly any extra money to create really good classroom libraries. Every teacher needs hundreds of leveled books in his or her classroom to be effective with read-alouds and independent reading. They need both fiction and nonfiction. Without that, we really can't meet all of the standards.

The recommendation for quality trade books was followed by the need to purchase class sets of supplemental phonics, spelling, and vocabulary materials. The elementary principals noted the need for the phonics materials while all survey participants identified the need for additional spelling and vocabulary resources.

Survey Findings

The results from this study highlight several keys to materials selection. First, information matters. The administrator or supervisor needs to be informed about the materials and their use. They wanted to be sure that the materials aligned curriculum, instruction, and assessment. Further, the administrator needs to arrange for this information to be secured and shared with teachers and community members as decisions are made.

Second, participation matters. The results of this survey are very clear: Administrators believe that teachers, specialists, and community members must be involved in the selection process. As one administrator stated, "I have the authority to make the decision. However, I don't have to use the materials. If I really want the materials used well, I need to make sure that those closest to the result of the decision are involved in the decision-making process."

Third, extended resources matter. While these leaders identified many instructional materials they would purchase with additional dollars, very few of them identified the need for computer software, children's magazines, or media as part of their materials selection. This is interesting, given the number of teachers who use technology and media in their classrooms (e.g., Fisher, Lapp, & Flood, 2000; Van Leeuwen & Gabriel, 2007), and we wonder if these extended resources were not considered be-

cause they are not traditionally purchased with "textbook" money.

Are There Additional Considerations?

We believe that many principals, like the ones surveyed, will ask the literacy specialist, peer coach, or lead teacher to assist with materials selection. It is important to note that the selection of materials is highly dependent on local literacy guidelines, standards, and instructional beliefs of the teachers who will use the materials. For example, if teachers are expected to read aloud every day to their students, they must have quality, interesting materials to do so. Similarly, if teachers are expected to provide guided reading instruction, they require a number of leveled texts and appropriate assessment materials. The following sections of this chapter focus on selecting various materials for the classroom, including basals and textbooks, children's literature, children's magazines, media, and assessments.

SELECTING BASALS AND TEXTBOOKS

Why Use Basals or Textbooks?

While there have been evaluations and criticisms of basals, anthologies, and textbooks (e.g., Case, Ndura, & Righettini, 2005; Flood & Lapp, 1986; 1987; Hiebert, Martin, & Menon, 2005; Hoffman, Sailors, & Patterson, 2002; Martinez & McGee, 2000; Moss & Newton, 2002), they are still the most significant component of the literacy curriculum (Fawson & Reutzel, 2000; Hoffman et al., 1998) because of the range of possible lessons that they provide and their comparatively low cost (when compared with independently purchasing multiple copies of the same selections).

At the secondary school level, the administrator is often less involved in the review or selection of textbooks that are used in the classroom. A district committee of content area specialists and teachers often adopts textbooks used in high school. However, more and more often, administrators and their faculties ask for and are given the opportunity to choose among a number of adopted textbooks in a subject area. Additionally, secondary school administrators and supervisors can review and select books to supplement the primary textbook.

What Counts as a Basal or Textbook?

Most basals or textbook series are programs that consist of several components including student and teacher editions that are designed for use in Grades 1–6 or 8. Traditionally, they include a collection of emergent literacy materials, several "little books" for beginning reading instruction, and at least one student textbook per grade level. Current basals focus on age-appropriate, quality text selections with pictures and illustrations. Supplementary or companion materials to a core basal program often include sets of library books, which relate to thematic units under study. Often these will include other books by authors appearing in the basals or full versions of excerpts contained there. Other materials include classroom assessments, such as informal inventories, rubrics for writing, and checklists of a variety of types. A variety of technology components are also included in modern basals. Interactive software for independent practice in comprehension or writing is common as are technology-based assessment, record keeping, and lesson planning systems.

Current basals attempt to embrace the entire language arts spectrum including listening, speaking, reading, and writing. They also attempt to provide activities that integrate the language arts with the content area curriculum. Activities span a wide range of language and literacy skills, including vocabulary, text structures, comprehension, and fluency. Lessons are generated from narrative texts, informational texts, poetry, e-texts, and other texts that students may encounter in their out-of-school life. These lessons are directly related to standards.

Student Edition. The most important part of any basal is the content of the books the students read. The contents of the student editions have changed considerably over the past several decades; current editions reflect a wide range of cultures and genres. The variety of genres in children's texts include informational texts, and many selections are complete or excerpted works of major authors. Levels are designated in an attempt to ensure a grade-level match with the reading competency of the students.

Companion libraries or lists of supplementary books are offered to help teachers provide materials that match students' levels. Technology extensions are also common in current basals.

Teacher Edition. The teacher edition of the past ranged from a low of 672 pages to a whopping 1,035 pages. Current teacher's editions are more compact, helpful guides designed to present systematic, explicit instructional examples and suggestions. Additionally, teacher editions often provide a range of alternative grouping, extension, and assessment activities; home involvement connections; and ideas for working with GATE (Gifted and Talented Education) students, students with special needs, and those who are learning English as a second language. More innovative teacher editions also include curriculum connections to assist teachers in planning thematic lessons as well as technology connections and Web sites.

How Can Basals Be Selected?

Figure 7.1 contains a checklist with a list of questions literacy leaders should ask before purchasing a basal series. This checklist can serve as a basis for evaluating differences among texts. The basal with the best score may not necessarily be the best choice for a school, but the checklist will provide the selection committee with information to discuss during their deliberations.

SELECTING CHILDREN'S LITERATURE

Why Use Children's Literature?

Literature encourages students to learn about people whom they may never meet and to visit places that they may never see in their lifetime. As Galda and Cullinan (2006) note, literature is both a window and a mirror to the world. Teachers use literature as a significant part of the reading/language arts program for at least three reasons: modeling of language structures, connecting lessons to students' prior knowledge, and motivating readers (e.g., Fisher, Flood, & Lapp, 2003; Roser & Martinez, 1995).

Figure 7.1. Criteria for Basal or Textbook Selection

Name of Basal _____ Publisher _____

Philosophy   Scale (1 = weak; 5 = excellent)

1. Is the program based on accessible, current research?   1   2   3   4   5
2. Does it have a philosophy that is compatible with yours?   1   2   3   4   5
3. Does it address the literacy needs of your population?   1   2   3   4   5
4. Does it encourage reading for enjoyment?   1   2   3   4   5

Content of the Student Text

5. Are there a variety of types of selections and genres?   1   2   3   4   5
6. Are selections grouped by themes?   1   2   3   4   5
7. Are texts leveled?   1   2   3   4   5
8. Are questions that involve an array of thinking strategies included? 1   2   3   4   5
9. Are many cultures represented?   1   2   3   4   5
10. Are selections systematically sequenced?   1   2   3   4   5
11. Is vocabulary presented, discussed, and practiced in a way that promotes
    reading independence?   1   2   3   4   5
12. Do comprehension skill and strategy lessons promote independence? 1   2   3   4   5

Practice Books

13. Are activities related to text selections?   1   2   3   4   5
14. Are instructions and examples clear enough to foster student independence? 1   2   3   4   5
15. Are skills presented in a spiral format (e.g., grammar, comprehension,
    phonics)?   1   2   3   4   5

Teacher Edition

16. Are before, during, and after reading strategies included?   1   2   3   4   5
17. Is instruction thoroughly explained and modeled?   1   2   3   4   5
18. Are skills initially contextualized?   1   2   3   4   5
19. Is there a systematically presented phonics sequence?   1   2   3   4   5
20. Do comprehension skills build from concrete to abstract?   1   2   3   4   5
21. Are consistent routines suggested that aid classroom management and
    instruction?   1   2   3   4   5
22. Is a week-by-week and a five-day planner included that provides a week-
    at-a glance overview of what is to be taught?   1   2   3   4   5
23. Are teacher and student editions numbered exactly the same?   1   2   3   4   5
24. Is a copy of the student's page included on the teacher's page? 1   2   3   4   5

Supplementary Materials

25. Are there big book and matching little books?   1   2   3   4   5
26. Are there sets of leveled little books?   1   2   3   4   5
27. Are there tapes of songs and poems?   1   2   3   4   5
28. Are there alphabet, word, and sentence strips?   1   2   3   4   5
29. Is there useful software?   1   2   3   4   5
30. Is a CD-ROM teacher planner system included?   1   2   3   4   5

Assessment

31. Are pre/post assessments in various formats (oral/written) included for
    each unit?   1   2   3   4   5
32. Are the end-of-lesson assessments included?   1   2   3   4   5
33. Do assessment selections (fiction and exposition) match those of
    standardized tests?   1   2   3   4   5
34. Do assessments incorporate response formats similar to those appearing
    on standardized tests?   1   2   3   4   5
35. Is instructional information provided that enables regrouping based on
    assessment?   1   2   3   4   5

                                                     TOTAL: _____

It is important to note that books that are selected for classroom use should support the goals, themes, languages spoken in the classroom, and the reading fluency of students. Strickland, Walmsley, Bronk, and Weiss (1994) found that basal reading anthologies, containing the very best children's literature, are used jointly with the classroom libraries in classrooms throughout the United States. One's concept of what counts as a text continues to expand (Diamondstone, 2000; Wade & Moje, 2000). Once basal funding has been spent, many principals believe that the next task is to select other children's narrative and informational literature.

What Counts as Children's Literature?

Each year, thousands of new books for children are published; tens of thousands more are still in print. The field of children's literature is expanding rapidly with children having significantly greater access to quality books. There are a number of sources that may help teachers identify appropriate materials. For example, book reviews in journals such as the *Journal of Children's Literature*, *The Horn Book*, *School Library Journal*, and *Book Links* provide educators with information about new books as well as previously published titles.

In addition to finding children's literature through these magazines and journals, several awards are given each year that highlight quality new books and may help teachers locate appropriate materials. The Newbery Award is based on literary quality, while the Caldecott Award is given for quality illustrations. Committees that read all of the books published during the year select the medal and honor winners. The Coretta Scott King Award is presented annually to both an African American author and an African American illustrator for outstanding contributions to children's literature. The Orbis Pictus Award is given for exceptional nonfiction writing for children and youth. Organizations such as the International Reading Association and the National Council of Teachers of English have established committees that annually develop lists of notable books. IRA's Teacher's Choices is a national project involving teachers in the selection of books for use across the curriculum. The Teacher's Choices lists are published annually in *The Reading Teacher*.

How Can Children's Literature Be Selected?

The following criteria may help with the selection of children's literature:

1. Books chosen for classrooms should cover a wide variety of genres, including folktales, tall tales, fables, myths, legends, poems, fantasy, realistic fiction, historical fiction, science fiction, informational texts, and other nonfiction books. Books should depict a variety of family structures and perspectives on the world. Good writing and engaging illustrations or photographs in a wide array of genres will elicit thoughtful responses from children and also opportunities to venture to unique discoveries and places.
2. Narrative selections should provide examples of well-developed characters, interesting language, and engaging plots. Literacy leaders must also be aware of gender, racial, and ability stereotypes that might exist within the text. Literary quality of the selection should have been demonstrated by reviews, awards, and trusted word-of-mouth recommendations.
3. Informational selections should represent the physical, social, and biological world accurately and in ways that engage students' minds. As with narrative selections, literacy leaders must be aware of the stereotypes that might exist with the texts. Figure 7.2 identifies criteria for selecting informational texts.
4. A wide range of difficulty levels and topics should be a part of every classroom library. This will ensure that readers can grasp concepts and ideas with and without guidance.

SELECTING CHILDREN'S MAGAZINES

Why Use Children's Magazines?

Children need to become proficient at reading a wide range of genres if they are to be literate as adults. To this end opportunities must be provided for them to read periodicals written for their grade and interest levels. Children's magazines have been

Figure 7.2. Criteria for Informational Text Selection

Name of Book _____ Publisher _____

Graphics and Illustrations   Scale (1 = weak; 5 = excellent)

1. Do the graphics enhance the overall experience with the book?	1 2 3 4 5
2. Do the pictures add to the information being learned?	1 2 3 4 5
3. Do the graphs extend the information being learned?	1 2 3 4 5
4. Do the charts extend the information being learned?	1 2 3 4 5
5. Is the information in the pictures, graphs, and charts consistent with the printed information in the text?	1 2 3 4 5
6. Are the graphs and charts well labeled?	1 2 3 4 5
7. Are the graphs and charts convened in an easy-to-read format?	1 2 3 4 5

Cohesiveness

8. Is the printed text written in a style that is friendly to the reader?	1 2 3 4 5
9. Does the text contain cohesive devices across paragraphs and sections (e.g., *next, then, therefore, however*)?	1 2 3 4 5
10. Does the text have a clear shared plan for conveying information to its readers?	1 2 3 4 5
11. Does the text contain enough information to answer the questions it raises?	1 2 3 4 5

Special Features

12. Does the text have a table of contents?	1 2 3 4 5
13. Does the text have a glossary of words with meanings?	1 2 3 4 5
14. Does the text have an index?	1 2 3 4 5
15. Does the text have effective headings?	1 2 3 4 5
16. Does the text have effective subheadings?	1 2 3 4 5
17. Does the text have labels where necessary?	1 2 3 4 5

Vocabulary

18. Does the text use appropriate grade-level language?	1 2 3 4 5
19. Does the text include special attention to new and unfamiliar words?	1 2 3 4 5
20. Does the text promote easy learning of content-bearing words?	1 2 3 4 5
21. Does the text display the most important words that are to be learned?	1 2 3 4 5
22. Does the text show relations among content words?	1 2 3 4 5

Text Accuracy

23. Are the concepts presented in the text accurate (historically, scientifically)?	1 2 3 4 5
24. Is there a bias in the presentation of information in the text?	1 2 3 4 5
25. Is the writing style conducive to presenting information accurately?	1 2 3 4 5

TOTAL:

developed to address this need. Many children's magazines provide readers with up-to-date articles about the world around them and are a great source of nonfiction, informational reading.

What Counts as Children's Magazines?

Children's magazines come in many forms and styles. There are some very popular magazines for elementary age students such as *Highlights* and *Weekly Reader*. In addition, there are children's magazines targeted toward specific markets such as *Music Express*, *Sports Illustrated for Kids*, *American Girl*, and *Kids Discover*. Further, there are magazines for older students such as *Teen Life*, *Music Alive*, and *Teen People*. Figure 7.3 provides a list of children's magazines by grade level and their Web sites. To identify additional titles in children's magazines, simply search the World Wide Web for "children's magazines."

Figure 7.3. Children's Magazines

Grades K–2

Spider: http://spider.tm/may2001/checkem.shtml

Humpty Dumpty: http://hallmags.com/store/search.php?searchindex=magazines&search=humpty

Jack & Jill: http://hallmags.com/store/search.php?searchindex=magazines&search=jack+jill

Sesame Street Magazine: http://www.sesameworkshop.org

Grades 3–5

Cricket: http://www.cobblestonepub.com

Ranger Rick's Nature Magazine: http://www.nwf.org/rangerrick

Your Big Backyard: http://your-big-backyard.mags4cheap.com/magazines

Wild Animal Baby: http://wild-animal-baby.mags4cheap.com/magazines

Disney Adventures Magazine: http://magsonthenet.com/disad.html

Zoobooks: http://www.zoobooks.com

Nick Jr.: http://nick-jr.mags4cheap.com/magazines

Kids Discover: http://kids-discover.mags4cheap.com/magazines

Weekly Reader: http://www.weeklyreader.com

Sports Illustrated for Kids: http://www.sikids.com

National Geographic World: http://www.nationalgeographic.com/media/world

National Geographic Kids: http://www.nationalgeographic.com/kids

Archaeology's Dig: http://www.digonsite.com/

Highlights: http://www.highlightsforchildren.com

Grades 6+

Music Express: http://www.cherrylane.com

Odyssey: http://www.odysseymagazine.com

Time for Kids: http://www.timeforkids.com

Music Alive: http://www.cherrylane.com

Stone Soup: http://www.stonesoup.com

Teen People: http://www.teenpeople.com

Teen Titans Go: http://www.magsonthenet.com/tetigomasu.html

Teen Newsweek: http://www.weeklyreader.com/teennewsweek

Black Beat: http://www.blackbeat.com

Latin Girl: http://www.latingirlmag.com

Footsteps: http://www.footstepsmagazine.com

Twist: http://www.twistmagazine.com

Nickelodeon: http://www.magsonthenet.com/nickelodeon.html

Teen Voices: http://www.teenvoices.com/tvhome.html

Jet: http://www.jetmag.com/assembled/home.html

Black Belt: http://www.magsdirect.com/blackbelt.html

How Can Children's Magazines Be Selected?

When selecting periodicals for a particular grade level, you may want to consider the criteria outlined in Figure 7.4 in order to ensure that you have addressed the range of literacy among the students.

SELECTING MEDIA

Why Use Media?

Standards documents in English/Language Arts now frequently note the importance of visual literacy as a component of a comprehensive and balanced literacy curriculum. Over the past decade, research on the effects on achievement when using multiple forms of media has grown significantly.

Visual representations of complex ideas help students organize information (Frey & Fisher, 2004; Mayer, 1990). Developing concept or semantic maps is one strategy used by teachers because it provides insights on students' knowledge about the topic (Armbruster, 1996; Valerio & Readence, 2000).

In addition to concept maps and character webs, teachers use art, illustrated vocabulary, videos, and computer Web sites to assist students in creating visual representations and in understanding text (Flood, Lapp, & Heath, 2008). Media literacy, especially the use of videos, films, and computers, has become a mainstay for many teachers. There is evidence that even a single, short powerful film can alter perceptions and behaviors (e.g., Eisenman, Girdner, Burroughs, & Routman, 1993). There is also evidence that easy-to-use software programs facilitate revision processes of writers (Haas, 1989). In other words, media and technology are powerful instructional materials that should be considered in the selection process.

What Counts as Appropriate Media?

Media comprise a variety of traditional and nontraditional, print and nonprint sources, including videos, films, computer software, Internet sites, graphics, and songs. We consider these sources together because in classrooms they are used to supplement textbooks and basals. While there are many forms of media, the two most common are videos and software programs (see also Chapter 15).

Videos. Realizing the value of video as an instructional media is sometimes difficult for administrators who are not sure of the educational significance. The criteria outlined in Figure 7.5 will enable a principal's participation in the selection of videos/DVDs.

Figure 7.4. Criteria for Magazine Selection

Magazine Title _____					
	Scale (1 = weak; 5 = excellent)				
1. Is current information provided?	1	2	3	4	5
2. Is a wide range of interest areas covered?	1	2	3	4	5
3. Is there a range of text difficulty within a periodical?	1	2	3	4	5
4. Do the graphics support the text?	1	2	3	4	5
5. Are various types of graphics included (e.g., photographs, drawings, illustrations, cartoons)?	1	2	3	4	5
6. Is there a range of genres (e.g., stories, poems, essays, cartoons, experiments, puzzles)?	1	2	3	4	5
7. Are students invited to submit their writing, poetry, art?	1	2	3	4	5
8. Does the content support the curriculum goals?	1	2	3	4	5
9. Are instructional suggestions offered to the teacher?	1	2	3	4	5
10. Will the content motivate students to read?	1	2	3	4	5
	TOTAL:				

Figure 7.5. Criteria for Video/DVD Selection

Title _____

	Scale (1 = weak; 5 = excellent)
1. Does the video/DVD support curricular goals?	1 2 3 4 5
2. Are there corresponding text materials?	1 2 3 4 5
3. Is there an instructor's manual?	1 2 3 4 5
4. Are the graphics appropriate for the target grade level?	1 2 3 4 5
5. Is the language grade-level appropriate?	1 2 3 4 5
6. Does the publisher provide a viewer's guide?	1 2 3 4 5
7. Is the information presented in the video/DVD historically or scientifically accurate?	1 2 3 4 5
8. Does the video/DVD display people in respectful ways?	1 2 3 4 5
9. Does the video/DVD encourage students to read more about the topic?	1 2 3 4 5
10. Is the video reasonably priced?	1 2 3 4 5
	TOTAL:

Software. As the studies on technology suggest, educational software is another type of material that can aid students in acquiring and expanding literacy. The criteria in Figure 7.6 can be used to select and match software with instructional goals.

GOING LIVE: HOW ONE PRINCIPAL'S TEAM SELECTED MATERIALS

We had the opportunity to observe the process of materials selection at Oak Park Elementary School in San Diego. In assuming the task of selecting a basal, the Materials Focus Group (named by the principal in collaboration with her staff) decided to try to involve the other teachers in staff development and the search for a basal that would best fit with their philosophy about literacy development. Under the leadership of the principal, the 15- to 20-member focus group met regularly to orchestrate the staff development and adoption process. Over the course of a year and a half, monthly workshops on language, literature, and learning given to the entire staff by focus group members and outside experts were interspersed with presentations by publishers' representatives who were invited to display materials at the district level.

Everyone was gaining a broader view and, consequently, was able to look at basal materials with an informed view of how literacy develops. Finally the choice was narrowed to two balanced literacy basals. Next the committee had to look closely to determine which one best met the adoption criteria that had evolved through the staff development and screening process. As they finished their work, the committee had to make a recommendation to the school board for final approval.

Supplementary materials were also selected by grade-level teams at Oak Park who brought their selections to share with the focus group. The sharing of information about materials as a whole is important in order to ensure that the entire school knows what is available for different classrooms at various levels of literacy. The principal then allocates funding to each grade level and allows them to purchase the supplemental materials that they wish to use at their grade level.

SELECTING ASSESSMENT INSTRUMENTS

Assessment instruments that are used in conjunction with the materials that are selected for students also need to undergo the same scrutiny. Assessment tools must be tied to content standards. Standards should frame the discussion of the assessments and evaluation instruments that are used to determine the effectiveness of literacy materials. This is not a small task; criteria have to be established from the standards that are useful in

Figure 7.6. Criteria for Software Selection

Title _____					
	Scale (1 = weak; 5 = excellent)				
1. Does the topic match curriculum goals?	1	2	3	4	5
2. Do the instructional strategies and content complement our philosophy?	1	2	3	4	5
3. Is the material interactive?	1	2	3	4	5
4. Is instructional feedback provided?	1	2	3	4	5
5. Is the material easy to navigate?	1	2	3	4	5
6. Are the directions language and user friendly?	1	2	3	4	5
7. Can the material be used independently by the student?	1	2	3	4	5
8. Can the program be reentered without starting over?	1	2	3	4	5
9. Are the skills levels appropriate for the student population?	1	2	3	4	5
10. Is learning enhanced by the graphics?	1	2	3	4	5
11. Is there an evaluation component?	1	2	3	4	5
12. Is a class spreadsheet available?	1	2	3	4	5
13. Is there a way to ensure student privacy?	1	2	3	4	5
14. Are additional extension lesson plans or materials included?	1	2	3	4	5
15. Can technical support be easily secured?	1	2	3	4	5
TOTAL:					

determining the overall efficacy of the assessment instruments as well as the fit with the programmatic materials.

Previous studies have documented a significant mismatch between tests and text selections; the tests that accompanied many of the classroom materials and the more formal assessment tests simply did not match the types of texts included in programs nor did the tests match the literacy levels of the programs (Flood & Lapp, 1986, 1987). Instructional materials today should include a number of opportunities for teachers to check for understanding, including the integrated use of formative assessments, diagnostic assessments, and summative assessments (Fisher & Ivey, 2006; Many & Jakicic, 2006).

CONCLUSION

While the majority of teachers use many different types of materials, the mainstay is a large library of trade books (single and multiple copies) and components of a major basal or anthology. The target material must be assessed to determine its alignment with state content standards, school goals, and student needs. This chapter has attempted to offer insights about the principal's role in the important process of selecting materials for the schoolwide literacy effort.

As we have noted throughout this chapter, the role of the principal, the instructional leader, is very complex since it encompasses working with teachers, parents, other policy makers, and building support personnel, and most important of all creating a safe, supportive, school learning environment for the students. To this end, it is important to reemphasize that students of all ages learn in classrooms where they are engaged. Guthrie (1996) identifies many factors that promote engagement. Selecting appropriate, motivating materials is one of the most significant of these. We have therefore offered research-based insights as well as criteria related to effective materials selection. Additionally, we have illustrated how effectively a classroom literacy environment functions when the teacher and principal are cooperatively engaged in the selection of literacy materials.

REFERENCES

Armbruster, B. B. (1996). Considerate texts. In D. Lapp, J. Flood, & N. Farnan (Eds.), *Content area reading and* learning: Instructional strategies (pp. 47–57). Needham Heights, MA: Allyn & Bacon.

Case, R. E., Ndura, E., & Righettini, M. (2005). Balancing linguistic and social needs: Evaluating texts using a critical language awareness approach. *Journal of Adolescent & Adult Literacy, 48*, 374–391.

Diamondstone, J. V. (2000). A view of what a text can be: Encouraging novel perspectives. *Journal of Adolescent & Adult Literacy, 44*, 108–120.

Eisenman, R., Girdner, E., Burroughs, R., & Routman, M. (1993). Attitudes of Mississippi college students toward David Duke before and after seeing the film "Who Is David Duke?" *Adolescence, 28*, 527–532.

Fawson, P. C., & Reutzel, D. R. (2000). But I only have a basal: Implementing guided reading in the early grades. *The Reading Teacher, 54*, 84–97.

Fisher, D., Flood, J., & Lapp, D. (2003). Material matters: Using children's literature to charm readers (or why Harry Potter and the Princess Diaries matter). In L. M. Morrow, L. B. Gambrell, & M. Pressley (Eds.), *Best practices in literacy instruction* (2nd ed., pp. 167–186). New York: Guilford Press.

Fisher, D., & Ivey, G. (2006). Evaluating the interventions for struggling adolescent readers. *Journal of Adolescent & Adult Literacy, 50*, 180–189.

Fisher, D., Lapp, D., & Flood, J. (2000). How is technology really used for literacy instruction in elementary and middle-school classrooms? In T. Shanahan & F. V. Rodriguez-Brown (Eds.), *49th Yearbook of the National Reading Conference* (pp. 464–476). Oak Creek, WI: National Reading Conference.

Flood, J., & Lapp, D. (1986). Types of writing in basal readers: The match between texts and tests. *Reading Research Quarterly, 21*, 284–297.

Flood, J., & Lapp, D. (1987). Forms of discourse in basal readers. *Elementary School Journal, 87*, 229–306.

Flood, J., Lapp, D., & Heath, S. B. (Eds.). (2008). *Handbook of research on teaching literacy through the communicative and visual arts* (Vol. 2). New York: Macmillan.

Frey, N., & Fisher, D. (2004). Using graphic novels, anime, teen magazines, and the Internet in an urban high school English class. *English Journal, 93*, 19–25.

Galda, L., & Cullinan, B. E. (2006). *Literature and the child* (6th ed.). Belmont, CA: Wadsworth/Thomson Learning.

Guthrie, J. T. (1996). Educational contexts for engagement in literacy. *The Reading Teacher, 49*, 432–445.

Haas, C. (1989). Does the medium make a difference? Two studies of writing with computers. *Human Computer Interaction, 4*, 149–169.

Hiebert, E. H., Martin, L. A., & Menon, S. (2005). Are there alternatives in reading textbooks? An examination of three beginning reading programs. *Reading & Writing Quarterly, 21*, 7–32.

Hoffman, J. V., McCarthy, S. J., Elliott, B., Bayles, D. L., Price, D. P., Ferree, A., & Abbott, J. A. (1998). The literature-based basals in first-grade classrooms: Savior, Satan, or same-old, same-old? *Reading Research Quarterly, 33*, 168–197.

Hoffman, J. V., Sailors, M., & Patterson, E. U. (2002). Decodable texts for beginning reading instruction: The year 2000 basals. *Journal of Literacy Research, 34*, 269–298.

Many, T. W., & Jakicic, C. (2006). A steadily flowing stream of information gives teachers much-needed data. *Journal of Staff Development, 27*(1), 46–48, 50–51.

Martinez, M. G., & McGee, L. M. (2000). Children's literature and reading instruction: Past, present, and future. *Reading Research Quarterly, 35*, 154–169.

Mayer, R. (1990). When is an illustration worth ten thousand words? *Journal of Educational Psychology, 82*, 715–726.

Meyer, R. J. (2002). Captives of the script: Killing us softly with phonics. *Language Arts, 79*, 452–461.

Moss, B., & Newton, E. (2002). An examination of the informational text genre in basal readers. *Reading Psychology, 23*, 1–13.

Posner, G. (2004). *Analyzing the curriculum* (3rd ed.). Boston: McGraw-Hill.

Roser, N., & Martinez, M. (Eds.). (1995). *Book talk and beyond: Children and teachers respond to literature*. Newark, DE: International Reading Association

Strickland, D., Walmsley, S., Bronk, G., & Weiss, K. (1994). *School book clubs and literacy development: A descriptive study* (Report #2.22). Albany: State University of New York, National Research Center on Literacy Teaching and Learning.

Valerio, P. C., & Readence, J. E. (2000). Promoting independent study strategies in classrooms of the twenty-first century. In K. D. Wood & T. S. Dickinson (Eds.), *Promoting literacy in grades 4–9* (pp. 331–343). Boston: Allyn & Bacon.

Van Leeuwen, C. A., & Gabriel, M. A. (2007). Beginning to write with word processing: Integrating writing process and technology in a primary classroom. *The Reading Teacher, 60*, 420–429.

Wade, S. E., & Moje, E. B. (2000). The role of text in classroom learning. In M. L. Kamil, P. Mosenthal, P. D. Pearson, & R. Barr (Eds.), *Handbook of reading research* (Vol. 3, pp. 609–627). Mahwah, NJ: Erlbaum.

CHAPTER 8

Observing the Reading Teacher

Key to Coaching; Key to Supervision

Bill Harp

One of the greatest changes in the reading profession since the publication of the previous edition of this book in 2002 is the growth in importance and practice of the role of the reading coach (see Chapters 2 and 3). A recent International Reading Association study ("IRA Surveys Coaching," 2006) showed that 67% of the coaches surveyed reported they work solely with teachers. Another 25% reported they work with both teachers and students. Coaching is a collaborative, supportive practice; not a supervisory practice. Here we will explore the importance of reading teacher observation in both the support function of coaching and the evaluative practice of supervision. The main topics discussed in this chapter include

- Effective observation of the teacher of reading as key to both coaching and supervision
- The Reading Lesson Observation Framework as a model for schools to use in designing their own observation frameworks
- A five-step process designed to maximize the professional development of reading teachers

COACHING COMPARED TO EVALUATION

In schools committed to offering the best possible literacy instruction, data are collected not only on pupil performance but on teacher behavior as well. The data collected on student performance ranges from informal and anecdotal to high-stakes standardized test data. Likewise, data collected on teacher performance ranges from that which the teacher collects through observation of students and reflection to that collected by a peer in a collaborative enterprise, to that collected by a coach committed to supporting the teacher's growth, to that collected by a supervisor who is making critical employment decisions. Careful, informed, and insightful teacher observation plays a key role in most of the data collecting efforts. The purposes for which the data are collected, how the data are analyzed, and how the conclusions are drawn from the data vary greatly depending on whether the focus is coaching or evaluation.

Before we look at the specifics of coaching and evaluation, we need to consider the role of the reading specialist. *Teaching All Children to Read: The Roles of the Reading Specialist* (IRA, 2000), a position statement of the International Reading Association, broadly defines the roles of the reading specialist as instruction, assessment, and leadership. The leadership function is delineated as managing re-

sources for teachers, administrators, and parents; providing staff development for teachers and paraprofessionals; and managing literacy program development and coordination. The roles of the reading specialist do not include evaluation that results in decisions regarding employment, tenure, salary, or advancement. This should be within the purview of administrators with the power to hire and fire faculty. Though reading specialists should not be engaged in high-stakes evaluation, it is instructive to look at the comparison of coaching with evaluation.

Coaching

The position statement of the International Reading Association entitled *The Role and Qualifications of the Reading Coach in the United States* (2004) offers the following definition of coaching taken from Poglinco et al. (2003):

> Coaching provides ongoing consistent support for the implementation and instruction components. It is nonthreatening and supportive—not evaluative. It gives a sense of how good professional development is.
>
> It also affords the opportunity to see it work with students. (p. 42)

The position statement (IRA, 2004) goes on to further define the roles of the reading coach:

> There are many activities that reading coaches engage in, from informal activities—such as conversing with colleagues—to more formal ones such as holding team meetings, modeling lessons, and visiting classrooms. It is critical that reading coaches understand that coaching may range from activities that help teachers develop or increase their knowledge about a specific issue to activities that focus on implementation issues (p. 3).

It is in the cycle of the coach's teaching demonstration lessons followed by observing the teacher implementing instruction that the observation of the teacher is critical. In the coaching role, the purpose of the observation is always to collect data to help the teacher enhance performance or implement new curricula and instructional strategies.

Evaluation

While the coaching component includes aspects of teacher evaluation, evaluation is usually associated with selection, training, improvement, and advancement of teachers. It is the selection and advancement of teachers that are clearly beyond the role of the reading specialist or coach. These high-stakes activities are used for decision making by the teacher, the evaluator, and the organization. Critical components of the evaluation process are (a) methods, instrumentation, and sources of evidence; (b) the training and expertise of evaluators; and (c) structural features of the evaluation process, such as who evaluates, when and how often, how data are combined and aggregated, what purposes evaluation is intended to serve, how judgments are communicated, and what follow-up is planned (Darling-Hammond, 1990).

Shared Role

Central to both quality coaching and evaluation is observation. It is difficult if not impossible to conceive of either quality coaching or quality evaluation that does not include careful, knowledgeable observation of the teacher at work. However, observation alone is not enough. The observer must have deep understandings of what to look for, and this must be accompanied by careful scrutiny of the data by the teacher with the assistance of the coach or evaluator.

Figure 8.1 illustrates the similarities and differences in the processes of coaching and evaluation. As you can see, both quality coaching and quality evaluation begin with goal setting and informed observation. The end results vary, but the processes begin at the same critical place: informed observation.

INFORMED OBSERVATION OF THE READING TEACHER

Brian Cambourne (2000) has been observing literacy classrooms as an ethnographer for 9 years. He offers the following conclusion after all of these observations:

These classroom were very complex settings. I don't think I'll ever fully understand this complexity, nor

Figure 8.1. Comparison of Coaching and Evaluation

Coaching	Evaluation
Observational goal setting, purpose setting, identification of data to be collected	Observational goal setting, purpose setting, identification of data to be collected
Informed observation	Informed observation
Data analysis with the teacher	Data analysis with the teacher
Demonstration/model teaching	
Debriefing and planning for future observations	Debriefing and planning for future observations
Continued coaching and staff development	Debriefing and writing of plan for improvement
	Continued work on plan for improvement or termination

will I understand how teachers manage to orchestrate it in ways that promote productive literacy learning. The best I can do is provide some preliminary insights to the nature of this complexity. (p. 512)

Cambourne (2000) asserts that the best way to understand the complexity of the literacy classroom is to make sense of the following aspects of classrooms he has observed:

1. The inanimate physical paraphernalia present in the setting
2. The human behaviors that take place in the midst of these paraphernalia
3. The programs (i.e., routines and events) that typically occur within the setting

The central message in Cambourne's work is that while teachers skillfully manipulate the paraphernalia of teaching reading, the most powerful thing the teacher manipulates is the discourse that pervades the classroom. Of this discourse Cambourne (2000) says:

The discourse features I identified could be grouped under a general heading that I described as strong "proreading/prowriting" ethos. By ethos I mean something that is akin to climate, atmosphere, tone, and other such terms. Each one describes a rather ubiquitous, ethereal "thing" that pervades all that takes place in the setting but is not immediately obvious to observers and is difficult to capture in language, except in broad terms. One only becomes aware of it after prolonged immersion in the settings where it occurs. (p. 513)

We need to be certain that our observations of the reading teacher consider this climate. Cambourne (2000) identified six basic expectation messages being constantly communicated in the classrooms he observed. A coach or evaluator may want to consider his list (paraphrased here) in examining the discourse in classrooms being observed:

1. Becoming an effective user of literacy is extremely worthwhile and will further the purposes of your life.
2. All members of this learning community are capable of becoming readers and writers. No one can fail.
3. The best way to learn is to share and discuss your learning problems with others—take risks, make approximations, and reflect on the feedback you get.
4. All statements, comments, and judgments must be justified using plausible and sensible arguments and examples.
5. It is safe to try things out in this setting.
6. You must take responsibility for your own learning. Take the lessons and demonstrations of others and make them your own.

Several conclusions seem inescapable here. In observing the work of reading teachers we need to focus as much on the learners as on the teacher. We need to examine the paraphernalia, the human behavior, and the routines and events that take place in the classroom, with particular attention to the nature of the discourse—discourse that establishes an atmosphere, a climate, a tone that is proreading and prowriting.

We need to engage teachers in this faculty development process in a variety of ways including peer observations, portfolios, and reflection. In order to have teachers involved in the process, we need to give them choices, focus on activities, and strive for authenticity.

Choice

Reading teachers must be permitted to exercise choice in the staff development process. Ownership of one's own growth as a teacher invites (if not requires) reflective practice. Reflective practice leads to the teacher identifying his or her next learning steps—the next step of personal growth to take. The development process for the reading teacher must offer opportunities for choice in the direction and scope of changes in practice.

Choice is critical to the development process in another dimension as well. We have recognized that if learners are to take ownership of their learning, they must be empowered to evaluate their own learning, based on work samples they help choose, and against criteria they help establish (Harp & Brewer, 2005). The development process for reading teachers must offer opportunities to evaluate their own work, to offer samples of their work, and to help identify the criteria against which their work will be evaluated.

Yet another aspect of choice comes into play in the growth of the reading teacher. Teachers are becoming more and more skillful at looking at their learners as readers and writers. In the process, teachers are beginning to ask their own research questions. The teacher as researcher is becoming accepted practice. As researchers, reading teachers behave reflectively: asking questions, seeking answers, and contributing to educational theory and practice. Their classrooms become teaching and learning laboratories. The questions the reading teacher identifies for research reflect another aspect of choice in the professional life of the teacher. The support process for the reading teacher should examine the choices a teacher makes as a researcher. The process must be attentive to the activities in the learning environment as well.

Activity

The role of the teacher is to create, in collaboration with the learner, the environment that encourages active reading, investigating, experimenting, thinking, writing, and speaking. In supporting the work of the teacher, attention must be focused on the nature of the activities he or she creates for learners. Two issues seem critical here: (1) the proreading/

prowriting atmosphere the teacher creates and (2) the degree to which the lessons the teacher designs reflect current understandings about best practice. The atmosphere in the room can be evaluated by carefully observing and listening, engaging learners in dialogue, and being present in that culture for extended periods of time.

A beautiful example of teachers collaborating to identify what should or might be observed in their work is the Reading Lesson Observation Framework (RLOF), developed by the Central Dauphin School District in Harrisburg, Pennsylvania (Henk, Moore, Marinak & Tomasetti, 2000). Development of the RLOF began with the staff agreeing upon goals for the literacy program and then developing shared understandings of effective literacy practices. This was accomplished by careful study of the research literature and by reflection and dialogue among all of the staff. Once the effective practices had been agreed upon, teams of teachers were engaged in creating the classroom observation framework consistent with these practices. Of the Central Dauphin framework, the authors reporting on the process say:

> Knowing that effective change requires years of ongoing staff development and support, the RLOF remains a working document within the district. Teachers use it as a basic guidepost for their reading instruction. They recognize that the framework represents an organized set of recommended principles and practices that can lead to better reading instruction for their children. They also realize that it serves as a blueprint for their continued professional development since they can decide which components and aspects will be addressed in the future. (p. 363)

The Reading Lesson Observation Framework is an excellent example of an observation guide related directly to reading. It is provided in Figure 8.2 in the hope that you will use it as a springboard for discussion and development of an observation framework designed or adapted by the teachers with whom you work. Two things are critical here: (1) Any framework developed must represent agreed-upon best practices in reading, and (2) there must be opportunity for teacher choice in what is included and how it is used. Please note that within the Classroom Climate component of the RLOF, consideration is given to the proreading/prowriting element. Within each component there is space for teachers to add elements.

There are other useful observation guides available. The Boulder Valley School District in Colorado has created an observation guide to help teachers focus on the degree to which issues of diversity are sensitively met in classrooms (Sobel, Taylor, & Anderson, 2003). As our classrooms become increasingly diverse, this consideration gains importance.

Authenticity

When you examine the elements within each component of the Reading Lesson Observation Framework, you will see that authenticity plays an important role in these observations of the reading teacher. Just as we expect the teacher to orchestrate authentic learning activities for children, we should expect authenticity in the criteria by which the work of the reading teacher is observed. *Authentic* in this context means "real." Authenticity in the development of the reading teacher means we examine the learning environment to draw conclusions about the nature of teaching and learning. We look at the nature of the environment, the activities of the learners, and the work of the teacher there. Teachers in training as literacy coaches have commented on their reactions to using the RLOF. Both of the coaches quoted below used the framework to observe another teacher's instruction.

> As I first looked at the Reading Lesson Observation Framework, it appeared somewhat complicated, with its numerous pages and multiple components. However, as I analyzed the criteria the framework was looking for, I could tell that it was based on criteria for sound reading instruction. The design and simplicity made it straightforward to use in observing the lesson and the classroom climate.

> Generally, I found the framework to be quite comprehensive. Most all components of a quality lesson were included under appropriate headings. I do, however, feel that it is important to remember that not every characteristic listed can be present in every lesson.

Figure 8.2. The Reading Lesson Observation Format

Teacher _____   Observer _____

School Year _____   Date of Observation _____   Observation # _____

Observation occurred: Before reading _____   During reading _____   After reading _____

	O	C	R	N
Component I. Classroom Climate				
A. Many different types of authentic reading materials such as magazines, newspapers, novels, and nonfiction works are displayed and are available for children to read independently.	☐	☐	☐	☐
B. The classroom has a reading area such as a corner or classroom library where children are encouraged to go to read for enjoyment.	☐	☐	☐	☐
C. An area is available for small-group reading instruction.	☐	☐	☐	☐
D. Active participation and social interaction are integral parts of reading instruction in this classroom.	☐	☐	☐	☐
E. The classroom environment indicates that reading and writing are valued and actively promoted (e.g., purposeful writing is displayed, journals are maintained, Word Walls are used, book talks and read-alouds by teacher occur regularly).	☐	☐	☐	☐
F.	☐	☐	☐	☐
G.	☐	☐	☐	☐
Component II. Prereading Phase	O	C	R	N
A. During the prereading discussion, the teacher asked the children to preview the text by having them read the title of the selection, look at the illustrations, and then discuss the possible contents of the text.	☐	☐	☐	☐
B. Children were encouraged to activate their background knowledge through the use of K-W-L charts, webs, anticipation guides, and so on.	☐	☐	☐	☐
C. By generating a discussion about the topic before reading the selection, the teacher created an interest in the reading.	☐	☐	☐	☐
D. The teacher introduced and discussed the new vocabulary words in a meaningful context, focusing on those new words that were central to the understanding of the story.	☐	☐	☐	☐
E. The children were encouraged to state or write predictions related to the topic of the reading selection.	☐	☐	☐	☐
F. Before reading occurred, the teacher helped the children identify the type of material that was to be read to determine what their purpose should be for reading it.	☐	☐	☐	☐
G. The objective for the reading lesson was clearly identified for the children, along with how the objective related to previous lessons.	☐	☐	☐	☐
H. The teacher continually assessed children's prereading discussion and made appropriate adjustments.	☐	☐	☐	☐
I.	☐	☐	☐	☐
J.	☐	☐	☐	☐
Component III. Guided Reading Phase	O	C	R	N
A. At appropriate points during the reading of the selection, the children were asked to evaluate their initial predictions.	☐	☐	☐	☐
B. The children were asked to identify or read aloud portions of text that confirmed or disproved predictions they had made about the selection.	☐	☐	☐	☐
C. The comprehension discussion focused on the purposes that were established for reading the selection.	☐	☐	☐	☐
D. An appropriate mix of factual and higher-level thinking questions were incorporated into the comprehension discussion.	☐	☐	☐	☐
E. During the reading lesson, the teacher modeled fluent reading and then encouraged the children to read fluently and with expression.	☐	☐	☐	☐

(continued)

Figure 8.2 *(continued)*

	O	C	R	N
Component III. Guided Reading Phase (continued)				
F. The teacher encouraged the children to adjust their reading rate to fit the material.	☐	☐	☐	☐
G. The teacher monitored the children and gave proper assistance and feedback while they read or completed practice activities.	☐	☐	☐	☐
H. The teacher modeled and encouraged the use of new vocabulary during the discussion.	☐	☐	☐	☐
I. The children were encouraged to use a variety of word study strategies (e.g., words within words, context, syllabication) to decipher the meaning of unknown words as appropriate.	☐	☐	☐	☐
J. The children were encouraged to use appropriate comprehension monitoring and fix-up strategies during reading (e.g., paraphrasing, rereading, using context, asking for help).	☐	☐	☐	☐
K. The teacher reminded the children to make use of their knowledge of text structure (e.g., fictional story grammar, nonfiction text structures).	☐	☐	☐	☐
L. The teacher periodically assessed the children's ability to monitor meaning.	☐	☐	☐	☐
M.	☐	☐	☐	☐
N.	☐	☐	☐	☐
	O	C	R	N
Component IV. Postreading Phase				
A. During the postreading discussion, the children were asked to read aloud sections of the text that substantiated answers to questions and confirmed or disproved predictions they had made about the selection.	☐	☐	☐	☐
B. The teacher asked the children to retell the material they had read, concentrating on major events or concepts.	☐	☐	☐	☐
C. The children were asked to explain their opinions and critical judgments.	☐	☐	☐	☐
D. The teacher had the children provide a written response to the reading (e.g., written retelling, written summarization, written evaluation).	☐	☐	☐	☐
E. Children were encouraged to use new vocabulary in written responses. Examples and modeling were provided by the teacher.	☐	☐	☐	☐
F. Writing was used as a natural extension of reading tasks.	☐	☐	☐	☐
G. The teacher continually monitored children's comprehension and provided appropriate feedback.	☐	☐	☐	☐
H.	☐	☐	☐	☐
I.	☐	☐	☐	☐
	O	C	R	N
Component V. Skill and Strategy Instruction				
A. The teacher provided a clear explanation about the structure of the skill or strategy to be learned and described when and how it could be used.	☐	☐	☐	☐
B. The teacher modeled the use of the skill or strategy so children were able to see how it would be used in an appropriate situation.	☐	☐	☐	☐
C. Any direct teaching of a phonemic element was immediately followed by children using the skill in a meaningful context.	☐	☐	☐	☐
D. Explicit skill and strategy instruction was provided and applied in the context of the reading selection.	☐	☐	☐	☐
E. The children were encouraged to use before, during, and after reading strategies as appropriate.	☐	☐	☐	☐
F. Reading skill and strategy instruction moved children toward independent use through scaffolding.	☐	☐	☐	☐
G.	☐	☐	☐	☐
H.	☐	☐	☐	☐

(continued)

Figure 8.2 *(continued)*

Component VI. Materials and Tasks of the Lesson	O	C	R	N
A. The selections used for the reading lesson were appropriate for children of this ability and grade level.	☐	☐	☐	☐
B. The reading materials represented authentic types of texts.	☐	☐	☐	☐
C. Reading materials and tasks reflected a sensitivity to the diverse learning needs of the children.	☐	☐	☐	☐
D. The amount and type of independent work was appropriate for the level of the children and instructional goals it was designed to achieve.	☐	☐	☐	☐
E. Independent work often contained open-ended questions that encouraged children to enhance and extend their understanding of the selection.	☐	☐	☐	☐
F. The literacy tasks the children were asked to perform during the lesson were meaningful and relevant.	☐	☐	☐	☐
G. The children engaged in various modes of reading during the lesson (e.g., silent, oral, guided, shared).	☐	☐	☐	☐
H. The teacher provided opportunities for the children to read for enjoyment.	☐	☐	☐	☐
I. Children were encouraged to respond personally or creatively to the reading material.	☐	☐	☐	
J. A balance existed in the reading lesson between teacher-initiated and student-initiated activities.	☐	☐	☐	☐
K Reading materials and tasks were organized around themes when appropriate.	☐	☐	☐	☐
L.	☐	☐	☐	☐
M.	☐	☐	☐	☐

Component VII. Teacher Practices	O	C	R	N
A. The teacher focused on reading as a meaningful process.	☐	☐	☐	☐
B. The instructional techniques used by the teacher and the ways they were executed reflected an awareness of recommended practices.	☐	☐	☐	☐
C. Children were grouped appropriately and flexibly.	☐	☐	☐	☐
D. The teacher's management of the reading lesson provided for active student engagement.	☐	☐	☐	☐
E. The pace and flow of the various phases of the reading lesson represented an effective use of time.	☐	☐	☐	☐
F. The teacher's instruction was sensitive to the diversity of children's experiences and their social, cultural, ethnic, and linguistic needs.	☐	☐	☐	☐
G. The teacher actively promoted the integration of the language arts in this lesson.	☐	☐	☐	☐
H. The teacher encouraged the children to take informed risks and promoted safe failure.	☐	☐	☐	☐
I. The teacher's conferences with children were timely, focused, and positive in nature.	☐	☐	☐	☐
J. Authentic assessment practices were used in this lesson.	☐	☐	☐	☐
K. The teacher's planned goals, actual instruction, and assessment practices were aligned.	☐	☐	☐	☐
L.	☐	☐	☐	☐
M.	☐	☐	☐	☐

Key to Checklist

O = Observed	This component was observed and was judged to be of *satisfactory* quality.
C = Commendation	This component was observed and was judged to be of *very high* quality.
R = Recommendation	This component either was not observed or was judged to be of *unsatisfactory* quality.
N = Not applicable	This component was *not observed* because it was not appropriate for the lesson.

Therefore, the presence of the "N" box—not applicable—was an important aspect. With regards to the content of the identified characteristics, I feel that, for the most part, they were both observable and measurable, although I did find a very few to be somewhat vague and difficult to detect in just one observation.

You may find the RLOF as useful as these coaches have. The framework is just one piece in a series of events designed to enhance a teacher's instruction.

SUGGESTED SEQUENCE OF ACTIVITIES

The following is a set of activities in which the reading teacher and coach might engage in the development process. The list is presented here only as one possibility, not as a definitive prescription. The activities engaged in by the teacher and coach should be agreed upon in advance and designed to best meet the needs of the teacher. The five-step process outlined here includes creating a professional portfolio, conducting an environmental scan, writing a self-assessment and goals statement, conducting a reading lesson observation, and engaging in an observation conference. Each of the steps is described below.

Step One: Professional Portfolio

The reading teacher assembles a portfolio to document strengths and draw conclusions about his or her next learning goals. All teachers might include artifacts from their action research. The teacher working with emergent readers might include running records, developmental reading checklists, writing samples, developmental writing checklists, samples of children's writing, copies of the Reading Lesson Observation Framework collected over time, and summaries of anecdotal records.

The teacher working with developing and fluent readers in Grades 3 through 5 may include many of the items listed above and additionally samples of work produced by children as part of themes or integrated units, records of genres children have read and written, and documentation of children's

progress in meeting the challenges of content area reading including research using print and electronic media.

The teacher working with middle school children may include many of the items listed for upper elementary teachers. The teacher working in remedial reading settings would probably only include an adapted version of the Reading Lesson Observation Framework.

Teachers working with students beyond the middle school level might include many of the items listed above and a variety of critical and analytic pieces from across a wide range of genres, well-researched term papers, and pieces documenting highly advanced use of computer and electronic media. An adaptation of the Reading Lesson Observation Framework would likely only be used in remedial settings. Beyond the emergent reader stage, running records would be a good way to document work with struggling readers.

Teacher portfolios are seen as a way to relieve some of the pressure on principals in the era of No Child Left Behind. Much of the responsibility for collecting data on the teacher's work shifts from the principal to the teacher. When teachers are charged with the responsibility of collecting portfolio data across time, they are continually attuned to thinking about their own professional development, and they have data ready to share with the principal throughout the year. Attinello, Lare, and Waters (2006) report on the success of a districtwide implementation of teacher portfolios in which teachers and administrators perceived that portfolios were more accurate and comprehensive than the traditional snapshot observations with promise for promoting professional growth.

Step Two: Environmental Scan

The teacher of reading joins the coach in doing an environmental scan of the classroom, documenting evidence of conditions that promote literacy. These conditions should be determined in advance at the district or school level consistent with philosophy and curriculum goals. The examples included here are drawn from the now-classic work of Cambourne (1988) who identified conditions conducive to literacy learning. He helped us understand that the conditions that foster learning oral language and the conditions that facilitate coming to fluency in reading and writing are the same. Thus the conditions that exist to facilitate oral language learning must exist to promote fluency in literacy.

At the elementary school level, all seven of Cambourne's Conditions, described here, should be included in the scan:

1. *Immersion.* As learners of oral language, we were constantly immersed in language. Many parents talk to children who are in the womb. We assign intentionality to the gurgles of newborns. Just as these very young children are immersed in oral language, so must emergent and developing readers be immersed in texts of all kinds. Evidence of the existence of this condition would be a classroom in which print is used for a variety of purposes: informing, persuading, directing, controlling. The classroom library is well stocked and includes the publications of class members.

2. *Demonstration.* Each time the oral language learner was immersed in language, the use of language was demonstrated. Literacy learners need many demonstrations of how texts are constructed and used. It seems easy for teachers to demonstrate reading, but children need to be read to many times during the day, not just for 15 minutes after lunch. However, teachers seem to have difficulty demonstrating writing. This is probably because we have received so few demonstrations of writing ourselves. By demonstrating writing, I mean actually showing children how you think through and execute the process of writing a piece.

Cambourne makes the critical point that unless children are engaged with immersion and demonstration, little learning will occur. *Engagement* implies that the learner is convinced that he or she is a potential doer or performer of the demonstrations, that learning these things will be beneficial, and that this new learning can be tried out without fear of harm if the performance is not "correct."

3. *Expectation.* Parents of young children fully expect that their toddlers will make tremendous leaps toward oral language fluency and will accomplish the task within a few years. Rarely do parents (barring unfortunate circumstances) worry about their children coming to fluency in oral language.

Why, then, do some parents respond so negatively when young children spell a word the best they can at the time or make a mistake when reading orally? Teachers of reading must have high expectations that children will learn to read and write, and at the same time help parents (and others) value the importance of successive approximations.

4. *Responsibility.* Parents are often grateful that they do not have to teach their children to speak. In fact, in coming to fluency in oral language, children take responsibility for their own learning. They appreciate the need for clear, useful communication and modify their language to maximize its use. Children can also be responsible for learning to read and write. We need to help children decide what their next learning steps are to be and how they will take them.

5. *Use.* As oral language users, we practiced our control over language in very real ways—to get things done and to get our needs met. In the reading/writing classroom children need many daily opportunities to practice reading and writing in ways that are real, communicative, and authentic. Probably no one reading this text has, as an adult, drawn three rectangles on a piece of paper and then practiced addressing envelopes in the rectangles. Why not? Because this is a truly inauthentic exercise. We address envelopes for the purpose of mailing something. Children need nonartificial ways to use reading and writing.

6. *Approximation.* In most families, certain words or phrases that a youngster approximated were deemed so charming, they become part of that family's vocabulary. When the 2½-year-old approached with a plate at a 45-degree angle and said, "Mommy, cookies all gonded, all gonded," Mommy didn't reply with, "Now, honey, that isn't the way we would say that." Mommy responded to the communication and probably enjoyed the child's approximation of standard speech. Why is it that parents who were so charmed by approximation in oral language are so disturbed by their children's approximation in reading and writing? Mistakes are a natural, developmental part of all learning. Knowledgeable teachers of reading see the mistakes as road signs that lead to better under-

standing of the developing reader and writer. Such teachers are very careful about how they respond to approximations.

7. *Response.* Cambourne asserts that learners must receive feedback on their attempts at reading and writing that is relevant, appropriate, timely, readily available, nonthreatening, and with no strings attached. We must help children understand that mistakes are a natural part of learning, that mistakes help them define what they need to learn next. The responses parents and teachers make to the child's efforts in literacy are critical factors in success.

The environmental scan is most effective when the teacher of reading joins with a coach to conduct the scan. This process of collegial observations of teachers' classrooms has proven effective at all grade levels. Bushman (2006) reports on the success of a process in which he has teachers walk with him through other teachers' classrooms and then meet with the teachers to collegially discuss what was observed. He reports that this process encourages teachers to reflect and share.

Figure 8.3 illustrates how an environmental scan form for the elementary school level is used. This scan was completed by third-grade teacher, Whitney Elkins. You will note that Whitney and her coach have taken great care in the details of the scan. The last page of the figure is Whitney's written commentary on the process. Notice when reading Whitney's reflection that the process of conducting the scan afforded her opportunities to affirm her good work and set some important goals.

The elements in the environmental scan illustrated in Figure 8.3 suggest that third-grade children are approximating less with increased fluency in both reading and writing. There probably are fewer teacher demonstrations of reading and writing, and possibly more demonstrations by children. Arguably, the nature of responses from the teacher change.

At the middle school and high school levels, the environmental scan should include expectation, responsibility, and use as defined above. At all grade levels, we should be looking for evidence in the classroom climate of a proreading/prowriting climate by the nature of the discourse. We should

also seek evidence that Cambourne's (2000) six expectation messages (described earlier) are present.

Step Three: A Written Self-Assessment

The reading teacher is asked to write a self-assessment of strengths as a teacher, and to identify desired next learning goals as a professional. This self-assessment and goals statement may be included in the portfolio the teacher assembles in Step One.

Step Four: The Reading Lesson Observation

The final aspect of observing the work of the reading teacher is the use of the Reading Lesson Observation Framework or, ideally, a framework designed in your school or district. Teachers would have the choice of getting this feedback from a grade-level colleague, a peer mentor, the principal, or a coach. If the framework is being used several times throughout the school year, the teacher could select one from the beginning, middle, and end of the year to include in the portfolio, rather than having the framework used as a separate step in the evaluation process.

Step Five: The Observation Conference

Here the teacher and coach meet to explore the contents of the portfolio, review the data from the environmental scan and lesson observation, and agree on the teacher's strengths, next learning goals, and a plan for meeting those goals.

USE OF THE FIVE-STEP PROCESS IN BOTH COACHING AND EVALUATION

Although the five-step process outlined above was framed as being useful in coaching situations, it is also applicable in evaluation situations. In coaching situations, the teacher and coach are collaborating to help the teacher make continued improvement in the art and craft of teaching in a situation with job security. In evaluation situations, the focus is on collecting data on the performance of a probationary teacher to make decisions about reappointment or of a weak teacher to aid in im-

Figure 8.3. Whitney Elkin's Third-Grade Environmental Scan

Condition	Classroom Evidence
Immersion	• Classroom library is substantial, well stocked, and contains books from variety of genres, both fiction and nonfiction. • Magazines, brochures, and reference materials are also available for student viewing throughout the classroom. • Wall display of graphics with the words "What's going on in our World, Nation, State, County, City, School, Classroom" shows various categories for which students bring in news reports, flyers, articles, advertisements, and so on to share with the class and then hang under the appropriate category. Students can view this "news wall" with a large variety of different texts. • Teacher uses words to provide information to students on a variety of displays throughout the room including bulletin boards, charts, labels, rules display, calendars, and so on.
Demonstration	• Teacher has posted schedule detailing daily read-aloud time. • A growing "caterpillar" around the room is created by constantly adding circles, on which a book title is written along with the individual who read the book. Many are listed as "class" indicating that this book was read aloud by the teacher. • Posters of writing samples, book summaries, brainstormings, tips, and so on have been modeled by the teacher on large chart paper and are prominently displayed on the wall. • Teacher has collaboratively written a story with the entire class on the computer and this is transferred to the TV screen so that it can be viewed by the whole class.
Expectation	• Student work samples are displayed throughout the room. • Achievement certificates, issued when students have met reading goals, are exhibited on a bulletin board. • Student achievement folders are maintained and kept in sight on a shelf. These folders are sent home weekly with teacher comments on students' progress.
Responsibility	• Students have personal reading goals for each 9-week period. They are individually responsible for completing these throughout the period. These assignments are tracked on a chart that the students are responsible for checking off. • A checklist for completing independent reading assignments is posted for students to complete on their own. • Students have created a checklist for personal writings on a cut-out of their own handprint. Teacher has laminated these, and they are displayed on student desks.
Use	• Daily sustained silent reading is incorporated into the posted schedule. • Teacher has created a reading center for students to use during independent reading after other assignments are finished or during free time.
Approximation	• Displayed student work reveals that mistakes are "acceptable" as they do not prevent a piece from being successful. Displays help students understand that our writing is a work in progress, and especially in "on-demand" writing, "best guesses" in spelling are okay.
Response	• Displayed student work reveals positive and appropriate comments from teacher.
Prereading/ Prewriting Climate	• Illustrated student writing pieces are exhibited in the classroom as well as in the hallway. • Teacher-created literature center is comfortable and inviting with a rug, bean bag chairs, and pillows. • Teacher has a table for interest reading where books are displayed that relate to topics that are currently being studied in various subjects. For example, during a science unit on the human skeletal system, the table would contain both informational books, nonfiction books on bones, as well as fiction books such as mysteries about skeletons. • Students have unlimited availability to a variety of writing materials for independent writings. These materials are openly displayed on a shelf for students to get as needed. The materials include a variety of papers such as notebook paper, tablet paper, designed paper (an example would be an outline of a dinosaur with lines inside for writing), pencils, and colored pencils. Construction paper is also available for "publishing" writing into book form.

Figure 8.3. (*continued*)

Teacher's Reflection:

After completing the environmental scan of my third-grade classroom, I was pleasantly surprised. I have always made every effort to ensure that my classroom was child centered, literacy rich, and emotionally positive, and I work daily to incorporate this philosophy into my lesson plans. However, I was initially unsure how much environmental evidence of this would be directly visible on the surface of my classroom. After completing the scan, I was pleased to learn that it was, in my opinion, very present. In addition to learning what aspects of my classroom I should certainly maintain, I was also able to gain ideas of what would be important additions to consider.

I believe I exhibited a multitude of examples of immersion. Throughout my classroom I found a variety of texts types to be used for multiple purposes—entertainment, informational, instructional, and so on. These included not only books, but also other publications such as magazines, newspapers, brochures, flyers, dictionaries, thesauri, and encyclopedias. I also used labels and signs that contained both graphics and text to communicate rules, expectations, reminders, and so on.

Likewise, I use modeling in nearly every lesson I conduct and thus had adequate samples of demonstration. I am fully aware of the benefits and necessities of both reading and writing interactively with students, and I have many of those products displayed for students to refer to as needed. Also, within my writing lesson, I consistently write sample stories with my students as a class. I am fortunate to have access to an Averkey, a device that transfers images from the computer screen to the TV screen, so my students can "see" the process we go through as I type stories that sometimes become quite lengthy as the students become more involved.

On the other hand, while this scan revealed areas that I felt were strengths of my environment, I was also able to see aspects that could be improved. For example, I found it very difficult to see visible samples of approximation or response. While I certainly seek to use appropriate oral responses and reward approximations, I didn't see many observable evidences of this in the environment, other than my responses on displayed student work. These are areas that I believe I should incorporate more tangible examples that students could clearly see. Goals for improving these areas are the following:

- Post motivating and encouraging posters or proverbs about making mistakes, such as "If at first you don't succeed, try and try again!" "Practice makes perfect!" and "It takes a lot of lemons to make lemonade!"
- Create a "My Best Work" wall on which students can choose one piece of writing to display. It will be at eye-level or lower for students so that peers can read each other's work. It will also have a blank front cover on which others can write positive comments or share their favorite thing about the piece.
- Add students' published work to the classroom library and interest table.
- Create a separate classroom writing center where students can sit with easy access to the writing materials they need.

Overall, I feel that the environmental scan confirmed that my classroom meets most of Cambourne's conditions and is thus conducive to literacy learning. By enhancing my room with the additions that will improve the areas of weakness, I feel that I can offer my students the advantages that will stimulate growth and help maximize their potential.

provement and avoid termination. Coaching and evaluation are radically different scenarios, with different goals and very different affective components. However, the power and importance of careful, informed, and insightful teacher observation are critical in both cases.

In both coaching and evaluation situations, the professional portfolio may be used to document student performance and teacher work. The environmental scan can be used for careful examination of the prowriting, proreading classroom environment and culture. In both situations a written self-assessment by the teacher is useful. In the coaching situation, the self-evaluation is used to set goals for future professional development activities. In the evaluation situation, it may be a critical early step in which the teacher presents a self-assessment to the supervisor. The supervisor makes comments in response to the teacher's evaluation. The teacher and supervisor will agree on some weaknesses and goals, and may have to negotiate others. In most situations, the supervisor has the authority to insist on certain goals for improvement. These discussions then set the stage for a series of observations of the teacher's work and observation conferences. Here the roles of the coach and supervisor take very different turns.

In the coaching situation continued observations, follow-up conferences, and even demonstration lessons by the coach are intended to improve the teacher's already acceptable performance. In the supervision situation, the negative evaluation of the teacher by the supervisor can result in a written plan for improvement. This plan could include coursework, professional development activities, changes in planning activities, and changes in teaching behaviors. The cycle of observations and observation conferences following the writing of the plan for improvement are highly focused only on whether or not the teacher has successfully implemented the plan. The stakes are very high here. The results will either be continued employment or termination. Again, careful, informed, and insightful teacher observation is key.

CONCLUSION

Effective observation of teachers of reading at work with children is essential to both the profes-

sional development work of the reading coach and the evaluation work of the supervisor. The reading coach should not be involved in the evaluation of the reading teacher, but should be working collaboratively with that teacher to enhance instruction. The supervisor, while also working to enhance instruction, is using the collected data to make decisions about the reading teacher's competencies. The Reading Lesson Observation Framework is recommended for adaptation and use in observing the engagement of the reading teacher with children. This framework, combined with a professional portfolio, an environmental scan, a written self-assessment, and an observation conference, is recommended as a five-step process of professional development.

REFERENCES

Attinello, J. R., Lare, D., & Waters, F. (2006, June). The value of teacher portfolios for evaluation and professional growth. *NASSP Bulletin, 90*(2), 132–152.

Bushman, J. (2006, March). Teachers as walk-through partners. *Educational Leadership, 63*(6), 58–61.

Cambourne, B. (1988). *The whole story: Natural learning and the acquisition of literacy in the classroom.* Auckland, New Zealand: Ashton Scholastic.

Cambourne, B. (2000). Observing literacy learning in elementary classrooms: Nine years of classroom anthropology. *The Reading Teacher, 53,* 512–515.

Darling-Hammond, L. (1990). Teacher evaluation in transition: Emerging roles and evolving methods. In J. Millman, & L. Darling-Hammond (Eds.), *The new handbook of teacher evaluation: Assessing elementary and secondary school teachers.* London: Sage.

Harp, B., & Brewer, J. A. (2005). *The informed reading teacher: Research-based practice.* Columbus, OH: Prentice-Hall Merrill.

Henk, W. A., Moore, J. C., Marinak, B. A., & Tomasetti, B. W. (2000). A reading lesson observation framework for elementary teachers, principals, and literacy supervisors. *The Reading Teacher, 53,* 358–369.

International Reading Association (IRA). (2000). *Teaching all children to read: The roles of the reading specialist.* Newark, DE: Author.

International Reading Association (IRA). (2004). *The role and qualifications of the reading coach in the United States.* Newark, DE: Author.

IRA surveys coaches. (2006, April). *Reading Today, 23*(5), 1–3.

Poglinco, S. M., Bach, A. J., Hovde, K., Rosenblum, S., Saunders, M., & Supovitz, J. A. (2003). *The heart of the matter: The coaching model in America's choice schools.* Philadelphia: Consortium for Policy and Research in Education.

Sobel, D. M., Taylor, S. V., & Anderson, R. E. (2003). Teacher evaluation standards in practice: A standards-based assessment tool for diversity-responsive teaching. *The Teacher Educator, 38*(4), 285–302.

CHAPTER 9

Professional Development

Maryann Mraz, Jo Anne L. Vacca, and Jean Payne Vintinner

As curriculum standards and assessment mandates have changed in recent years, so too professional development has undergone transitions. In the wake of policy initiatives, such as the No Child Left Behind Act of 2001, those responsible for overseeing reading programs must deliver professional development programs that effectively respond to changing expectations. This chapter discusses the following aspects of professional development:

• Characteristics of high-quality professional development

- The role of administrators in professional development
- Strategies to support change (including school-based professional development, university-school collaboration, teacher research, portfolios, and National Board for Professional Teaching Standards certification)
- Guidelines for professional development programs

CHARACTERISTICS OF HIGH-QUALITY PROFESSIONAL DEVELOPMENT

What constitutes high-quality professional development? The findings of a 2-year study by the National Foundation for the Improvement of Education (NFIE) indicate that gains in teacher learning are greatest when schoolwide faculty collaborate to examine student performance results and decide collectively what steps need to be taken to improve those results (Renyi, 1998).

In an analysis of schools and school districts that succeeded despite socioeconomic challenges, effective professional development was designed to directly impact student learning needs that were relevant to specific schools. Teachers and administrators began by working collaboratively to clarify the standards on which students would be assessed. Next they reviewed student-achievement data in order to identify standards which were not currently addressed satisfactorily. Then they developed and consistently assessed instructional strategies to help students meet those standards (Schmoker, 2002).

Similarly, Richardson (2003) identified seven characteristics that were evident in successful professional development initiatives. Professional development was most successful when it

- Was schoolwide
- Was long-term and included follow-up
- Encouraged collegiality
- Sought consensus among participants on goals
- Received support from administrators
- Received adequate funding for materials, consultants, and staffing
- Acknowledged participants' existing beliefs and instructional practices

In the final analysis, "high-quality professional development is not a program or an activity, but an ethos—a way of being where learning is suffused throughout the teachers' working lives" (Renyi, 1998, pp. 73–74).

THE ROLE OF THE ADMINISTRATOR

Research consistently supports the link between effective professional development and increased student achievement (Paez, 2003). The primary role of administrators (principals, academic coordinators, or literacy coaches) in the professional development process is one of enabling teachers to talk about teaching and to build upon their existing knowledge of teaching and learning in order to improve their own instructional practices. Being knowledgeable about the characteristics of professional development can lead to greater, more meaningful involvement of administrators and teachers in the entire professional development process (Lieberman, 1995).

Administrators must be active and informed participants on the professional development team. An administrator should be able to meaningfully discuss educational research and theory with other team members and model teaching practice based on this research and theory (George, Moley, & Ogle, 1992). The administrator should be committed to the program and eager to collect data, conduct observations, provide teachers with opportunities to observe one another, provide the resources needed to experiment with new strategies, and reflect with the rest of the team on what is happening in the classroom. The administrator must sustain change through his or her continuing presence in workshops, immediate response to teachers' concerns, and spirit of celebration over successes (Courtland, 1992).

In order for professional development initiatives to succeed, it is essential that these programs receive consistent support from administrators at the building and district levels (Morgan et al., 2003). Administrators can be supportive of professional development in many ways. One resource that is often in short supply for teachers is time. Teachers need time during the school day to discuss the needs of their students, as well as their visions of the broader needs of their school, and to collaborate on ways in which those needs can be effectively addressed (Paez, 2003). Careful arrangement of planning times may facilitate the formation of study groups or planning groups among the faculty. Part of periodic staff meetings can be set aside for sharing questions, observations, and concerns about a project (Clyde, Condon, Daniel, & Sommer, 1993).

A systemwide commitment to change could be demonstrated by support for release time, reimbursement for conferences, and establishment of local workshops. By incorporating paid curriculum days into the summer and school-year calendars, time can be allotted for teachers to discuss issues and develop collaborative solutions for meeting student needs (Folio, 1999). Providing teaching materials to support literacy, access to technology resources, a video library of model lessons, and a print library for teacher study of literacy issues also illustrate the administrator's commitment to change. Growth-oriented evaluations, based in part on self-assessment, can allow teachers to develop their own professional growth plans for meeting individual and district standards (Curry, 2000; see also Chapter 8).

Just as students must be partners in the construction of their knowledge, so must teachers have a voice in both the process and the content of professional development (Pahl & Monson, 1992). Teacher input must be "sought, valued, and considered" (Henk & Moore, 1992, p. 48) during the process of implementing curricular initiatives. Some administrators have cited teachers' own fear of risk taking as an obstacle to instructional innovation (Mraz, 2000). These curriculum directors and assistant superintendents emphasized the need to include building administrators, such as principals and literacy coaches, in professional development initiatives. One explained, "The building administrator is the prime mover in that process. If you have a principal who's dynamic, who doesn't spend a lot of time in the office, who is willing to learn more and get resources, that whole building structure can change" (Mraz, 2000, p. 47). For example, in one district, principals participated not only in the reading program selection process, but also in the professional development programs that were designed to teach teachers how to implement the new reading program. By attending these sessions, administrators gained an understanding of how the reading program operated and how its implementation could be effectively monitored. As a result, when teachers had questions about how to use the new materials, principals were able to assist.

GENERAL STRATEGIES TO SUPPORT CHANGE

Change can be uncomfortable and demanding, and the rate of change can vary depending on the nature of the change required and the willingness of participants to undertake it. Moving toward the goal of effective literacy education "requires teachers who are empowered, careful thinkers about their day-to-day interaction with students—teachers who are able to reflect on their practice" (Vacca, Vacca, & Bruneau, 1997, p. 445). To support teachers as they continue to develop professionally, a number of strategies are useful (Folio, 1999; Kelleher, 2003; King & Newmann, 2000; Levy & Murname, 2004; Lewis, 2002; Richardson, 2003; Vacca, Vacca, & Bruneau, 1997):

- Peer collaboration to develop instructional strategies and assessments
- Observations in one another's classrooms in one's own or another building
- Mentoring programs for new teachers or experienced teachers who are new to a grade level
- Small-group seminars that include time for reflective dialogue
- Reading and discussion of professional literature with colleagues
- Peer support teams (peers share questions, concerns, and ideas for solutions as they seek to implement changes in their teaching and literacy programs)
- Peer coaching (feedback is given to teachers by teachers as strategies are applied with students)
- Lesson demonstrations
- Guided practice (a literacy coach leads participants in applying strategies)
- Opportunities to attend conferences or to hear speakers on topical issues
- Follow-up sessions related to conferences or workshops attended

- Threaded discussions via e-mail
- A professional development Web site where teachers can share resources, ideas for lesson plans, and relevant data

In addition to the general strategies for supporting change, there are a number of more expansive strategies that can be used to support teacher growth and student achievement. School-based professional development, university-school collaboration, teacher research, portfolios, and the National Board for Professional Teaching Standards process are discussed below.

School-Based Professional Development Initiatives

As the result of watching students struggle to comprehend textbooks and achieve limited success on state and national standardized assessments, Vance High School in Charlotte, North Carolina, recently started a school-based initiative to raise students' reading abilities and overall achievement. In their analysis of student data, teachers noted that many students had difficulty understanding the materials provided across content areas within the state's curriculum. Unfortunately, the majority of these high school teachers had received little or no formal instruction on how to support reading in a content area class.

To address this problem, teachers and administrators worked together to form a schoolwide reading program that was integrated across subject areas and included several of the general strategies recommended to support change. Beginning early in the school year, all teachers were required to participate in in-service instruction, during which literacy specialists explained how to assess students' reading ability and provide instruction that would be accessible to students of all ability levels. English teachers administered informal reading tests and shared the results with the entire faculty, providing all teachers with a benchmark of each student's present abilities. The school media specialist provided a workshop in finding curriculum materials that were matched to students' reading levels. Each department and content area was responsible for creating reading strategies that would support their specialized content and work within the school district's

course of study and pacing guides. Teachers in all content areas participated in professional development that discussed strategies (for example, anticipation guides, two-column note taking, and discussion activities) that would engage students in interacting with content area texts throughout all phases of the reading process: before, during, and after reading.

The teachers chose to focus on those strategies that could be applied across content areas and that would enable students to focus on using strategies to understand subject area content. Teachers formed peer support teams to discuss their observations and reflections with one another. For example, ReQuest (Manzo, 1969) became a popular strategy because it helped students, including English language learners, to improve comprehension and metacognition. They also found the use of think-alouds and graphic organizers to be helpful in classes such as science and technology that required the use of highly specialized vocabulary: Teachers had a framework for discussing complicated processes and engaging in peer coaching, while students had a visual aid for recording information.

Over the course of a school year, literacy specialists provided 2 days of professional development workshops. School personnel provided 3 or 4 additional days of instruction and practice for teachers, which included opportunities to follow up on concepts presented in formal workshop sessions. While some were initially resistant to the additional responsibility of reading instruction in a secondary classroom, most teachers were responsive to this professional development initiative, particularly as gains in students' achievement and motivation became evident.

University-School Collaboration: Professional Development Schools

A major support system can result when pre-K–12 and university educators develop collaborative and sustained relationships designed to support teacher growth and address the needs of schools and communities (Orr, 2006). The Professional Development School (PDS) model is an increasingly valued vehicle for achieving collaboration between universities and school districts. Professional Development Schools seek to improve the preparation of new teachers, provide ongoing faculty development for experienced teachers, direct inquiry at the improvement of teaching practice, and enhance student achievement (National Council for Accreditation of Teacher Education, 2006). These partnerships support teachers in becoming knowledgeable practitioners who are able to reflect on their teaching practice and implement responsive instructional practices (Miller, Duffy, Rohr, Gasparello, & Mercier, 2005).

The University of North Carolina at Charlotte, for example, has established PDS partnerships with eight schools in three different school districts. A university faculty member serves as a liaison for each school. The school administrator appoints a school representative to serve as an on-site coordinator. Together a team of faculty and administrators from both the university and the school establish goals for the partnership and subsequently formulate plans, including assessment measures, to meet those goals.

The types of initiatives implemented through the PDS partnerships vary depending on the needs of each school. For example, some partnerships are focused on instructional projects, such as training teachers to conduct writing workshops with their students or establishing tutoring opportunities for students. Through other partnerships, methods courses, which are part of a preservice teacher education sequence, are conducted by university faculty at the school site. Classroom teachers are involved in the training of preservice teachers. Graduate-level classes are offered at some PDS sites for teachers who are pursuing advanced degrees through university programs. Opportunities to attend workshops and in-service programs are regularly offered to teachers who are not enrolled in a degree program. Funding for some initiatives is typically provided to the PDS school by the university.

Opportunities for professional development beyond the school site are available to teachers through PDS partnerships. For example, some teachers have collaborated with university faculty to present the findings of studies conducted at the PDS school, as well as experiences with PDS initiatives, at regional, state, and national conferences, including the annual National PDS Conference. Additionally, by hosting student-teacher candidates in yearlong internship programs, the PDS partnership can serve as a valuable recruitment tool for school administrators who are seeking to hire new faculty members.

Teacher as Researcher: Action Research

Often tied to the university-school collaboration model is *action research*, the practice of teachers in the classroom investigating questions that they have generated about teaching and learning. This type of practice-centered inquiry begins with the questions "What do I think?" and "How will I know?" Teacher-researchers gather evidence in their classrooms to test their hypotheses and then evaluate their results (Gove & Kennedy-Calloway, 1992). The steps in an action research sequence are shown in Figure 9.1.

What better person to raise questions about practice, test assumptions, and evaluate results on students' learning than the classroom teacher? For example, after noticing that adolescent struggling readers often seemed unmotivated to practice reading, several teachers decided to create opportunities for these students to participate in reading instruction that had a purpose beyond themselves. High school students were paired with nearby elementary students for cross-age peer tutoring. The specific research question became "Would students' attitudes toward reading and reading instruction improve as the result of their participation in a peer-tutoring program?"

In order to create a benchmark of students' present attitudes and interests, a reading survey was administered to identify how students felt about reading and about themselves as readers, their perceived importance of reading and writing in their lives, and the type of reading they enjoyed. Students were also given an informal reading assessment to determine their reading levels. The same process was administered at the end of the program to determine growth or change as the result of the project.

At the beginning of the program, most students recognized that reading was important but few saw themselves as proficient readers and did not enjoy the process. After discussing students' interests and ability levels, the teachers selected materials for the tutoring sessions. The high school students were presented with *Alice in Wonderland* and asked if they would be willing to work with their younger counterparts to tutor them in reading. This allowed the teenagers to work with a text that was at their reading

Figure 9.1. Action Research Sequence

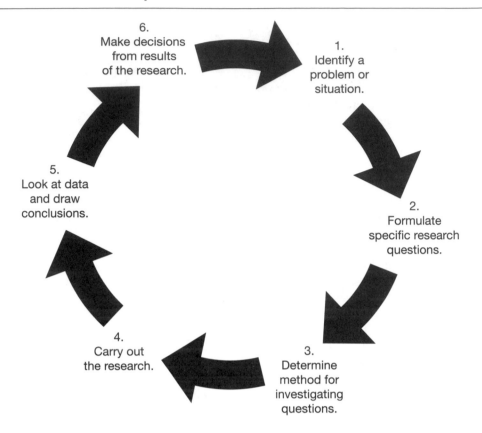

level without being insulted by the content. The adolescents repeatedly practiced the text until they had mastered the material, and then ventured to the elementary school to work with their young partners.

Each adolescent was paired with a fifth grader based on reading scores; the highest senior was placed with the highest elementary counterpart in order to leave room for the greatest percentage of growth based in the zone of proximal development (Vygotsky, 1962). Some special accommodations had to be made for both elementary and high school students requiring special services or exhibiting uncooperative personality styles.

The high school students traveled to the neighboring elementary school six times for approximately an hour and a half each visit. During these sessions, all students would read the text, and then high school students were responsible for leading a discussion based on predetermined questions.

Older students then helped their younger partners create a written response to a prompt modeled after the state's writing test. The younger students used this as a draft for a future writing assignment and presented their work to the class.

Overall, students' reading scores improved, as did their responses on the survey. Students spent more time on task and exhibited a higher level of comprehension of content. They also realized the importance of reading. The project was successful in that the students enjoyed the social aspect of working with others and took pride in their increased reading skills and in their ability to be of help to others, often telling their peers and teachers about their tutoring experiences.

As the teacher-researchers reflected on their experiences throughout the action research project, they noted that it was sometimes difficult to keep the adolescent readers on track when working with their younger partners. Other challenges included finding resources to facilitate the meetings of the two groups of students; gaining administrative permission to leave one campus and enter another; and justifying the use of class time to work on alternative curriculums. Together, they sought solutions to these challenges. Based on their research, teachers found that the interaction between the groups was beneficial to both the adolescent and to the younger readers. They decided to collaborate on future projects that would build upon this growth by using informational texts, content area materials, and extended writing experiences with peer tutoring.

Action research, and the sharing of its findings with colleagues, creates a problem-solving mind-set in teachers and empowers them to improve instructional practices in order to improve the educational process and the outcomes of that process for students (Hall, 2005). According to teachers who have participated in practice-centered inquiry, three trends have emerged: (1) There is greater involvement in teaching; (2) collegiality among members of the research team is enhanced; and (3) focused, data-based feedback is generated.

Portfolios

The portfolio can be an especially versatile teaching and learning tool. Different types of portfolios can be used for evaluating the progress of learners in the classroom, for preparing preservice teachers as they seek to link theory with practice, and for selecting prospective teachers to fill classroom positions. Portfolios can also be used by teachers as a professional development tool to assess their own progress in implementing a program or in documenting accomplishments.

Just as educators are encouraged to view their students as active participants in the process of reading and writing, administrators of reading programs should encourage teachers to be active participants in their own professional development. Teacher portfolios can be a collaborative evaluation tool and can serve as the basis for discussions between administrators and teachers on topics such as instruction, classroom management, and student assessment. From these portfolio-based discussions, administrators and teachers can work together to develop a teacher's professional growth plan (Curry,

2000). Folio (1999) explains that such conversations should be a focused means of exchanging and processing ideas and skills.

To introduce the concept of teacher portfolios, an administrator may choose to gather the teachers together to discuss the expectations for personal portfolio development. The group would then meet periodically to share the material from their portfolios and the experiences they have had in selecting this material. This dialogue gives educators a firsthand experience with a strategy they may use with their students and also encourages teachers to reflect on their own continuing development.

Certification by the National Board for Professional Teaching Standards

An independent, nonprofit organization for the voluntary certification of highly accomplished teachers, the National Board for Professional Teaching Standards (NBPTS, 2006) purports that high standards for teaching performance will enhance student achievement. Participating in the NBPTS process is a way for teachers to engage in a series of professional development experiences that require them to assess and reflect on their own teaching practices.

Preparation of a portfolio is one key requirement in the process that is intended to provide evidence of a candidate's exemplary teaching practice. Four portfolio entries document the candidate's classroom practice. These entries include samples of student work, evidence of the candidate's service to the profession, evidence of effective two-way communication with the parents of their students, and videotapes of interactions between the teacher and students. Six remaining entries are completed in a summer assessment at a computer lab in which teachers have 30 minutes to respond to specific questions pertaining to content knowledge and classroom pedagogy.

Portfolio entries and assessment exercises focus on relevant teacher issues such as communicating with parents and meeting diverse learner needs. Entries are scored by teachers who have attended an intensive training workshop and have qualified to score by demonstrating an understanding of the National Board standards, the directions to candidates, and the scoring guides. Scoring is based on the collection of a candidate's responses: video-tapes, student work samples, and the candidate's written responses to assessment exercises. Each of these pieces of evidence helps evaluators assess a candidate's work in light of the conscious, deliberate, analytical, and reflective criteria the National Board standards endorse.

Administrators are not required to be involved in the NBPTS process. However, as teachers compile evidence of leadership and collaborative accomplishments within their educational community, most choose to include their administrator as a reference. At the district level, many schools have developed support groups for teachers within their district as they engage in the NBPTS process. Candidates have described such groups, as well as mentoring from teachers who have successfully completed the process, as invaluable. Guidance and mentoring can help candidates to better understand the process and its requirements. For example, one support group through Cleveland State University (one of several northeast Ohio universities offering such groups) met once a month in the early stages of the NBPTS process, twice a month toward the end, and additional times to prepare for the summer assessment.

State policies and appropriations for NBPTS support vary, but more commonly include monetary incentives for attaining NBPTS certification, release time to prepare for and complete the process, license portability from state to state, and license renewal or CEU credits. While tangible rewards can provide an incentive for pursuing National Board certification, candidates report intrinsic benefits as they reflect on the NBPTS process. "I learned a lot about myself as a teacher," one candidate explained. "It validated my teaching practices," said another.

GUIDELINES FOR PROFESSIONAL DEVELOPMENT PROGRAMS

The successful planning and implementation of a professional development program is a collaborative effort. It requires reflection, on the part of both teachers and administrators, about the current needs and strengths of the school's program. Together, the members of the school team can then coproduce a systematic plan for meeting those mutually agreed-upon needs. The following section offers guidelines for generating and implementing such a plan.

Before making any consequential decisions, administrators need data-based information. Next they need to work with participants in goal setting. Studies have confirmed the importance of including teachers (Holloway, 2003) and administrators (Morgan et al., 2003; Mraz, 2000) in all phases of the professional development program. When both groups have a say in targeting goals for improvement, a balance across individual, instructional, school, and school district priorities is more achievable.

One of the most efficient and effective ways to engage in professional development planning is to follow a model that is both systematic and participatory. It should be orderly and flexible and depend on input from those most directly involved. Above all, a cyclical design is conducive to collaboration among teachers, administrators, coordinators, and committees. A plan such as this virtually assures that professional development will be tailored to meet participants' needs.

Another way for administrators to plan professional development for their school or district is to focus on the following questions in designing the professional development program:

- What is the current situation?
- What baseline data do we have?
- What needs to be improved?
- Why do we want improvement in a particular area?
- Why are teachers and administrators doing what they are doing in the classroom?
- How can we begin to make changes in the status quo?
- How should we initiate professional development?
- How should we proceed with professional development?

As a rule, planning proceeds in phases, beginning with a proposal, often based on assessment data or revised standards, to initiate change in the school's reading program. This phase of planning should rely on information and ideas from several sources, particularly the group for whom professional development is intended.

Needs assessment enables the administrator and planning committee to identify needs, attitudes, interests, and potential resources. Two types of assessment surveys designed to collect information from the faculty are provided, one for primary-grade teachers in Figure 9.2, and one for intermediate-grade teachers in Figure 9.3. At this point in the planning process, basic goals and objectives can be set. The next phase—the actual implementation of content and process—soon follows.

The implementation of professional development centers on delivery of the program. It should occur over a series of planned activities with appropriate follow-up, lasting anywhere from a month to a year or two. To work effectively with teachers, administrators need to be open to new ideas and demonstrate strategies and techniques for improving instruction. Interpersonal skills, as well as one's basic delivery and knowledge base, are important, whether conducting a workshop or assisting in an action research project. The following are some personal characteristics that are associated with effective presenters at professional development sessions (Vacca & Vacca, 1999):

- Demonstrates enthusiasm and interest in the topic
- Stimulates excitement

- Relates in an open, honest, and friendly manner
- Answers questions patiently
- Does not talk down to participants
- Displays a sense of humor

As literacy coaches are more frequently called upon to take on the role of staff developer, they, too, need to be confident and collaborate with teachers on ways to work effectively together toward shared goals. Professional development leaders need a tolerance for ambiguity and a realization that participants are involved in a learning effort.

One of the most practical ways to implement a professional development project is to incorporate the process of change with the best principles of adult learning. Essentially, adults go through a change process beginning with unfreezing or showing readiness for change, next moving forward and gaining experience, then refreezing or reevaluating the need for change, and finally incorporating changes into the environment or routine. Implementing professional development with this process in mind allows reading supervisors and literacy coaches to introduce a range of action-oriented instructional options to participating teachers. The key to effective delivery is involvement through hands-on activities such as role-playing, demonstration teaching, observations,

Figure 9.2. Survey of Needs and Concerns for Primary-Grade Teachers

Directions: At our last faculty meeting, primary-grade teachers indicated that effectively implementing reading groups is a common concern. Please number in order of importance (1 = least important; 5 = most important) the areas in which you would like to receive additional help in order to successfully implement reading groups as part of your reading instruction. Then, answer each question as thoroughly as possible.

_____ Forming flexible groups

_____ Selecting appropriate reading material

_____ Identifying appropriate before-reading strategies

_____ Engaging students in meaningful literacy tasks when not in teacher-led instruction

_____ Assessing and recording students' progress

1. What is your area of greatest concern about small-group reading instruction?

2. In what aspect of using small-group reading instruction do you feel most competent?

Figure 9.3. Survey of Competency Needs for Intermediate-Grade Teachers

Directions: Our revised standards for reading comprehension put greater emphasis on actively engaging students throughout all phases of the reading process (before, during, and after). Indicate whether or not you would like assistance in each area of competency related to reading comprehension in the intermediate grades.			
Competency	*Level of Need*		
	I feel confident in this area.	I would like a little more help here.	I would like lots of help here.
1. Activating background knowledge to develop a frame of reference			
2. Showing students how to generate their own questions			
3. Involving students in the processes of predicting and verifying			
4. Engaging students in group discussions			
5. Sensitizing readers to sources of information where answers to questions can be found			
6. Using literature in response groups and in journal writing			

interviewing, and problem-solving groups, which afford teachers opportunities to experience how theoretical information can be applied to their own classroom practice. For example, as the teachers experience the process of learning to read by playing the role of reader and experiencing new strategies and materials, the leader explains the how and why of selecting techniques to use in a program. The leader will need to sustain the rapport that was established in the beginning and vary the choice of activities, remembering that no single technique will be effective in all situations.

Frequent and informal evaluation by participants can help keep the professional development on track. Simple rating scales to provide information on the perceived value and usefulness of sessions should help the leader decide on modifications that will enhance the planned implementation of profes-

sional development sessions. Feedback at the end of each session might be a two-way street, with both the staff developer and teachers exchanging suggestions for future directions. Evaluation in this context, then, becomes an integral and responsive part of the professional development implementation.

CONCLUSION

Of all the advances in professional development, the refocusing of attention on the role of the teacher as professional is likely to have the most significant impact. Teacher growth and change is most likely to occur when teachers perceive professional development as relevant to the contexts in which they teach (King & Newmann, 2000). Administrators have the potential to play a pivotal role in actualizing professional development programs that will support the advancement of teachers as professionals and, in turn, the quality of educational opportunities offered to students.

REFERENCES

Clyde, J., Condon, M., Daniel, K., & Sommer, M. (1993). Learning through whole language: Exploring book selection and use with preschoolers. In L. Patterson, C. Santa, & K. Smith (Eds.), *Teachers are researchers: Reflection and action* (pp. 42–50). Newark, DE: International Reading Association.

Courtland, M. C. (1992). Teacher change in the implementation of new approaches to literacy instruction. In J. Vacca (Ed.), *Bringing about change in schools* (pp. 30–36). Newark, DE: International Reading Association.

Curry, S. (2000). Portfolio-based teacher assessment. *Thrust for Educational Leadership, 29*(3), 34–37.

Folio, E. (1999). What are teachers talking about? Peer conversations as professional dialogue. *ERS Spectrum, 17*(1), 16–22.

George, J., Moley, P., & Ogle, D. (1992). CCD: A model comprehension program for changing thinking and instruction. In J. Vacca (Ed.), *Bringing about change in schools* (pp. 49–55). Newark, DE: International Reading Association.

Gove, M., & Kennedy-Calloway, C. (1992). Action research: Empowering teachers to work with at-risk students. In J. Vacca (Ed.), *Bringing about change in schools* (pp. 14–22). Newark, DE: International Reading Association.

Hall, P. (2005). A school reclaims itself. *Educational Leadership, 62*(5), 70–73.

Henk, W., & Moore, J. (1992). Facilitating change in school literacy. From state initiatives to district implementation. In J. Vacca (Ed.), *Bringing about change in school*. (pp. 44–48). Newark, DE: International Reading Association.

Holloway, J. H. (2003) Research link: Linking professional development to student learning. *Educational Leadership, 61*(3), 85–87.

Kelleher, J. (2003). A model for assessment-driven professional development. *Phi Delta Kappan, 84,* 751–756.

King, M. B., & Newmann, F. M. (2000). Will teacher learning advance school goals? *Phi Delta Kappan, 81,* 576–580.

Levy, F., & Murname, R. J. (2004). A role for technology in professional development? Lessons from IBM. *Phi Delta Kappan, 85,* 728–734.

Lewis, A. C. (2002). School reform and professional development. *Phi Delta Kappan, 83,* 488–489.

Lieberman, A. (1995). Practices that support teacher development. *Phi Delta Kappan, 76,* 591–596.

Manzo, A. V. (1969). The ReQuest procedure. *Journal of Reading, 11,* 123–126.

Miller, S., Duffy, G. G., Rohr, J., Gasparello, R., & Mercier, S. (2005). Preparing teachers for high-poverty schools. *Educational Leadership, 62*(8), 62–65.

Morgan, D. N., Saylor-Crowder, K., Stephens, D., Donnelly, A., DeFord, D. E., & Hamel, R. (2003). Managing the complexities of a statewide reading initiative. *Phi Delta Kappan, 85,* 139–145.

Mraz, M. (2000). The literacy program selection process from the perspective of school district administrators. *Ohio Reading Teacher, 34*(2), 40–48.

National Board for Professional Teaching Standards (NBPTS). (2006). Retrieved August 3, 2006, from http://www.nbpts.org/resources/research

National Council for Accreditation of Teacher Education. (2006). *Professional development schools*. Retrieved June 12, 2006, from http://www.ncate.org/public/pdsImportant.asp?ch=133

Orr, M. T. (2006). Mapping innovation in leadership preparation in our nation's schools of education. *Phi Delta Kappan, 87,* 492–499.

Paez, M. (2003). Gimme that school where everything's scripted! One teacher's journey toward effective literacy instruction. *Phi Delta Kappan, 84,* 757–763.

Pahl, M., & Monson, R. (1992). In search of whole language: Transforming curriculum and instruction. In J. Vacca (Ed.), *Bringing about change in schools* (pp. 6–12). Newark, DE: International Reading Association.

Renyi, J. (1998). Building learning into the teaching job. *Educational Leadership, 55*(5), 70–74.

Richardson, V. (2003). The dilemmas of professional development. *Phi Delta Kappan, 84,* 401–406.

Schmoker, M. (2002). Up and away. *Journal of the National Staff Development Council, 23*(4), 10–13.

Vacca, R. T., & Vacca, J. L. (1999). *Content area reading: Literacy and learning across the curriculum* (6th. ed.). New York: Longman.

Vacca, R. T., Vacca, J. L., & Bruneau, B. (1997). Teachers reflecting on practice. In J. Flood, S. B. Heath, & D. Lapp (Eds.), *Handbook for literacy educators: Research on teaching the communicative and visual arts* (pp. 445–450). Newark, DE. International Reading Association.

Vygotsky, L. S. (1962). *Thought and language.* Cambridge: MIT Press.

CHAPTER 10

Assessment of Reading Programs

Barbara A. Kapinus

The context for assessment in reading has changed vastly in the years between the first edition of this book in 1989 and now. The trend, at that time, toward more authentic assessment has almost vanished due to the demand for all students to be assessed in a manner that allows

for quick turnaround of scores for reporting. The role of teachers in the development of large-scale assessments has disappeared as states have sought quick assessment development that can be done very cost-effectively by large commercial assessment enterprises. There are indications that there has been a slowdown in the trend toward reliance on simplistic, commercially prepared reading assessments, but not a dead stop. Concern about authenticity of assessment tasks is reappearing as recognition of the need for assessment to focus on skills and knowledge relevant to twenty-first-century life beyond school. Educators are beginning to call for fewer, broader standards rather than many, highly specific standards. There are indications that policy makers might be hearing this. The expertise of teachers is recognized as essential for classroom learning, and there is hope that highly knowledgeable teachers will be asked to participate in the development of large-scale assessments. However, teachers and administrators must cope with the current realities, and that is what this chapter is about.

I provide considerations and guidelines for using assessments as data sources for educational decisions at the school and classroom level in a context of heavy emphasis on large-scale assessments with high stakes. There are five main topics:

- The issues and impact of the current role of large-scale assessment for accountability
- Data-driven decision making in the school
- Data-driven decision making in the classroom
- Partnerships with parents
- Putting it all together

The goal of all assessment is to support effective teaching and learning. This purpose is accomplished by documenting the individual accomplishments of students and looking at how individuals and groups of students are performing in order to determine student progress and the success of instructional approaches, programs, school organization, and state and local policy. This chapter addresses assessment on a large scale, at the school level and at the classroom level, since the purposes and processes of each, while ultimately focused on the goal stated above, differ in some important ways. Classroom assessment directly informs instruction and should be useful to students, parents, and teachers, all of whom can be involved in directly promoting the reading achievement of individual students. School assessment guides classroom and school practices. Large-scale assessment, on the other hand, must inform the public and policy makers who are not as interested in specific instructional implications

of the results for individuals but rather in whether the overall curriculum and school programs are effective. It is usually tied to public accountability and must be rigorously, publicly defensible to a far greater degree than classroom assessment. As a consequence of these different orientations, there are different constraints, at least at present, on the types of activities that can be used in each type of assessment.

REALITIES OF LARGE-SCALE ACCOUNTABILITY ASSESSMENT

In many schools, especially public schools, accountability drives testing and assessment, and it is a truism that what gets tested gets taught. Large-scale testing with results made public has been an increasingly emphasized aspect of education for over two decades. The assessment demands of the Elementary and Secondary Education Act (ESEA) of 2000, better known as the No Child Left Behind Act (NCLB), have accelerated the trend. The law requires that the results of testing in every grade are reported as percentages of students reaching set achievement standards of progress.

The tests are usually composed of multiple-choice items. If there are any constructed response items, they are few and frequently not very thought provoking. Current large-scale reading assessments, with the exception of the National Assessment of Educational Progress (NAEP), give few opportunities—sometimes none—for students to demonstrate critical thinking, problem solving, and rich understandings of what they read.

The emphasis on accountability based on achievement on two tests—mathematics and reading—has led to a narrowing of the curriculum. Much of the school day in elementary schools is devoted to reading instruction that emphasizes discrete skills in reading tasks and little time is left for instruction in science, social studies, health, art, and music. This ultimately threatens to limit students' comprehension development since a reader cannot understand a passage about science or social studies if the concepts covered in the passage are unknown or only vaguely understood (Hirsch, 2003, 2006).

Engagement and motivation of teachers as well as students is challenged. Teachers and administrators are, in many instances, discouraged by the demands of testing every student every year in mathematics and reading. Teachers and administrators also are very concerned that the success of their school is judged on math and reading scores alone, with little consideration given to the diversity of culture, economics, language, and home background that students bring through the doors of the school and into their classrooms. Even when progress in student achievement is made in the face of seemingly insurmountable difficulties and lack of resources, it is all too often not enough to meet current accountability demands.

Assessments are supposed to address and be aligned with standards for what students should know and be able to do. However, present content standards have become checklists of highly specific basic skills and pieces of knowledge rather than statements of what students should know and be able to do as a result of rich knowledge and high-level thinking skills. In turn, many current accountability assessments address only the skills and knowledge from standards that lend themselves to paper-and-pencil tasks, usually multiple-choice items. Thus what gets tested and consequently emphasized is a narrow aspect of reading literacy.

The Partnership for 21st Century Skills (2006) is calling for assessments to address students' ability to use critical thinking, creative thinking, and problem solving on tasks that also require the application, not simply recall, of information. The assessments need to have tasks that reflect real-world activities such as finding, gathering, organizing, and summarizing or presenting information from a variety of text sources including the Internet.

It is a reality for many schools that unless their students perform well on large-scale assessments, they are faced with decreases in resources, a siphoning off of students who choose alternative schools, and restrictions in curriculum and materials. Consequently, it is understandable that schools would be mainly focused on the tests, preparing for them and responding to the results. While such efforts are understandable and even necessary, some schools are misusing large-scale assessments in the following ways:

- Using large-scale data to make diagnostic decisions about individual students. Large-scale as-

sessments were not designed for this purpose but rather for determining whether students have met certain criteria of performance. They do not have enough items or the types of items that provide reliable information on the individual needs of students. In addition, the testing situation, especially for younger students, is not reflective of the contexts in which students are usually asked to perform. Finally, comprehension assessment, the main aspect of reading assessed, is not based on a well-articulated theory of comprehension and is limited in scope and utility (RAND Reading Study Group, 2002).

- Narrowing the curriculum to emphasize only what is on the assessments. When schools emphasize higher order thinking and rich literacy, they perform better on large-scale assessments than schools that take a narrow focus (Taylor, Pressley, & Pearson, 2002).

- Focusing mainly on those students who can easily be brought up to the mandated level of achievement with an effort that emphasizes the skills and knowledge on the large-scale assessment (Booher-Jennings, 2006).

However, a substantive amount of time is spent on preparing for and administering large-scale assessments, and there are ways that the data can be useful. Some of these include

- Showing where there are achievement gaps across specific groups of students such as English language learners or economically disadvantaged students. Sometimes the achievement problems of these students are missed. While they might be making progress according to classroom assessments, they might need additional instruction to accelerate their learning and begin to close the gap between their achievement and that of other students.

- Reexamining the curriculum areas where student results indicate weaker achievement for the standards reflected on the assessment. For example, if an overall classroom score shows a weakness in recognizing details that support a specific conclusion, then the teacher should give a set of classroom tasks to determine which students have mastered this, which ones show some skill, and which ones do not have understanding and skill in this area. The teacher should design instruction to meet the needs of these students.

- Providing an outside yardstick for student achievement. There are schools where students appear to be doing well on classroom assessments, but those assessments might be too easy. It is good for teachers and students to see progress on classroom assessments, but progress is not enough if students are not being given access to curriculum that develops skills that are considered essential and that put them on equal footing academically with students in other schools.

Stiggens and Knight (1997) provide the following advice on standardized tests:

> We urge you to keep these tests [standardized, large-scale] in perspective. They are highly visible and carry a lot of weight in the schooling process. Considerable pressure for both teachers and students is typically associated with their use. Just remember that, even with their obvious political and media appeal, they represent only a fraction of one percent of the assessments students experience in school. The rest happen in the classroom under the control of their teachers. Further, while standardized tests certainly do inform important decision makers, it is those *day-to-day classroom assessments* that inform students, teachers, and parents. (p. 63)

EFFECTIVE, USEFUL ASSESSMENT AT SCHOOL

In spite of the problems brought on with the overemphasis and misuse of large-scale assessments, there are important ways in which teachers and administrators can develop and maintain an assessment system that supports student achievement and learning that leads to rich literacy and a continuously improving school literacy context. So what does a school do to cope with the pressures of accountability testing and still strive to implement a rich literacy curriculum to all students?

The overall school context should be one of data-driven decision making. This does not mean cold application of statistics linked to large-scale accountability tests or even a system of assessment provided on computers for students to march through. It means that teachers and school staff are continuously

gathering, examining, and discussing a range of data that indicate what is working and what is not, who is achieving and who is not, why things work, and why students are not achieving. The data are not just test scores. It can include a variety of areas that need to be continuously examined.

In its best form, data-driven decision making includes the use of teacher-led inquiry groups or study groups to examine student work and school data to determine how best to adapt and improve classroom instruction, school activities and schedules, and parent involvement to promote student learning. Data-driven decision making can be applied to the whole school reading program and to classroom instructional decision making.

Schools can use large-scale data to "back map" to classroom instruction and track progress. When results come back to a school from a large-scale assessment such as a state test, teachers should meet in groups and identify areas that could be strengthened. For example, at one school, fourth-grade teachers found that students were having trouble with identifying good summary statements. They decided to list, or back map, the skills involved. Teachers from kindergarten through Grade 4 worked together. They included such skills as grouping and naming common characteristics of objects in kindergarten, giving the lesson learned in stories such as fables in Grade 1, providing a one-sentence lesson summary with teacher support in Grade 2, writing a summary paragraph about a science topic in Grade 3, and writing a summary statement of stories and social studies readings in Grade 4. In grade-level groups they planned activities to use and types of data they would collect, share, and discuss with each other at subsequent meetings. The meetings would be focused on tracking student progress, examining the effectiveness of instruction, and planning changes and adaptations, especially for specific student needs.

Schools should not rely only on large-scale data to inform instruction and the policies and contexts of the school. There are many areas that impact student achievement, and the school can choose a focus or a set of areas to examine in order to promote student learning. Figure 10.1 presents some of the areas for data gathering by the entire staff at a school in order to build understanding of and make informed decisions about student learning.

Figure 10.1. Some School Data Areas and Questions

Attendance	Who is not coming to school regularly?
	What are the causes of absence or lateness?
	Is attendance increasing or decreasing?
Parents	How many and which parents have attended back-to-school night?
	How many and which parents have attended PTA meetings?
	How many and which parents have attended parent-teacher conferences?
	Who has volunteered? What are the reasons for volunteering or not volunteering?
	Are parents becoming more or less involved?
	What are parents' major concerns with the school?
Safety	What is the number of student conflicts?
	Where and when do they usually take place?
	Are there concerns for the safety of students from other students?
	Are there concerns about the physical setting and safety?
Schedule	How is instructional time being allotted?
	Do students have sufficient breaks each day for activities such as music, exercise, and art?
	What changes in schedule will improve student learning and teacher effectiveness?
Curriculum	What do the data from large-scale assessments tell us about our curriculum and instructional emphases?
Access	Are certain groups of students not achieving? What problems impede their success?
Attitudes	Do teachers have high expectations for all students?
	Is there a context of professional collaboration and mutual support?

DATA-DRIVEN CLASSROOMS

A data-driven classroom is not necessarily governed by numbers. There are many types of data that can inform instructional decisions. An interview with a student or parent can provide data that will help a teacher adapt instruction or the instructional context to support that student's achievement in reading. Types of data that can be used to inform classroom decision making include the following:

- Interviews with students about their progress and their goals
- Interviews with students about their reading preferences
- Observations of students discussing their reading
- Charts of students' improvement in fluency, including number of sight words

- Students' reflections on their small-group discussions
- Students' reading response logs
- Samples of work picked by the teacher, the students, or both
- Special projects
- Interviews or surveys of students on their perceptions of self-efficacy
- Interviews with parents
- Notes from parents about students' reading habits or discussions at home

The list of questions with one student's responses that appears below is from a bulletin board at Forest Edge Elementary School, Fairfax, Virginia, in January 1989. These questions show the type of information that can be gathered over time to track changes in the attitudes and understandings of students. They can document increased understanding of the reading process and growing ownership of their reading on the part of students.

1. *What does someone have to do to be a good reader?* They have to write good. Good readers make good sentences. Good readers make mistakes and they fix them.
2. *How have you improved as a reader these 9 weeks?* I go back to the beginning and start again. I try to read to the end. I think about the reading.
3. *What reading goal will you set for yourself for the next 9 weeks?* I'll try to sound out the hard things I can't read.

Classroom assessment should be designed to allow the detection of patterns and growth in skills and knowledge. This means examining the usefulness of assessment tasks and classroom data collection to continuously monitor important aspects of learning. Research supports the importance of student progress monitoring in the classroom:

> When teachers use systematic progress monitoring to track their students' progress in reading, mathematics, or spelling, they are better able to identify students in need of additional or different forms of instruction, they design stronger instructional programs, and their students achieve better. (Fuchs & Fuchs, 2002, p. 1)

Some classroom assessments are beginning to reflect a move toward constructivist classrooms where teachers and students are partners in the processes of learning, assessing, and building common understandings. Teachers in these classrooms use assessment approaches that increase both the understanding of students and the teachers' understandings of themselves and their teaching. For example, to culminate a unit in geography students might be asked to write a reader-friendly article about the country or area studied and explain the characteristics of their text they believe will help their readers understand the ideas of the article. Such an activity allows students to apply their knowledge of reading, writing, and geography in complex and creative ways. The teacher will also learn about the students' understanding of reading, writing, and geography from the activity.

As teachers use a wider variety of assessment tools in their classrooms and as they assess more complex aspects of reading, they are challenged to bring it all together. Managing a classroom system of assessment can be as challenging as managing a statewide system. One approach is the use of portfolios. The use of classroom portfolios continues mainly in schools not weighed down by the demands of accountability testing. Unfortunately, those schools are seldom the ones that serve at-risk, less privileged populations. Even where teachers do use portfolios, there are often misunderstandings about them. Teachers often believe that collecting students' work in some physical receptacle is the critical feature of using portfolios. However, the work collected in portfolios should allow for students and teachers to discuss and negotiate understandings of progress; in the classroom, this conversation leads to the establishment of mutually accepted goals. This discussion and the focus on goal setting and improvement over time are essential ingredients in a portfolio approach in the classroom.

The process of examining progress with respect to goals and revising or reestablishing goals is at the core of portfolio use. Teachers need to have clear, challenging goals for their students that provide benchmarks for determining progress. Teachers in a multistate project, the Primary Level Assessment System, have developed such benchmarks. Based on materials used in the Upper Arlington schools in Ohio, the following set of benchmark descriptors are for an early stage of a "developing reader":

- Selects appropriate reading material with some support
- Begins to keep a list of books read
- Retells and discusses text with teacher support
- Comments upon patterns, characters, plot, and setting with prompts; may compare or contrast his or her experiences with the story
- May make connections with the literature
- Makes predictions using book language and story elements
- Self-corrects most miscues that interfere with meaning
- Able to problem-solve new words in a variety of ways: by rereading the sentence, phrase, or preceding work; by analogy; by sounding out; and so forth

- Reads in multiple-word phrases
- Is beginning to read for longer periods of time on his or her own
- Views self as a reader

In using portfolios, teachers must be aware of their goals and keep them as a focus if they are to ensure students a reliable assessment of real progress. Without such focus, portfolios can support aimless education, unfocused activity, and even capricious evaluation.

Finally, it is important for teachers to work together to maintain a vision of the literacy they want students to develop that goes beyond the demands of the assessments used for accountability. The rubric in Figure 10.2 represents a general goal for reading comprehension that can be used for examining classroom discussions, response journals, and responses to open-ended questions about reading. Figure 10.3 provides a support for preparing students to respond to open-ended questions by helping them understand what makes a good response. It is useful in guiding discussions of students' answers to questions. However, even these are only part of what needs to be addressed in developing highly literate students. There is a list of resources at the end of this chapter that provides additional ideas. Teachers should set aside meeting time at regular intervals to discuss what they need to include in their instruction and data gathering.

PARENTS AS COLLABORATORS

Schools are becoming increasingly committed to forging partnerships with parents in the task of helping students become literate. Teachers are asking parents to provide information on home reading habits and discussion. When they meet with parents, they share portfolios or work samples, demonstrating specific areas of growth rather then reporting only numbers and scores. Parents bring as wide a range of backgrounds to teacher conferences as their children bring to classrooms. However, there are many ways to involve parents in assessments and to inform them of the instructional program and its goals. Parents can help keep track of reading at home. They should be invited to write

regular responses about their children's work and teachers' comments that their children bring home.

Schools can educate parents to see new ways for students to demonstrate learning through exhibitions, portfolios of work, and conversations about their work, their growth, and their goals. A science fair project is one example of this. It provides an opportunity for parents to see how well students plan, understand content, and present information using summaries and graphic displays. A group project focused on a community problem is another means of showing parents students' skills in gathering, selecting, organizing, and presenting information while using higher level thinking and problem solving.

PUTTING IT TOGETHER IN A COHERENT PROGRAM

At present, there is a trend in schools and classrooms to use commercial materials such as basal tests or computer packages aligned with state standards to determine and keep track of student progress. These systems even provide suggested instruction, taking that "burden" from teachers. The problem with these systems is that teachers have little ownership and even less say about decisions about curriculum and instruction for groups and individuals. The process of examining and making sense of data is essential for high-performing schools. Creating internal, school-specific benchmarks for determining students' progress toward accountability goals provides a focus for systematic, ongoing assessment aligned with state expectations. Back mapping—determining the enabling skills and knowledge needed to accomplish large-scale accountability goals—enables teachers to consider the needs of students and the curriculum in order to set periodic benchmarks for reaching those goals. Data should be gathered not only on how well students are meeting the benchmarks but also on how well the school and classrooms are facilitating student learning. Heidi Hayes Jacobs (2004) reminds educators: "Good data on students, a method of responding to the information, and consistency of response—these are the three elements of a sound focus on student achievement" (p. 115).

Figure 10.2. Rubric for Reading Comprehension

Note: These criteria can be applied as required by the activity. Not every activity calls for all the possible behaviors described in this generic rubric.

0 = No evidence of construction of meaning.

1 = Some evidence of constructing meaning, building some understanding of the text. Presence of defensible, and possibly some indefensible, information.

2 = A superficial understanding of the text, with evidence of constructing meaning. One or two relevant but unsupported inferences.

3 = A developed understanding of the text with evidence of connections, extensions, or examinations of the meaning. Connections between the reader's ideas and the text itself are implied. Extensions and examinations are related to the text, but explicit references to the text in support of inferences are not present. When more than one stance is possible, the response may remain limited to one stance.

4 = A developed understanding of the text with evidence of connections, extensions, and examinations of meaning. Connections between the reader's ideas and the text are explicit. Extensions and examinations are accompanied by explicit references to the text in support of inferences. When possible, the response indicates more than one stance or perspective on the text; however, only one stance is substantially supported by inferences to the text.

5 = A developed understanding of the text with evidence of connections, extensions, examinations of meaning, and defense of interpretations. Connections between the reader's ideas and the text itself are explicit. Extensions and examinations are accompanied by explicit references to the text in support of inferences. When possible, the response indicates more than two stances, all substantially supported by references to the text.

6 = A complex, developed understanding of the text with evidence of connections, extensions, examinations of meaning, and defense of interpretations. Connections between the reader's ideas and the text itself are explicit. Extensions and examinations are accompanied by explicit references to the text in support of inferences. Responses indicate as many stances as possible based on the activity, all substantially supported by references to the text. These responses reflect careful thought and thoroughness.

Even the best of assessments, whether large-scale or classroom-based, are only useful if they provide relevant, reliable information for making sound educational decisions. Administrators and teachers need to question the data from assessments. For example, improvement in overall reading scores in a school can mask ongoing problems with groups of students who are not making progress. When school data on student achievement is disaggregated by economic, gender, or cultural groups, or by previous achievement, patterns sometimes emerge that indicate problems such as the following:

• Students from certain cultural or economic backgrounds may not be making gains in reading achievement.
• Students who are already high achievers might account for most of the gains a school shows,

while struggling readers might be actually losing ground, or vice versa.
• Boys might be making significantly less progress than girls in some areas of reading.

Teachers need to ask similar questions of data from classroom assessments. Again, impressive performance by students who began the year with advanced skills and knowledge might mask a lack of progress on the part of other students. Detecting student achievement patterns and making inferences about those patterns in order to plan programs and instruction are activities that administrators should share with teachers and teachers should share with students. Explaining to parents both school and classroom decisions on scheduling, programs, materials, and instruction, based on assessment data, can promote parental support and involvement.

Figure 10.3. Target In On Complete Answers

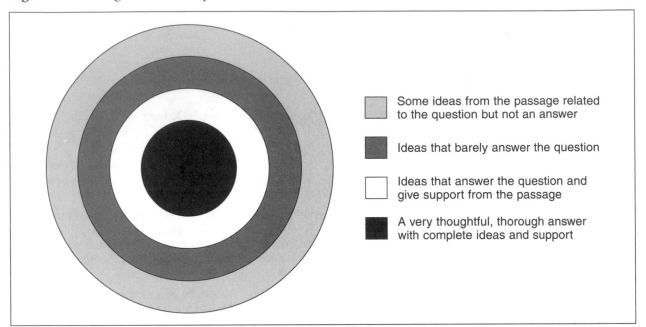

Some ideas from the passage related to the question but not an answer

Ideas that barely answer the question

Ideas that answer the question and give support from the passage

A very thoughtful, thorough answer with complete ideas and support

CONCLUSION

Assessments should offer insights into the goals of education and ways to reach those goals for educators at all levels, from national to the classroom. These insights must be developed by each educator, individually and collaboratively. Ideas, goals, and guidelines cannot be simply handed down by policy makers or administrators. This means that an approach such as data-driven decision making cannot really be set in place quickly through a district or state mandate. A cookbook for assessment is no more appropriate than a cookbook for instruction. Teachers need to be decision makers and problem solvers in assessment. And teachers are not the only people who need to understand reading assessment. Educational leaders at all levels need to engage all the parties involved in education—students, parents, teachers, administrators, and policy makers—in the process of reflecting on the match between educational goals, instructional practice, and assessment approaches. A deep understanding and clarification of these areas on the part of individuals is necessary for successful evaluation that truly enhances education for all students. Policy makers and administrators can and

must provide the time, resources, opportunities, and encouragement for the development of the understanding necessary for successful assessment of reading programs and the effective use of assessment data. It is important to always remember that the goal of schooling is not test results but a complete and rich education.

REFERENCES

Booher-Jennings, J. (2006, June). Rationing education in an era of accountability. *Phi Delta Kappan, 87,* 756–761.

Fuchs, L. S., & Fuchs, D. (2002). *What is scientifically based research on progress monitoring?* Technical Report. Nashville, TN: Vanderbuilt University.

Hirsch, E. D. (2003, Spring). Reading comprehension requires knowledge: of words and the world: Scientific insights into the fourth-grade slump and stagnant reading comprehension. *American Educator, 27,* 10–13, 16–22, 28–29.

Hirsch, E. D. (2006, Spring). Building knowledge: The case for bringing content into the language arts block and for a knowledge-rich curriculum core for all children. *American Educator, 30,* 8–21, 28–29, 50.

Jacobs, H. H. (Ed.). (2004). *Getting results with curriculum mapping.* Alexandria, VA: Association for Supervision and Curriculum Development.

No Child Left Behind Act of 2001 (NCLB). Pub. L. No. 107-110, 115 Stat. 1425 (2002).

Partnership for 21st Century Skills. (2006, March). *Results that matter: 21st Century Skills and high school reform.* Retrieved October 2, 2006, from author's Web site under resources publications at www.21stcenturyskills .org

RAND Reading Study Group. (2002). *Reading for understanding: Toward an R&D program in reading comprehension.* Santa Monica, CA: Author.

Stiggens, R., & Knight, T. (1997). *But are they learning? A common sense parents' guide to assessment and grading in schools.* Portland, OR: Assessment Training Institute.

Taylor, B. M., Pressley, M., & Pearson, D. (July, 2002). *Research-supported characteristics of teachers and schools that promote reading achievement.* Washington, DC: National Education Association.

RECOMMENDED RESOURCES

Asp, E. (2000). Assessment in education: Where have we been? Where are we headed? In R. S. Brandt (Ed.), *Education in a new era* (pp. 123–157). Alexandria, VA: Association for Supervision and Curriculum Development.

Barrentine, S. J. (Ed.). (1999). *Reading assessment principles and practices for elementary teachers: A collection of articles from the Reading Teacher.* Newark, DE: International Reading Association.

Brandt, R. (Ed.). (1998). *Assessing student learning: New rules, new realities.* Alexandria, VA: Association for Supervision and Curriculum Development.

Bredekamp, S., & Rosegrant, T. (1992). *Reaching potentials: Appropriate curriculum and assessment for young children.* Washington, DC: National Association for the Education of Young Children.

Calhoun, C. (2004). *Using data to assess your reading program.* Alexandria, VA: Association for Supervision and Curriculum Development.

Elmore, R. F., & Rothman, R. (1999). *Testing, teaching, and learning.* Washington, DC: National Academy Press.

Fehring, H. (Ed.) (2003). *Literacy assessment: A collection of articles from the Australian Literacy Educators' Association.* Newark, DE: International Reading Association.

Glazer, S. M., & Brown, C. S. (1993). *Portfolios and beyond: Collaborative assessment in reading and writing.* Norwood, MA: Christopher-Gordon.

Harp, B. (Ed.). (1993). *Assessment and evaluation in whole language programs* (abr. ed.). Norwood, MA: Christopher-Gordon.

Herman, J. L., Aschbacher, P. R., & Winters, L. (1991). *A practical guide to alternative assessment.* Alexandria, VA: Association for Supervision and Curriculum Development.

International Reading Association. (1995). *Reading assessment in practice: A book of readings.* Newark, DE: Author.

Marzano, R. J., & Kendall, J. S. (1998). *Implementing standards-based education.* Washington, DC: National Education Association.

McTighe, J., & Ferrara, S. (1998). *Assessing learning in the classroom.* Washington, DC: National Education Association.

Reeves, D. B. (2005). *101 questions and answers about standards, assessment, and accountability.* Englewood, CO: Advanced Learning Press.

Reeves, D. B. (2006). *The learning leader: How to focus school improvement for better results.* Alexandria, VA: Association for Supervision and Curriculum Development.

Stiggins, R. J. (1998). *Classroom assessment for student success.* Washington, DC: National Education Association.

Valencia, S. W., McGinely, W., & Pearson, P. D. (1990). *Assessing reading and writing.* In G. G. Duffy (Ed.), *Reading in the middle school* (pp. 124–146). Newark, DE: International Reading Association.

PART IV

INTERCONNECTIONS

A reading program's richness comes from its diversity of components and students. In order for it to work effectively, it must work together with all facets of the school and community to create and improve literacy. This part of the book includes six chapters that provide leaders of literacy with the necessary tools to create a fully effective program that attends to the diversity of students and the communities in which they live.

Chapter 11, written by Julie K. Kidd and Karen Bromley, identifies ways to promote writing with reading and learning. Information about writing in relation to reading and issues that influence writing instruction and assessment in relation to the standards movement are presented. Specific guidelines are offered for developing writing goals, curriculum, and instruction. Also included in this chapter are ideas for helping teachers to engage in their own professional development to become better instructors of writing.

In Chapter 12, Junko Yokota, William H. Teale, and Ruth E. Quiroa address literacy development for culturally diverse populations. Given that more and more children from diverse ethnic, cultural, and linguistic backgrounds are entering our schools each year, the authors discuss different perspectives on educating such children, and how the social constructivist model best promotes diverse students' literacy learning. In addition to presenting ideas for examining one's own cultural identity and beliefs, eight guidelines are provided to help administrators and literacy leadership personnel assist teachers with the classroom climate that they create and the educational activities that they offer.

Given the large and growing numbers of students who speak a home language other than English and

the urgency of preparing teachers to work with linguistically diverse students, Chapter 13, written by Mary Elizabeth Curran, focuses specifically on culturally responsive teaching for the English language learner population. This chapter discusses the concepts of linguistic diversity and linguicism in classrooms, and describes ways in which teachers can be prepared to acknowledge differences, understand how linguistic and cultural differences influence learning, and adapt instruction to accommodate these differences.

In Chapter 14, Jennifer L. Goeke and Kristen D. Ritchey discuss the literacy learning problems of students with disabilities and other at-risk populations. Research-based understandings about learning disabilities are presented. A detailed description of a response-to-intervention model (RtI) is offered as a process for assessing and instructing students with reading problems. Guidelines for administering and supervising practices to help students with literacy learning problems also are provided.

Chapter 15, written by Shelley B. Wepner, Liqing Tao, and Linda Labbo, discusses how leaders of literacy can help promote teachers' use of technology for literacy instruction. This chapter explains what leaders of literacy should know technologically so they can support teachers in helping students become multiliterate. Specific ideas and guidelines are provided to assist teachers in using technology for instruction and assessment, along with suggestions for creating a professional development plan for teachers that prepares them for implementing such ideas.

The final chapter of this book, Chapter 16, written by James V. Hoffman and Misty Sailors, describes what literacy specialists can do to help teachers change instruction for the purpose of helping students learn. With an emphasis on creating a culture of change within the school by working closely with teachers, administrators, and parents, this chapter presents 10 principles to guide the evaluation and change process. The premise is that teachers will change when change works from where teachers are functioning.

This last part of the book suggests that important links or interconnections to different programs, initiatives, and populations are essential for a reading program's success in today's society.

CHAPTER 11

Promoting Writing with Reading and Learning

Julie K. Kidd and Karen Bromley

As administrators and supervisors work with teachers to develop and implement literacy programs that promote writing with reading and learning, one question is prevalent: How can administrators and supervisors help teachers invite students to write, enjoy writing, learn as writers, and write well in a range of forms for a variety of purposes and audiences? This question is significant because it recognizes the importance of the support that supervisors and administrators provide for teachers and also identifies the overall goals of a sound writing program. Although on the surface the question appears rather simple, district- and school-level administrators and supervisors are aware of the complexity of designing and implementing writing programs. They realize the need to take action grounded in research-based decisions, but are also cognizant of the fact that these decisions and actions are influenced by current issues and policies. In an effort to help administrators and supervisors make informed decisions, this chapter is organized around four topics:

- Issues that influence writing instruction and assessment
- Knowledge about writing and the reading-writing-learning connection
- Guidelines for developing writing goals, curriculum, and instruction
- Professional development

As each topic is explored, five educators share their insights that illustrate key points. Ann and Mary are supervisors of literacy programs. Ann is a curriculum specialist for reading, and Mary is an English language arts supervisor. They work in neighboring urban school districts that are culturally, linguistically, and socioeconomically diverse. Lulu and Vicki are administrators. Lulu is an elementary principal in the same district as Ann. Vicki is an assistant principal and a former reading specialist in a large, affluent, metropolitan school district. Don is a professor of English and the director of the local National Writing Project site at a large state university located near the school districts where Ann, Lulu, Mary, and Vicki work. They hope that sharing their thoughts will help administrators and supervisors support teachers in the creation and implementation of sound writing programs.

ISSUES THAT INFLUENCE WRITING INSTRUCTION AND ASSESSMENT

In past decades, writing instruction and assessment have shifted from stressing skills and the written product to emphasizing the writing process, to focusing on a balanced approach that embraces both process and product. Writing instruction and assessment continue to evolve as more is known about writing and practices that promote writing. Although educators would like to believe that current practices are based on current research and reflect what teachers, administrators, and supervisors know fosters student writing, the fact is that writing instruction and assessment are also influenced by current policies, issues, and trends. In light of this reality, administrators and supervisors need to be aware of the factors that influence decisions and seek ways to ensure that sound practices are put into place regardless of prevailing trends or policies.

Recently, supervisors and administrators have responded to a variety of factors that influence writing instruction in their districts. These include current research on writing; trends in professional development; societal issues, such as literacy in the twenty-first-century workplace; and state and federal mandates. Vicki, like many school administrators, is concerned about the pressures placed on administrators, teachers, and children as a result of the No Child Left Behind Act of 2001 (NCLB) and the emphasis on state-mandated accountability systems. Vicki doesn't deny the value of "accountability measures to ensure that schools are providing sound instruction." However, she is "concerned about the pressure of preparing young children to 'perform' on a multiple-choice test to measure writing." She takes exception to tests that are "not an authentic measure of children's ability to write."

On the other hand, Mary, a district-level supervisor, believes that state standards have had a positive effect on writing instruction and assessment in her district. Although she hasn't seen many changes at the secondary level, she notes that a positive outcome is that elementary teachers are advised "to instruct more and assign less." She believes that state standards and the evaluation of students' writing at particular grade levels have encouraged teachers "to pay more attention to student writing."

Ann and Lulu also feel the effects of NCLB and the state assessment system. Lulu, as an elementary principal, believes that current policies have a wide-reaching effect on curriculum and instruction, and in many ways "these policies dictate what teachers and administrators do." Ann, as a curriculum specialist, recognizes the effects of state and federal mandates, but also raises other issues.

She asserts that "writing is a critical component of literacy that has been neglected as we have placed more and more emphasis on reading." However, she feels that "current research is having an impact on writing instruction," and "the apparent outcome is that we are beginning to realize that we must place more emphasis on writing instruction." She is also concerned about adolescent literacy, including whether students leave high school prepared to meet the demands of the workforce of the twenty-first century.

Don works closely with teachers, administrators, and supervisors and agrees that state standards and NCLB influence writing instruction at all levels of education. However, he contends that there are other forces affecting writing instruction, including research on teaching writing and the availability of meaningful professional development for teachers offered by professional associations such as the National Writing Project and the National Council of Teachers of English. He is optimistic about the writing instruction students receive from teachers who are knowledgeable and well-informed. But he worries about the quality of instruction from teachers who are swayed by opinions at the expense of making well-informed, research-based instructional decisions.

All five of these educators are affected by current policies and trends and are concerned about issues related to writing and writing instruction. They recognize that research, issues, and policies affect the decisions they make when working with teachers to develop and implement sound writing programs. Because research evolves, issues shift, and policies change, the factors affecting their decisions today will be different in the future. Therefore, they all feel it is important for supervisors and administrators not only to be aware of current policies and issues, but also to be knowledgeable about writing, the reading-writing-learning connection, and sound instructional practices.

KNOWLEDGE ABOUT WRITING AND THE READING-WRITING-LEARNING CONNECTION

As a curriculum specialist for reading, Ann recognizes that "reading, writing, and thinking are all interconnected." However, she finds that writing is a component of literacy that is often neglected. One of Ann's challenges is "helping teachers across content areas hone their skills in teaching and integrating writing into the content areas." She believes that, in order to help teachers and improve programs, administrators and supervisors need knowledge of the writing process and the reading-writing-learning connection. To encourage the integration of writing across the curriculum, supervisors and administrators must have the knowledge to respond to these questions about the writing process and the relationship among reading, writing, and learning.

What Is the Writing Process?

Writing is a complex process that involves planning, drafting, revising, editing, and publishing text. Because writing involves the writer, possible collaborators, and an audience, it is a social and cultural process that is influenced by social conventions and cultural practices (Hayes, 2004). This means that as part of the planning or reflective process, writers take into account the audience and purpose for writing, decide on a form or genre of writing, and generate and organize ideas for writing. As writers draft, they produce text, read the text produced, reflect, and produce additional text (Hayes, 2004). In doing so, they may revise by adding, deleting, changing, or rearranging the written text. In addition, they may edit or make changes to the text to ensure correct capitalization, punctuation, grammar, and spelling. The final draft is considered the published copy and is shared with the intended audience.

How Are Reading and Writing Related?

Reading and writing are interactive and complementary processes; in the real world, they function together. Both readers and writers must know word meanings and spelling. Readers read what writers write. For a reader, the reading-writing interaction involves constructing a writer's message (Kintsch, 2004). For a writer, it involves alternating roles as reader and writer. A writer is usually a reader—often reading others' work before writing. Writing about something read can give the writer a deep appreciation both of what was read and how it was written. Writers read their own work throughout the writing process (Hayes, 2004). Students continually alternate roles as readers and writers as they move back and forth between the two to interpret and use language to learn.

How Does Writing Promote Learning?

Writing involves the eye, the hand, the head, and the heart. Writing is a tool for thinking that allows students to connect ideas and information about things they already know, and it allows for the creation of new knowledge (Farnan & Dahl, 2003). Writing gives students concrete evidence of their feelings, observations, and actions, and it lets them revisit and review these ideas. It enables them to "make inferences, draw upon prior knowledge, and synthesize material" (Gammill, 2006, p. 760). By writing, students can explore the known and the new, and they can manipulate language to communicate with themselves and others. When students read and write in the content areas of science, social studies, and math about ideas that are important to them, they process ideas and information more deeply and have a better chance of remembering that material than by just listening or reading.

What Needs to Be Considered When Planning Instruction?

While reading and writing overlap, they are not mirror images of each other and their integration does not automatically lead to learning. This means that although it makes sense to integrate reading and writing in meaningful ways, it is also essential to provide direct instruction in the skills and strategies of each process for students at all levels. For example, third graders may need explicit instruction in creating good leads and conclusions, and tenth graders may need instruction in the use of their senses and precise vocabulary to create imagery in their writing. This kind of direct instruction may be isolated from reading, but may also be integrated with reading through the use of real literature. For example, third-grade teachers and their students can read and compare the work of authors like Pam Conrad, Seymour Simon, and Arnold Lobel, and teachers can model lessons using this literature to show students how these authors write leads and conclusions. Tenth-grade teachers and students can read the poetry of Edgar Allen Poe or

Emily Dickinson, and teachers can model lessons with this literature to show students how these writers evoke images. This thoughtful approach to integrated instruction includes direct explanation, instruction, and practice that can lead to enhanced learning of the targeted writing skills and strategies.

GUIDELINES FOR DEVELOPING WRITING GOALS, CURRICULUM, AND INSTRUCTION

For teachers to effectively integrate writing into the curriculum in ways that enhance writing development and promote learning across the content areas, teachers, administrators, parents, and students need to know what is to be accomplished. These goals reflect thoughtful consideration of writing development research, state standards and assessments, and what is valued by members of the school community. They take into account the cultural and linguistic diversity of students as well as their diverse abilities. These goals guide instructional decisions and are the basis for establishing criteria used for assessing and evaluating student progress.

Likewise, teachers and administrators must be knowledgeable about effective ways to reach the goals. One way is to develop curriculum and plan instruction that builds across students' academic careers. To achieve this, some districts assemble a districtwide committee of administrators, supervisors, parents, teachers, and students. Other districts support school-based efforts involving principals, reading specialists, literacy coaches, teachers, students, and parents. Collaborating to develop a shared vision is important, as Engel and Streich (2006) assert, because "if every teacher is to be held accountable, every teacher's voice should be heard" (p. 676).

In Ann's district, one school used a collaborative approach that involved all teachers in the development of writing goals and curriculum. Over the course of several years, the reading specialist, acting as the facilitator, met with grade-level teams of teachers to develop and refine a writing curriculum that built upon the writing skills and strategies introduced to and practiced by students in previous grades. As the teachers communicated across grade levels, a shared vision and a common language evolved. Family members were invited to meetings held both during the day and in the evening. The purpose of these meetings was to provide information to families about the writing goals and curriculum and to elicit feedback used to further refine and develop the curriculum.

As this group developed writing goals, they relied on key resources to inform their decisions. They began by examining research on writing development, the state standards, standardized test blueprints, their own knowledge of what students can and should do, and what the members of the school community value. With goals established, they decided upon the content of the curriculum, developed and selected assessment tools, and explored teaching practices that would meet the needs of their culturally, linguistically, and ability diverse students. As they proceeded through this process, they drew from the work of Atwell (1998), Calkins (1994), Graves (1994), Spandel (2005), and Tompkins (2004).

Through collaboration and research, school communities can make deliberate and informed decisions that result in goals, curriculum, and instruction that is consistent, meaningful, and well developed. The outcome of this work might be the development of goals similar to the ones listed here:

- *Fluency*—to write easily, legibly, and quickly enough to communicate with an audience, whether it be oneself or others
- *Competence*—to write accurately and proficiently in a variety of forms or genres for difference purposes and audiences
- *Independence*—to choose and enjoy writing and possess the necessary skills and strategies to be able to write on one's own with a minimum of help and support

Once goals are identified, the next step is to develop curriculum and plan and implement instruction using guidelines shown in Figure 11.1. Each of these guidelines is discussed in more detail below.

Recognize Students' Diverse Cultures, Languages, and Abilities

Students bring to their writing the richness of their cultural knowledge, linguistic backgrounds, and diverse abilities. *Cultural knowledge* is defined as "the concepts, explanations, and interpretations that students derive from personal experiences in their homes, families, and community cultures" (Banks, 2006, p. 204). Teachers can better teach their students by building upon these funds of knowledge and becoming acquainted with students and their families within the context of their home and community (Dworin, 2006; Moll & Gonzalez, 2004). One way to do this is to promote two-way communications between school and the home and community that "help families understand school programs" and "help schools understand families' cultures, strengths, and goals" (Hidalgo, Siu, & Epstein, 2004, p. 645). By understanding the richness of families' experiences and literacy practices, teachers can provide opportunities for students to build upon their home literacy practices as they write about what is known and link new information to the knowledge they possess. Teachers can also enhance learning by recognizing and building upon students' diverse cognitive strengths, including those not traditionally recognized in schools (Sternberg, 2006). Sternberg explains, "When we teach students in a way that fits how they think, they do better in school" (p. 33).

Create an Environment That Provides Writing Tools, Time, and Models

Creating an environment that fosters writing entails setting aside time to be devoted to writing. Isolated skill instruction can be accomplished in short segments of time, but integrated instruction focused on meaningful learning with application in authentic contexts requires larger blocks of time (Bromley, 2003). This kind of instruction also requires appropriate tools and models provided in an environment that promotes writing as a stimulating and engaging activity. One way to create this type of atmosphere is to schedule a consistent time for writing workshop (Atwell, 1998; Calkins, 1994; Moore, 2004). Using a workshop approach to teaching writing and reading includes such activities as minilessons; work time for planning, writing, and revising; conferring with peers, response groups, and the teacher; and share sessions and publication celebrations (Calkins, 1994; Moore, 2004; Tompkins, 2004).

Figure 11.1. Guidelines for Developing Sound Writing Goals, Curriculum, and Instruction

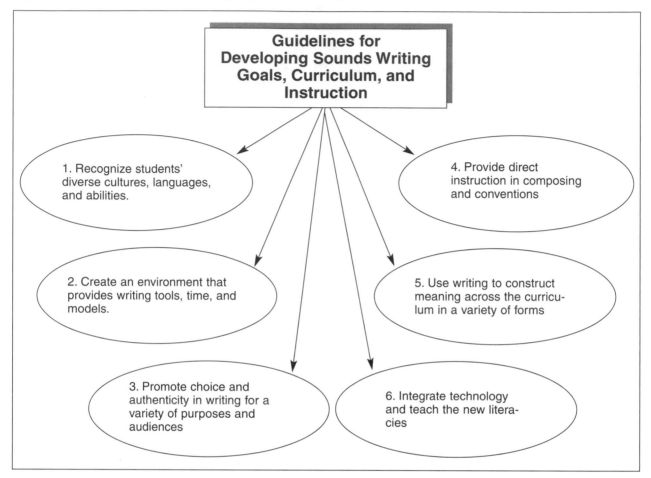

Promote Choice and Authenticity in Writing for a Variety of Purposes and Audiences

Writing for lots of different reasons and audiences builds fluency, competence, and independence (Bromley, 2003). Students need to write for various purposes: to entertain, inform, persuade, and narrate. They also should have opportunities to write for a variety of audiences, including, for example, their peers, parents, teachers, businesses, and people across the country and around the world as well as themselves. K–12 students need opportunities to become proficient writers on the Internet and with word processors as well as with the traditional paper and pencil or pen. Extending

literacy beyond traditional print should be a significant part of a strong writing program.

In addition, finding a balance between process writing that incorporates choice and authenticity with on-demand writing required in state assessments is also important. On-demand writing is writing students do that has a time limit and often includes a prompt that must be addressed (see Appendix A at the end of this chapter). Process writing focuses on teaching children to plan, draft, revise, edit, and publish for an audience and often spans the course of several days or weeks. Although on-demand writing may ask students to plan, draft, edit, and publish, there is often little time for students to revise their written work. In both types of writing, teachers concentrate on the conventions of writing, which includes spelling, punctuation, format considerations, legibility in handwriting, and ease in keyboarding.

Provide Direct Instruction in Composing and Conventions

Another aspect of sound writing instruction is direct and systematic instruction accompanied by time to write (Bromley, 2003). Embedded in integrated instruction should be opportunities for lessons, guidance, and practice that allow students to become accomplished writers. For example, third-grade students may need specific instruction on organizing their writing into paragraphs, and eighth-grade students may benefit from lessons on transitioning among paragraphs. Instruction that includes explanations, modeling, guided practice, and independent practice helps students identify strengths and needs in their own writing and put new or refined skills into practice as they write.

Use Writing to Construct Meaning Across the Curriculum in a Variety of Forms

K–12 students should write in every genre to show what they have learned and to build new knowledge in science, social studies, math, and other content areas (Bromley, 2003). This includes, for example, journal writing, expository writing, or creative writing. For example, tenth-grade students can use poetry in social studies to relate the agony of war as they study world conflicts, or second graders can write persuasive letters to a community leader about the need for a hiking and biking trail along a local river. Another key focus is the genres or types of writing everyone will teach. Typically, a K–12 writing curriculum includes four types of writing: expository, persuasive, descriptive, and narrative (see Appendix B at the end of this chapter). Most good writing in everyday life contains elements of each of the four types. For example, a well-written newspaper article about a national park may be expository in style overall but include descriptive imagery, a narration of the park's history, and a persuasive style to influence readers to visit the park. Teaching the four types of writing separately makes sense, but the ultimate goal is for students to use elements of the four types together to produce well-crafted writing.

Integrate Technology and Teach the New Literacies

As supervisors and administrators work with teachers to implement sound writing instruction, use of technology and technology integration is an important part of the conversation. Educators have recognized the support that technology provides for writing. In fact, many are able to point out the advancements of the available technology equipment and the increased use of technology tools to support writing and learning. For example, administrators, like Vicki, note the "increased use and availability of laptop computers, more computers in the classroom, and the use of smart boards" when discussing technology use in their schools. Others, like Ann, Lulu, and Mary, mention word processing, desktop publishing, drawing and painting, hypermedia, and presentation software as well as online programs that support writing. Still others discuss the use of digital cameras, camcorders, and digital voice recorders as tools for promoting writing. And some refer to students' use of e-mail, instant messaging, and the Internet when discussing the integration of technology and writing.

In addition to thinking about technology as a useful tool, supervisors and administrators also focus on the integration of technology with writing. When doing this, they identify the skills and strategies students need to communicate proficiently using technology. It is important to consider the implications of preparing students who will enter a twenty-first-century workforce that is highly reliant on accessing and communicating information through e-mails, the Internet, and multimedia. Educators need to respond by providing instruction in the new literacies, the literacy skills and strategies required to communicate via ever-changing technologies. Leu, Kinzer, Coiro, and Cammack (2004) go on to explain: "Clear, rapid, and effective communication that takes advantage of the networked information contexts of ICTs [information and communication technologies] will be central to our students' success. We need to know how to support students in achieving these abilities" (p. 1603). Therefore, it is not sufficient for supervisors and administrators to focus only on the tools to support writing. They must also stay informed about the changing technologies and the new literacies needed for students to communicate successfully (see also Chapter 15).

PROFESSIONAL DEVELOPMENT

Ann, Lulu, Mary, and Vicki all recognize the importance of keeping on top of current trends, issues, and policies in writing. They believe that being aware of the research on writing helps administrators and supervisors support their teachers and make informed and deliberate decisions. Mary explains, "I think that reading current research helps to modify knowledge, in this case knowledge about writing. Trends come and go, so I try not to grab onto new ideas too quickly."

Engaging in Professional Development

Although it is not always easy to stay abreast of new developments, they find that one of the best ways to stay informed is through professional organizations. Many administrators and supervisors of literacy programs belong to the following organizations and read the journals they publish, which include articles and studies about research and practices in teaching writing:

- International Reading Association (IRA) (www .reading.org)
  The Reading Teacher (for elementary teachers)
  Journal of Adolescent and Adult Literacy (for middle and high school teachers)
  Reading Online at www.readingonline.org (an electronic journal for K–12 educators)
  Reading Research Quarterly (for literacy research on all levels)
- National Council of Teachers of English (NCTE) (www.ncte.org)
  Language Arts (for elementary teachers)
  English Journal (for middle and high school teachers)
  Research in the Teaching of English (for literacy research on all levels)
- Association for Supervision and Curriculum Development (ASCD) (www.ascd.org)
  Educational Leadership (for K–12 educators)

Mary also suggests that administrators and supervisors become involved in research organizations like the National Reading Conference (NRC). By joining the NRC listserv, Mary is able "to see what the hot topics are" as questions are posed and responses are posted.

Ann believes that reading professional books and attending conferences and workshops also enable her to stay informed. Professional books give Ann a chance to delve into specific topics and gain ideas for how to put research into practice. Conferences and workshops give her an opportunity to reaffirm or refine current practices in her school district and learn about new approaches. While attending conferences, she makes an effort to talk with colleagues who are dealing with similar issues. She also spends time looking at products and talking with vendors to become more aware of the products available to support teachers. She thinks, "Staying informed is key because there are new products being developed all of the time and not all are of the same quality. So being knowledgeable gives us a way to evaluate and compare products, as well."

Recognizing that it is a challenge for supervisors, especially those working with pre-K–12, to be fully knowledgeable about materials, approaches, and strategies appropriate at all grade levels, Mary stresses the importance of relying on teachers to stay informed and help make decisions. She explains, "I also listen to English teachers whom I respect. I never taught at the secondary level, so the teachers keep me informed." Lulu echoes this sentiment for school-based administrators. She finds it is a challenge for principals to be fully aware of the current trends and issues in all content areas, including literacy. Therefore, Lulu recommends that principals rely upon their building reading specialists and literacy coaches for guidance and as a resource for supporting teachers. In her school, reading specialists not only provide her with information, they also work with teachers and model effective writing strategies and approaches.

Promoting Professional Development for Teachers

Making it possible for reading specialists and literacy coaches to work with teachers in their own classrooms is one way supervisors and administrators ensure that teachers engage in professional development that is responsive to their needs and is part of an ongoing journey. In Mary's district, they have hired a writing coach to specifically work with elementary teachers. They recognize that as reading specialists and literacy coaches share their expertise with teachers in their own classrooms with their own students, teachers are able to see how particular approaches and strategies work with their students and try them out for themselves. When reading specialists and literacy coaches work with teachers in their classrooms, they teach model lessons, coteach lessons with classroom teachers, observe and respond to teachers, provide materials and ideas, coplan strategies for guided reading and writing, assess students, and provide training on topics teachers request (Dole & Donaldson, 2006). This model of professional development builds in the support necessary for teachers to refine their teaching practices and promotes the confidence to try out new ideas.

In addition to drawing upon the resources within the school, Lulu allocates funds to bring presenters into the building, for teachers to attend conferences, and to purchase resources that support an effective writing program. Her school district, like others, also works with local universities to provide teachers with opportunities to enroll in graduate programs that focus on literacy. Teachers engaged in graduate studies expand their knowledge about literacy, make connections between theory and practice, reflect on ways to enhance literacy instruction, and apply effective instructional practices. For many teachers, graduate work is either the beginning or continuation of a long-term commitment to develop professionally.

Several major movements initiated by teachers and supported by school districts and universities give teachers opportunities to chart their own courses for professional development: the National Writing Project (NWP), teacher-research groups, and teacher study groups. One common thread across the three initiatives and their variations is that teachers form communities of writers engaged in thoughtful inquiry, reflection, discussion, and action around literacy-related issues.

The National Writing Project is a professional development model supported by the university where Don works, the nearby community college, and the school districts where Ann, Lulu, Mary, and Vicki work. The project was designed "to improve the teaching of writing and improve learning in the nation's schools" (National Writing Project, n.d.). It "recognizes the primary importance of teacher knowledge, expertise, and leadership" (Northern Virginia Writing Project, n.d.). Don explains that local writing project sites create communities of writers because the courses and institutes offered are all about teachers teaching teachers and teachers being writers. Mary has been a long-time supporter of the project and has encouraged teachers to enroll in courses. More recently, her district has arranged to have courses taught at schools within the county. Ann believes it is a successful model and also encourages teachers to enroll in the courses. She supports the writing project because teachers are engaged in the writing process and learn to see themselves as writers as well as teachers of writing. Teachers who view themselves as writers are more likely to model and write for and with students. She explains, "If a teacher is in touch with her own writing process, it is much easier for her to help students improve their writing."

Teacher-research groups, such as the Teacher-Researcher Network in Vicki's district, are also instrumental in creating communities of writers engaged in learning and writing. Teachers involved in teacher-research take an inquiry approach to enhancing writing in their own classrooms. As part of the process of learning about and improving writing, they share and discuss their ideas, questions, and findings with other teachers engaged in research. They work together to connect theories and research about writing with their everyday practices. Ultimately, they share their research through oral presentations and written papers. In this way, teachers form a community of learners and writers as they themselves teach, write, and learn.

Another way to form a community of writers is through teacher study groups. In Ann's district, teachers who are eager to learn and improve their practice form small, voluntary groups to read and discuss professional books. Typically, teachers choose the book, and the district purchases and distributes copies. Groups often meet once a week for 30–45 minutes right before school to discuss two or three chapters at a time and enjoy coffee and bagels. From these discussions, some teachers form small support groups for their own writing. Study groups can subtly and positively influence teacher knowledge and practices in teaching writing.

CONCLUSION

Ann, Lulu, Mary, and Vicki are committed to promoting student writing with reading and learning. They are fully aware of the challenges of supervising and administering school- and districtwide English language arts programs, especially in a time when schools are held accountable for the achievement of their students. They understand the importance of being knowledgeable about writing and the connections among writing, reading, and learning. They also recognize the importance of engaging families in the instructional process and drawing upon the richness of students' cultural knowledge, linguistic backgrounds, and diverse abilities. Developing writing programs based on long-range goals and sound writing instruction is a focus of the work they do. To that end, they stay up-to-date with the literacy field and advances in technology. They also provide opportunities for teachers to engage in professional development that keeps them informed of literacy research and practices and encourages them to be involved in communities of writers.

APPENDIX A:
QUESTIONS AND ANSWERS
ABOUT ON-DEMAND WRITING*

1. What is on-demand writing?

    *   On-demand writing is time-restrictive writing. It is the writing process in an accelerated and compacted form.

2. Why should educators be concerned about on-demand writing?

    *   On-demand writing is the type of writing most adults engage in on a daily basis. If schools are in the business of preparing students for life,

it makes sense that the writing curriculum focus on developing this skill.

*   The increased on-demand writing expectation found on all state assessments encourages us to examine how to develop student skill and fluency in on-demand writing. All state exams ask students to respond to challenging questions by writing coherent, well-developed, logical answers that are supported with content area facts and/or text details in a restricted time. In other words, student writing skills are being put to the test of time.

3. What are some examples of on-demand writing?

    *   In the classroom: short responses to literature and content texts, assignments in social studies, science, and math, as well as assignments for homework and classroom assessment purposes.

    *   On state exams: short responses, extended responses, thematic essays, and responses to document-based questions and scaffolded questions.

4. How is the on-demand writing process different from the general writing process?

    *   True implementation of the writing process includes recursive steps that require ample time for students to
        Plan
        Produce several drafts
        Conference with critical friends and the teacher
        Revise
        Edit
        Share published work

    *   In on-demand writing, the first copy the writer produces is usually the final copy. The restriction of time promotes a more linear writing process that requires the writer to prioritize tasks as follows: (1) planning, (2) writing, and (3) editing. Because of the time restriction there is little "wiggle" room with the process of on-demand writing.

5. Does this new emphasis on on-demand writing mean teachers should stop teaching the writing process?

---

*Created by Louise Cleveland, Curriculum Coordinator, Vestal Central Schools.

Absolutely not! Again, it is important to emphasize that on-demand writing is a version of the writing process. It is very important that students have ample time to learn about the art of writing through the steps of the writing process. In fact, this is the best preparation for on-demand writing. However, students should not be required to use the writing process with all classroom assignments. Many assignments lend themselves to teaching and practicing the on-demand writing process, for example, short responses to literature and content area assignments. If ample time is given to modeling the thinking and organizing needed for on-demand writing, student writing skill and fluency in on-demand writing can improve.

6. How can we help students become proficient on-demand writers?

There are many ways to improve student ability to produce coherent, well-developed, and logical writing in a brief time period. Among them are

- Teach and model the writing process through the use of think-alouds, write-alouds, and critiques of exemplars. Regular practice teaches students the art of writing.
- Help students
  Understand the purpose of the writing task
  Select the best planning/organizing structure
  Learn how to use the structure in their writing

Our ultimate goal should be to move students toward independence in selecting and using a few useful planning/organizing structures. It is critical that students understand the graphic organizer as a logical precursor to effective writing. Clever and cute graphic organizers do not always support logical and thoughtful writing. Ideally, a K–12 writing program provides a sequential and developmentally appropriate continuum of instruction in several basic graphic organizers.

- As a class, regularly examine the differences and similarities between on-demand writing and the writing process.
- Help students plan for and assess their own writing and the writing of others by having them use rubrics you create together. State

assessments provide one model for developing them.

APPENDIX B: FOUR TYPES OF WRITING

Expository Writing. Writing to explain, inform, make factual information clear, or tell how a process happens. Students do this kind of writing most often.

Elements

- A main idea clearly stated or implied
- Information that supports and develops the main idea
- A clearly ordered sequence of facts and details
- A specific audience in mind

Examples

- Messages
- Invitations
- Announcements
- Directions
- Paragraphs
- Explanations
- Reports
- Learning logs

Persuasive Writing. Writing to convince or persuade. It is done to change the opinion of others or influence someone's actions.

Elements

- An opinion clearly stated
- Supporting facts and examples as evidence
- Logical and orderly arguments
- Vivid and specific vocabulary
- Language and tone appropriate for the target audience

Examples

- Advertisements
- Product descriptions
- Sales pitches
- Tributes

- Travel brochures
- Letters
- Essays
- Editorials
- Book reviews

Descriptive Writing. Writing that develops images by using precise sensory words and phrases. It is used in expository writing to present facts clearly (e.g., the life cycle of a butterfly) and in persuasive writing to present and support an opinion (e.g., the need for a hiking trail along the riverbank in a community).

Elements

- Precise, vivid vocabulary that describes accurately
- Sensory images (sights, sounds, smells, tastes, textures)
- Effective use of comparisons (metaphor, simile, personification)
- Clear images/pictures that have unity and focus
- Organization and logical sequence

Examples

- Sentences and paragraphs that are parts of a story, report, essay, advertisement, or letter
- Poems
- Biographical sketches
- Essays
- Editorials
- Reports
- Letters

Narrative Writing. Writing that tells a story or gives an account of events. It can be fiction or non-fiction and can be a retelling, new version, sequel, or original account.

Elements

- An introduction and conclusion
- Plot or sequence of events told in order
- A character, setting, event to care about in first sentence
- A conflict or problem to solve
- Setting that makes sense and helps the story
- Vivid, exact words

- Theme that everyone understands and can relate to

Examples

- Autobiographies
- Biographies
- Stories
- Story summaries
- Nonfiction accounts
- Plays
- Journals
- Learning logs
- Letters
- Reports
- Book character conversations
- Sequels or new chapters or episodes

Acknowledgments. The authors extend special thanks to Ann Anderson, Curriculum Specialist for Reading, and Lulu Lopez, Principal, Alexandria City Public Schools, Alexandria, Virginia; Mary Zolman, Supervisor for K–12 Language Arts, Arlington Public Schools, Arlington, Virginia; Vicki Duling, Assistant Principal, Fairfax County Public Schools, Fairfax, Virginia; Don Gallehr, Northern Virginia Writing Project Director, George Mason University, Fairfax, Virginia; and Louise Cleveland, Curriculum Coordinator, Vestal Central Schools, Vestal, New York for generously sharing their ideas and insights.

REFERENCES

Atwell, N. (1998). *In the middle: New understandings about writing, reading, and learning.* Portsmouth, NH: Heinemann.

Banks, J. A. (2006). *Cultural diversity and education: Foundations, curriculum, and teaching.* New York: Pearson Education.

Bromley, K. (2003). Key components of sound writing instruction. In L. Gambrell, L. M. Morrow, S. Neuman, & M. Pressley (Eds.), *Best practices in literacy instruction* (pp. 143–165). New York: Guilford Press.

Calkins, L. (1994). *The art of teaching writing.* Portsmouth, NH: Heinemann.

Dole, J. A., & Donaldson, R. (2006). "What am I supposed to do all day?": Three big ideas for the reading coach. *The Reading Teacher, 59,* 486–488.

Dworin, J. E. (2006). The family stories project: Using

funds of knowledge for writing. *The Reading Teacher, 59,* 510–520.

Engel, T., & Streich, R. (2006). Yes, there is room for soup in the curriculum: Achieving accountability in a collaboratively planned writing program. *The Reading Teacher, 59,* 660–679.

Farnan, N., & Dahl, K. (2003). Children's writing: Research and practice. In J. Flood, D. Lapp, J. R. Squire, & J. M. Jenson (Eds.), *Handbook of research on teaching the English language arts* (pp. 993–1007). Mahwah, NJ: Erlbaum.

Gammill, D. M. (2006). Learning the *write* way. *The Reading Teacher, 59,* 754–762.

Graves, D. H. (1994). *A fresh look at writing.* Portsmouth, NH: Heinemann.

Hayes, J. (2004). A new framework for understanding cognition and affect in writing. In R. B. Ruddell & N. J. Unrau (Eds.), *Theoretical models and processes of reading* (5th ed., pp. 1399–1430). Newark, DE: International Reading Association.

Hidalgo, N. M., Siu, S., & Epstein, J. L. (2004). Research on families, schools, and communities: A multicultural perspective. In J. A. Banks & C. A. McGee Banks (Eds.), *Handbook of research on multicultural education* (pp. 631–655). San Francisco: Jossey-Bass.

Kintsch, W. (2004). The construction-integration model of text comprehension and its implications for instruction. In R. B. Ruddell & N. J. Unrau (Eds.), *Theoretical models and processes of reading* (5th ed., pp. 1270–1328). Newark, DE: International Reading Association.

Leu, D. J., Kinzer, C. K., Coiro, J. L., & Cammack, D. W. (2004). Toward a theory of new literacies emerging from the Internet and other information and communication technologies. In R. B. Ruddell & N. J. Unrau (Eds.), *Theoretical models and processes of reading* (5th ed., pp. 1570–1613). Newark, DE: International Reading Association.

Moll, L. C., & Gonzalez, N. (2004). Engaging life: A funds-of-knowledge approach to multicultural education. In J. A. Banks & C. A. McGee Banks (Eds.), *Handbook of research on multicultural education* (pp. 699–715). San Francisco, CA: Jossey-Bass.

Moore, M. T. (2004). Issues and trends in writing instruction. In R. D. Robinson, M. C. McKenna, & J. M. Wedman (Eds.), *Issues and trends in literacy education* (3rd ed., pp. 201–219). New York: Pearson Education.

National Writing Project. (n.d.). *About NWP.* Retrieved September 21, 2006, from http://www.writingproject.org/about

Northern Virginia Writing Project. (n.d.). Available from http://www.nvwp.orgs/public/print/doc/about/missun.csp

Spandel, V. (2005). *Creating writers through 6-trait writing assessment and instruction* (4th ed.). New York: Pearson Education.

Sternberg, R. J. (2006). Recognizing neglected strengths. *Educational Leadership, 64*(1), 30–35.

Tompkins, G. E. (2004). *Teaching writing: Balancing process and product* (4th ed.). Upper Saddle River, NJ: Pearson/Prentice Hall.

Chapter 12

Literacy Development for Culturally Diverse Students

Junko Yokota, William H. Teale, and Ruth E. Quiroa

The statistics are clear: U.S. society in general and school classrooms in particular are significantly more diverse than they were a generation ago and will become even more so in the coming decades. As of 2005, approximately one-in-three U.S. residents were non-White. The percentages of Latinos, African Americans, and Asians in the population all rose during the period from

1995–2005. Four states (Hawaii, New Mexico, California, and Texas) along with the District of Columbia are now majority-minority in terms of their population, and five states (Maryland, Mississippi, Georgia, New York, and Arizona) have minority populations of 40% or more (U.S. Census Bureau, 2006).

Of great significance to U.S. educators is the growing number of English language learners, documented in a recent study by the U.S. Department of Education (2004). The numbers of limited English proficient students in Grades K–12 increased over 60% between the academic years 1993/94 to 2004/05. Currently, around one in five children in U.S. schools has at least one foreign-born parent, and approximately the same percentage of children ages 5–17 speak a language other than English at home (Forum on Child and Family Statistics, 2007). Latinos now comprise the largest (42.7 million) and fastest growing minority group in the country (U.S. Census Bureau, 2006). Even states that don't have particularly large numbers of Latinos are experiencing substantial percentage increases in Latino children which means that teachers who have never before had English language learners in their classes now do.

Thus, educating ethnically or culturally diverse children and children who are English language learners is no longer an issue merely for urban school districts or for schools in Texas and California; teachers in virtually all parts of the United States now work with children from diverse backgrounds, and many of the teaching force (who remain, despite the increasing student ethnic and cultural diversity, predominantly middle-class Anglo Americans [National Collaborative on Diversity in the Teacher Force, 2004; National Education Association, 2003]) are finding themselves underprepared with respect to how to educate these children effectively (Cochran-Smith & Zeichner, 2005; Hoffman & Pearson, 2000; International Reading Association, 2005; Rogers, Marshall, & Tyson, 2006).

It is, and has been for many years, a statistical fact that students of diverse backgrounds lag significantly behind their mainstream peers in literacy achievement (Perie, Moran, & Lutkus, 2005). These differences are evident by the early elementary years and increase as students move through the grades. What is equally important to realize, however, is that ethnic, cultural, or linguistic variances are not automatic determinants of academic performance in reading and writing. There is ample evidence that students from diverse backgrounds can achieve at levels comparable to and even beyond those of mainstream students (Au, 1993, 1998b, 2005; Cunningham, 2007; Taylor & Pearson, 2004). Attributing low achievement to diversity is essentially an act of "blaming the victim" and abdicates the responsibility for teaching all students. We need to understand such variances and consider how best to support the literacy development of students from diverse backgrounds.

Administrators and literacy leadership personnel play a critical role regarding how issues of diversity are addressed in the classroom. Being well-informed about the various issues surrounding the education of students from diverse populations allows administrators, reading specialists, and literacy coaches to take a leadership role in the decisions that must be made. To assist in them in this endeavor, this chapter presents

- A brief definition of types of diversity
- Support for the social constructivist model with and for diverse students
- The need to consider our own cultural identity and beliefs
- Recommendations of educational implications

TYPES OF DIVERSITY

When discussing students who are different from the mainstream population, we frequently identify three types of diversity: ethnic, cultural, and linguistic. A brief description of each type of diversity is provided here, along with a summary of the understandings about each of these types of diversity that are helpful to educators.

Ethnic Diversity

Ethnicity basically refers to ancestral roots. But more important, ethnicity is the core by which people often share a sense of belonging to a group. Ethnic group membership implies a shared history that affects the way in which people live today

(Gollnick & Chinn, 1990). It is usually most desirable to identify ethnicity as specifically as possible. For example, it is preferable to refer to students as being Japanese, Cuban, or Navajo rather than Asian, Hispanic, or Native American. One issue to keep in mind is that the acceptable name for some ethnic groups is based on highly individual preference: For example, depending on individual preference, a person of Mexican descent living in the United States may prefer to be called Mexican American, Latino, Hispanic, or Chicano.

Cultural Diversity

Culture is defined as a system of values, beliefs, and standards that guides people's thoughts, feelings, and behavior. Culture is not static, but rather is a dynamic process by which people make sense of their lives. Cultural understanding is learned and shared by members of the cultural group (Au, 1993). Values and behaviors shared by cultural groups are not completely homogeneous (they are adapted by subgroups and individuals), but each member of the cultural group adheres to a common core of the culture's values and behaviors. The boundaries by which cultures are defined may be based on ethnicity, religion, philosophy, geographical region, or other common ground, or some combination of these factors.

Linguistic Diversity

Two broad types of linguistic diversity can be identified: multilingualism and dialect differences. *Multilingualism* refers to the ability to speak more than one language. *Dialect differences* are variations of the English language (e.g., African American Vernacular English [Green, 2002; Smitherman, 2000]; Southern dialect). Linguistic factors like these often play a critical role in school learning because uses of language by different groups of people can result in miscommunication owing to differences in interpretation or one group's attitudes toward another group's way of speaking. When mainstream "standard" rules of communication are imposed on all, students from nonmainstream backgrounds often feel a sense of rejection since language is so much a part of one's identity.

APPROACHES TO EDUCATING DIVERSE POPULATIONS OF STUDENTS

Understanding these different types of diversity is important foundational knowledge that can help educators develop ethnosensitivity, a critical disposition for having success in reaching diverse populations. Although it may be unintentional, many mainstream U.S. educators have assumed that the cultural and linguistic norm of their background is to be maintained, even denying or marginalizing race as an important factor in literacy education (Willis, 2003). As a result, they interpret the actions and speech of their students according to that norm (Farr, 1991). Such ethnocentrism needs to be replaced by ethnosensitivity if children from diverse populations are to succeed in learning to read and write well. Ethnosensitivity takes the perspective that all students are competent in the language and culture in which they were raised. When students possess a cultural background or linguistic pattern that is different from that of the mainstream, it should not be considered a deficit, but rather a difference (Au, 1993; Farr, 1991; Gay, 2000). For many students of diverse heritage, there is a mismatch between the experiences they have in their homes and the experiences they have at school (Rueda, 1991). These differences become problematic when they conflict with what is expected in schools, and therefore are interpreted by educators as deficits to be overcome. A priority need, then, is to eliminate prejudices against such variation and bring about the understanding that cultural and linguistic variation is natural. Understanding the naturalness of variance is only a first step, however; it is equally important to recognize the value that variance offers.

Beyond the brief definition of the types of diversity, it is helpful to consider various approaches to how children are educated in schools. Numerous models have been proposed, but we have found useful the perspective taken by Au (1993), in which she identifies the transmission model and social constructivist model.

Transmission Model

Transmission models are based on the belief that all students learn in the same manner, "absorbing" knowledge that is transmitted to them. Transmission models tend to reflect the teacher's background experiences, which are often largely based on mainstream values. Therefore, it is not surprising that the transmissions are better received by students who are from a background similar to the teacher's. When failure occurs in this situation for students of diversity, the typical remedy has been to place them in highly structured remedial programs. Most often, these programs focus narrowly on teaching "the basics" of decoding and word recognition, believing that diverse students lack ability or experience to also learn higher level comprehension, vocabulary, and writing strategies. As a result, the children get a heavier dosage of what they have already experienced as failure. Students of diversity report a high degree of "transmission teaching" (Nieto, 2003a), despite the fact that such a focus on "transmitting the basics" denies them the time and opportunity to engage in higher level thinking (Au, 1998a).

Social Constructivist Model

Based on the understanding that all learners come to school with literacy knowledge of some type, the social constructivist model acknowledges that the kind of literacy knowledge and the way in which each learner develops literacy differs from student to student (Erickson, 1991). In the most basic sense, *constructivism* in literacy learning refers to the understanding that meaning is created through the interaction of reader and text. Literacy is seen as embedded in social contexts. Learners in the social constructivist model are active participants in constructing their own learning, based on their own backgrounds and interests. Students set goals and actively create their own paths for literacy learning. The teacher's role is to teach, guide, and support students so that they successfully pursue their literacy development. This support includes instruction in specific areas of literacy development as well as creating contexts that enable students to explore many facets of oral and written language so that they create personalized understandings and strategies.

Au (1998b) defines students' *ownership* of their own literacy as valuing it enough to have a positive attitude about literacy, choosing to make literacy a part of their lives even outside of school, and

being engaged in the process. A visitor to a constructivist classroom may perceive the level of active student participation to be noisy. However, structure and organization are found in the variety of reading/writing activities occurring and in the materials being used by students.

1. Why Does the Social Constructivist Model Work for Students of Diverse Backgrounds? The social constructivist model defines literacy learning by considering how people think and construct knowledge in the various social contexts in which literacy is used. Because of their variety of social and cultural experiences with literacy prior to schooling, students of diverse backgrounds inevitably have varying understandings of literacy and ways of thinking about literacy. The social constructivist model endorses literacy instruction that takes such backgrounds into consideration, makes connections, and builds literacy based on the backgrounds students already have (Langer, 1991). Specific reasons the social constructivist model is particularly well suited to students of diverse backgrounds include the following:

- Students can select some of their own reading material.
- Students can write and speak on topics of their choice.
- Students have the opportunity to select some of the types of literacy activities in which they wish to participate.
- Literacy-related skills are contextualized in meaningful ways.

When students of diverse backgrounds have choices regarding their reading materials, topics for writing and speaking, and literacy activities, the opportunity to tap into their individual backgrounds becomes an option. It is then more likely that students will be able to make meaningful connections between their backgrounds and literacy learning in schools.

In a discussion of the best ways to educate African American learners at risk, Strickland (1994) suggests that literacy learning should

- Start early and continue throughout life
- Be used to make meaning out of our world

- Take place through active involvement and use
- Be influenced by one's language and cultural background
- Be influenced by social context

These recommendations endorse the social constructivist model as appropriate.

2. What Precautions Should Be Taken When Employing the Social Constructivist Model for Students of Diverse Backgrounds? Clearly, the social constructivist model has many advantages for students of diverse backgrounds, as well as for mainstream students. Nevertheless, there are potential pitfalls that should be avoided when employing the model. Students from mainstream families acquire the basic codes of literacy at home and put them into practice at school. However, students who have acquired their literacy from a code other than standard English may need explicit instruction to acquire the skills expected. In order to have lifetime access to the expectations of the culture of power, all students must be able to communicate in standard English. Explicit instruction is often the most effective and efficient method of explaining how and why things work the way they do (Spangenberg-Urbschat & Pritchard, 1994). Explicit instruction may seem to conflict with the role of teachers as facilitators, but since a facilitator meets the needs of students, students cannot be held accountable for knowledge that has never been made available to them. This does not imply that direct instruction of skills in isolation is being advocated. Delpit (1988) cites Siddle in stating that direct instruction minilessons taught in the context of meaningful activities are most effective.

Although emphasizing the process of learning is quite valuable, there is also a need to emphasize product; ultimately, it is the product that society will judge (Delpit, 1988). Often, the standards of mainstream culture are used to make these judgments. A teacher will assume different roles in helping students achieve these end goals, sometimes acting as facilitator and guiding students in their own personally meaningful learning, and at other times offering explicit instruction.

Most literacy-related components of the social constructivist model are supportive of diversity in learners. However, not all activities appropriate for the mainstream population within the construc-

tivist model should also be assumed to be appropriate for the diverse population. For example, Reyes (1991) studied the use of dialogue journals and literature logs in a sixth-grade bilingual classroom. Although the students were able to communicate effectively with their teacher, gains in mastering the conventions of standard English writing were not made as rapidly as could be accomplished through direct instruction. Such activities should not necessarily be dropped as inappropriate, but instead they should be altered to fit the differing needs of diverse students.

Another example of the differing roles for teachers who teach diverse students is the need for explicit teacher assistance when students are unable to make choices on their own (Reyes, 1991). An example cited by Au (1993) is that of a student who is asking for help in selecting a library book and is told by the teacher to continue looking alone. The student's subsequent failure to find an appropriate book is interpreted as a lack of motivation. What is interesting is that the selecting of a book is viewed with less guidance than some other choices to be made in life. For example, children are generally given much guidance on how to select the proper foods in order to have a balanced meal; parents would not consider allowing a child to eat only sweets all day, but would insist on the child's making more nutritious choices. A student who is having difficulty making a book selection alone is analogous to our entering a foreign restaurant for the first time, being offered any choice on a multipage menu in a foreign language, and trying to select a meal among dishes we have never tasted. Most adults would ask for assistance from or recommendations from an "expert"—the server, another guest, or anyone who seems to have more knowledge about the choices we are presented. The expert asks informed questions to determine what your preferences might be, and then offers assistance in helping limit the number of choices by making a few recommendations, along with explanations of each item. Choosing becomes more manageable with such guidance.

Likewise, children who have limited background in making personal book selections should be encouraged to seek the assistance of those they perceive as having the expertise and experience in making such choices. When the school curriculum offers opportunities for students to discuss authors and illustrators and to share personal book recommendations, students are likely to consider these factors and more successfully make choices when faced with selecting a book independently (Hiebert, Mervar, & Person, 1990).

SELF-EXAMINATION OF CULTURAL IDENTITY AND BELIEFS

Teachers from the dominant White culture often view themselves as simply "American," with an apologetic stance of being cultureless since only "others" have culture (Schmidt, 1999). Such a belief may not seem particularly problematic at first glance but a deeper consideration of such a stance reveals how teachers with cultural isolation lack understanding and put students of diverse backgrounds at an educational disadvantage (Apol, Sakuma, Reynolds, & Rop, 2002/03; Howard, 2006). For one thing, such thinking can lead to viewing race as a problem intrinsic only to people of color and therefore unimportant to teachers of the dominant White culture (Willis, 2003). Additionally, this notion that culture belongs to "others" contributes to the belief that individuals with strong cultural identities are not quite American. A lack of understanding of one's own cultural grounding (and everyone has a cultural grounding) makes it impossible to understand how students' cultural identities and literary traditions and practices play a critical role in literacy learning. More important, it creates blinders to the hidden literacy curriculum of teacher behavior and interaction patterns (Hernández, 2001) that maintain structural inequalities in classrooms and schools.

Critical Race Theory stems from the work of anthropologists, sociologists and historians and is based on the fundamental understanding that race matters, and that inequities are often based on beliefs about superiority and inferiority related to issues of race and economics (Ladson-Billings, 1999). Not acknowledging this inequity and its impact on social and school issues is to put on blinders; instead, these issues must be recognized and consciously dealt with through educational policies and in practice (Ladson-Billings & Tate, 1995). Edu-

cators who endorse critical race theory believe that the goal is to work toward social justice. As Willis (2003) points out, ignoring race ensures the centrality and privilege of the White race as the norm in literacy instruction.

One way that schools and teachers have attempted to address issues of diversity in classrooms has been by including thematic units of study such as "Holidays Around the World," (usually in December) or "African American History" (in February). Banks (2003) has called this the Additive Approach to multicultural education and notes that it usually "results in the viewing of ethnic content from the perspectives of mainstream historians, writers, artists, and scientists" (p. 232). The danger here is that the cultural content presented in multicultural books or units of study may end with "narcissistic self-reflection" rather than a change in perspective toward others (Cai, 2002, p. 16). Teachers may also focus on practical aspects of implementation rather than the cultural and historical significance of textual content (Apol et al., 2002/03).

Although important, supplementing existing curriculum to include multicultural texts and themes without significant changes to classroom implementation practices as well as to teacher knowledge of and perspectives toward race, culture, and language likely will not effectively create culturally responsive instruction. Simple changes in curriculum do not enable teachers to recognize or validate the many ways in which children of diverse backgrounds may transport and transform cultural material across symbolic and social borders in their writing (Dyson, 2003) or in their literary responses (Enciso, 1997). Rather, students' differing paths to literacy, ways of interacting with texts, and reading and writing abilities in multiple languages may still be viewed as disruptions to instruction or even as subversive threats to power and authority.

Banks (1999) notes, "Teachers cannot transform schools until they transform themselves" (p. xi). Toward this end, individual and school-based changes in relation to race and language begin with deep examinations of what Enciso (1997) calls "cultural maps," or personal backgrounds, beliefs, and attitudes. When educators take time for such self-reflection, then they can consider how their personal background, beliefs, and attitudes affect their teaching and their relationships with their students

(Willis & Lewis, 1998; Xu, 2001). In addition, schools and districts can begin to reflect on the focus and scope of mission statements to ensure that these explicitly address issues of diversity, particularly in relationship to literacy. Reflective processes begin with honestly questioning one's own assumptions, as well as acknowledging the limitations of culturally conditioned perceptions of truth (Howard, 2006). Nieto (2003b) outlines specific guidelines for literacy researchers and teachers interested in racial justice: (a) Develop insight and awareness about the role of race and racism in the classroom and in one's own identity; (b) work up the courage to change classroom curriculum and instruction; (c) assume a stance of humility; and (d) engage in social change.

EDUCATIONAL IMPLICATIONS: GUIDELINES FOR PRACTICE

The discussion of an appropriate model for the literacy education of diverse populations has important implications for classroom climate and educational activities. First, educators can acknowledge diversity as a factor that can enrich students' literacy development. Second, although many similarities and parallels exist between literacy development for mainstream populations and students of diverse backgrounds, there must be an understanding that some differences exist as well. Willingness to understand these differences will be reflected in the effectiveness of instruction. Discussions of eight specific ways in which the literacy needs of diverse student populations can be effectively met follow here.

1. *Create a Culturally Responsive Language and Literacy Community.* A culturally responsive classroom environment provides an ethos that is conducive to advancing students' literacy learning while recognizing and supporting diverse backgrounds. When students of diverse backgrounds live in a different world at home from that which exists in the school, they must change from one world to another when going between the two settings (Phelan, Davidson, & Cao, 1991). Au (2006) suggests that students will be able to manage this boundary crossing better if they become active and constructive participants in their literacy instruction.

A classroom that has a culturally responsive language and literacy environment is one in which there is an ethos of support, cooperation, and collaboration. All languages and dialects spoken by students are respected, and when possible, represented in the materials and activities available to students. Most important, all students feel "safe" and equal as members of a community. This implies the need for creating a stronger sense of belonging than simple tolerance offers. Being an equal member of a community implies relationships that are reciprocal and family-like. Group members make an emotional investment in the learning successes as well as the difficulties of each member.

2. *Connect Student Background to Literacy Instruction.* This statement is true for all students, but it is especially important to recognize the background knowledge and experiences of culturally diverse students because this background may be perceived by others as irrelevant or deficient. There are two aspects to connecting student background to literacy instruction and activities. First, there is a need to connect classroom literacy materials and activities to the background knowledge and experiences of students, since it is more likely that print materials encountered in schools will relate to the background knowledge and experiences of the mainstream population. One strategy is to include materials or activities relating to the backgrounds of diverse students. Another is to make the connections for current materials and activities more explicit. For example, in one suburban school, second graders were assigned to write a description of their Thanksgiving meal, and the papers were posted on bulletin boards when parents arrived for an open house activity. A Japanese woman who had recently arrived in the United States was horrified to find that her son had written a very brief paragraph describing the beans and rice dish that their family had eaten the previous Thursday, a simple meal since the father had been away on a business trip; besides, Thanksgiving was not a holiday they celebrated in their culture. The teacher could have connected student background to literacy instruction and asked students to discuss different kinds of special meals their families had at important celebrations (not only Thanksgiving), and thereby be more inclusive of different

cultural celebrations that include special meals. Creating such connections between school instruction and students' background makes learning more personally important.

The next aspect, basing literacy growth on students' background, goes beyond the initial connection made. Literacy-related activities should have a basis in the cultural background held by the child. Students can be encouraged to make personal connections and responses to their reading. Encouraging students to tell stories from their own backgrounds can be one way to accomplish this. Books that are strongly rooted in culturally based experiences can provide good reading material as well as serving as the springboard for speaking and writing experiences. *Family Pictures/Cuadros de Familia* (1990) by Carmen Lomas Garza is a bilingual book reflecting a Mexican American family's experiences. Other books that would pair well with this one are *The Relatives Came* (1985) by Cynthia Rylant, about an Appalachian family's reunion, and *We Had a Picnic This Sunday Past* (1998) by Jacqueline Woodson, about an African American family reunion. After reading a variety of books on family gatherings, students could interview family members, tell or write about their own family experiences, and even create their own family album of remembered family gatherings. When students read a book like *Leon's Story* (Tillage, 1997), they come to realize that personal life stories can be engaging and powerful. And students who read *I Love Saturdays y Domingos* (Ada, 2002) will find a girl who embraces her bicultural heritage and describes loving relationships with both her grandparents who are Latino and her grandparents who are European American. Students can learn to value the contributions of oral histories and the histories of their own communities. If their stories of family and community are valued in school, students develop pride and a sense of self-empowerment in contributing to the classroom the stories from their own backgrounds (Willis & Lewis, 1998).

3. Acknowledge and Access the First Language, and Add English As Another Language.

In 1984, Ruíz outlined a three-pronged framework related to language orientations in policy planning that is still highly relevant to literacy educators and schools, namely: language-as-problem, language-as-right,

and language-as-resource. The language-as-problem perspective views linguistically diverse children and families as "at risk" and in need of "fixing" to ensure assimilation to the dominant society and the attainment of academic success. This assimilationist position expects individuals of diverse linguistic and cultural backgrounds to become part of the great "melting pot" (Ferdman, 1990), and often results in deliberate efforts to eradicate students' native language or dialect to conform to "standard" English (Jalongo, 2003). The language-as-right perspective is a reaction to the assimilationist deficit view of language, presenting goals of full participation and equal representation at all levels. Seen as a fight for justice and language preservation, this viewpoint may not adequately address the socioeconomic (class) and intradiversity issues that play significant roles in academic success. In contrast, the language-as-resource orientation goes beyond language rights to emphasize the reshaping of dominant attitudes about language and language groups, of developing language skills, and of conserving such linguistic resources. Here, bilingualism and multilingualism are seen as beneficial resources, important for all aspects of academic success. In essence, language-as-resource is a pluralistic position that capitalizes on the child's first language or dialect but also endorses mastery of the dominant language in the culture (Jalongo, 2003). Language-as-resource is additive in that it recognizes the worth of the first language and adds English as another language for communication. The value of maintaining the first language should be made clear to students. Students also need to understand that effective communication in the language of the mainstream is important for success in many situations. Some believe that diversity in dialect should be accepted; others argue that this denies some students access to the language of power (Delpit, 1988).

Students entering school with a language other than English as their first language, may find that English is the exclusive language developed in school. In such cases, the native language does not become developed in a formal sense. Consequently, students may never learn to improve that first language to the extent of using it effectively for full communication in their adult lives. A point for consideration: what happens during the time period before English becomes proficient enough to become the language in which content learning can take place?

Bilingual education is an enormous field of study by itself, but these issues go beyond the scope of this chapter and will be discussed in Chapter 13. The main issue that educators need to keep in mind is that whenever possible, students should be supported in continuing to learn their first language (Snow, Griffin, & Burns, 1998).

Samway and McKeon (1999) provide an in-depth list of myths and misconceptions related to English language learners. Several myths that they debunk include the following:

- Students who do not speak English are found only in large, urban areas.
- Children learn second languages quickly and easily.
- The younger the child is, the more skilled he is in acquiring a second language.
- The more time students spend in a second-language context, the quicker they learn the language.
- Children have acquired a second language once they can speak it.
- All children learn a second language in the same way.
- Children are not able to learn content-area subjects until they learn English.
- Parents of English language learners are not interested in how well their children are doing in the classroom.
- It is too difficult to involve second-language parents and families when most of the teachers are monolingual English speakers.

In order to avoid the beliefs embodied in these and other myths about linguistically diverse students, it is important to gain basic understandings about language acquisition, legal requirements for educating linguistically diverse students, and placement, program, and assessment information. Most of all, it is important to keep in mind that language is a significant part of people's sense of self. The manner in which linguistic diversity is viewed by the school shapes the attitudes students accept about their own language.

4. Give Students Opportunities To Talk and Establish An Oral Communicative Competence. Students

need opportunities to engage in meaningful language use in order to develop competency in oral communication. Oral language competency can serve as the basis through which all learning can take place. In order to develop communication skills, students need opportunities to listen and to talk in a variety of contexts for a variety of reasons. Some students, particularly those whose first language is other than English, need extra time to phrase their thoughts before feeling prepared to express them through speech. Teacher feedback should focus primarily on the content of what was said, with selective feedback on how it was said. Scaffolding can provide temporary frameworks for students as they build their levels of competence (e.g., Cummins, 1989; Watts-Taffe & Truscott, 2000).

The ability to communicate orally allows students to connect to one another and to become a part of the classroom community. In *My Trouble Is My English,* Fu (1995) recalls her own experiences as a foreign student in a graduate English department. In this context she listened and read but hardly ever joined in the conversations in class. When she entered a doctoral program in reading and writing instruction at the University of New Hampshire, she found herself pulled into the community of learners who sought to engage her as a member— one who would respond, express opinions, question, and laugh with the group. What Fu found was that her professors and classmates validated her talk, and she no longer felt like an outsider to class discussions. This kind of engagement in talk helps students feel empowered in their ability to communicate, encouraging them to practice and thereby develop competency.

5. Provide Assessment that Accurately Reflects Students' Strengths and Weaknesses, Focusing on Literacy Achievement and Expecting Students to Be Successful. Ladson-Billings (Willis & Lewis, 1998) calls for focus on academic achievement, with teachers and students expecting success. Assessment, then, should provide feedback that leads to successful achievement. However, traditional assessment practices do not necessarily reflect the true strengths and weaknesses of students from diverse populations. They may instead merely lead to teachers' attributing problems to student weaknesses, and even to labeling and segregation. This results in a "gatekeeping" function of allowing some to have entry into educational experiences, but not others. In addition, it promotes a tracking system in which students, once labeled as in the low group, tend to stay in a particular track for the rest of their school careers. When administrators and literacy leaders look at their own schools, they should see if the percentage of students of diverse backgrounds who are in remedial programs parallels the ethnic balance of the school as a whole or if there is a disproportionately large number of students in those programs.

There is also a need to consider advocacy-oriented assessment that locates the problems in the social and educational context, instead of in the students, and seeks to change the instructional situations (Allington, 1991). One example of the need for assessment to match student background is evident from a study by Applebee (1991). He cites statistics that indicate students tend to fare better on testing that reflects their particular ethnic background. For example, when responding to a question on Langston Hughes' poetry, 53% of the African American students answered the question correctly, but only 35% of the White students and 27% of the Latino students did so. When students appear to give a wrong response, teachers should try to determine how the student arrived at that response and gain insight into the student's thinking (Watts-Taffe & Truscott, 2000). Thus instruction that follows can be informed by assessment.

6. *Establish Strong School, Home, and Community Connections.* The importance of a strong school, home, and community connection is virtually without debate. However, a misconception is that when the home and community differ from the mainstream population, there is little interest or willingness from home or community in school involvement. The truth of the situation is that typically there are factors that inhibit the participation of homes and communities of diversity (Yokota Lewis, 1988), and when these factors are addressed and the reasons for their hesitation dispelled, families and communities often find themselves very actively involved in their neighborhood schools. Moll (1992) talks about the notion that all families have "funds of knowledge" that they can contribute to the educational enterprise of the school. What Moll and his colleagues discovered in their work with Latino families was that these "funds of knowledge" often go unrecognized because they are typically nontraditional sources of knowledge, such as that possessed by migrant workers or the woman who is a local *curandera,* or folk healer. When these "funds of knowledge" are invited into the school community, home-school connections improve dramatically because the contributions of formerly disenfranchised communities are recognized. Furthermore, typically, parents and the community are asked to provide support for the instructional program in ways identified by the school.

When Keenan, Willet, and Solsken (1993) invited community participation, they changed their school's focus to look for ways to adapt and support families according to their identified needs. They identify four ways in which such change can occur: discovering parents' talents and teaching capabilities, overcoming fears of difference, trusting curriculum to emerge through conversation, and constructing equitable relations with parents. Schmidt (1999) discusses the following ways to strengthen family involvement: avoid educational jargon, encourage families to provide insights about their children, share student work, encourage families to visit the school, and encourage families to share their knowledge of the community. Schmidt also encourages teachers to help families understand the culture and structure of the school, and understand whom to call in various situations.

In Japan nearly all mothers are members of parent-teacher organizations and operate an extensive volunteering network. The same mothers, when coming to the United States, are usually not involved in PTAs. Causes cited for their not being involved in the U.S. PTAs include a sense of not "belonging" owing to cultural and linguistic barriers, a lack of understanding about how American schools operate, and not being solicited for assistance. When asked about being involved in their children's schools, the mothers expressed interest and willingness, provided that the barriers cited be removed (Yokota Lewis, 1988). Goldenberg and Gallimore (1995) found Latino immigrant parents tended to regard formal education as the way to social and economic mobility, and they tended to support the efforts of their children's literacy learning when it was made explicit to them. Based on the program called Transformative Family Literacy,

Ada, Campoy, and Zubizarreta (2001) identified specific principles for engaging Latino parents in family literacy. These principles include the following:

- Parents as the first and most constant educators of their children
- Parents' home language as a valuable resource for children's oral language and cognitive development
- Parents as valuable allies for children's emotional and social development
- Parents' need to experience the pleasure and relevance of reading in order to be more inclined to share books with their children

Picture books are an accessible medium for all parents. As parents and children share their thinking in the context of such books, their writing, stories, and self-confidence all grow (Ada et al., 2001).

7. Include Multicultural Literature as Reading Material in the Classroom and as a Catalyst for Discussions of Diversity. Multicultural literature, when culturally authentic, offers insights into how cultures function. "Culturally conscious" literature reflects cultural groups through values, perspectives, language, and artifacts of the group depicted (Sims, 1982). Students from the cultures represented feel a sense of self-esteem as they see their lives reflected in literature. Through reading, students from other cultural groups can gain insight into cultures and their values and beliefs. Regardless of their backgrounds, all students will gain from the broadening of the literary canon to include multicultural literature that reflects a diversity of views.

A survey of the literature being read in high schools indicated that students were required to read basically the same works by White, male Anglo-Saxons that were required nearly a hundred years ago, when literature was seen as a vehicle to reduce diversity and promote a common set of values (Applebee, 1991). However, if literature is to be regarded as having power not only to influence the values of individuals but also to "redirect the course of society as a whole" (p. 234), the need for diversity of literature is clear. Rosenblatt's (1938) belief that literature provides access to the feelings, beliefs, and values that help individuals make choices

in developing their personal philosophies, also calls for dignifying, through inclusion in the curriculum, literature reflecting the lives of diverse students.

When including multicultural literature in the classroom, the following considerations are important to keep in mind:

- Include multicultural literature in all aspects of the curriculum.
- Include a diversity of cultural, ethnic, and linguistic groups.
- Include a balance of genres: folklore, poetry, historical fiction, informational, contemporary fiction, biography, and picture books.
- Include a balance of books set in other countries, as well as those of diverse groups in the United States. (Yokota, 1993)

Another important understanding is the role of picture books as an accessible format for all ages. Good illustrations offer support for visual literacy, going far beyond text alone in helping readers of all backgrounds to better understand the concepts. The text in picture books can be easily read aloud, offering another type of support to those who have a wider capacity for orally presented information than for written text. In addition, the minimal text limits the amount of information presented, allowing time for amply offering background support and discussing concepts in ways that improve understanding of a topic. One example of an informational picture book that works on multiple levels for many age groups is David Smith's *If the World Were a Village: A Book About the World's People* (2002). In this book, Smith poses a theoretical village of 100 people, and using the concept of percentage, explains how language, economics, and lifestyles are represented in the world by translating this into numbers that children are more likely to grasp.

Literature that has text in a language other than English holds an important place among books made available to students of diverse backgrounds. When a bilingual book or two versions of a book in different languages is made available to students who are bilingual, they see both of their languages represented and have the opportunity to comparatively study the two languages. Translated international literature, originally published in a non-English language, offers a different opportunity. It presents a culture and language natively depicted by people from the original country of publication, and then allows the English translation to make it available to a wider audience. Readers may be able to read a book that originated in the country of their own heritage or from the heritage of their classmates.

Multicultural literature can also serve as a catalyst for discussions of diversity. Often, the characters in multicultural literature face the same issues that students of diversity in a classroom face. Through such literature, both students of diversity and students from the mainstream population can vicariously experience these lives. An example of a book that reflects the experiences of many teens of Indian heritage is *Born Confused* by Hidier (2002). One teen reader exclaimed that this book so accurately reflected her own experiences in balancing the pull of her life among mainstream American teens with that of her traditional parents who immigrated from India that she immediately bought copies for all her cousins. Other books more broadly reflect the experiences of many students of diversity, regardless of the country from which they come. A picture book example is Allen Say's *Grandfather's Journey* (1993). Although the book is about an immigrant from Japan, readers who are first generation immigrants from other countries exclaim that they know just how this man must have felt because they share those feelings too. Through literature of this type, readers have the opportunity to discuss issues regarding how diversity affects the lives of characters.

An example of how linguistic diversity is viewed by speakers of more than one language is found in Laurence Yep's (1991) *The Star Fisher*. The Chinese-born mother repeatedly tells her American-born children to "speak only Chinese" in the home. She supports their success in learning English at school, but fears that her children will not retain their family's home language. The mother expresses concern that as the children's English improves, their Chinese will diminish, and she will no longer be able to communicate effectively with her own children. This does not arise from lack of desire to learn English on the mother's part, but rather from fear of losing higher levels of verbal communication between parent and child. This fear is very real and valid, not only in this story but also among bilingual people today. For example, the first author of this chapter has been raised with Japanese as her first and home language, but with English as her school and adult language; this affects communication with various family members, including her parents, on some difficult issues because their stronger language is not the same.

The perspective of bilingualism presented in *The Star Fisher* is one that adult readers will understand. On the other hand, students who read this book may instead empathize with the children in the story who are told they must always speak to each other only in Chinese when they would prefer to use the language of school instruction. Students may also relate to what it is like to have parents rely on children when English communication for parents is difficult. Educators reading books such as Yep's *The Star Fisher* will find themselves empathizing with the characters' dilemma and will stop wondering at each conference time, "Why can't a parent who has lived in this country for so long communicate at a child's conference in English?"

Discussion can help illuminate a book's theme, broaden perspectives, and deepen understanding. When students of diverse backgrounds identify with a book, it may allow them to feel empowered in discussions. But discussions can also be met with hostility, resistance, and surface prejudices that author Toni Morrison (1992) calls "willful critical blindness." Students of diverse backgrounds may feel silenced in such cases. In other instances, students from the mainstream may become patronizing or make responses they believe to reflect tolerance but reveal a lack of sincere understanding (Harris, 1994; Rogers & Soter, 1997). Earlier, we emphasized the importance of talking with peers, and we do not negate that here. Although literature discussions with peers are a powerful way to come to new understanding, the role of the teacher cannot be overlooked. A perceptive teacher can sensitively mediate discussion when it appears to go in directions that are problematic. On the other hand, some teachers may overlook the power of posing questions that focus the discussion on issues of diversity. Ladson-Billings (2003) found through her research that teachers who failed to notice racial issues posed in books and neglected to pose questions in discussions missed important opportunities to address a main theme in a book such as *The Watsons Go to Birmingham–1963* (Curtis, 1995) or teachers who, through their silence on racial issues, seemed to endorse the problematic notion of "color blindness" as presented in books like *Maniac Magee* (Spinelli, 1990).

8. *Provide Extensive Professional Development Opportunities and Support in Issues Related to Ethnic, Cultural, and Linguistic Diversity.* Ongoing staff development is necessary to support educators who are working to meet the literacy needs of students of diversity. When students' backgrounds differ from the educators' backgrounds, there is need for additional support in learning about these differences and how to best support literacy learning in each case. First and foremost, all educators will benefit from expanding knowledge about various cultures in general. Reading books like Julia Alvarez's *Before We Were Free* (2002), which describes life under a dictatorship in 1960s Dominican Republic, or Deborah Ellis's *The Breadwinner* (2001), which describes life under the Taliban regime, expands our understanding of worlds very different from what most U.S. educators have experienced. Teachers can be helped to understand their students by reading An Na's *A Step from Heaven* (2001), which depicts an immigrant child's experience in coming to the United States and learning a new language and a new culture that the parents enthusiastically embraced and then struggled in the disappointing reality of such a dramatic move. Beyond reading about other cultures, engaging as actively as possible in communities of diversity will expand the experiential background for educators. Doing research on the cultural background of students and attempting to learn some simple language phrases acknowledges the educator's willingness to learn about students' backgrounds and is likely to be appreciated by students. In particular, listening to the stories and learning from the parents will be very valuable in establishing improved levels of communication.

It is a reality that good instruction is good for all students, and that good instruction is based on the quality of planning and reflection teachers give to their instruction. To that end, Watts-Taffe and Truscott (2000) developed a questionnaire to promote the practice of reflection and to serve as an impetus for change. In addition to taking time for self-reflection, teachers benefit from opportunities to engage in discussion about issues facing students of diversity. An ongoing support group offers teachers a regularly scheduled time to discuss the issues they may individually be pondering in their separate classrooms. Resources and opportunities for growth are critical in order for teachers to act upon their desire to provide culturally relevant instruction.

CONCLUSION

This chapter's purpose has been to introduce selected issues about literacy development for culturally diverse students, briefly discuss their educational implications, describe examples, and offer recommendations. Being well-informed about the various factors surrounding the education of students from diverse populations allows educators to take a leadership role in the decisions that must be made. Most important, those in leadership positions should advocate an open, ongoing discussion of these issues among teachers, parents, and students.

Many of the responses to the challenge of educating diverse children tend toward what may be called a technical approach, one that perceives this as an issue of transmitting to such children what they have been lacking in areas of background knowledge, vocabulary, and skills related to phonemic awareness, comprehension, phonics, and so forth. Such an approach essentially operates from a deficit model. We hope that this chapter has demonstrated that although children benefit from extra attention and extra instruction, a deficit approach that so often characterizes attempts to work with diverse children does little to help them learn to read and write; often, it contributes to a lack of engagement in literacy and ultimately to high numbers of school dropouts. Instead, approaches that foreground the diversity and differences of children and regard these differences as resources stand a better chance of engaging such children and raising their literacy skill.

One issue that administrators and literacy leaders can profitably consider is how various policies and mandates affect the literacy learning that goes on in classrooms. Federal or state legislation or district mandates may leave little room for negotiating the implementation of such decisions. Therefore, those who are in positions of influencing such policy making and implementation need to have a thorough understanding of literacy development that is responsive to diversity (Nieto, 2003a; Samway & McKeon, 1999). Au (2003) calls for leaders to speak out on issues for which there exists a research-based theoretical stance on how best to meet the literacy development needs of students of diverse backgrounds. Without such voices, political forces can bring about consequences that will affect students and teachers, consequences that are not based on research evidence or related to the learning or achievement of diverse students, but are based on politics.

Many of the instructional and curriculum recommendations made in other chapters of this book apply equally well for students of diverse backgrounds. Recommendations for improving the literacy learning of students of diverse backgrounds are specifically geared to meet their needs. However, many of these principles are also applicable to mainstream students and can be helpful to all students, regardless of their background. It should be noted that although all students deserve the best literacy instruction possible, at present there is a notable difference in the quality of instruction offered (Allington, 1991). The additive stance (Cummins, 1986) implies that the home language and culture are not to be replaced but broadened, so that students will be able to function in both the home and their ethnic community as well as in the mainstream culture and the school. Ladson-Billings (Willis & Lewis, 1998) notes the importance of teachers understanding more than what and how to teach diverse students. Teachers need to realize why it matters and make a commitment to offer all students the best instruction possible. This commitment goes beyond the call for "tolerance" or "social justice"—it implies that emotional investments are made in supporting the literacy success of each student.

REFERENCES

Ada, A. F., Campoy, I., & Zubizarreta, R. (2001). Assessing our work with parents on behalf of children's literacy. In S. Hurley & J. V. Tinajero (Eds.), *Literacy assessment of second language learners* (pp. 167–186). Boston: Allyn & Bacon.

Allington, R. L. (1991). Children who find learning to read difficult: School responses to diversity. In E. H. Hiebert (Ed.), *Literacy for a diverse society: Perspectives, practices, and policies* (pp. 237–252). New York: Teachers College Press.

Apol, L. Sakuma, A., Reynolds, T. M., & Rop, S. K. (2002/03). "When can we make paper cranes?": Examining pre-service teachers' resistance to critical readings of historical fiction. *Journal of Literacy Research, 34,* 429–464.

Applebee, A. N. (1991). Literature: Whose heritage? In E. H. Hiebert (Ed.), *Literacy for a diverse society: Perspectives, practices, and policies* (pp. 228–236). New York: Teachers College Press.

Au, K. H. (1993). *Literacy instruction in multicultural settings.* Fort Worth: Harcourt Brace Jovanovich.

Au, K. H. (1998a). Constructivist approaches, phonics, and the literacy learning of students of diverse backgrounds. In T. Shanahan & F. V. Rodriguez-Brown (Eds.), *47th Yearbook of the National Reading Conference* (pp. 1–21). Oak Creek, WI: National Reading Conference.

Au, K. H. (1998b). Social constructivism and the school literacy learning of students of diverse backgrounds. *Journal of Literacy Research, 30,* 297–319.

Au, K. H. (2003). Literacy research and students of diverse backgrounds: What does it take to improve achievement? In C. Fairbanks et al. (Eds.), *52nd Yearbook of the National Reading Conference* (pp. 85–91). Oak Creek, WI: National Reading Conference.

Au, K. H. (2006). *Multicultural issues and literacy achievement.* Mahwah, NJ: Erlbaum.

Banks, J. (1999). Series foreword. In G. R. Howard (Ed.), *We can't teach what we don't know: White teachers, multiracial schools* (p. xi). New York: Teachers College Press.

Banks, J. (2003). Approaches to multicultural curriculum reform. In J. A. Banks & C. A. McGee Banks (Eds.), *Multicultural education: Issues and perspectives* (4th ed., pp. 225–246). Hoboken, NJ: Wiley.

Cai, M. (2002). *Multicultural literature for children and young adults: Reflections on critical issues.* Westport, CT: Greenwood Press.

Cochran-Smith, M., & Zeichner, K. M. (2005). *Studying teacher education: The report of the AERA Panel on Research and Teacher Education.* Mahwah, NJ: Erlbaum.

Cummins, J. (1986). Empowering minority students: A framework for intervention. *Harvard Educational Review, 56,* 18–36.

Cummins, J. (1989). *Empowering minority students.* Sacramento: California Association for Bilingual Education.

Cunningham, P. (2007). High-poverty schools that beat the odds. *The Reading Teacher, 60,* 382–385.

Delpit, L. D. (1988). The silenced dialogue: Power and pedagogy in educating other people's children. *Harvard Educational Review, 58,* 280–298.

Dyson, A. H. (2003). *The brothers and sisters learn to write: Popular literacies in childhood and school cultures.* New York: Teachers College Press.

Enciso, P. E. (1997). Negotiating the meaning of difference: Talking back to multicultural literature. In T. Rogers & A. O. Soter (Eds.), *Reading across cultures: Teaching literature in a diverse society* (pp. 13–41). New York: Teachers College Press.

Erickson, F. (1991). Foreword. In E. H. Hiebert (Ed.), *Literacy for a diverse society: Perspectives, practices, and policies* (pp. vii–x). New York: Teachers College Press.

Farr, M. (1991). Dialects, culture, and teaching the English language arts. In J. Flood, J. M. Jensen, D. Lapp, & J. R. Squire (Eds.), *Handbook of research on teaching the English language arts* (pp. 365–371). New York: Macmillan.

Ferdman, B. M. (1990). Literacy and cultural identity. *Harvard Educational Review, 60,* 181–204.

Forum on Child and Family Statistics. (2007). *America's children in brief: Key national indicators of well-being, 2006.* Retrieved May 8, 2007, from http://childstats .gov/pubs.asp?yr-ac2006

Fu, D. (1995). *My trouble is my English: Asian students and the American dream.* Portsmouth, NH: Heinemann.

Gay, G. (2000). *Culturally responsive teaching: Theory, research and practice.* New York: Teachers College Press.

Goldenberg, C., & Gallimore, R. (1995). Immigrant Latino parents' values and beliefs about their children's education: Continuities and discontinuities across cultures and generations. In M. L. Maehr & P. R. Pintrich (Eds.), *Advances in motivation and achievement: Culture, motivation, and achievement* (Vol. 9, pp. 183–228). Greenwich, CT: JAI Press.

Gollnick, D. M., & Chinn, P. C. (1990). *Multicultural education in a pluralistic society* (3rd ed.). Columbus, OH: Merrill.

Green, L. J. (2002). *African American English: A linguistic introduction.* New York: Cambridge University Press.

Harris, V. J. (1994). Multiculturalism and children's literature: An evaluation of ideology publishing, curricula, and research. In C. K. Kinzer & D. J. Leu (Eds.), *Multidimensional aspects of literacy research, theory, and practice. 43rd Yearbook of the National Reading Conference* (pp. 15–27). Chicago: National Reading Conference.

Hernández, H. (2001). *Multicultural education: A teacher's guide to linking context, process, and content* (2nd ed.). Upper Saddle River, NJ: Merrill/Prentice Hall.

Hiebert, E. H., Mervar, K. B., & Person, D. (1990). Research directions: Children's selection of trade books in libraries and classrooms. *Language Arts, 67,* 758–763.

Hoffman, J., & Pearson, P. D. (2000). Reading teacher education in the next millennium: What your grandmother's teacher didn't know that your granddaughter's teacher should. *Reading Research Quarterly, 35,* 28–44.

Howard, G. R. (2006). *We can't teach what we don't know: White teachers, multiracial schools* (2nd ed.). New York: Teachers College Press.

International Reading Association. (2005). *Prepared to make a difference: Research evidence on how some of America's best college programs prepare teachers of reading.* Newark, DE: Author.

Jalongo, M. R. (2003). *Early childhood language arts.* Boston: Allyn & Bacon.

Keenan, J. W., Willett, J., & Solsken, J. (1993). Focus on research: Constructing an urban village: School/home collaboration in a multicultural classroom. *Language Arts, 70,* 204–213.

Ladson-Billings, G. J. (1999). Preparing teachers for diverse student populations: A critical race theory perspective. *Review of Research in Education, 24,* 211–247.

Ladson-Billings, G. J. (2003, November). *Still playing in the dark: Whiteness in the literary imagination of children's and young adult literature.* Paper presented at the annual conference of the National Council of Teachers of English, Detroit, MI.

Ladson-Billings, G., & Tate, W. F. (1995). Toward a critical race theory of education. *Teachers College Record, 97,* 47–68.

Langer, J. A. (1991). Literacy and schooling: A sociocognitive perspective. In E. H. Hiebert (Ed.), *Literacy for a diverse society: Perspectives, practices, and policies* (pp. 9–27). New York: Teachers College Press.

Moll, L. (1992). Funds of knowledge for teaching: Using a qualitative approach to connect homes and classrooms. *Theory Into Practice, 31,* 132–141.

Morrison, T. (1992). *Playing in the dark: Whiteness and the literary imagination.* Cambridge, MA: Harvard University Press.

National Collaborative on Diversity in the Teacher Force. (2004). *Assessment of diversity in America's teaching force: A call to action.* Washington, DC: National Education Association. Retrieved 1/6/07 from http://www.nea .org/teacherquality/images/diversityreport.pdf

National Education Association. (2003). *Status of the American public school teacher: 2000–2001.* Washington, DC: Author. Retrieved 1/6/07 from http://www .nea.org/edstats/images/status.pdf

Nieto, S. (2003a). *Affirming diversity: The sociopolitical context of multicultural education* (4th ed.). New York: Longman.

Nieto, S. (2003b). Afterword. In S. Greene & D. Abt-Perkins (Eds.), *Making race visible: Literacy research for cultural understanding* (pp. 201–205). New York: Teachers College Press.

Perie, M., Moran, R., & Lutkus, A. D. (2005). *NAEP 2004*

trends in academic progress: Three decades of student performance in reading and mathematics. Retrieved December 23, 2006, from http://nces.ed.gov/pubsearch/pubsinfo.asp?pubid=2005464

Phelan, P., Davidson, A. L., & Cao, H. T. (1991). Students' multiple worlds: Negotiating the boundaries of family, peer, and school cultures. *Anthropology & Education Quarterly, 22,* 224–250.

Reyes, M. de la Luz. (1991). A process approach to literacy instruction for Spanish-speaking students: In search of a best fit. In E. H. Hiebert (Ed.), *Literacy for a diverse society: Perspectives, practices, and policies* (pp. 157–171). New York: Teachers College Press.

Rogers, T., Marshall, E., & Tyson, C. A. (2006). Dialogic narratives of literacy, teaching, and schooling: Preparing literacy teachers for diverse settings. *Reading Research Quarterly, 41,* 202–224.

Rogers, T., & Soter, A. O. (Eds.). (1997). *Reading across cultures: Teaching literature in a diverse society.* New York: Teachers College Press.

Rosenblatt, L. (1938). *Literature as exploration.* New York: D. Appleton Century.

Rueda, R. (1991). Characteristics of literacy programs for language-minority students. In E. H. Hiebert (Ed.), *Literacy for a diverse society: Perspectives, practices, and policies* (pp. 93–107). New York: Teachers College Press.

Ruíz, R. (1984). Orientations in language planning. *NABE Journal, 8*(2), 15–34

Samway, K. D., & McKeon, D. (1999). *Myths and realities: Best practices for language minority students.* Portsmouth, NH: Heinemann.

Schmidt, P. R. (1999). Know thyself and understand others. *Language Arts, 76,* 332–340.

Sims, R. (1982). *Shadow and substance.* Urbana, IL: National Council of Teachers of English.

Snow, C., Griffin, P., & Burns, S. (1998). *Preventing reading difficulties in young children.* Washington, DC: National Research Council.

Smitherman, G. (2000). *Talkin' that talk: Language, culture, and education in African America.* London: Routledge.

Spangenberg-Urbschat, K., & Pritchard, R. (Eds.). (1994). *Kids come in all languages: Reading instruction for ESL students.* Newark, DE: International Reading Association.

Strickland, D. S. (1994). Educating African American learners at risk: Finding a better way. *Language Arts. 71,* 328–336.

Taylor, B. M., & Pearson, P. D. (2004). Research on learning to read at school, at home, and in the community. *The Elementary School Journal, 105,* 167–181.

U.S. Census Bureau. (2006). *Nation's population one-third minority.* Retrieved December 19, 2006, from http:

//www.census.gov/Press-Release/www/releases/archives/population/006808.html

U.S. Department of Education. (2004). The growing numbers of English Proficient students, 1993/1994–2003/2004. Retrieved September 23, 2007, from http://www.ncela.gwu.edu/policy/states/reports/statedata/2003LEP/GrowingLEP_0304.pdf

Watts-Taffe, S., & Truscott, D. M. (2000). Using what we know about language and literacy development for ESL students in the mainstream classroom. *Language Arts, 77,* 258–264.

Willis, A. I. (2003). Parallax: Addressing race in pre-service literacy education. In S. Green & D. Abt-Perkins (Eds.), *Making race visible: Literacy research for cultural understanding* (pp. 51–70). New York: Teachers College Press.

Willis, A. I., & Lewis, K. C. (1998). A conversation with Gloria Ladson-Billings. *Language Arts, 75,* 61–70.

Xu, S. H. (2001). Preservice teachers in a literacy methods course consider issues of diversity. *Journal of Literacy Research, 32,* 505–532.

Yokota, J. (1993). Issues in selecting multicultural children's literature. *Language Arts, 70,* 156–167.

Yokota Lewis, J. (1988). *Home literacy environment and experiences: A description of Asian American homes and recommended intervention.* Unpublished doctoral dissertation, University of North Texas, Denton, TX.

CHILDREN'S BOOKS CITED

Ada, A. F. (2002). *I love Saturdays y domingos* (E. Savadier, Illus.). New York: Atheneum.

Alvarez, J. (2002). *Before we were free.* New York: Knopf.

Curtis, C. L. (1995). *The Watsons go to Birmingham–1963.* New York: Delacorte.

Ellis, D. (2001). *The breadwinner.* Toronto: Groundwood.

Garza, C. L. (1990). *Family pictures/Cuadros de familia.* San Francisco: Children's Book Press.

Hidier, T. (2002). *Born confused.* New York: Scholastic.

Na, A. (2001). *A step from heaven.* New York: Front Street.

Rylant, C. (1985). *The relatives came* (S. Gammell, Illus.). New York: Macmillan.

Say, A. (1993). *Grandfather's journey.* Boston: Houghton Mifflin.

Smith, D. J. (2002). *If the world were a village: A book about the world's people* (S. Armstrong, Illus.). Toronto: Kids Can Press.

Spinelli, J. (1990). *Maniac Magee.* Boston: Little Brown.

Tillage, L. W. (1997). *Leon's Story* (S. L. Roth, Illus.). New York: Farrar, Straus, Giroux.

Woodson, J. (1998). *We had a picnic this Sunday past* (D. Greenseid, Illus.). New York: Hyperion.

Yep, L. (1991). *The star fisher.* New York: Morrow.

CHAPTER 13

Culturally Responsive Teaching for English Language Learners

Mary Elizabeth Curran

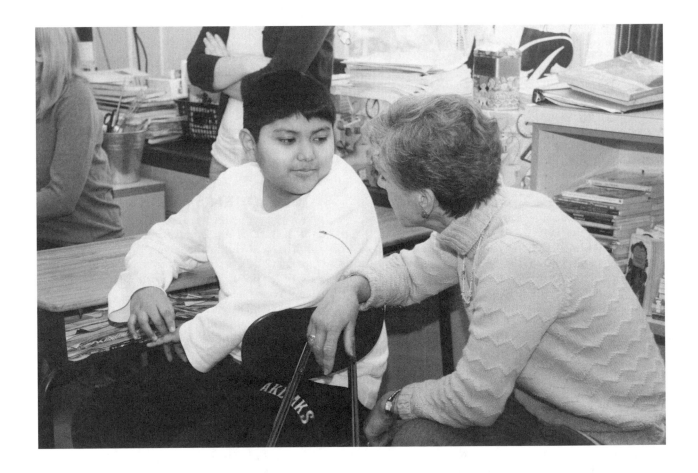

Marilyn, an experienced reading specialist, agreed to be shadowed by a reading specialist candidate preparing for certification. As Marilyn described a typical day and her activities, she gave a brief profile of each learner with whom she worked in a fourth-grade class. After talking about most of the students, Marilyn turned her attention to two 10-year-old girls who were sitting at a little round table in the back of the classroom. "And, those two," she said, pointing to the two students who had recently immigrated to the area with their families from Egypt, "I just don't know what we can do to help them. They don't understand anything, and they can't read or write English yet. The ESL teacher works with them. She takes them out for instruction one or two times a day. The rest of the time, they work together over there at that table on worksheets from their teacher, or things the ESL teacher leaves for them to do."

We know that reading and writing proficiently in English is indispensable for success in school, on the job, and in most facets of everyday life in the United States. For students who come from linguistically diverse backgrounds where English is not the primary language of the home, this means they will need additional support in the classroom to foster their literacy development in English. However, many educators, as illustrated in Marilyn's comments in the above vignette, have not received adequate professional development to prepare them to work effectively with their linguistically and culturally diverse students (August & Shanahan, 2006). Lacking preparation, educators may feel frustrated or at a loss about how best to help these students, especially as the English language learner (ELL) population is rapidly growing. To aid reading/literacy specialists, supervisors, administrators, and teacher educators as they design literacy instruction and programs and prepare teachers to best meet the needs of ELLs, this chapter provides information about the following topics:

- Linguistic diversity and linguicism
- Cultural differences and the educational experience
- Culturally responsive teaching for English language learners

LINGUISTIC DIVERSITY AND LINGUICISM

The urgency for educators to be prepared to work with linguistically diverse students in U.S. classrooms is essential given the large and growing numbers of students who speak a home language other than English. In a period of 20 years, from 1979 to 1999, the number of ELLs increased by over 100%, from 6 to 14 million students (National Center for Education Statistics [NCES], 2004). As indicated in Chapter 12, one in five children speak a language other than English at home.

The total number of languages spoken across the United States is quite dramatic and diverse. Kindler (2002) reports that more than 460 languages were reported as spoken in student homes. Of these languages, the most frequently spoken in ELLs' homes were Spanish (72%), Asian languages (21%), and other European languages (10%). Recent statistics show that the largest numbers of ELLs can be found in prekindergarten through third grade (44%), then middle grades (35%) and high school (19%). ELLs are found in all states with California, Texas, Florida, New York, Illinois, and Arizona having the largest enrollments. Given that almost 1 of every 10 students across the nation has limited English proficiency (in some urban areas, as much as 21% of all students), today's reading educators must be prepared to regularly serve these students' needs (Kindler, 2002).

Like all students, ELLs deserve an education that prepares them for success in today's society. However, the reality is that these students often do not perform well in U.S. schools and drop out at a rate three to five times higher than the rate for students who speak English at home (NCES, 2004). In spite of the fact that reading specialists, supervisors, administrators, and teacher educators will be working in schools that serve ELLs, as previously noted, educators in general have expressed feeling underprepared to work with this population. A survey from the National Center for Education Statistics (1997) found that only 20% of teachers feel "very well prepared" to work with ELLs. Of teachers who reported working with ELLs in their classes, only 30% have received any type of professional development that focused on this topic. It is possible to consider teachers' underpreparation to work with this population as an effect of linguicism.

Linguicism is parallel to terms we are more familiar with, like *racism, sexism,* and *classism*; terms that describe discrimination based on race, sex, or class. *Linguicism* was coined by Skutnabb-Kangas (1988) to mean "ideologies and structures which are used to legitimate, effectuate and reproduce an unequal division of power and resources (both material and nonmaterial) between groups which are defined on the basis of language" (p. 13). In other words, it is discrimination on account of language, and the fact that ELLs often do not receive adequate or appropriate educational support can be seen as a type of linguicism.

For example, if there were more concern about ensuring equitable access to educational achievement for ELLs, there would be more attempts on the behalf of teacher education and in-service professional development programs to offer training in meeting their needs. In addition, we would more readily see examples of how educational institutions are working to support ELLs' first language and culture in the classroom. However, the reality is that as of 2000, only 19% of language minority students received any instruction in their native language. At the same time, many bilingual education programs have been eliminated (Kindler, 2002). Research has shown that teachers who are prepared to work with ELLs and who affirm and support their students' first languages and cultures have best results with this population (Gandara, 1995; Portes & Rumbaut, 1996; Zentella, 1997). What may be a more important indicator for students' achievement than the fact that these students speak English as an additional language, may be *"the way in which teachers and schools view students' language"* (Nieto, 2004, p. 216; italics in original) and how well prepared they are to work with linguistically and culturally diverse students.

Nieto (2004) writes that ELLs have often been viewed as a problem and the value of their native languages and cultures has been disregarded. While there are multiple social, cultural, historical, and economic factors that influence ELLs' academic achievement, it is possible that teachers' lack of preparation in successful practices for working with ELLs and their attitudes toward the learners may lead to detrimental practices that are not ideal for their literacy development and contribute to their lower performance and high dropout rates. In this chapter, we will focus on ways educators involved in the teaching of reading can work to combat linguicism through engaging in culturally responsive pedagogical practices aimed at providing equitable opportunities for educational success.

CULTURAL DIFFERENCES AND THE EDUCATIONAL EXPERIENCE

To teach for the success of children from diverse linguistic, cultural, racial, and social-class backgrounds, teacher educators have addressed the need to foster the predispositions, knowledge, and skills to engage in what has been called "culturally responsive teaching" (Gay, 2000), "culturally relevant pedagogy" (Ladson-Billings, 2001), and "diversity pedagogy" (Sheets, 2004). All of these pedagogical approaches call for the need to make instruction more culturally appropriate for learners. To engage in culturally responsive teaching requires changing one's attitudes, knowledge base, and behavior. First, one must acknowledge that cultural differences exist. Second, one needs to become aware of how these differences influence the educational experience and make the necessary changes to his or her pedagogical practices. In the following sections, what is meant by each of these stages will be discussed in more detail.

Acknowledging That Cultural Differences Exist

To be able to understand the depths of the cultural differences that exist among people, we first need to understand that we are all cultural beings, with our own beliefs, biases, and assumptions about human behavior. Often it is easy to apply this concept to those we see as belonging to other cultures; however, it is important that we begin with an examination of our own culture as well. Our tendency to focus on others and find their cultural differences as remarkable or even strange comes from our ability to ignore the strangeness and uniqueness of our own culture. Like fish in the water, we often feel that our own culture is natural, normal, and right, while interpreting other cultural phenomena as abnormal and incorrect. This naturalization and lack of awareness of our first culture confines us to an ethnocentric worldview in which we are limited to interpreting all cultural phenomena and behaving solely from within our own cultural framework.

We must extend our examination of our first cultures to an articulation of the cultural values implicit in the Western, White, middle-class orientation of U.S. schools, such as the emphasis on individual achievement and accountability, meritocracy, and efficiency. Reading educators, in addition, need to examine the often unarticulated cultural practices around literacy, such as reading from left to right and from left cover to right cover of a book, getting a library card, using a library, and telling or reading bedtime stories, which belong to many mainstream English-speaking readers. By bringing the cultural orientations that steep our educational system and literacy practices to a conscious level, we can more clearly understand how pedagogical practices are culturally mediated and how cultural biases influence how we interpret (or misinterpret) the behaviors of our culturally different students. This knowledge will aid us as we consider the best way to teach them so that they have equitable access to educational success. When we begin to examine and understand ourselves, we are doing the groundwork so that we can move from operating out of an ethnocentric orientation limited to seeing the world through the lens of our first culture to a broader, ethnorelative framework from which we can begin to accept and adapt to cultural difference (Bennett, 1993).

While learning about our own first cultures, we must also work to learn more about the cultural, racial, ethnic, class, and other differences that exist among people. We must take an active role in our own education to learn about differences and resist the impulse to see "everyone as the same." We are *not* all the same; and claiming that we are promotes a color-blind attitude, which in the name of fairness and impartiality actually might be limiting one's ability to perceive and accept differences (Nieto, 2004). The U.S. Supreme Court in the *Lau v. Nichols* decision of 1974 is an excellent example of how color blindness can be used to deny differences. In this case, the San Francisco School Department was sued for not providing their many Chinese-speaking students with an equal education. The school department claimed that they were providing an equal education because the students received exactly the same teachers, instruction, and materials. However, the U.S. Supreme Court ruled against the department, reasoning that for non-English-speaking children, using the same resources as the English-speaking students did not provide them with equal access to course content and learning opportunities. The case established the right of students to differential treatment based on their language minority status. This example demonstrates how we must first acknowledge biases within our own cultural practices if we are to subsequently adapt those practices in the interests of students from other linguistic or cultural backgrounds.

To become culturally responsive, we must also gather cultural content knowledge. We must learn, for example, what first languages our students speak, what communicative practices govern their use of language, what previous educational experiences they have had, what their culture's norms for literacy practices are, and how their culture treats time and space. Through gathering this information, we can demonstrate our openness and willingness to learn about the cultures and languages that are important to our students and their families. We also need to learn about the practices they are familiar with, and begin to understand more about their beliefs and values. This knowledge will help us understand the cultural discontinuities that may exist between the students' home and school cultures so that we can help bridge that gap. While gathering this information, it is important that we remain aware of the ethnocentric tendency to stereotype or essentialize groups as static, monolithic, and homogenous by not acknowledging the tremendous variation within cultural groups.

In addition to learning about first and other cultures, culturally responsive teaching requires that teachers understand the ways that schools reflect and perpetuate discriminatory practices of the larger society. We must understand how differences in race, social class, gender, language background, and sexual orientation are linked to power. We need to recognize that the structure and practices of schools (e.g., rigid tracking, instructional practices, unevenly distributed resources, standardized testing) can privilege select groups of students while marginalizing or segregating others.

Becoming Aware of How Linguistic and Cultural Differences Influence Learning

Another important component in becoming a culturally responsive educator is understanding the ways that learning is influenced by linguistic and cultural differences. In addition to gaining a better understanding about ourselves and others, we must learn more about the following:

- The second-language acquisition process
- The ELLs in our classrooms
- The role of the first language and culture in the learning process

The Second-Language Acquisition Process. Second-language acquisition occurs when one learns a language within the context of the second-language community. That is, unlike foreign language learning in which one studies a language outside of the context in which it is used, the second-language learner is situated within the culture of the target language. The immersion experience of the second-language learner is helpful because, ideally, the learner receives plenty of input and opportunities to produce language in the new language. Of key importance is making sure that learners have language-rich experiences in their new language community.

Scholars in the field of second-language acquisition highlight the importance that learners receive what Krashen (1981) called "comprehensible input." Comprehensible input is language made comprehensible through context, such as language linked to gesture, realia, or a clear communicative activity. For example, if a child is on the playground, waiting in line to go down a slide, and another child turns and points for him to climb the ladder, saying "It's your turn," the context (the physical setting, the gestures, and so forth) helps the child understand what the language means. Krashen adds that when comprehensible input is combined with input that is at a slightly higher level than what a learner currently comprehends (what he called "i + 1") a learner is able to add new knowledge to his repertoire. For example, if in the above scenario, the next time the learner hears his peers say, "It's your turn. Hurry up!" and they proceed to push him to get on the slide, the learner will begin to understand that *hurry up* has to do with a sense of urgency and speed.

In addition to input, scholars like Swain (1985) have written about the importance of opportunities to produce language. Swain writes how when learners produce either comprehensible or incomprehensible output, they have the chance to test hypotheses about how language works. For example, if a learner says, "it's my turned" (when meaning "it's my turn"), his peers' subsequent laughter, correction, or negative feedback ("it's *turn*, silly!") will inform the learner that his hypothesis was wrong and needs adjusting. In this way, language used either correctly or incorrectly and the subsequent communicative success or failure will provide growth opportunities for the learners' developing language system. Scholars have also claimed that it is essential for learners' development that they engage in this type of trial and error, what Long (1985) has called the "negotiation of meaning," while they work toward communication.

While having opportunities to receive language input, produce language output, and negotiate meaning are crucial, scholars in the field of language acquisition have recently also demonstrated the importance of participation in the new language community (Pavlenko & Lantolf, 2000). This perspective is grounded in a sociocultural approach to language learning that, drawing upon the ideas of Vygotsky (1978), sees learning as a social phenomenon in which one first learns through interactions on an intrapersonal plane, and then later assimilates this new knowledge at the interpersonal level. This means that it is essential that learners be actively included in target language activities, ideally with scaffolded support so that they can move from legitimate peripheral participation to full participation (Lave & Wenger, 1991). From this perspective, learning a language is not simply the acquisition and production of new linguistic forms and functions; it also entails interacting with experts in the community, becoming recognized as a member, and participating in new linguistic communities. In our previous example on the playground, the learner was interacting with his peers, experts in U.S. playground language and culture. This could be an ideal learning context. However, if the peers decided instead to tease him, not let him play, and exclude him, their actions could have a dramatic impact on his ability to access an optimal learning environment.

It is important that all educators understand the complicated process of second-language acquisition. As Brown (2000) writes,

> Learning a language is a long and complex undertaking. Your whole person is affected as you struggle to reach beyond the confines of your first language

and into a new language, a new culture, a new way of thinking, feeling, and acting. Total commitment, total involvement, a total physical, intellectual, and emotional response are necessary to successfully send and receive messages in a second language. (p. 1)

Learning a second language and culture is taxing and all encompassing. To best support their ELLs, reading educators need to be aware of the demanding and overwhelming nature of the activity in which these students are involved.

The English Language Learners in Our Classrooms. Each ELL needs the opportunity to participate in language-rich (in terms of input, output, and meaning negotiation) experiences for learning to occur. However, to best design learning environments for these students, we need an understanding of the unique perspective of the English language learner. In this case, it is very helpful if we have had the experience of learning an additional language and living outside our first culture ourselves. That experience would help us understand, on some level, the responses to being immersed in a new language and culture that many of our ELLs may be experiencing.

Children entering schools in the United States, especially if it is for the first time, are overwhelmed as they encounter new people, a new language, new sights, and new smells. It is only natural, when confronted with such newness, that they may experience what has commonly been called *culture shock*, in which after an initial phase of excitement, an individual may become anxious, disoriented, and frustrated. This may lead to loss of self-esteem, depression, anger, withdrawal, or mental fatigue (Brown, 2000). Teachers and administrators need to be aware that while these students are in the process of adapting to the new language and culture, responses like these are normal, and they need to be careful not to belittle or dismiss signs of culture shock. They also need to keep in mind that individuals' responses will vary, due to the degree of similarity and difference between their home and school culture, their length of time in the United States, the emotional support available for them at home and school, their previous experiences in their home cultures, and their individual personalities. In addition, we need to remember that children immigrate along with their families and may not

have willingly chosen to come to the Unites States, or they may be arriving after experiences of severe trauma in their first culture.

As can be imagined, it is very difficult to learn to read and write in a new language when one is feeling anxious or unmotivated, or has low self-esteem. Krashen (1981) proposed that learners best "acquire second languages when they obtain comprehensible input and when their affective filters are low enough to allow the input in" (p. 62). Krashen and others have claimed that affective and social-emotional variables influence second-language acquisition. As a result, many urge teachers not to force learners to produce language too quickly; instead, they are urged to allow students a "silent period," similar to what we experience in the early stages of first-language acquisition, when one is exposed to language knowledge through listening and understanding and there is no demand that one speak immediately.

In addition to the diverse ways ELLs may respond to the stress of living in a new culture, an interesting finding in a recent review of the literature on literacy and second-language learners is that there is a also great variability among ELLs and their literacy backgrounds (August & Shanahan, 2006). While we are aware that all learners have their own strengths and weaknesses, studies have shown that "English-language learners are more variable by far in the kinds of knowledge they bring to the literacy classroom than are English-only children" (p. 631). Some English language learners may arrive in the United States with strong literacy skills in their first language; others may not know how to read in their first language. Some may not be familiar with the Roman alphabet and aspects of English orthography (like reading from left to right across a page). Others may have had some prior exposure to English as a foreign language or lingua franca in their country.

The Role of the First Language and Culture in the Learning Process. Educators understand the importance of linking new knowledge to previously learned information, a practice that is often called *scaffolding*. This holds for language and culture learning as well. "One's native language is a foundation for future learning," writes Nieto (2004, p. 214). The maintenance and support of students' native languages have been shown to be an asset in their academic achievement (Gandara, 1995; Portes & Rumbaut, 2001; Zentella, 1997). Nieto (2004) and Lippi-Green (1997) both use the metaphor of a foundation to show that just as any building needs a solid foundation to sustain the stress of the tons of building materials it will support, students who arrive at school speaking a language other than English need to use the language they already know as the foundation for their future learning. Otherwise, "it would be as if the strong foundation that had been created were abandoned and the building materials were placed on top of a sand lot across the street. Needless to say, the building would crumble in short order" (Nieto, 2004, p. 214).

Unfortunately, teachers and administrators often do not acknowledge or build upon ELLs' native languages and cultures, probably because they hope to push English acquisition as soon as possible. However, educators need to realize that this push for English could be occurring at the cost of missing the opportunity to integrate new input (English and U.S. cultural knowledge) into existing cognitive structures created through first-language and cultural experiences. In addition, this may also perpetuate the message that educators do not value ELLs' first languages and cultures.

While many educators push for fast English language acquisition, the reality for many English language learners is that it is a long, iterative process. While some learners may demonstrate nativelike conversational skills—what Cummins (1981) called BICS, or basic interpersonal communicative skills— after 2 or more years of exposure to English, the kinds of English skills necessary for academic achievement—CALP, or cognitive academic language proficiency—may take 5 or more years to match the performance of native English speakers (Collier, 1987).

Cummins (1981) writes that both types of language skills, BICS and CALP, are necessary for functioning in school environments. BICS consists of the context-rich language skills and functions that allow students to communicate in everyday social contexts. CALP, in contrast, is made up of the context-reduced communication and thought processes needed to perform school tasks that are abstract and decontextualized, like comprehending a lecture, answering multiple-choice questions on a test, and writing an essay. These tasks are more difficult for ELLs because there are no concrete cues to aid them in their comprehension (i.e., there is not comprehensible input). Developing CALP requires complex growth in many linguistic and cognitive areas simultaneously. This fact and studies that show the benefits of first-language maintenance have led scholars like Cummins and others to support programs in which students do not have to transition into English too abruptly so that they can build upon the cognitive and linguistic fundamental skills they have learned in their first language as a foundation for subsequent learning.

Additionally, one's learning is also influenced by the cultural attitudes, behaviors, and values learned through socialization into a first culture (Nieto, 2004). Our culture influences our interactional and communicative styles. For example, this affects how comfortable we are with silence, our expectations about who should speak in classrooms, and things like eye gaze and body movements (raising hands to answer questions). At the same time, while it is also important to remember that our culture influences us, we must remember that it does not determine who we are. We need to be mindful of the tension between recognizing cultural tendencies and stereotyping all individuals of a certain culture. We are all differently socialized into our cultures and have adopted or adapted some cultural norms to our own needs. However, an awareness of these culturally conditioned tendencies helps us bridge cultural discontinuities between home and school cultures when needed.

CULTURALLY RESPONSIVE TEACHING

Equipped with an understanding of one's first and other cultures and having considered the way linguistic and cultural differences influence learning, an educator can then make the effort to adapt his or her pedagogy for the maximum benefit of ELLs. While pedagogical approaches used with native speakers are also effective with ELLs, research suggests that adjustments to these approaches are needed to have maximum benefit with ELLs (August & Shanahan, 2006). This is the heart of culturally responsive pedagogy: making accommodations to one's pedagogy to promote the learning of students from diverse linguistic and cultural backgrounds. In practice, this means that an educator must consider what additional or different efforts will help ELLs learn better. In this section, we will focus on the kinds of accommodations one can make when teaching, planning, or administering reading programs. Specifically we will focus on how teachers and administrators should

- Draw upon the first language and culture as a resource
- Use appropriate teaching strategies
- Use assessments to inform their teaching
- Plan professional development opportunities with ELLs in mind

Draw Upon the First Language and Culture as a Resource

Knowing that environments that value students' first language and cultures are more conducive to their learning, reading educators need to help build a school community that affirms the linguistically and culturally diverse backgrounds of their students. This can happen in many ways and on many levels, but it will not happen without a conscious effort. Some ways to do this include providing some instructional support in the first language, using multicultural literature, and promoting and valuing multilingualism for all.

Instructional Support in the First Language. When possible, it is important to provide some instruction for ELLs in their native language. ELLs who are instructed in their native language as well as English have been shown to perform better, on average, on measures of English reading proficiency than those instructed only in English (August & Shanahan, 2006). Research shows that ELLs can make positive transfer of their previous learning into their English studies, and direct instruction as to similarities and differences between the first language and English has also shown to be helpful. For example, Spanish speakers can be instructed as to which particular phonemes and combinations of phonemes used in English do not exist in Spanish. Working in and making connections to their first language offers them links to previously learned knowledge, like

definitions and cognates with which they are already familiar. Clearly, to be in a position to help readers make such connections between languages, reading educators need to learn more about the first languages and literacy practices of their students.

Multicultural Literature. Another way to demonstrate the value of ELLs' first language and culture is the use of culturally meaningful and familiar texts. These texts facilitate comprehension because they make connections to students' background knowledge. See Chapter 12 for a discussion of the importance of including multicultural literature, examples of texts, and important considerations to keep in mind when making selections. In addition, many lists of multicultural texts are available to aid in the selection process (e.g., see Barreras, 1997; Muse, 1997; Nieto, 2004).

The use of multicultural literature also sends a message to the broader school community that diverse language and cultural backgrounds are valued. For example, having children read and discuss the picture book *My Name is Yoon* by Helen Recorvits (2003) serves this purpose. This beautifully illustrated book describes a Korean girl's decision-making process as she searches for a new name for herself after arriving in the United States. The book's message of the importance of keeping her original name makes a powerful statement of the value of Yoon's first language and culture.

Multicultural literature can also be used to help teachers and all students understand the overwhelming and all-encompassing task of learning a second language. Books like *I Hate English* by Ellen Levine (1995) allow readers to enter the world of ELLs. In this book a Chinese girl initially resists English, preferring to speak Chinese. The story demonstrates some of the typical responses of new immigrant children to the United States, like feelings of anxiety and homesickness. Stories like this one can be useful when working with ELLs and native-English-speaking students to help them understand more about the second language and culture acquisition process.

Valuing Multilingualism. To show their appreciation and affirmation of students' first languages and cultures, educators need to promote the value of multilingualism. While fostering English literacy development, educators can also spread the message that speaking other languages is valuable. This requires a reorientation from viewing ELLs as problem students to seeing them as community resources and role models. One simple but important way some educators have chosen to do this is through the language they use to speak about ELLs. For example, calling learners "ELLs" promotes the notion that learners are acquiring an additional language, while using the labels "LEP (limited English proficiency) students" or "linguistic minority students" can be seen as discriminatory in that they orient to the students as being somehow deficient or lesser.

The acceptance, valuing, and affirmation of linguistic and cultural diversity can make students feel more comfortable in their learning environment, and this may lead to lowering their affective filters and reducing anxiety and discomfort (Krashen, 1981). In this way a school climate that promotes multilingualism may contribute to creating the necessary social and emotional states that are conducive for ELLs' acquisition and participation in English. It is hoped that this attitude would also lead to the promotion of multilingualism for all, so that administrators would consider instructional options that would foster additional language acquisition for all students and staff—for example, strengthening existing world language programs or developing a dual immersion program. When multilingualism becomes a schoolwide value, ELLs will be learning within a context designed for them to flourish.

Adapt Instructional Strategies

As is the case with all new readers, research shows there are clear benefits when educators provide ELLs with an understanding of and practice in the key components of the reading and writing process (i.e., phonemic awareness, phonics, fluency, vocabulary, and text comprehension). The findings show, however, that in the case of ELLs this type of training, while helpful, only fosters word-level skill development, not text-level skill development (August & Shanahan, 2006). With ELLs, instructors need to provide more than a focus on reading and writing skills. Specifically, they must engage the learners in an extensive English development program that sees oral proficiency as critical. The most effective literacy programs with ELLs are those that

serve dual purposes: They provide intentional instructional support of oral language development in English, aligned with high-quality literacy instruction. In other words, when reading specialists work with ELLs, they need to consciously be working to foster their students' literacy skills and their English development in general.

To do this, reading educators must make an effort to engage students in language-rich literacy practices that offer ELLs the opportunity to receive comprehensible input, produce output, negotiate meaning, and participate actively as members in literacy activities. To help make written and oral input comprehensible for ELLs, visual support for texts is essential. Reading specialists can foster comprehension by carefully picking texts with helpful illustrations, or by drawing and creating illustrations themselves. Use of the chalkboard, gestures, realia, and other visual aids help ELLs link to the meaning in print. In addition, teachers should provide models for classroom procedures and exercises for their ELLS. They can either provide the model themselves, or have students demonstrate. They must also think about important background information readers rely on to understand a text that newcomers to the culture may not have. For example, ELLs may not be familiar with folktales, popular culture, or common formulaic expressions such as "Once upon a time," which serve as background knowledge for most English readers. Working with ELLs, instructors need to realize what background knowledge they might take for granted, and then work to find ways to make this knowledge comprehensible for the learner. The more the instructor works to make the language contextualized, the more likely it will become comprehensible input. Of course, this kind of support is important for all students, but it is even more necessary for ELLs, who without it, may find themselves lost in a sea of incomprehensibility.

It is important to point out that providing comprehensible input to ELLs alone will not be sufficient for language acquisition if ELLs are not considered active and valued members of the school community. This means that they must be included in classroom and school activities and not given other projects to occupy their time—a worksheet for example—while other students engage in group activities. To signal their full membership in the classroom community, ELLs should be seated toward the middle and up front in the room. This will help immerse them in the various interactions between the teacher and their peers. Importantly, they will have the opportunity to observe their more experienced classmates, while the teacher can also observe them carefully to assess their level of comprehension and adaptation.

Planning collaborative learning and pair-work projects are other good ways to include ELLs in classroom activities. Common literacy activities, like literature circles, group story mapping, or readers' theatre, are optimal for providing opportunities for the language-rich interactions ELLs need to acquire English. When ELLs are provided with clear models and roles, these types of activities can offer ideal language learning settings in which learners actively participate in processing input, producing output, and negotiating for meaning. With ELLs who are very new to English, a good strategy is to give them roles with little language production (like illustrator or timekeeper). This allows them to participate with their peers and receive input, while reducing the anxiety they might feel from having to produce language. Once ELLs have the skills to produce English, it is important to extend longer periods of wait time in response to questions and in verbal and written exchanges.

Use Assessments to Inform Teaching

An important research finding to keep in mind when working with ELLs is that the reading difficulties they experience appear to be more a function of individual differences than their language-minority status (August & Shanahan, 2006). Moreover, compared to native-English-speaking learners, ELLs are more likely to vary in the kinds of knowledge they bring to the literacy classroom. Given this, instructors need to work hard to understand more about each individual ELL's strengths and weaknesses so that they can consider which strategies will best meet the learner's needs. This requires careful informal and formal assessments of the ELLs' reading abilities, and it also requires assessing their language proficiency in English in different skill areas (listening, speaking, reading, and writing). In addition, assessments should be be done in the ELLs' first language to inform educators about their

prior knowledge and literacy skills in the first language (Perogoy & Boyle, 2001). August & Shanahan (2006) discuss how especially important it is that assessments with ELLs are carefully crafted so that assessors respond to specific criteria, instead of drawing their opinions about learners from little data or stereotypes they may unconsciously hold about learners.

Create Professional Development Opportunities

To be able to put all the previous recommendations into practice, it is crucial that reading educators receive additional professional development so that they can understand more about students' first languages and cultures, how their backgrounds influence their learning, and how to adapt instruction to best serve those readers' needs. As we already know, educators in general do not have enough background in this area. The following are important recommendations from the literature regarding the kinds of professional development activities that are most helpful.

Practical applications. The urgent need for professional development focusing on how to best serve ELLs was a key finding in August's (2006) review of literature on literacy and ELLs. When planning professional development activities, consider that the type that researchers found to consistently best serve teachers' needs were those that "provided opportunities for hands-on practice with teaching techniques readily applicable in their classrooms, in-class demonstrations with their own or a colleague's students, or personalized coaching" (p. 4). These findings highlight how important it is that administrators who plan professional development activities work closely with providers so that the training is practical and provides concrete information for participants. Administrators need to clearly inform professional development providers about their specific teacher and student populations and their needs, and they also should work closely with providers to design the workshops and ask for specific details before the training. That way they can help design a learning experience that will leave participants with relevant and meaningful information that they can put to use.

Collaborations. Reading educators who work with ELLs have two jobs: fostering literacy and English language development. Because of this, it is important that they work to build relationships with experts who can assist them. August's (2006) review found that the quality of reading instruction for ELLs improves when educators work collaboratively with English-as-a-second-language (ESL) teachers, special education teachers, and resource specialists. Reading educators need to reach out to their colleagues, and administrators need to help provide an infrastructure to support these efforts. They can, for example, provide time for meetings or hire more ESL teachers and bilingual teachers and staff who speak the first languages of the school's ELL population. August also found that outside collaborations with university researchers and teacher educators are also helpful, and cites findings from several studies that suggest that when outside "change agents" work with teachers, classroom practices improve (p. 4). In addition, there are other important potential collaborators with a wealth of information about the ELLs' first language and culture and their literacy development—the parents. Studies consistently show that the parents of ELLs express the willingness and have the ability to help their children succeed, but schools tend to underestimate and underutilize the parents' interest, motivation, and potential contributions. Administrators and teachers need to reach out to parents and find creative ways to draw upon their knowledge and support.

CONCLUSION

To teach for the success of the ELLs in today's classrooms, educators must work to reach all of their learners by engaging in culturally responsive pedagogy. This requires that we learn more: about ourselves, our students, and how to adapt our pedagogy to bridge the difference. Teacher educators have long been aware that the way most teachers teach is the way they have been taught. Even after training in new methodologies and techniques, they often revert to doing things the old way, the way that is comfortable (Lortie, 1975). However, culturally relevant pedagogy is not about doing what is comfortable and best for teachers; it is about doing what is comfortable and best for the students. Cul-

turally responsive pedagogy requires that we make changes in order to bridge the gap between home and school cultures and adapt our pedagogy to the specific needs of our students. The goal is that culturally responsive pedagogy will enhance ELLs' engagement, motivation, and participation so that they will stay in school and be successful learners.

REFERENCES

August, D. (2006). *Executive summary: Developing literacy in second-language learners: Report of the National Literacy Panel on Language-Minority Children and Youth.* Retrieved February 21, 2007, from http://www.board_ofed.idaho.gov/lep/NatlLiteracyPanel4Langminority.pdf.

August, D., & Shanahan, T. (Eds.). (2006). *Developing literacy in second-language learners: Report of the National Literacy Panel on Language-Minority Children and Youth.* Mawhah, NJ: Erlbaum.

Barreras, R. (1997). *Kaleidoscope: A multicultural booklist.* Urbana, IL: National Council of Teachers of English.

Bennett, M. J. (1993). Toward ethnorelativism: A developmental model for intercultural sensitivity. In R. M. Paige (Ed.), *Education for the intercultural experience* (pp. 21–71). Yarmouth, ME: Intercultural Press.

Brown, H. D. (2000). *Principles of language learning and teaching* (4th ed.). White Plains, NY: Addison Wesley Longman.

Collier, V. P. (1987). Age and rate of acquisition of second language for academic purposes. *TESOL Quarterly, 21,* 617–641.

Cummins, J. (1981). The role of primary language development in promoting educational success for language minority students. In California State Department of Education (Ed.), *Schooling and language minority students: A theoretical framework* (pp. 3–49). Los Angeles: Evaluation, Dissemination and Assessment Center, California State University.

Gandara, P. (1995). *Over the ivy walls: The educational mobility of low-income Chicanos.* Albany: State University of New York Press.

Gay, G. (2000). *Culturally responsive teaching: Theory, research, and practice.* New York: Teachers College Press.

Kindler, A. L. (2002). *Survey of the states' limited English proficient students and available educational programs and services: 2000–2001 summary report.* Washington, DC: National Clearing house for English Language Acquisition.

Krashen, S. (1981). *Second language acquisition and second language learning.* Oxford, UK: Pergamon.

Ladson-Billings, G. (2001). *Crossing over to Canaan: The journey of new teachers in diverse classrooms.* San Francisco: Jossey-Bass.

Lave, J., & Wenger, E. (1991). *Situated learning: Legitimate peripheral participation.* Cambridge, UK: Cambridge University Press.

Levine, E. (1995). *I hate English.* New York: Scholastic Books.

Lippi-Green, R. (1997). *English with an accent: Language, ideology, and discrimination in the United States.* New York: Routledge.

Long, M. (1985). Input and second language acquisition theory. In S. Gass & C. G. Madden, (Eds.), *Input in second language acquisition* (pp. 337–393). Rowley, MA: Newbury House.

Lortie, D. C. (1975). *Schoolteacher: A sociological study.* Chicago: University of Chicago Press.

Muse, D. (1997). *The New Press guide to multicultural resources for young readers.* New York: New Press.

National Center for Education Statistics (NCES). (1997). *1993–94 schools and staffing survey: A profile of policies and practices for limited English proficient students.* Washington, DC: U.S. Department of Education, Office of Educational Research and Improvement.

National Center for Education Statistics (NCES). (2004). *The condition of education, 2004 Education Statistics Quarterly, 6* (1&2). Retrieved February 21, 2007, from http://nces.ed.gov/programs/quarterly/vol_6/1_2/7_1.asp

Nieto, S. (2004). *Affirming diversity: The sociopolitical context of multicultural education.* Boston, MA: Allyn & Bacon.

Pavlenko, A., & Lantolf, J. P. (2000). Second language learning as participation and the (re)construction of selves. In J. P. Lantolf (Ed.), *Sociocultural theory and second language learning* (pp. 155–177). New York: Oxford University Press.

Peregoy, S. F., & Boyle, O. F. (2001). *Reading, writing, & learning in ESL: A resource book for K–12 teachers.* New York: Addison Wesley Longman.

Portes, A., & Rumbaut, R. G. (2001). *Legacies: The story of the immigrant second generation.* Berkeley: University of California Press.

Recorvits, H. (2003). *My name is Yoon.* New York: Farrar, Straus, & Giroux.

Sheets, R. H. (2004). *Diversity pedagogy: Examining the role of culture in the teaching-learning process.* Boston: Allyn & Bacon.

Skutnabb-Kangas, T. (1988). Multilingualism and the education of minority children. In T. Skutnabb-Kangas & J. Cummins (Eds.), *Minority education. From shame to struggle* (pp. 9–44). Clevedon, UK: Multilingual Matters.

Swain, M. (1985). Communicative competence: Some roles of comprehensible input and comprehensible output in its development. In S. M. Gass & C. G. Madden (Eds.), *Input in second language acquisition* (pp. 325–353). Rowley, MA: Newbury House.

Vygotsky, L. (1978). *Mind in society: The development of higher psychological processses* (M. Cole, V. John-Steiner, S. Scribner, & E. Souberman, Eds.). Cambridge, MA: Harvard University Press.

Zentella, A. C. (1997). *Growing up bilingual: Puerto Rican children in New York.* Malden, MA: Blackwell.

CHAPTER 14

Reconfiguring General and Special Education to Meet the Needs of Struggling Readers

The Promise of Response to Intervention Models

Jennifer L. Goeke and Kristen D. Ritchey

In recent years, the literacy development of students with learning problems has come more prominently into national focus. Teachers and administrators face increased responsibility for their students' learning outcomes as a result of state and federal accountability mandates (e.g., high-stakes testing and No Child Left Behind). Simultaneous pressures exist in at least two important areas. First, many more students with disabilities are being included in general education classrooms than ever before. Nearly 96% of students with disabilities are educated in regular education school buildings, and approximately 76% of students are educated in general education classrooms for at least 40% of the school day. Of that percentage, approximately 28% of students with disabilities are educated in general education classes full-time (U.S. Department of Education, 2003). Second, many teachers are entering classrooms without adequate preparation for teaching students who require more than typical instructional practices (Kozleski, Pugach, & Yinger, 2002), although general education teachers now have increased responsibility for teaching students with disabilities, often in collaboration with special educators, reading specialists and coaches, and other personnel. The collision of heightened scrutiny with increased demands leaves many teachers and administrators frustrated as to how they can effectively meet the instructional needs of struggling readers.

In many general education classrooms, the illusion persists of two distinct groups of students: "disabled" vs. "normally achieving." With the exception of students formally identified with disabilities, educators often continue to assume homogeneity among very diverse students who do not share the same skills, motivation, proficiency in English, background knowledge, or experience. Students who have difficulty learning to read and write are not confined to poor, urban, and rural schools; they exist in nearly every general education classroom. Difficulties with reading and language skills are the most common of all learning problems; Congressional testimony has indicated that 6% of school-age children will experience learning difficulty, particularly in the area of reading (U.S. Department of Education, 2003). Therefore, many students without disabilities—those at-risk for reading failure, culturally diverse and English language learners,

and low-achieving students—can benefit from effective instructional programs in literacy. Administrators and supervisors of reading programs play a key role in determining how students with literacy learning problems fit into the current instructional landscape of classrooms and schools. This chapter addresses these issues and will discuss the following:

- The literacy learning problems of students with disabilities and other at-risk populations
- Effective literacy instruction that meets the needs of students with disabilities and others
- Response-to-Intervention (RtI) models as an emerging paradigm in meeting the literacy learning needs of all students
- Guidelines for administration and supervision practice related to students with literacy learning problems

THE LITERACY LEARNING PROBLEMS OF STUDENTS WITH DISABILITIES

When discussing students with literacy learning problems, two major types of disabilities are typically identified: speech/language disorders and learning disabilities that include reading, writing, and mathematics disorders. Related behavioral disorders such as attention deficit hyperactivity disorder (ADHD) are not learning disabilities per se; however, students with ADHD often experience similar difficulties accessing classroom instruction and progressing at a rate comparable to their same-age peers. A brief description of characteristics exhibited by students with the most prominent disabilities is provided in Figure 14.1. This is not intended to be an exhaustive list of all problems students might exhibit, but rather a description of those most likely to be found in general education classrooms. Below is a brief summary of research-based understandings about learning disability (LD).

Many aspects of speaking, listening, reading, and writing overlap and build upon the same cognitive abilities. It is not surprising, then, that students can be diagnosed as having more than one area of disability. For example, the ability to understand spoken language also interferes with the development of language, which may in turn hinder

Figure 14.1. Characteristics of Students
with Disabilities

Learning Disabilities (LD)

- Poor academic achievement in reading, writing, and/or math despite average to above-average intelligence

- In comparison to classmates, significant lag in developing skills in one or more academic areas (e.g., focusing attention on print, phonological awareness, recognizing the sounds associated with letters, understanding vocabulary and grammar, building ideas and images, comparing new ideas to what is already known, storing ideas in memory)

- Difficulty distinguishing and using sounds in spoken words (e.g., reading the word "cat" by sounding out the letters c-a-t)

- Difficulty with rhyming (e.g., rhyming "cat" with "hat") or more advanced phonological awareness tasks such as segmentation (e.g., identifying isolated phonemes in the word "cat" as /c/ /a/ /t/)

- Difficulty with writing structures, vocabulary, grammar, fine motor coordination, and working memory skills

- Problems with written expression (e.g., spelling and/or composing complete, grammatically correct sentences)

- Problems with comprehension of text, especially in later grades as the focus of literacy instruction shifts from word identification to reading comprehension (later emerging RD)

- Limited vocabulary growth as students get older

- Difficulty with motor skills or coordination, or related disorders

- Motivational and self-esteem issues as a result of repeated academic failure, especially as students get older

Speech Language Impairments (SLI)

- Difficulty producing speech sounds, using spoken language to communicate, and/or understanding what other people say

- Persistent misuse of sounds, words, or language structure, past the point at which such errors are considered developmentally appropriate

Emotional and Behavior Disorders (EBD)

- Behavior that is extreme in comparison to social or cultural norms

- Maladaptive behavior that is chronic/ongoing, and exhibited in a variety of settings

- Problems from emotional disorders (e.g., affective disorder, depression, anxiety, schizophrenia, bipolar disorder) and behavioral disorders (e.g., ADHD, conduct disorder, aggression, antisocial behavior)

- Externalizing behavior (e.g., aggression, impulsivity, acting out) or internalizing behavior (e.g., social withdrawal, depression, inattentiveness) or some combination of both

---

the process of learning to read. A single gap in a student's academic skill acquisition can disrupt many areas of learning activity.

Learning disabilities involve difficulty collecting, organizing, or acting on verbal and nonverbal information. Most commonly, a student with LD has trouble understanding or using written or spoken language. Such difficulty is believed to be due to a neurological difference in brain structure or functioning. School is often the setting where a child's learning disability first becomes apparent. The disparity between the student's intelligence and his or her school performance highlights the learning difficulty. Students with LD do not have low intelligence; in fact, they typically have average to above-average intelligence. Their academic performance, as measured by standardized tests, is below what would be expected of a student of their IQ, age, and grade level. A student with LD may score poorly on tests, but low test scores are due to a problem with learning, not low intelligence.

Traditionally, identifying a student with a learning disability (or other disability) required a complex evaluation procedure. For decades, the accepted method of identifying students with LD has been the IQ-achievement discrepancy approach. Controversy was ignited, however, when this approach failed to validly identify students (see Vellutino, Scanlon, & Lyon, 2000 for further discussion). In addition, the often lengthy nature of this identification process meant that many struggling learners could not receive intervention until they were formally identified with LD. In many cases, students received services only after years of repeated school failure. The 2004 reauthorization of the Individuals with Disabilities Education Improvement Act (IDEA) provides the opportunity to address the inadequacies of the IQ-achievement discrepancy formula for identifying students with learning disabilities and intervening appropriately.

Many scholars and policymakers proposed the use of a response-to-intervention (RtI) model as an alternative or supplement to the IQ-achievement discrepancy formula. The rationale for RtI is that students who respond poorly to otherwise effective interventions have learning deficits that require more intensive intervention to accelerate their progress (Fuchs, 2003). RtI models are considered to hold multiple advantages over the traditional IQ-achievement discrepancy approach. The two most important of these advantages are that improved interventions for all students can be implemented early in the educational process, and that effective early intervention will result in a reduced subset of students eventually being identified with LD. The following section provides a more detailed description of RtI.

WHAT IS A RESPONSE TO INTERVENTION MODEL?

RtI was operationalized by some of the most prominent scholars in education (see, for example, Fuchs, 1995; Fuchs & Fuchs, 1998; Speece & Case, 2001; Vellutino et al., 1996). Although it specifically refers to a multitiered, individualized assessment and intervention process, at its core, RtI is about effective teaching. Despite the widespread focus on early intervention for reading problems and the establishment of phonological awareness training as a core component of reading instruction in the early grades, many literacy programs remain tailored toward students who are—or will easily become—literate. As a result, there are increasing numbers of students in general education classrooms who need more than "typical" literacy instruction in order to learn to read. Some of these students are eventually identified with LD, while others may be labeled as low achievers. In reality, many of these students are the victims of impoverished literacy instruction.

Recognizing that what is often accepted as "typical" literacy instruction leaves many students out, RtI models work first to provide highly effective teaching for all students, including those with special needs, within the general education classroom. Even before students are formally identified with a disability, those who need help learning to read receive additional and progressively more intensive intervention. For example, Tier 1 intervention may consist of the general education teacher briefly modeling and explaining a reading strategy for the entire class. At Tier 2, this intervention may be intensified to include more explicit use of cognitive modeling, scaffolding, and increasingly complex repeated practice, using modified text, with a smaller group of learners. At the most intensive

level, Tier 3, a comprehensive strategy instruction curriculum may be implemented in an individual or small-group setting. This system allows teachers to quickly identify students who may need help and work to provide early support that may make identification for special education unnecessary.

Although RtI models are implemented with some variation, there are attributes common to many RtI model implementations. Table 14.1 presents a detailed description of a typical three-tiered RtI model, along with recommendations for best practice by administrators and supervisors at each tier. Core characteristics of RtI include the following:

- Multiple tiers of increasingly intensive student-focused intervention
- Implementation of a high-quality, research-based curriculum in the general education classroom
- Instruction delivered by professionals other than the classroom teacher
- Implementation of scientifically based interventions of varied duration, frequency, and time
- Continuous progress monitoring of student performance to pinpoint difficulties, document progress, and determine if modifications to the intervention are necessary (Figure 14.2 presents a brief summary and examples of the role of progress monitoring in RtI.)
- Systematic assessment of the fidelity of treatment intervention

A distinguishing feature of RtI models is the extent to which intervention is individualized. There are two iterations of Tier 2 and Tier 3 interventions. The first, the problem-solving model, is a secondary research-based intervention that is designed specifically for an individual student (e.g., remediation of deficits with sight word vocabulary and accompanying progress monitoring). In such cases, treatment fidelity—the extent to which the intervention is delivered in the most consistent, effective manner—is assessed by monitoring that the intervention is implemented as designed (e.g., that the instruction is provided the recommended three times per week, that the sessions last the determined amount of time, and so on). The second iteration, the standard treatment protocol approach, uses a research-based intervention designed for students with similar learning problems (e.g.,

Table 14.1. Description of a Typical RtI Model

	Tier 1	*Tier 2*	*Tier 3*
Description	Comprehensive curricular and instructional reading programs and strategies for all students	Instruction designed to enhance and support primary intervention (for students identified at risk and/or who have not responded to Tier 1)	Specifically designed and customized reading instruction that is extended beyond the allocated reading time, may require extensive and ongoing intervention (for students who have not responded adequately to Tier 1 and Tier 2)
Who delivers the instruction?	General education teacher with appropriate support from other reading professionals and administrators	To be determined by the school, but could include general education teacher, reading professionals, special education teacher, or other qualified expert	To be determined by the school, but could include general education teacher, reading professionals, special education teacher, or other qualified expert
Where does instruction take place?	General education classroom	Appropriate setting within schools (e.g., general education classroom or reading specialist classroom)	Appropriate setting within schools (e.g., general education classroom or reading specialist classroom)
How are students assessed?	Students are assessed using Curriculum Based Measurement or other assessments at least three times a year to determine if they are meeting benchmarks	Progress monitoring at least twice per month on targeted skill to ensure response to Tier 2	Progress monitoring at least twice per month on targeted skill to ensure response to Tier 3

Responsive Reading Instruction; Denton & Hocker, 2006). A standard protocol is then applied while fidelity of implementation is assessed. In this instance, the fidelity of implementation also includes whether the intervention was implemented as designed (e.g., all instructional components were included in intervention; lesson scripts were followed, and so on). There are advantages and disadvantages to each of these approaches. In problem-solving models, there is more emphasis on the teacher's professional judgment to determine how and when to make instructional changes. In a standard protocol, there is little opportunity for deviation from the standard instruction, resulting in greater treatment fidelity.

In the following sections, we illustrate how one particular approach to the RtI process might work by presenting a series of vignettes. What is notable across the series of vignettes is the extent to which

research-based literacy instruction practices are implemented with increasing intensity.

Tier I. Effective Teaching for All Students and Ongoing Progress Monitoring

Ms. Farmer is a first-grade teacher in a diverse suburban school. She begins the day with large-group circle time on the carpet. First, she leads a direct instruction lesson on segmentation. Students use cheerleader pom-poms to "cheer out" each sound in a list of words. Next, she reviews previously learned letters, letter sounds, and keywords for each letter (s, /s/, snake). As she reveals each colorful card, the students respond chorally as they trace the letter in the air. Students are instructed on the new sound/spelling for the day using a keyword; then they decode

Figure 14.2. The Role of Ongoing Progress Monitoring in RtI

What is progress monitoring? Progress monitoring is an assessment system designed to determine if students are making adequate growth in important indicators. A frequently used progress monitoring approach is curriculum-based measurement (CBM; see Deno, 1985). CBM originated as a special education tool, but has been applied within general education contexts. While CBM measures are relatively easy to develop, two widely available, Internet-based systems include the Dynamic Indicators of Basic Early Literacy Skills (DIBELS; Good & Kaminski, 2003) and AIMSweb (Edformation, 2006).

How is screening conducted? All students are screened using brief (1–2 minutes) assessment procedures to identify which students are at risk for reading failure. Typically, students performing below the 25th percentile (on school-based or state normative standards) on the beginning-of-year screening, students with past records of deficits, as well as students recommended by parents or classroom teachers, are identified. These students might also be assessed in more depth using diagnostic assessments.

Examples

    A. The team of first-grade teachers screen all students using the Word Identification Fluency assessment (Fuchs & Fuchs, 2001) in September. This measure asks students to read a list of 50 randomly selected sight words in one minute and counts the number of words read correctly. The scores from two assessment probes are averaged, and students reading less than 15 words per minute are identified.

    B. The third-grade team of teachers (including the classroom teachers, reading specialist, and special education teacher) screen all students using Oral Reading Fluency (ORF) in September, January, and May. They use passages from DIBELS which consist of stories at the third-grade level. Students read two stories each for one minute and their scores are averaged. The lowest 25% of students are designated as at-risk and are provided with additional instruction.

    C. Seventh grade students are given a maze passage from the AIMSweb system. The maze passage is a story that has every seventh or ninth word deleted. For each deletion, three choices are provided, and students circle the choice that fits the sentence. Students have three minutes to read the passage and identify the correct word. Students in the lowest 25% are identified as at-risk and requiring further attention.

How is progress monitored during Tier 2 and Tier 3? When engaged in Tier 2 and Tier 3 interventions, assessments are administered more frequently (weekly, biweekly) using the same assessments. Multiple, alternate forms are available or can be developed.

words with that pattern and read sentences containing those words. Ms. Farmer calls a few students, one at a time, to a small table where she conducts some quick curriculum-based measurement assessments (e.g., letter name fluency, word identification fluency, and so on).

Later in the day, students are once again seated on the carpet as Ms. Farmer leads them through several rounds of a segmentation and blending exercise using the Elkonin Blocks procedure. All students have a few plastic disks laid out in front of them. Ms. Farmer provides a word and students chorally segment it into sounds, moving a block toward them for each sound or segment of the word that they hear. The students then work together to spell the word as Ms. Farmer writes it on a small whiteboard in front of them. Work on segmentation and blending continues later as Ms. Farmer pulls small guided reading groups to the round table to provide individualized instruction using the same technique. Four to five students read a short, leveled text and then work to segment and blend new words they identify from the story. Ms. Farmer has identified several students who appear to have early difficulties with learning to read. For several weeks, she closely monitors their progress through CBM and daily small-group work.

Tier 1 instruction in Ms. Farmer's first-grade classroom can be described as research-based because

- Ms. Farmer uses a validated reading curriculum that includes all components of reading, including instruction in phonological awareness, phonics, vocabulary, fluency, and comprehension.
- Ms. Farmer provides direct, explicit instruction in phonological awareness, word identification, and other aspects of reading; includes multiple opportunities to practice new skills; and uses large- and small-group instructional configurations.
- Ms. Farmer's supervisor closely monitors her implementation of the reading curriculum, documents that the program is implemented with fidelity, and supports her use of new instructional practices through mentoring and professional development.
- Ms. Farmer monitors her first graders' responsiveness to instruction at Tier 1 by assessing students once each week using an alternate form of CBM.

What Reading Professionals Need to Know About Tier 1. As stated previously, one of the primary reasons for the development of RtI was the provision of high-quality primary literacy instruction in the general education classroom. In the vignette above, it is clear that Ms. Farmer has been provided with the professional development and curriculum necessary to provide high-quality literacy instruction to all students. Had this not been the case (i.e., instruction in key areas was not being provided, curriculum was being used inappropriately, many students were not making adequate progress), Tier 1 intervention would occur at the "classroom level" or "teacher level" in an effort to improve the literacy instruction provided to all students.

Effective implementation of Tier 1 intervention requires reading personnel to engage teachers in frank discussion about what currently constitutes best practice in reading instruction. Much of this discussion extends to reflecting on what has become "typical instruction" in many classrooms, and identifying how such practices may marginalize some students. Many teachers already implement effective Tier 1 literacy instruction, as evidenced by most, if not all of their students making adequate literacy growth. When more than a handful of students are not being successful, however, the problem may reasonably be attributed to the instruction delivered to the entire class. In this case, interventions target whole-class reading instruction. Assessment of Tier 1 intervention should occur at least three times a year, but may be done as frequently as once a week.

Tier 2. Problem Solving for Students Who Need Additional Help

In the next vignette, the teacher reaches beyond her own classroom to seek collaboration in designing appropriate intervention for three students who continue to have reading difficulty.

Ms. Farmer has identified three students who are still not making adequate progress in developing decoding skills. On CBM measures, these students have not met the January benchmark established for sound-symbol relationships. To address these concerns, Ms. Farmer and a school-based Problem-Solving Team, made up of teachers, the literacy coach, an administrator, and a parent representative, meet to discuss the students and make plans for how to address their needs. Because the three students have similar difficulties reading words with short and long vowel patterns, the literacy coach, Mrs. Lopez, tailors a small-group intervention specifically to their needs. She begins small-group instruction within the general education classroom as a supplement to their existing guided reading groups and adds several activities to target these skills during center time. She works with these students 4 days a week for 15 minutes each day. The Elkonin box procedure is implemented in combination with other activities, to strengthen students' skills in the identified area of weakness. She continues to collect assessment data on the students' progress and monitors the fidelity of the interventions. After one month of this intervention, two of the three students are able to read words with long and short vowel patterns with 90% or more accuracy and are considered "caught up" with their classmates. The Problem-Solving Team meets a second time to discuss the progress of Casey, who is not responding to the additional intervention. Tier 2 instruction continues for another 4 weeks for Casey and Charlie, a newly identified student who has begun to have difficulty.

What Reading Professionals Need to Know about Tier 2. This vignette highlights several things that are important for administrators and supervisors to know about Tier 2. The intended purpose of Tier 2 intervention is to supplement, enhance, and support literacy instruction for specific students who have been identified as at-risk at Tier 1. Thus Tier 2 instruction should be tailored explicitly to the instructional needs of those students. Tier 2 interventions can be implemented by the general education teacher in the context of the daily instructional program or as a separate program delivered by appropriate personnel identified by the school. A key aspect of Tier 2 intervention is that the person delivering the instruction—whether the classroom teacher or a specialist—is highly trained in the intervention program and can deliver it with fidelity.

Tier 2 intervention can include many different types of instruction. For example, a school may choose to implement a commercially available intervention such as the struggling readers strand of their adopted reading curriculum. Alternatively, they may choose to design their own Tier 2 intervention program that includes instructional components that have been identified as scientifically based (e.g., the Elkonin box procedure referred to above). The key consideration is that any component of a uniquely developed Tier 2 program should be research-based and closely monitored so that instructional decisions are validated by data.

As with Tier 1, implementation of Tier 2 should be closely monitored for fidelity to ensure that students' instructional needs are being met. When intervention for struggling readers is attempted within the general education classroom, it is often implemented in an inconsistent or haphazard way. The reasons for this are clear: the day-to-day complexity of working classrooms prevents even the most well meaning teachers from adhering to a consistent program of academic intervention. Distractions and interruptions ranging from fire drills to assemblies can be difficult for classroom teachers to control. As a result, students often struggle to make adequate progress. In many cases, their failure is not due to lack of effort or responsiveness or the choice of an inappropriate or inadequate intervention. Rather, the intervention was not implemented as designed. A related issue is that teachers

may require additional training in order to implement Tier 2 instruction effectively. Administrators and supervisors can play a key role in supporting treatment fidelity by designing schedules that provide swaths of uninterrupted instructional time and by providing high-quality professional development around novel instructional practices.

Tier 3. Problem Solving for Students Who Fail to Respond at Tier 2

In the final vignette, a student with ongoing difficulty receives even more intensive intervention, as well as evaluation for special education, at Tier 3.

Mrs. Lopez has implemented the Tier 2 instructional program with fidelity for 8 weeks, and Charlie has made some slow and inconsistent progress. He continues to have difficulty with all aspects of phonological awareness (i.e., cannot blend three or four isolated sounds to produce a word, difficulty isolating initial phonemes in words). An additional meeting is scheduled to discuss his progress with the Problem-Solving Team. At this point, a more specialized instructional approach is discussed. The team also decides that an educational evaluation to determine if Charlie has a disability is warranted. In the meantime, Charlie begins working with Ms. Barwick, the reading specialist, who is trained in the Lindamood Phonological Sequencing Program (LIPS) program. The LIPS is a intensive instruction program designed to explicitly teach phonological awareness, and the program is implemented for 30 minutes a day, 5 days per week. A student from another classroom who is experiencing the same types of difficulty joins Charlie for these sessions. Ms. Barwick carefully coordinates with Ms. Farmer to make it all work. After 4 weeks in the program, Charlie is making more consistent progress, and the intervention is continued for another 4 weeks. At the 8-week point, the Problem-Solving Team is reconvened to discuss the results of Charlie's evaluation for special education services. The test results highlight considerable deficits in Charlie's literacy development. Rather than identifying him for special education, however, the team decides to continue monitoring Charlie until the end of the marking period in light of his progress with the LIPS intervention. At that point, Charlie's entire instructional program will be reviewed and special education identification reconsidered.

What Reading Professionals Need to Know about Tier 3. In keeping with the increasing intensity of the RtI model structure, Tier 3 represents the most intensive and individualized level of intervention designed for students who fail to respond at Tiers 1 and 2. The intensity of Tier 3 is reflected in instruction that is specifically designed to address a student's area of weakness and provided individually, more frequently, and for longer periods of instructional time. As with Tier 2, Tier 3 does not necessarily dictate the use of specialized programs or curricula. Reading professionals may be the best judges of a student's instructional needs and how to develop an appropriate program that complements the reading curriculum of their school, rather than developing or implementing a new curriculum.

Progress monitoring data continues to be collected during Tier 3 intervention to track the student's growth and make instructional decisions. As illustrated in the vignette, if the student makes adequate progress, he or she continues with Tier 3 intervention until the Problem-Solving Team decides it is no longer needed. As long as the student is progressing, he or she may continue in cycles of Tier 3 intervention for as long as necessary. Of course, some students do not respond satisfactorily to Tier 3 intervention. In such a case, the team could either continue to monitor the student's progress in additional cycles of Tier 3 intervention or refer the student for special education evaluation. RtI models differ with respect to the point at which special education evaluation is initiated (see Marston, 2005, for further discussion of how many tiers are needed within RtI). Some models embed evaluation within the tiers (e.g., if a student fails to respond to one cycle of Tier 3 intervention, evaluation is initiated), whereas others reserve evaluation as the final step once the multitiered efforts have been exhausted. In either case, the number of students referred for special education evaluation is intended to be significantly reduced by the increasing intensity of intervention within the tiers.

INTERVENTION BEYOND THE PRIMARY GRADES

Effective intervention in the primary grades can prevent or improve reading problems in many students. However, some students, including some of those with learning disabilities, may need more intensive instruction beyond the primary grades. In normally achieving readers, phonemic awareness is well developed by the end of first grade, and basic phonics skills are solidified by the end of Grade 3. As a result, these areas are not typically included in general education literacy instruction beyond the third grade. After the primary grades, reading instruction typically consists of vocabulary development and a variety of comprehension skills needed for competent reading at the upper grades. Unfortunately, students with reading disabilities often experience difficulties with phonemic awareness and phonics that persist into the middle and even secondary grades. Poor reading fluency is also common among older students with LD, even those whose difficulties with phonemic awareness and phonics have been successfully remediated. Poor fluency is especially problematic in the upper grades because it impairs comprehension, decreases motivation to read, and makes it difficult for students to keep up with the increased reading demands of their classes (Meyer & Felton, 1999).

The body of existing research on RtI models focuses primarily on reading instruction and intervention in the elementary grades; less is known about how RtI models might be implemented with older students (i.e., in middle and high school). Nonetheless, research-based recommendations have been made regarding effective reading instruction for older students (Gersten, Fuchs, Williams, & Baker, 2001; Lovett et al., 2000; Rankin-Erickson & Pressley, 2000; Torgesen et al., 2001). These recommendations target the major areas of reading difficulty experienced by older students: comprehension, vocabulary, and fluency.

For struggling older readers, instruction in reading comprehension should include the use of specific comprehension strategies. These include summarization, using context to determine word meanings, and using text structure to facilitate comprehension (e.g., understanding that the headings and subheadings in an expository science text provide information that helps with comprehension). Students should also develop an understanding of literary devices and themes. In some cases, teachers may need to substitute oral comprehension activities for typical reading and writing tasks. Because some students' oral comprehension far exceeds their reading comprehension, oral comprehension activities allow such students to demonstrate skills that would not be evident in their reading and writing. If teachers do substitute oral comprehension activities, they should continue to remediate specific reading weaknesses that will help students to become capable, independent readers.

Vocabulary instruction should include both explicit instruction (i.e., direct teaching of key vocabulary words) and indirect exposure to new vocabulary (e.g., encouraging wider reading so that students are confronted with a variety of new words). Finally, instruction that specifically targets fluency is extremely important for older readers.

In summary, the importance of specific reading-related skills tends to change according to students' grade level and stage of reading development. The abilities needed to be a successful middle or high school reader are not the same as those required for success in the primary grades. Response to intervention programs may not serve to eradicate later emerging or persistent reading problems. As with younger students, schools need to systematically assess older readers' strengths and weaknesses and provide targeted intervention in the identified areas of difficulty. It is important to note that reading intervention for older students should be based on the precise nature of the disability (e.g., whether it is a comprehension problem or a lack of phonemic awareness or phonics skills) rather than on the overall grade level of the student (Leach, Scarborough, & Rescorla, 2003).

GUIDELINES FOR ADMINISTRATION AND SUPERVISION PRACTICE

This review has presented RtI as an alternative to traditional methods used for identifying students with learning disabilities. The discussion of a more appropriate model for literacy intervention has important implications for administrators and supervisors. The following recommendations relate directly to the two major features of the RtI approach: implementation of effective academic interventions in general education and measuring students' response to those interventions.

Stay Up-to-Date on Scientifically Based Interventions

One role of administrators and supervisors is to review their school's current literacy materials and practices and select or recommend instructional strategies, materials, or interventions to be used at Tiers 1, 2, and 3. The notion of certain literacy instruction practices as "scientifically based" has been a source of controversy among scholars and practitioners in recent years. Some authors openly question the notion and intent of a "scientific basis" (Garan, 2005), others argue for the establishment of a rigorous research agenda to validate the scientific basis of our instructional practices (Lyon, 2005), while still others might argue for their own preferred instructional practices to be considered scientific. Nonetheless, several decades of research combined with the collective experience of literacy professionals indicate that certain characteristics of literacy instruction promote progress in learning to read and write, especially for students who have disabilities or may be at risk for reading failure (International Reading Association, 2002). These include the following:

- Explicit instruction in the major components of reading (e.g., phonological awareness, fluency, word recognition, vocabulary, comprehension)
- In the primary grades, explicit instruction in phonological awareness and phonics
- Opportunities to read decodable and authentic texts
- Access to varied genres of high-quality text
- In the secondary grades, instruction in learning strategies for reading and writing, especially those related to expository text
- For older students, continued remedial support that is delivered in an age-appropriate fashion
- Vocabulary development

- Implementation of instruction with fidelity (i.e., it is consistent, intensive, and sustained)
- A minimum of 90 minutes per day of literacy instruction (Chard, Vaughn, & Tyler, 2002) and up to 2 hours or more per day

Table 14.2 lists features and examples of scientifically based instruction at each tier of RtI.

Provide Ongoing, Responsive Professional Development for All Educators

Professional development is critical to the implementation of any schoolwide instructional programs in literacy, including those specified by a three-tiered RtI model. General education teachers may need professional development as they learn to implement novel instructional practices and to choreograph whole-group, small-group, and individual instruction. Despite the inclusion of students with disabilities and other diverse learning needs in general education, their teachers may have little knowledge of how to effectively teach such students. Historically, teacher education programs in general education have not included core content on special education issues or instructional practices, leaving many teachers ill-equipped to teach students with disabilities adequately, if not well (Kozleski et al., 2002). Similarly, many secondary teachers lack preservice training in basic reading instruction and may need additional skills to teach reading within the content areas. Because treatment fidelity is an integral part of RtI, professional development should extend beyond typical "workshop" presentations and include ongoing observation, mentoring/coaching, and constructive feedback on implementation of instructional practices. Administrators and supervisors also may need professional development to keep abreast of current developments in scientifically based literacy practices, assessment tools, and coordinating the complexities of schoolwide literacy interventions. Research has shown that administrator support is a key factor in the success of instructional reforms (Wagner, 2001).

Develop Communities of Practice

One consequence of RtI is a culture of shared responsibility among educators for the success of all students. Historically, intervention for students with disabilities has been viewed as the sole domain of special education. Once a student was identified for special education, there may have been little collaboration between general and special education professionals. RtI models have shifted perceptions about who is responsible for struggling students, occasionally blurring the boundaries between the roles and responsibilities of different educators. What was traditionally viewed as the domain of the special educator, for example, may now be the responsibility of a reading specialist, literacy coach, or tutor. In addition, a portion of special education funding can now be used for early intervention and prevention for students who have not yet been identified with disabilities (IDEA, 2004). The effects of these challenges on students with learning problems, the professionals who serve them, and their schools have yet to be fully understood.

Innovative models of literacy intervention provide new challenges for how administrators and supervisors work together with teachers and other reading professionals. A positive working relationship is required among all participants in RtI, and can be difficult to achieve. Here the role of administrators and supervisors cannot be underestimated. Respect for others' expertise, effective communication, ongoing reflection and problem solving, and common planning time are all essential as partners assume new roles and establish communities of practice. This work may extend to communicating with parents, who are often unaware and uninvolved in the design of their child's instructional program, particularly when special education is not yet a part of the child's education.

A related challenge to the establishment of communities of practice is that many classroom teachers are accustomed to a high degree of professional autonomy. The importance of progress monitoring and treatment fidelity to RtI means that teachers may feel that their individual "styles" of teaching are compromised in favor of more prescriptive forms of teaching. While these concerns are legitimate, administrators and supervisors can help teachers to strike a reasonable balance between creativity and precision in their teaching. Finding constructive ways to use data and assessment information is key to improving teachers' instructional programs and the response of all students.

Table 14.2. Features of Scientifically Based Instruction in RtI

Features of Scientifically Based Instruction	Tier 1	Tier 2	Tier 3
Explicit	√	√	√
Whole-class	√		
Small-group	√	√	√
Individual	√		√
Multiple opportunities for practice, in varied settings	√	√	√
Delivered with fidelity by trained personnel	√	√	√
Sustained	√	√	√
Examples (see Denton, Fletcher, Anthony, & Francis, in press; O'Connor, Harty, & Fulmer, 2005)	Whole-class instruction in the major components of reading; teacher modeling and scaffolded guided practice of reading skills and strategies	Small-group instruction 3 days a week Phonological awareness and early alphabetics in kindergarten and decoding instruction in Grade 1	Daily small-group or individualized instruction specifically designed for the student
Programs	Commercially available literature series that meets scientific-basis criteria	Responsive Reading Instruction (Denton & Hocker, 2006); Proactive Early Intervention in Reading (Mathes, Torgesen, Menchetti, Wahl, & Grek, 1999)	Phono-Graphix (McGuiness, McGuiness, & McGuiness, 1996); Read Naturally (Inhot, Mastoff, Gavin, & Hendrickson, 2001)

Note. Both descriptive examples and commercial programs are listed in order to illustrate the choices available when choosing or designing interventions for Tiers 2 and 3. Although these examples were validated as Tier 2 and Tier 3 intervention by their respective researchers, they are *not* intended as recommendations.

CONCLUSION

Although RtI models represent a significant advance in our instruction of all students and our intervention with those who struggle with reading, some facets of RtI remain unknown. Questions continue to arise as RtI emerges from its origins as a provocative idea explored in the literature to an actual intervention being implemented in schools. For example, scholars and professionals continue to question and identify how RtI procedures will merge with existing special education policies and procedures. Also, the body of existing research on RtI models focuses primarily on reading instruction and intervention; less is known about how RtI models might be implemented with older students (i.e., in middle and high school) or in other content areas such as mathematics. We await research data to support the effectiveness of specific RtI models, in particular settings, for students with certain types of learning problems.

REFERENCES

Chard, D. J., Vaughn, S., & Tyler, B. J. (2002). A synthesis of research on effective interventions for building reading fluency with elementary students with learning disabilities. *Journal of Learning Disabilities, 35*(5), 386–406.

Deno, S. L. (1985). Curriculum-based measurement: The emerging alternative. *Exceptional Children, 52,* 219–232.

Denton, C. A., Fletcher, J. M., Anthony, J. L., & Francis, D. J. (in press). An evaluation of intensive intervention for students with persistent reading difficulties. *Journal of Learning Disabilities.*

Denton, C. A., & Hocker, J. (2006). *Responsive reading instruction: Flexible intervention for struggling readers in the early grades.* Longmont, CO: Sopris West.

Edformation, Inc. (2006). Assessment and improvement monitoring systems (AIMSweb). Eden Prairie, MN: Author.

Fuchs, L. S. (1995, May). *Incorporating curriculum-based measurement into the eligibility decision-making process: A focus on treatment validity and student growth.* Paper presented for the National Academy of Sciences Workshop on Alternatives to IQ testing, Washington, DC.

Fuchs, L. S. (2003). Assessing intervention responsiveness: Conceptual and technical issues. *Learning Disabilities Research and Practice, 18,* 172–186.

Fuchs, L. S., & Fuchs, D. (1998). Treatment validity: A unifying concept for reconceptualizing the identification of learning disabilities. *Learning Disabilities Research and Practice, 13,* 204–219.

Fuchs, L. S., & Fuchs, D. (2001). Using assessment data to account for and promote strong outcomes for students with disabilities. In D. Hallahan & B. Keough (Eds.), *Research and global perspectives in learning disabilities: Essays in honor of William Cruickshank* (pp. 93–110). Mahwah, NJ: Erlbaum.

Garan, E. M. (2005). Murder your darlings: A scientific response to the voice of evidence in reading research. *Phi Delta Kappan, 86,* 438–443.

Gersten, R., Fuchs, L. S., Williams, J. P., & Baker, S. (2001). Teaching reading comprehension strategies to students with learning disabilities: A review of research. *Review of Educational Research, 71,* 279–320.

Good, R. H., & Kaminski, R. A. (2003). Dynamic indicators of basic early literacy skills (DIBELS). Eugene, OR: University of Oregon Center on Teaching and Learning.

Individuals with disabilities education improvement act (IDEA). (2004). Retrieved September 13, 2006, from http://www.ed.gov/policy/speced/guid/idea/idea2004.html#law

Inhot, C., Mastoff, J., Gavin, J., & Hendrickson, L. (2001). *Read Naturally.* St. Paul, MN: Read Naturally.

International Reading Association. (2002). *Evidence-based reading instruction: Putting the National Reading Panel report into practice.* Newark, DE: Author.

Kozleski, E. B., Pugach, M., & Yinger, R. (2002). *Preparing teachers to work with students with disabilities: Possibilities and challenges for special and general teacher education.* Washington, DC: American Association for Colleges of Teacher Education.

Leach, J., Scarborough, H., & Rescorla, L. (2003). Late-emerging reading disabilities. *Journal of Educational Psychology, 95,* 211–224.

Lovett, M. W., Lacerenza, L., Borden, S., Frijters, J., Steinbach, K., & DePalma, M. (2000). Components of effective remediation for devel-opmental reading disabilities: Combining phonological and strategy-based instruction to improve outcomes. *Journal of Educational Psychology, 92,* 263–283.

Lyon, G. R. (2005). Why scientific research must guide educational policy and instructional practices in learning disabilities. *Learning Disability Quarterly, 28,* 140.

Marston, D. (2005). Tiers of intervention in responsiveness to intervention: Prevention outcomes and learning disabilities identification patterns. *Journal of Learning Disabilities, 38,* 539–544.

Mathes, P. G., Torgesen, J. K., Menchetti, J. C., Wahl, M., & Grek, M. K. (1999). *Proactive early intervention in reading.* (Teacher guides, daily lesson materials, and student activity books for first-grade reading intervention.) Columbus, OH: SRA/McGraw-Hill.

McGuiness, C., McGuiness, D., & McGuiness, G. (1996). Phono-Graphix: A new method for remediating reading disabilities. *Annals of Dyslexia, 46,* 73–96.

Meyer, M. S., & Felton, R. H. (1999). Repeated reading to enhance fluency: Old approaches and new directions. *Annals of Dyslexia, 49,* 283–306.

O'Connor, R. E., Harty, K. R., & Fulmer, D. (2005). Tiers of intervention in kindergarten through third grade. *Journal of Learning Disabilities, 38,* 532–538.

Rankin-Erickson, J. L., & Pressley, M. (2000). A survey of instructional practices of special education teachers nominated as effective teachers of literacy. *Learning Disabilities Research and Practice, 15,* 206–225.

Speece, D. L., & Case, L. (2001). Classification in context: An alternative to identifying early reading disability. *Journal of Educational Psychology, 93,* 735–749.

Torgesen, J. K., Alexander, A., Wagner, R. K., Rashotte, C., Voeller, K., & Conway, T. (2001). Intensive remedial instruction for children with severe disabilities: Immediate and long-term outcomes from two instructional approaches. *Journal of Learning Disabilities, 34*, 33–58.

U.S. Department of Education. (2003). *Twenty-fifth annual report to Congress on the Implementation of the Individuals with Disabilities Education Act.* Retrieved July 14, 2006, from http://www.ed.gov/about/reports/annual/osep/2003/25th-vol-1-sec-1.pdf

Vellutino, F., Scanlon, D., & Lyon, G. R. (2000). Distinguishing between difficult-to-remediate and readily remediated poor readers: More evidence against the IQ-achievement discrepancy definition of reading disability. *Journal of Learning Disabilities, 33*, 223–238.

Vellutino, F., Scanlon, D., Sipay, E., Small, S., Pratty, A., Chen, R., et al. (1996). Cognitive profiles of difficult-to-remediate and readily remediated poor readers: Early intervention as a vehicle for distinguishing between cognitive and experiential deficits as basic causes of specific reading disability. *Journal of Educational Psychology, 88*, 601–638.

Wagner, T. (2001). Leadership for learning: An action theory for school change. *Phi Delta Kappan, 82*, 378–383.

CHAPTER 15

Leading with Technology

Shelley B. Wepner, Liqing Tao, and Linda D. Labbo

Reading specialist Luke Orin works closely with his K–5 teachers to use technology to support and enhance their teaching. He is convinced that his teachers need to develop students' multi-literacies so that they can use both technology and traditional print media to communicate, access information, and learn. Luke collaborates with the district's technology coordinator to organize workshops at regular intervals throughout the year to develop teachers' skills. He wants to make sure that his teachers are competent with keyboarding, computer vocabulary, desktop navigation (find files, copy disks, use the control panel), web searching, word processing, and data management. He also wants to make sure that they experiment with using technology for literacy instruction, including the use of specific software packages and Web sites. He brings his mobile computer station to different classrooms to conduct demonstration lessons as a follow-up to the workshops. A technology specialist is available in his building to troubleshoot and assist with technological challenges.

Luke recently started a technology-based program with a local college that involves student teachers. The student teachers team teach with their assigned classroom teacher in his building for six literacy-based, technology lessons. The college supervisor, responsible for working with the student teacher, must be present for these lessons to offer assistance. Such a paradigm provides both incentive and support for the classroom teacher to use technology for literacy instruction. In return for hosting a student teacher, the classroom teacher is given a Smartboard and a portable lab of wireless computers for the classroom for the entire time that the student teacher is there.

In addition to promoting technology with teachers, Luke creates special technology-based programs for his students. He has his older student groups engage in virtual booktalks with students from other schools and other districts. He arranges the virtual booktalks with other reading specialists, and together they select specific books and develop questions and prompts for book discussions. His students are especially motivated to read and discuss the books assigned because of the virtual discussions with other students. He has his younger students reading electronic storybooks and working with the many Web-based activities related to these storybooks. All of his students use the computer for at least a third of the time that they work with him in a pull-out capacity.

Luke maintains the school's Web page for the reading program. He also maintains the school's electronic assessment system that includes records of students' formal and informal assessment results, anecdotal observations, and students' success with specific programs, materials,

and strategies. He uses the information from this system to initiate discussions with teachers and other specialists about students' learning trends.

Luke's work and leadership with technology is the result of his engaging in a time-consuming and painstaking learning process. He was willing to undertake this because he believes in the value of technology for literacy development, and knows that he needs to serve as a role model, motivator, and coach for his teachers to get them to use technology the way it should be used.

Luke has helped his teachers to add an important dimension to their teaching that definitely is in students' best interests. What do reading specialists, literacy coaches, and other reading personnel need to know to help their teachers and students use technology for literacy instruction? This chapter addresses this question as the following main topics are discussed:

- What leaders of literacy need to know about technology
- The development of students' multiliteracies
- Ideas for using technology for instruction and assessment
- Responsibilities of leaders of literacy for helping teachers use technology for literacy instruction

WHAT LEADERS OF LITERACY NEED TO KNOW ABOUT TECHNOLOGY

All of us use technology on a daily basis with different levels of navigational skill. We use cell phones, tape recorders, digital video recorders, and digital calendars for convenience, pleasure, and professional efficiency. Most of us do not read cover to cover the comprehensive, technical manual that accompanies these products. We simply cannot remember, and usually are not interested in remembering, all the details of these products' technical operations. Instead, we keep the manual somewhere close by and use it as the need arises. At the same time, we try to learn about the options that come with our technological products so that we can use them with as much ease as possible. Years of experience working with telephones, televisions, and other such products enable us to know enough about the purpose and basics that we can use technological upgrades almost immediately.

Much of this approach in using these everyday electronic devices applies to operating a computer. Years of experience with computers enable us to move from one brand of machine to the next, and from one computer upgrade to another, with a fair amount of ease. We use manuals and guides for information and tips about the unique features of a new platform or a new model, but seldom do we read them cover to cover.

Those new to technology are similar to those new to using other electronic devices in that certain levels of knowledge, skills, and practice are essential for developing independence with the machine. This section highlights basic technological knowledge and skills leaders of literacy need in three major areas: hardware and basic desktop commands, application programs, and electronic communication.

Knowledge of Hardware and Basic Desktop Commands

Our knowledge of computer hardware includes our ability to work with a central processing unit, monitor, keyboard, mouse, and printer. It also means working with disk drives, speakers, microphones, scanners, digital cameras, and video projection devices, especially if we are responsible for or called upon to demonstrate software or Web sites to students.

Navigating a computer desktop involves knowing how to start and shut down a system; how to find, open, copy, print, close, and save files to both the hard drive and storage media such as flash or floppy disks; how to install, open, and close programs; how to keep multiple programs in temporary memory; and how to use the operating system's control panel to adjust color, modify the design of a desktop, and change the date and time.

Knowledge of Application Programs

Application programs are the electronic tools of the trade. Word processing programs such as Microsoft Word enable us to write with greater flu-

ency, especially if we are facile with commands such as format, font, cut, copy, and paste. Multimedia tools such as PowerPoint help us to present ideas effectively and to help students do the same. Database management programs such as Microsoft Access help with class lists and student assignments; electronic spreadsheets such as Microsoft Excel help with grade calculations and budgets. Knowing how and when to use curricular applications for tutorial, drill and practice, and exploratory features for specific age and ability groups helps us work with students more effectively.

Knowledge of Electronic Communication

Communication commands, concepts, and software connect teachers and students to other people, places, and ports of information. Knowing how to use a Web browser such as Internet Explorer or Mozilla Firefox, how to send e-mail with attachments, how to use listservs, how to blog or do online journaling that is open to online visitors, and how to search for Web sites through search engines such as Google are vital for successful instruction and leadership in our field. Electronic communication generally falls into two broad categories: asynchronous, which is more like traditional written communication, and synchronous, which is more like traditional oral communication.

Asynchronous Communication. A time lag of some length characterizes asynchronous communication. The sender and receiver work independently, and each often waits to receive a message before composing and sending one. The communication style is therefore linear. It most typically occurs in writing, although voice messages also belong in this category. Examples of asynchronous communication include e-mail, key pals, distance learning, online instruction, and Web publishing.

E-mail is the most common form of asynchronous electronic communication. Its delivery time is fast, and the receiver can choose whether or when to respond. Beside speed, a benefit of e-mail is that one can communicate easily and cheaply with people in remote parts of the world. This easy and fast access motivates students to compose, read, and write, students who otherwise resist reading or writing much of anything at all in a traditional sort of assignment. Using the attachment function of e-mail can expand students' e-mail writing from the informal domain to formal writing. Key pals, or electronic pen pals, are typically students who use e-mail to correspond with students in other schools, providing students with extra opportunities of reading and writing.

Distance learning and online instruction are the electronic version of the correspondence courses of the past. Whether course content is provided through video, over the Internet, or in some combination as archived online lectures, electronic media makes it possible for people who are physically unable to meet in a traditional classroom to participate in a learning experience and a learning community.

Web publishing resembles the sharing of information in a journal article or term paper; it is a formal way of reporting on learning. But there are powerful differences. First, Web publishing allows for a much broader audience. Knowledge is not just delivered to one person but rather shared widely. Second, information that is published on a Web site can be enhanced with multimedia and usually cross-referenced to other material. These hyperlinks, created intentionally between one's knowledge and other sources, are indicators of the way technology enables learners to connect their knowledge with related ideas and resources. Blogging is a less formal but more interactive way of Web publishing, providing reading and writing experiences for all the participants through online personal journaling and commenting.

Synchronous Communication. Unlike asynchronous communication, synchronous communication happens in real time; the communication act is experienced simultaneously by sender and receiver. It is more like speech, even if the actual message is textual. Examples of synchronous communication include online chatting, instant messaging, teleconferencing, and electronic whiteboards.

Online chatting and instant messaging enable two or more people to enter text into an electronic space at the same time. Participants compose and post ideas in the same way a conversation flows at a dinner party. If there are more than two participants, a unified conversation can easily diverge into several threads of dialogue that coexist in the common space, much like two ends at a table breaking off into separate conversations.

Teleconferencing enables real-time oral conversations between widely dispersed participants. While teleconferencing offers a visual component, its use is somewhat restricted because it requires specific facilities on at least one site. A cheaper alternative would be to use Webcam technology. Electronic whiteboards, also called Smartboards, enable participants to view, comment on, or annotate material that "lives" on someone else's computer. Electronic whiteboards enable dispersed groups to work together on a presentation or project by seeing and editing that project at the same time, rather than sending drafts or versions around for review and revision. Extending the conferencing function into instruction, teachers use Smartboards for teaching in order to pull together different resources, handwrite on the board, and share board writing and resources with students as handouts and links in digital forms through networked, mobile computer labs.

In sum, these technological options offer access to new or additional resources for both teaching and learning. Teachers involved in professional listservs (asynchronous group e-mail) and e-mail with colleagues have an ever wider pool of ideas, recommended books, and tips about where to find good information on a particular topic. They may discover Web sites that have good maps or lesson plans to supplement a curricular unit. Teachers using technology are usually further motivated to keep up with instructionally relevant technology skills. Leaders of literacy need to help teachers realize the benefits of using technology and provide opportunities for teachers to explore them through professional development and through their own technology-based teaching.

THE DEVELOPMENT OF STUDENTS' MULTILITERACIES

Students use technology outside of school for entertainment, communication, and information.

Electronic devices such as cell phones, DVD players, IPODS, digital cameras, handheld computers, or desktop computers provide students with immediate access to people, ideas, and opportunities. The unique characteristics of technology requires users to develop corresponding skills to maximize their ability to use specific technologies. Educational technology often presents information in unique ways such as different pagination, animated graphics, and hypertextuality that requires students to develop multiliteracy skills in addition to their conventional literacy skills to access and maximize the use of such information.

Using Technology for School-Based Learning

Today's students need to become multiliterate so that they are equally facile in using traditional print, spoken language, and electronic media to function. Students who are multiliterate are flexible and resourceful and able to understand and use literacy and literacy practices with a range of texts and technologies to fully participate in a socially, culturally, and linguistically diverse world (Anstey, 2002; Anstey & Bull, 2006).

Today's teachers need to insure that their instruction is relevant to students by explicitly showing them the connection between their school-based world and lifeworld (Anstey & Bull, 2006). Teachers need to provide explicit modeling of technology use and, more important, engage students instructionally in various technology applications that are part of their life experience. Instructional procedures that build upon and promote students' lifeworld experiences with technology can create learning processes that are both cognitively constructive and internally motivating.

Communicating globally through electronic media is increasing students' interest in and use of the language arts of reading and writing. Key pals connect students with contexts and issues teachers previously had to fabricate on bulletin boards or evoke in filmstrips or videos. Many Web sites exist that are specifically designed for teachers who are looking for collaborative projects with schools all over the world, or for book discussions or curricular projects with students from such schools (see

U.S. Department of Education, 2006). These real-world communication opportunities stimulate nonwriters to create text and nonreaders to rush to school to read an e-mail posting.

Electronic research and presentation tools facilitate nonlinear searching for information and offer writers new strategies for organizing ideas and presenting information. Students are challenged to find and establish specific connections between ideas that are coherent and cognitively effective. Our challenge is to keep ahead of, or at least on par with, students so that we feel comfortable working collaboratively with them to share ideas and techniques.

Conducting online research has become a necessary skill for accessing information. Learning to search with Boolean operators is no longer an esoteric skill in the realm of the computer scientist, but rather a lifelong literacy skill. Teachers need to help students learn how to access and then sift through the huge amount of information available online and to establish more sophisticated and efficient selection and evaluation skills.

Even though many students may be facile with surfing the Web or accessing information, they need to apply research criteria and standards to online sources. The issues of giving credit to one's sources, staying within the limits of current copyright laws, and verifying the credibility and authority of a site are skills students need to learn to apply to online materials in the same way that they learn to apply them to print materials. The vast array of software and Web-based applications help students learn literacy skills and content knowledge across curricular areas (Wepner & Ray, 2000). These applications are especially useful when they are aligned with curricular goals and state standards. It is just a matter of sifting through Web site and software programs to locate the specific applications that will help students with the needed skills. A variety of commercial companies provide databases on software and on the Internet that match the specific content of curricular software with national or state curriculum standards (see Wasburn-Moses, 2006). Other Web sites, such as the California Learning Resource Network (http://www.clrn.org/home), differentiate software for subject and skill areas to help guide choices. Preview centers exist across the country in area education agencies, universities, and other publicly accessible sites where educators can review software before it is purchased. Moreover, most software companies offer 30–60-day preview policies to allow schools to return inappropriate software purchases.

> As part of the grant with his local college, Luke Orin created a Software–Web site Review Club, a group of teachers and students of varying ages and abilities who meet before and after school to review software and Web sites together and rate them according to specific characteristics. He uses this club to develop two annotated bibliographies, one for software and one for Web sites. The software bibliography includes information about location, platform compatibility, network capabilities, and the number of copies available within the district. The Web site bibliography is divided into sites that contain electronic books, sites about specific authors, and sites that focus on specific skills, and sites that focus on specific content.

Dealing with Access Issues

School districts must also grapple with important equity issues. How widely is technology really available to all students? What policies has your district put in place to ensure that all students have an equal opportunity to both learn how to use technology and to make use of that learned skill during and after school hours?

The so-called digital divide should end at the doorway of each school, whether it is a preschool or a high school, a classroom or a computer lab, a marine biology class or a remedial reading class, an urban, impoverished school or a suburban college preparatory showcase school. School district administrators should ask: Does each location have the same high-speed Internet connection? Do all locations have the same proportional number of computers with the same processor speeds and with the same peripheral devices? If not, why not?

Furthermore, district administrators should be able to ask questions about technology's usefulness and how to face the challenge of getting teachers to use them. Is technology in all of these locations being used to advance curricular achievement? Or do some schools continue to use software as a reward for early finishers (i.e., high-achieving students) or as a babysitter for students unable to participate in collaborative classroom work? Does the district choose to wink at the reluctance of some of the professional staff to embrace technology rather than to recognize that this reluctance restricts the opportunities for their students?

Leaders of literacy who are committed to the integration of technology into all areas of the curriculum need to take an active role in the distribution of computer hardware, software, training, and Internet access throughout the schools in a district. The following can serve as guidelines:

- Determine whether there are computers in each classroom or in computer labs, and/or laptop computers available for students and teachers' regular use.
- Tour the local public and college libraries in your area to make sure that students within your schools are learning the routines they will need to access material at these locations.
- Volunteer to serve on local committees that make decisions about what kinds of resources and research tools (DVD databases, subscription services, online catalogs, software, Internet access, or filtering software) are chosen for each site.
- Monitor the kinds of sign-up procedures for student computer use in place in each facility to ensure that all students have equal access to the learning, research, and communication tools that technology offers.
- Help your district or school establish "Acceptable Use Policies" to communicate with students about appropriate use of technology and to communicate with parents about your school's commitment to their children's safety and responsibility in using technology.

Technology, like any other instructional tool available, is only valuable when it is available consistently, fairly, and effectively for all learners. Efforts of leaders of literacy and teachers in ensuring technology access to all students for their learning would be an important step in promoting students' multiliteracies.

IDEAS FOR USING TECHNOLOGY FOR INSTRUCTION AND ASSESSMENT

Our goal is to help teachers see for themselves the value of technology for tailoring instruction and exposing students to new information and communication tools. Creative use of Web sites and software allows teachers to see the immediate benefits for students. Examples are provided below of teachers' use of Web sites and software along with guidelines for selecting and using such resources. Also discussed are ideas for using technology to support teachers' assessment efforts.

Web-Based Lessons

The teachers described in this section have incorporated Web sites into author studies, content area instruction, and general reading development. Third-grade teacher Kelly, for example, developed a Web-based author study on Kevin Henkes. She first read his book *Wemberly Worried* (2000) to her students, and then she had them go to the Web site about him (http://www.kevinhenkes.com) where they were to look for answers to questions about his life. She gave each student a small clipboard that contained index cards on which to note details about book titles, author biography, other works, and interesting information. Student pairs worked together at the Web site to research these four areas (Wepner, 2004).

On another occasion, Kelly developed a Web-based reading and science lesson. She had students read Mary Stolz's *Storm in the Night* (1998) as a springboard to a lesson on thunderstorms. She used students' responses from an initial exercise to develop questions for students to research at ThinkQuest's *Weather Gone Wild* (http://library.thinkquest.org/5818). Students worked in pairs to find answers to the questions that they were to note in their own teacher-made reporter folders, which again included index cards. As a follow-up, Kelly had a written worksheet for students to complete that was related to their research. Although the Web site is somewhat encyclopedic and has very few graphics, Kelly made sure that her students had a purpose for reading and had their own "reporter notebooks" to motivate them to do the work (Wepner, 2004).

Third-grade teacher Cheri developed a Web-based lesson using a Web site about the illustrator Jerry Pinkney (http://friend.ly.net/users/jorban/biographies/pinkneyjerry/index.htm). After students read *Jerry Pinkney: Achiever of Dreams* (Cooper, 1999) from their class reading anthology, they participated in an illustrator study by answering research questions on a worksheet that Cheri had created, such as What or who made Jerry Pinkney want to become an artist? Name three awards that Jerry Pinkney has won for his illustrations of children's books. As Cheri explained, this lesson took time because of the need to find the Web site, determine how to connect the information from the site to what students needed to learn, prepare an appropriate worksheet assignment, prepare the computers with the downloaded site, and organize the students into workable pairs (Wepner, 2004).

While Kelly and Cheri created their own Web-based lessons so they would be tailored to their reading anthology and curriculum standards, there are ready-made lessons and WebQuests for students to use for research. Dodge (1995) defines a *WebQuest* as "an inquiry-oriented activity in which some or all of the information that learners interact with comes from resources on the Internet" (p. 10). Dodge's own WebQuest site (http://webquest.sdsu.edu) along with *Kathy Schrock's Guide for Educators* (http://school.discovery.com/schrockguide/webquest/webquest.html) provide numerous examples of links to WebQuests for different grade levels and subjects.

While WebQuests provide specific activities for searching the Web, teachers can simply identify and use good Web sites for sustaining students' interest. First-grade teacher Mary found the Starfall Web site (http://www.starfall.com), a free service that supports children's learning to read with interactive books and rhyming word-family games that teach phonemic awareness, comprehension, vocabulary building, and spelling skills. First-grade teacher Kellyann found The Seven Continents Web site (http://www.cfschools.net/schools/veterans/218/t7con.html) where her first graders could take a virtual tour of the world. Second-grade teacher Nicole and her students celebrated Dr. Seuss online (http://www.seussville.com). The Seussville Web site highlighted things she had discussed with her students during their study of his works (Wepner, 2004).

Much has been written about the influence of the Internet on instruction (e.g., see Karchmer, 2001; Leu, 2000) because of the number of Web sites available for students. For example, there now are a number of Web sites that contain online stories and books (http://www.readwritethink.org, http://storiestogrowby .com, http://www.storyplus.com/Home.asp, and http://goodnightstories.com/stories .htm). Teachers need to discover for themselves that it is worth the time to have a Web-based lesson ready for the students. Good use of Web sites depends on the assignments and questions, and the age appropriateness of such assignments (Balajthy, 2000). It involves knowing what the students are developmentally ready to handle, and understanding the level of teacher guidance needed to help students feel successful. Although teachers cannot control the Web site's readability, and sites are not controlled for vocabulary the way published books are, teachers can still help students feel successful through their assignments.

If we want teachers to use Web sites effectively in their classrooms, we need to help them know how to do the following:

- Search for and bookmark appropriate Web sites.
- Adapt lessons to students' needs. Web site text is typically not leveled, and so it might not be appropriate for students' reading abilities.
- Develop assignments that help students process the information from the Web site.
- Make sure that Web sites are still up and running when they are ready to use them.
- Assess the value of the Web site by asking objective questions:
    Who is the author or producer of the site? What is his or her expertise?
    What is the author's affiliation? Is that relevant
    What is the purpose of the site, and does it fit students' needs?
    Who is the site's target audience? For what age group is the information appropriate?
    Is the page dated? When was the site last revised?
    What information on the site is important to the students' lesson, research, or assignment?
    Is the text readable, grammatically correct, and correctly spelled?

We also need to help teachers ask themselves the following questions when developing a Web site assignment:

- What is the purpose of making this assignment?
- Can the students navigate the Web site independently, or will they need assistance? If navigational assistance is needed, who is going to provide it?
- What is the level of keyboarding needed for working with a Web site? Appropriate Web site assignments at the primary level should not require more than letter position mastery. Web site assignments at the upper elementary grades can call for "touch typing" because students in these grades have developed the dexterity and finger span required (Sullivan & Sharp, 2000).
- What type of assignment is needed to maximize students' interaction with the Web site?
- What type of instruction is needed to help students work through the assignment?
- In the event that a technical problem affects students' use of the Web site, what arrangements can be made so the problem can be remedied?

Software-Based Lessons

Software most typically includes CD-ROMs and DVDs. Because they are commercially prepared as individual packages, software programs for reading and writing development are usually leveled in their text presentation and are appropriate for the targeted grade levels, which can be readily used by teachers for instructional purposes. However, unlike Web sites, software upgrades and simultaneous use by multiple users may be constrained by budget and license issues. Furthermore, software is usually created for an individual audience, making it more appropriate for individual learning. The most common examples of literacy software fall into four main categories: those that develop students' alphabetic skills, including letter knowledge and phonics; those that assist with fluency, vocabulary words, and comprehension; those that promote writing or help with writing; and those that focus on assisting special needs students. Given current technology opportunities, software is usually used in combination with the Internet and/or with traditional books. The following examples describe how each type of software is used.

Alphabetic Skills. In her preschool class of 12 students, Ruth used Chicka Chicka Boom Boom (1996) software and its namesake book by Bill Martin, Jr., and John Archambault (1989) to explore and consolidate her students' knowledge of letters. Ruth read the book aloud to her preschoolers so that they could hear the rhythms of sentences, in which letters were personified and performed repeated actions that highlighted the repeated sentence patterns. Children in her class sang along with her in reading the repeated phrase: "I'll meet with you at the top of the coconut tree." Afterwards, the students were given the opportunity to explore the book in the library corner and the software in the computer station with headphones at the back of the classroom. The color, animation, text-to-speech functions, and pagination hotspots of the software version allowed her children to control their pace through the digital book and further interact with the active letters in sequence as they replaced each other at the top of the coconut tree and eventually slid down to the ground. A teacher-created worksheet with a target letter such as *B* on the coconut treetop let students practice tracing the letter through crayon coloring. The lesson included teacher modeling, direct instruction of letters, student letter exploration with voice support from the computer, and additional kinetic stimulation through coloring the work sheet. The software supported and reinforced students' letter knowledge acquisition in a gamelike format.

Fluency, Vocabulary, and Comprehension. The software program Breakthrough to Literacy, Version 6.2 (2004), provided Ruth's students with animated talking books for the corresponding titles in print. Ruth read a big book from the program to her students every week. In using Raymond Briggs's *The Snowman* (1986), Ruth intended to improve her students' oral comprehension by talking about the story and explaining print concepts. She read aloud and did a think-aloud of the big book to highlight the correspondence between pictures and sentences, and identify environmental labels related to constructing a snowman built by the character, a lonely boy. Students then could read on their own the small books as well as the talking book *Snowman* on the computer to support their interaction with print and pictures. On the computer, individual students recorded and listened to their own retellings of the story. Ruth used these retellings for her own evaluation of students' oral comprehension later on.

Older students who use *Breakthrough to Literacy* can take advantage of the interactive features of the program such as controlled read alongs, recording of retellings, and animated graphics to develop fluency, vocabulary, and comprehension through individual or group work on and off the computer.

Writing. Third-grade teacher Chad used Kidspiration 2.1 (2006) to have students develop ideas for writing their stories. Kidspiration 2.1 is a software program created for K–5 learners to help build graphic organizers by combining pictures, text, and spoken words to represent thoughts and information. After having students read a story about blizzards in their class anthology, Chad demonstrated how the software program can be used to develop ideas. He then had his students work in pairs to create with their portable computers a Venn diagram of items that are useful, not useful, or useful to special groups for surviving the winter months. They used many of the symbols from the software's symbols library to include in their Venn diagram. He then guided them to use their Venn diagram to begin their informational story about items that they should consider having in order to survive the winter.

Other writing software packages that support students' writing development include: Kid Pix Deluxe 4 (2004), Print Shop 22 Deluxe (2006), Student Writing Center (2002), and StoryBook Weaver Deluxe (2004). As discussed in Chapter 11, such desktop publishing, drawing and painting, and presentation software packages should be integrated into a school's writing program to contribute to students' literacy development.

Assistance with Special Needs. Second-grade teacher Cathy used the computer program Dr. Peet's Talk/Writer (2002) to increase her English language learners' familiarity with English spellings. To help English language learners develop skills in writing English words, Dr. Peet's Talk/Writer says aloud a letter name when students press the letter key, and pronounces a whole word when the space bar is pressed. A talking picture dictionary lends extra help by matching the concepts in a picture with the words spoken. As students type their sentences, the software program says aloud what the students have typed. This feature helps students hear what they are writing. It is particularly useful for English language learners because it helps with their transition to English reading and writing at their individual paces. Cathy saw the benefit of having such a program for her second-language learners because it provides assisted reading and writing activities at their levels that enhance their understanding of English language. *Dragon Naturally Speaking 9* (2006) is another more advanced program for voice recognition and text speaking.

No matter what category of literacy software is considered for use, we need to help teachers give careful thought to the software's alignment with national and state standards for the appropriate grades, as with any type of instructional material. To make full use of software, a teacher should also consider a software's durability. For example, how easy is it to upgrade the software from the vendors? How easy is it to obtain a durable site license for running the software on one machine and multiple machines? We do not have to expect teachers to be experts of technology, but they should be savvy consumers of software.

Evaluation criteria for selecting software should be developed and used. Published guidelines can be adopted or adapted (e.g., see Wepner, Valmont, & Thurlow, 2000), or informal guidelines can be developed that address specific needs of the school. Because of the prevalence of CD-ROM storybooks, we offer the following evaluation criteria developed by Shamir and Korat (2006) as an example of the types of features to consider to facilitate effective use of software:

- Age level of the software, including story structure appropriateness such as simple plot or complex plot; and written register appropriateness such as literate language, font size, amount of text presentation on each screen, and highlighted written text
- Child-control features that allow for separate modes such as read and play and read alone; text reading options modes such as controlling where to read; dictionary option; print option; and options for activating illustrations

- Clear instructions that are simple and accurate, accompanied by illustrations, and expressed verbally
- Support of children's independence such that mastery of the program is achieved with minimal help
- Process orientation that promotes discovery, matches activations with story content, and includes a separate game mode
- Technical features that provide easy installation and handling

Technology for Assessment

Technology holds promise for literacy assessment. It has great capacity for capturing useful data, including the ability to record and store verbal information, track process data, categorize parsed verbal information syntactically and thematically, and provide a platform for standardized assessments. However, technology assessment is still limited to low-level, skill-based assessment. Assessments that employ solely multiple-choice questions and true-false questions, as is the case with standardized tests, can be performed through technology. Technology can assess students' responses to preset types of questions on phonics, vocabulary, and comprehension. Many commercial software packages include some type of low-level, skill-based assessment. For example, Breakthrough to Literacy has preset questions to assess students' comprehension and vocabulary, and can track students' progress in these areas.

Naturalistic and authentic assessments that are most informative to classroom teachers are not technologically available yet. Eventually, digital recording devices should be able to record students' oral reading and think-alouds for later analysis; voice recognition devices could be useful in capturing and transcribing students' retelling; and different types of software should be able to analyze students' writing samples.

Even when such technology is available for teachers' use, it will not be a replacement for their judgment. For example, in doing a running record, a miscue analysis, an oral phonemic awareness assessment, a think-aloud assessment of comprehension, or an analysis of a piece of writing, teachers would still need to use their own professional knowledge and judgment to understand their students' strengths and weaknesses in order to appropriately direct instruction. Technology will not really assess students' literacy competencies or truly determine students' processes for developing literacy. Teachers would still be the decision makers, but could be assisted by technological assessment tools. Leaders of literacy should help teachers understand the possibility and limitations of using technology for assessment, and help them grow into using such tools as they become available for helping assess students' literacy growth.

In concluding this section, we believe it is important to remember that, especially in the beginning, teachers take twice as long—if not more than that—to create lessons that use technology. Not only do they have to create the lesson plan for using technology, but they also need to have back-up lessons prepared in the event that the technology fails. As a student teacher said to one of us, "Preparing for technology-based lessons takes a lot longer than preparing for traditional lessons. I spent 2 hours looking at Web sites and an hour testing the computers." Whatever we can do to help teachers use technology constructively in their classrooms will contribute to their willingness to experiment and explore.

RESPONSIBILITIES OF LEADERS OF LITERACY FOR HELPING TEACHERS USE TECHNOLOGY FOR LITERACY INSTRUCTION

Let us clarify how quickly technology has been assimilated: In 1998, computers with Internet connections were in more than 90% of schools, and more than 40% of 4th- through 12th-grade classrooms (Becker, 1999; Schlager, 2000). As of 2003, nearly 100% of the nation's public K–12 schools and 93% of the classrooms had direct access to the Internet (Wells & Lewis, 2006). Moreover, in 2003, 82% of public schools were offering professional development to their teachers on how to integrate the Internet into the curriculum (Wells & Lewis, 2006). The ever-increasing presence of technology in the schools and the ever-growing opportunities for its instructional use make it compelling for leaders of

literacy to be aware of how its use affects teaching and learning, and how to promote technology for instruction and assessment. Ironically, the problems with the quantity and quality of technology use are the same problems that existed years ago: convenient access, professional development, and time. This next section describes what you can do to help yourself to help others use technology for literacy instruction.

Get Yourself Involved

In order to advocate for the use of technology, you need to appreciate its value and use it frequently enough to be aware of technology's integral role in the lives of students. After all, there isn't a company today that doesn't have a Web site. Local bus schedules and school bulletin boards are accessible on Web sites. Print, radio, and television ads include Web site addresses.

Use the K-W-L instructional framework (Ogle, 1986) to find out what you *know,* what you *want* to learn, and what you have *learned* and still need to learn. Then look for assistance from colleagues, friends, and family. Attend workshops and courses, especially those offered by your school district, universities, and professional organizations. Observe others using technology. Find a buddy you trust to introduce you to some of the rudimentary skills. Obtain a software package such as one of the many versions of Mavis Beacon Teaches Typing 17 (2005) or SpongeBob SquarePants Typing Software (2004) to help with keyboarding skills.

Look to colleges and universities for technology support and tutoring. As you seek assistance, identify the kind of expert you need: Web expert, machine expert, software expert, or systems expert. The technology field has become so complicated and specialized that any one "expert" in technology may not necessarily have the specific expertise that you need. Acknowledge that you need access, training, and time to really become proficient with technology. Be certain to get some form of professional development every year not only to learn about the latest technologies and accompanying application packages but also to fill in the gaps of what you still need to learn. Professional development could take various forms: workshops, participation in collaborative grant opportunities, short courses, online tutorials, participation in technology conferences, and consultation with local education colleges, schools, or departments.

The goal should be that technology is almost an invisible part of the curriculum. The focus should be not so much on technology itself but on its use as a resource for learning, data collection and analysis, and communication. If our teachers see that we are doing this for ourselves and for them, they in turn will do it for their students.

Part of our ability to deliver professional development to our teachers requires an awareness of what our school districts and schools, and neighboring schools and districts, expect from students. Informal needs assessments help to find out what is available in support, personnel, resources, and professional development, and what is actually happening in the classrooms, the labs, and the community. Observations, conversations, interviews, and e-mail with contacts within the district and outside the district help us gather information. It is then possible to use existing resources from our school districts, schools, and community agencies to help get started.

Luke Orin is fortunate to have state-of-the-art technology in his school and to work in an area where technology is valued by other school districts. You might be working in a school district that has very limited technology. If so, think of ways to look beyond your school and district for technology support. Look to colleges and universities to form a Professional Development School where the college's faculty have a vested interest in your teachers and students. Collaborate on grant writing to seek technology for your teachers. Luke's student teacher, technology-based project actually comes from a grant that was collaboratively written by his school and a local college.

Recommended Resources. An excellent resource for establishing competencies is the International Society for Technology in Education's (2007) publication, *National Educational Technology Standards for Students, Second Edition*. This guide identifies technology standards at each level, including English language arts, for both preservice teachers and pre-K–12 students which help determine what we need to know for the students that we teach, whether in pre-K–12 or teacher education.

Books, magazines, professional journals, and Web sites also offer information and insights about technology's influence on learning. *Growing Up Digital: The Rise of the Net Generation* (Tapscott, 2006) talks about the shift in learning paradigms resulting from the growth of the Internet, particularly from linear to hypermedia learning, and from instruction to construction and discovery (Rhodes, 2000). The American Association of Colleges for Teacher Education's monograph, *Log On or Lose Out: Technology in 21st-Century Teacher Education* (2000), addresses issues related to teaching and technology. Many of the issues—ethical and social use, commercialization in the classroom, and assessment—are the same issues that we as literacy educators need to address. The International Reading Association's book by Anstey and Bull (2006), *Teaching and Learning Multiliteracies: Changing Times, Changing Literacies*, introduces the concept of multiliteracies and its implications for instruction. The book provides examples of activities that can be implemented at the classroom or school level. A listing of Recommended Resources can be found at the end of this chapter.

Also be aware of any research that supports technology use for literacy development (e.g., Hasselbring, Goin, Taylor, Bottge, & Daley, 1997; Labbo, 1996; Shiah, Mastropieri, & Scruggs, 1995) as well as the undercurrents of skepticism that question technology's merits (e.g., Armstrong & Casement, 2001; Cordes & Miller, 1999; Healy, 1998). This helps you to become an informed consumer and decision maker as you get more and more involved.

Identify Significant Others Who Can Help You Move Forward

Find an expert teacher or technotutor in your school or district who can and will teach teachers the skills needed for working with technology. Technotutors are teachers with certain areas of technological expertise who make office calls to tutor faculty on, for example, creating Web pages or searching the Internet. Teachers know to contact a technotutor hotline for their queries, and a technotutor with the appropriate expertise gets assigned.

Form an in-school or across-school teacher network for support and assistance. For example, second-grade teacher Maria who uses computers in her class has found that she can use her prep time to meet with other teachers who share her interest in technology and discuss ways of using technology in their classes. The informal meetings have become very important for her to share her ideas, listen to others, and discuss what works and what does not work for their students and what technology skills their students are developing. Maria looks forward to, cherishes, and protects such time with her like-minded colleagues.

Work with others from both pre-K–12 and higher education interested in pursuing technology projects. For instance, sixth-grade language arts teacher Joan has students do electronic literature response journals, and uses graduate students from a literacy course to serve as electronic buddies to her students. These graduate students read the same books as the sixth graders and then communicate through e-mail about the books to help raise the sixth graders' level of response to the books that they read (Wepner, 2004).

Fourth-grade teacher Fred found a university faculty member who teaches a graduate-level educational technology course. She created an assignment to research appropriate Web sites for fourth-grade children on specific topics from the fourth-grade curriculum. Together, Fred and the faculty member determined specific characteristics needed for a Web site to be recommended.

There are also examples of professors of reading/language arts methods courses who pair their students with classes of students in local school districts. Roe (2000) paired her students with seventh graders in a middle school to discuss literature selections that both groups were reading. The partners communicated about the selections through regularly scheduled e-mail exchanges. The university students used this assignment as an opportunity to apply the literary analysis and reading strategies learned in the methods courses. In another course, Kariuki and Turner (2001) provided preservice teachers with laptop computers for a yearlong project in an elementary school. Preservice teachers used the computers to help elementary students create electronic portfolios. The use of the laptops created unique occasions for accomplishing several goals for the preservice teachers that include (a) providing quick access to computers, (b) developing confidence in technology-related teaching, (c)

being effective participants in the electronic information era, and (d) serving as a role model for classroom teachers.

Maring, Levy, and Schmid (2002) followed a cybermentoring approach to guide university-school partnerships. Cybermentoring is a form of online collaboration whereby preservice teachers use Internet communicative tools to mentor and support the learning of elementary students. The projects, which ranged in focus from writing newspaper articles to learning about dinosaurs, were centered on content and used technology as a tool to develop literacy strategies. The authors report that the projects were meaningful for all participants, produced integrated literacy and content area opportunities, and resulted in positive effects on students' learning outcomes.

Create a Professional Development Plan

A professional development plan for the teaching staff needs to be crafted similarly to the way we plan instruction for students. For instance, a combination of whole-group, small-group, and individual instruction, with ample time set aside for practice and feedback, should be planned. Teachers need to develop specific competencies by learning how to

- Use software and Web sites for the five components of reading: phonemic awareness, phonics, fluency, comprehension, and vocabulary
- Handle equipment, and use basic desktop and electronic applications for data management and the expression of ideas
- Communicate electronically with others through both asynchronous and synchronous modes
- Use the Web to conduct online research as a reference tool and an instructional tool
- Mix and match software, Web sites, and communication tools to develop appropriate assignments and material to accompany the use of technology during a lesson
- Prepare the lesson's sequence, taking into account students' technology skills, and organize the students for instruction
- Develop a mechanism for assessing students' achievements (Labbo, 2005; Pearman & Lefever-

Davis, 2006; Strong, Wepner, Furlong, & Wartenberg, 2000; Wasburn-Moses, 2006; Wepner, 2004)

These competencies help teachers meet the standards prescribed in the International Society for Technology in Education's *National Educational Technology Standards for Teachers: Preparing Teachers to Use Technology* (2002) that identify what teachers should be able to do in their classrooms.

Teachers will be motivated to become proficient with technology when it is easy and worthwhile to do. One incentive for teachers is to see the impact of technology on students' enthusiasm for learning. Another incentive is the creation of annual goals that teachers must accomplish, usually through a Professional Improvement Plan. The goals should be realistic, and need to be created with the principal so that they are part of a teacher's annual evaluation. Grade-level or content area teachers can get together to decide what they can reasonably accomplish with the resources available.

A buddy system can be created for teachers to help each other. For example, two third-grade teachers, Mimi and Christine, who are following the same curriculum in their classrooms created the same technology-based lessons together, helping each other develop interdisciplinary lessons, identify appropriate Web sites, and create worksheets and assignments (Wepner & Tao, 2002). Since they have to share the wireless, portable lab, they created a schedule that enables them to do their technology-based lessons at different times or on different days. They pool their instructional materials budget to get additional software, help each other with troubleshooting issues, and work together during their planning time and after school to review and revise their lessons to accommodate students' needs.

Teachers who are active users can use faculty meetings or professional development sessions to demonstrate what they are doing in their classrooms and to provide positive peer pressure. Tapping national resources, such as the Presidential Award for Reading and Technology, cosponsored by the International Reading Association and PLATO Learning (http://reading.org/association/awards/teachers_presidential.html), helps to reward those involved with inspiring technology initiatives. This

award honors educators in Grades K–12 who are making an outstanding and innovative contribution to the use of technology in reading education.

Access to trouble shooting is essential, whether it is a school-based person, a hotline, or someone from the community (e.g., a retired person) who can help. As with any change, it is important to celebrate steady, slow, and continuous progress, rather than push for an overnight overhaul of pedagogical practice.

It also is critically important to be sensitive to what it takes for a teacher to use technology. Two of us (Liqing and Shelley) actually examined ways in which classroom teachers' responsibilities change as a result of teaching with technology. We found through interviews and classroom observations that teachers' responsibilities shift considerably. They need to devote more time to their professional development to acquire the necessary technology and technical knowledge. They must spend more time planning and organizing for instruction and arranging for the availability and usefulness of equipment. They also need to come to accept that, even as veteran teachers, they are humbled by their lack of technology proficiency (Wepner & Tao, 2002).

Part of acknowledging the shifting responsibilities associated with integrating technology into the curriculum is figuring out what your teachers already know and are doing, and what skills and resources they need to acquire to function at the next level in their development. Figure 15.1 provides an observation checklist that you can use to determine your teachers' evidence of planning, knowledge, skills, technical skills, and instructional management. The checklist consists of frequency checks and descriptive observations. The frequency checks indicate the number of times that you observe evidence of an item within a category. Items within some categories such as planning probably would be observed only once. Any observations noted that do not fit into the checklist categories can be noted in descriptive terms under "Comments." This checklist can be used to determine individual, grade-level, content area, and schoolwide needs of your teachers. Once you use the checklist to determine both accomplishments and needs with technology, there are ways in which you can support teachers to cope with the expectation of using technology:

Figure 15.1. Observation Checklist

Teacher's name: _____	Date/time of observation: _____
Topic: _____	Number of students in class: _____

Time/Activity	**Evidence of Planning**	**Frequency**	**Comments**
	Checked out Web sites	_____	
	Planned for appropriate equipment	_____	
	Created schedule for students' time with computer	_____	
	Invited others into classrooms to help	_____	
	Worked out logistics of getting each student the same exposure to technology	_____	
	Other _____	_____	

	Evidence of Knowledge	**Frequency**	**Comments**
	Technology vocabulary used	_____	
	Keyboarding terms	_____	
	Word processing terms	_____	
	Internet terms	_____	
	Hardware terms	_____	
	Database terms	_____	
	Spreadsheet terms	_____	
	Communication terms	_____	
	CD-ROM/laserdisc terms	_____	
	Multimedia terms	_____	
	Other _____	_____	

	Evidence of Skills	**Frequency**	**Comments**
	Keyboarding	_____	
	Word processing	_____	
	Internet	_____	
	Hardware	_____	
	Database	_____	
	Spreadsheet	_____	
	Communication	_____	
	Other: _____	_____	

	Evidence of Technical Skills	**Frequency**	**Comments**
	Troubleshooting hardware	_____	
	Troubleshooting software	_____	
	Knowledge of person(s) to seek to fix problem	_____	
	Other: _____	_____	

	Evidence of Instructional Management	**Frequency**	**Comments**
	Pairing students	_____	
	Being available to students working on computers	_____	
	Going to "Plan B"	_____	
	Making sure students go to appropriate sites	_____	
	Giving students opportunities to explore	_____	
	Giving clear directions	_____	
	Creating worksheets for the Internet	_____	
	Training students to be independent	_____	
	Assessing students' computer skills (discussing internet)	_____	
	Other: _____	_____	

Source. "From master teacher to master novice: Shifting responsibilities in technology-infused classrooms," by S.B. Wepner and L. Tao, 2002, *The Reading Teacher, 55,* p. 645. Copyright © 2002 by the International Reading Association.

- Help teachers recognize that integrating technology into the literacy curriculum is an evolutionary process that has fits and starts in functionality and practicality.
- Facilitate planning, instructional, and assessment partnerships between teachers so that they help each other save time.
- Help teachers understand the "Plan B" phenomenon with technology in that teachers need to know how to immediately shift gears when something goes awry technologically.
- Work with administrators to get as much equipment and technical assistance as possible for teachers. Help identify grant opportunities and possible partnerships that could lead to funds for such resources.
- Work with administrators to develop professional development opportunities for teachers that include coursework, hands-on presentations, and coaching. Push to have someone in your building with technological expertise to serve as a coach and technical assistant for teachers.
- Work with teachers and administrators to determine available times during the day and week that can be used to develop technology-based lessons.
- Work with teachers and administrators to determine ways to promote technology use (e.g., provide time at each faculty meeting for teachers to share newly created technology-based lessons or have a technology tip of the week posted on school Web site) and ways to hold administrators and teachers accountable for helping to promote technology use in the schools.

CONCLUSION

Our leadership as professionals depends on our ability to be on the cutting edge of what is current in the field, not just with technology but in all aspects of literacy. As we change, we need to bring others along so we are in charge of determining how our students are taught. As we encounter issues of equity and use, we need to take the time to address them so that we determine technology's availability and accessibility. As we expand our definition of literacy to include electronic tools, we need to share our knowledge with our colleagues.

We need to grow with technology the way we do with other new developments in our field, especially during this era of standards-based education, high-stakes testing, and accountability so that we can continue to steer our programs and constituencies with near-perfect vision.

REFERENCES

American Association of Colleges for Teacher Education (Ed.). (2000). *Log on or lose out: Technology in 21st-century teacher education.* Washington, DC: American Association of Colleges for Teacher Education and the ERIC Clearinghouse on Teaching and Teacher Education.

Anstey, M. (2002). *Literate futures: Reading.* Coorparoo, Australia: State of Queensland Department of Education.

Anstey, M., & Bull, G. (2006). *Teaching and learning multiliteracies: Changing times, changing literacies.* Newark, DE: International Reading Association.

Armstrong, A., & Casement, C. (2001). *The child and the machine: How computers put our children's education at risk.* Beltsville, MD: Robins Lane Press.

Balajthy, E. (2000). Is technology worth my professional time, resources, and efforts? In S. B. Wepner, W. J. Valmont, & R. Thurlow (Eds.), *Linking literacy and technology: A guide for K–8 classrooms* (pp. 203–217). Newark, DE: International Reading Association.

Becker, H. J. (1999). *Internet use by teachers: Conditions of professional use and teacher-directed student use. Teaching, learning, and computing: 1998 national survey.* Irvine, CA, and Minneapolis, MN: University of California at Irvine and University of Minnesota, Center for Research on Information Technology and Organizations.

Breakthrough to Literacy, Version 6.2 [Computer software]. (2004). Coralville, IA: Wright Group/McGraw Hill.

Briggs, R. (1986). *The snowman.* London: Hamish Hamilton.

Chicka Chicka Boom Boom [Computer software]. (1996). New York: Davidson.

Cooper, I. (1999). Jerry Pinkney: Achiever of dreams. In *Signatures: Wings* (pp. 96–102). Orlando, FL: Harcourt Brace.

Cordes, C., & Miller, E. (Eds.). (1999). *Fool's gold: A critical look at computers in childhood.* Available at Alliance for Childhood Web site: http://www.allianceforchildhood.net/projects/computers/computers_reports_fools_gold_download.htm

Dodge, B. (1995). WebQuests: A technique for Internet-based learning. *Distance Educator, 1*(2), 10–13.

Dragon Naturally Speaking 9 [Computer software]. (2006). Burlington, MA: Nuance Communications.

Dr. Peet's Talk/Writer [Computer software]. (2002). New Smyrna Beach, FL: Interest-Driven Learning.

Hasselbring, T. S., Goin, L., Taylor, R., Bottge, B., & Daley, D. (1997). The computer doesn't embarrass me. *Educational Leadership, 55*(3), 30–33.

Healy, J. M. (1998). *Failure to connect: How computers affect our children's minds—for better and worse.* New York, NY: Simon and Schuster.

Henkes, K. (2000). *Wemberly Worried.* New York: Scholastic.

International Society for Technology in Education. (2007). *National educational technology standards for students, Connecting curriculum and technology.* Eugene, OR: International Society for Technology in Education. Retrieved September 2007, from www.iste.org/inhouse/nets/cnets/index.html

International Society for Technology in Education. (2002). *National educational technology standards for teachers: Preparing teachers to use technology.* Eugene, OR: International Society for Technology in Education. Retrieved April 2007, from http://www.iste.org/inhouse/nets/cnets/teachers/t_book.html

Internet Explorer [Computer software]. (1999). Redmond, WA: Microsoft.

Karchmer, R. A. (2001). The journey ahead: Thirteen teachers report how the Internet influences literacy and literacy instruction in their K–12 classrooms. *Reading Research Quarterly, 36*, 442–466. Retrieved May 2004, from www.ingentaselect.com/ira/00340553/v36n4/contp1–1.htm

Kariuki, M., & Turner, S. (2001). Creating electronic portfolios using laptops: A learning experience for preservice teachers, elementary school pupils, and elementary school teachers. *Journal of Technology and Teacher Education, 9.* http://www.questia.com/PM.qst?a=o&se=gglsc&d=5002438779&er=deny

KidPix Deluxe 4 [Computer software]. (2004). San Francisco, CA: The Learning Company.

Kidspiration 2.1 [Computer software]. (2006). Beaverton, OR: Inspiration.

Labbo, L. D. (1996). A semiotic analysis of young children's symbol making in a classroom computer center. *Reading Research Quarterly, 31*, 356–385.

Labbo, L. D. (2005). Books and computer response activities that support literacy development. *The Reading Teacher, 59*, 288–292.

Leu, D. J., Jr. (2000). Continuously changing technologies and envisionments for literacy: Deictic consequences for literacy education in an information age. In M. Kamil, P. Mosenthal, P. D. Pearson, & R. Barr (Eds.), *Handbook of reading research* (Vol. 3, pp. 743–770). Mahwah, NJ: Erlbaum.

Maring, G. H., Levy, E. W., & Schmid, J. A. (2002). Variations on a cybermentoring theme: Six literacy projects involving preservice teachers and students across grade levels. *Reading Online, 6*(4). Retrieved April 2007 from http://www.readingonline.org/articles/art_index.asp?HREF=maring2/index.html

Martin, B., Jr., & Archambault, J. (1989). *Chicka chicka boom boom.* New York: Simon & Schuster.

Mavis Beacon Teaches Typing 17 [Computer software]. (2005). San Francisco, CA: Broderbund/The Learning Company.

Ogle, D. (1986). K-W-L: A teaching model that develops active reading and expository text. *The Reading Teacher, 39*, 564–570.

Pearman, C. J., & Lefever-Davis, S. (2006). Supporting the essential elements with CD-ROM storybooks. *Reading Horizons, 46*, 301–313.

Print Shop 22 Deluxe [Computer software]. (2006). San Francisco, CA: The Learning Company.

Roe, B. D. (2000). Using technology for content area literacy. In S. B. Wepner, W. J. Valmont, & R. Thurlow (Eds.), *Linking literacy and technology: A guide to K–8 classrooms* (pp. 133–158). Newark, DE: International Reading Association.

Rhodes, E. M. (2000). The impact of technology on how we learn: Implications for teacher education. In American Association of Colleges for Teacher Education (Ed.), *Log on or lose out: Technology in 21st-century teacher education* (pp. 69–73). Washington, DC: Author.

Schlager, M. (2000). Communities of practice as catalysts for a revitalized teaching profession. In American Association of Colleges for Teacher Education (Ed.), *Log on or lose out: Technology in 21st-century teacher education* (pp. 202–208). Washington, DC: Author.

Shamir, A., & Korat, O. (2006). How to select CD-ROM storybooks for young children: The teacher's role. *The Reading Teacher, 59*, 532–543.

Shiah, R.-L., Mastropieri, M. A., & Scruggs, T. (1995). Computer-assisted instruction and students with learning disabilities: Does research support the rhetoric? *Advances in Learning and Behavioral Disabilities, 9*, 161–192.

SpongeBob Squarepants Typing Software. [Computer software]. (2004). San Francisco, CA: Broderbund/The Learning Company.

Stolz, M. (1998). *Storm in the night.* New York: HarperCollins.

Storybook Weaver Deluxe [Computer software]. (2004). San Francsico, CA: The Learning Company.

Strong, M. W., Wepner, S. B., Furlong, M. J., & Wartenberg, A. D. (2000). Philosophical dilemmas in undergraduate and graduate literacy programs. In *Literacy at a New Horizon: The Twenty-Second Yearbook: A peer reviewed publication of the College Reading Association* (pp. 131–145). Readyville, TN: College Reading Association.

Student Writing Center [Computer software]. (2002). San Francisco, CA: The Learning Company.

Sullivan, J., & Sharp, L. (2000). Using technology for writing development. In S. B. Wepner, W. J. Valmont, & R. Thurlow (Eds.), *Linking literacy and technology: A guide to K–8 classrooms* (pp. 106–132). Newark, DE: International Reading Association.

Tapscott, D. (2006). *Growing up digital: The rise of the Net generation.* New York: McGraw-Hill.

U.S. Department of Education. (2006). http://www.ed.gov/teachers/how/tech/international/guide_pg2.html).

Wasburn-Moses, L. (2006). 25 best Internet sources for teaching reading. *The Reading Teacher, 60,* 70–75.

Wells, J., & Lewis, L. (2006). *Internet access in U.S. public schools and classrooms: 1994–2005* (NCES 2007–020). Washington, DC: National Center for Education Statistics. Retrieved February 2, 2007, from http://nces.ed.gov/pubs2007/2007020.pdf

Wepner, S. B. (2004, May/June). Technology run amok: Top ten technoblunders. *Reading Online, 7*(6). Retrieved April 2007, from http://www.readingonline.org/electronic/elec_index.asp?HREF=wepner2/index.html

Wepner, S. B., & Ray, L. (2000). Using technology for reading development. In S. B. Wepner, W. J. Valmont, & R. Thurlow (Eds.), *Linking literacy and technology: A guide to K–8 classrooms* (pp. 76–105). Newark, DE: International Reading Association.

Wepner, S. B., Valmont, W. J., & Thurlow, R. (Eds.). (2000). *Linking literacy and technology: A guide to K–8 classrooms.* Newark, DE: International Reading Association.

Wepner, S. B., & Tao, L. (2002). From master teacher to master novice: Shifting responsibilities in technology-infused classrooms. *The Reading Teacher, 55,* 642–651.

RECOMMENDED RESOURCES

Books

Designed for Beginners

Kent, P. (2001). *The complete idiot's guide to the Internet* (7th ed.). Indianapolis, IN: Que Publications.

Helpful for Teaching and Professional Development

Adsit, J. N. (2004). *Technology-mediated professional development for teachers and school leaders.* Washington, DC: American Association of Colleges for Teacher Education.

    Provides the latest research on technology-mediated professional development programs for teachers and school leaders, and identifies a set of guidelines for assessing such programs.

Burgstahler, S., & Utterback, L. (2000). *New kids on the Net: Internet activities in elementary language arts.* Needham Heights, MA: Allyn & Bacon.

    Includes over 80 ready-to-use language arts worksheets with Internet activities.

Carlson, G. (2004). *Digital media in the classroom.* New South Wales, Australia: Focus Press.

    Demystifies various technologies in the classroom and offers useful examples for integrating technology in subject areas.

Carroll, M. (2004). *Cartwheels on the keyboard.* Newark, DE: International Reading Association.

    Uses a study of one teacher's integrated computer-based literacy instruction as a basis for providing ideas and lessons.

Karchmer, R. A., Mallette, M. H., Kara-Soteriou, J., & Leu, D. J., Jr. (2005). *Innovative approaches to literacy education: Using the Internet to support new literacies.* Newark, DE: International Reading Association.

    Presents stellar examples of Internet projects designed by teachers who have won the Ms. Rumphius Award, sponsored by the IRA's RTEACHEr listserv for K–12 educators (www.reading.org/resources/community/discussion.-rt-about.html).

Labbo, L. D., Love, M. S., Prior, M. P., Hubbard, B. P., & Ryan, T. (2006). *Literature links: Thematic units linking read-alouds and computer activities.* Newark, DE: International Reading Association.

    Provides a variety of classroom-tested, integrated activities that connect children's books with computer activities for pre-K–2 teachers.

Leu D. J., Jr., Leu, D. D., & Coiro, J. (2004). *Teaching with the Internet, K–12: New literacies for new times* (4th ed.). Norwood, MA: Christopher-Gordon.

    Offers ideas about how to effectively integrate the Internet into the classroom.

Provenzo, E. F., Jr., & Gotthoffer, D. (2000). *Quick guide to the Internet for education.* Needham Heights, MA: Allyn & Bacon.

    A handbook of facts and ideas for using the Internet.

Magazines and Journals

Information About Technologies for Classroom Use

Association for the Advancement of Computing in Education Journal (formerly *Educational Technology Review*) (http://www.aace.org/pubs/default.htm)

Journal of Technology and Teacher Education (JTATE) (http://www.aace.org/pubs/jtate/default.htm)
PC Magazine (http://www.pcmag.com)
Technology & Learning (http://www.techlearning.com)
T.H.E. Journal (http://www.thejournal.com)

Online Journals

Reading Online (http://www.readingonline.org)
Offers ideas and information for using technology for literacy development. This electronic journal, published by IRA, contains peer-reviewed articles and columns about the electronic classroom, international perspectives, and the new literacies.

The Reading Matrix (http://www.readingmatrix.com/journal.html)
Focuses on second-language acquisition and applied linguistics, and disseminates research to educators around the world. Explores issues related to reading, literacy in a broader sense, and other issues related to second-language learning and teaching.

English Online (http://english.unitecnology.ac.nz/resources/links/prof_reading.html)
Provides resources and recommendations for links to professional literacy resources and articles on the Web.

Reading Journals

The Reading Teacher
Publishes articles and columns that provide practical guides to integrate technology in elementary classrooms

Journal of Adolescent and Adult Literacy
Offers a department on the use of media literacy for middle school and secondary classroom instruction

Reading and Writing Quarterly
Provides a column on technology that addresses ways to use technology for regular and special education students

Journal of Literacy Research
Includes research and theoretical articles that investigate the technological dimensions of literacy

Learning and Leading with Technology
Publishes a learning connections section on ways in which technology can be used for language arts instruction

Web sites

Abcteach (http://www.abcteach.com)
Provides printables to use with language arts lessons and theme-based units. Some are free, and some require a membership fee to download.

Book-clubs-resource.com (http://www.book-clubs-resource.com)
Offers a guide to book clubs and book discussion groups

Doucette Index (http://www.educ.ucalgary.ca/litindex/)
Presents a list of books and Web sites about children's literature

Gallagher, C. (http://teachingheart.net/readerstheater.htm)
A fascinating Web site that presents lessons, print outs, links, units, readers theater scripts, and more

ReadWriteThink (http://www.readwritethink.org)
Developed by IRA, NCTE, and Marcopolo, this Web site provides lesson plans, standards, Web resources, and student materials needed to carry out lesson plans. One section is specifically geared to literacy engagements for learning language, learning about language, and learning through language.

Sites for teachers (http://www.sitesforteachers.org)
Provides access to hundreds of educational Web sites that are used by teachers and rated by their popularity. There is a section on information literacy lesson plans.

Teacher Planet (http://www.teacherplanet.com)
Provides 250 theme-based resources pages, including language arts and literature-based lessons

Teachers Network (http://www.teachersnetwork.org)
Connects teachers to improve student learning. Over 500 lesson plans created by teachers in English/language arts are part of the many resources provided on this site.

CHAPTER 16

Evaluation and Change

The Role of the Literacy Specialist in Guiding Program Improvement

James V. Hoffman and Misty Sailors

Things do not change; we change.
—Henry David Thoreau

Connie Luna has just been hired to serve as the reading specialist at Progreso Elementary School. The reading specialist position was created to promote positive changes in the school reading program. Connie is an experienced classroom teacher and has recently completed a reading specialist program at an area university. Progreso Elementary is a K–5 school located in the heart of a metropolitan area in the Southwest. The school serves families of Hispanic descent living right at or below the line of poverty. The 645 students, many of whom are classified as English language learners, are supported by 2 administrators and 44 staff members (34 teachers and 10 instructional aides). The majority of the teachers are of the same ethnicity as the students, and many have more than 20 years of teaching experience. There are five beginning teachers on this campus. Progreso Elementary School has struggled to meet state standards on reading achievement and has come under pressure from the district to raise scores. Connie is committed to the students and the parents in the community served by the school. Based on her initial observations in classrooms, Connie sees the need for change. However, she is concerned that the pressure for raising test scores will divert attention away from a focus on improving the quality of teaching. She is determined to help the teachers at Progreso Elementary School to become more effective and take ownership of the reading program. Connie wants to be a catalyst for positive change. She is developing a plan to work with teachers to improve the reading program in their school.

Why change? For many classroom teachers, the answer to this question may seem obvious: to improve the quality of literacy support we offer to our students. This stance likely reflects your personal perspective and experience as a classroom teacher. Take a moment to recall the number of different changes you made in your own classroom teaching. You explored book clubs, reading and writing workshops, comprehension strategy instruction, think-alouds, portfolio assessments, and on and on.

In some cases you struck out on your own; in other cases you collaborated with colleagues, and more than once you went against the grain in exploring instructional practices that were at odds with the expected. In almost every case you discovered that the original idea had to be modified along the way to better fit your specific context. Your students became your informants, your collaborators, and your teachers. Sometimes these changes were rooted in frustration with the shortcomings of the current practices. Sometimes these changes were rooted in some exciting new idea you read about or observed. Sometimes these changes grew out of a creative spark inside of you.

For other teachers, this kind of motivation to change may be less compelling. Of course, all teachers want their students to achieve, but for many teachers the path toward significant change is less clear. There are all kinds of forces that inhibit change and lead to the preservation of the status quo. "I don't want to rock the boat." "Things are just fine right now." "We tried that before and it didn't work." "I don't have time to do all the work required to change." Some of these statements may seem selfish and self-centered, but they are the reality for many teachers. As a literacy specialist, you will need to step outside your view and inside the views of others if you are to open them to other paths that invite change.

To assist you in guiding change, in this chapter we present

- A framework for thinking about the role of the literacy specialist in guiding program implementation
- A connection to the types of assessments that classroom teachers employ
- A practical discussion around the development of skills and strategies to work within a school to create a culture of change.

At Progreso Elementary, like any school, Connie found teachers who have been doing the same kind of teaching for years and years. Their classrooms look the same as they did when they started teaching. Life in their classrooms is, like the curriculum they offer, unaffected by the world outside. These teachers may appear confident on the surface. They quickly look with cynical eyes on any new proposals for change. Connie wonders, "Do they think they are that good?" "Do they know anything else?" "What excites them about teaching?" In some cases, these may be isolated teachers who close their door and just carry on. In other cases, these teachers may have formed groups that support their way of thinking and doing school.

Likewise at Progreso Elementary, Connie found teachers who are in a constant state of change. These are the teachers who never seem to have met a program they don't like. They try everything. They move furniture. They are excited with every new thing they are trying out. They are excited by change, but it is not always clear how their decisions about change are guided. Again, they may operate in isolation or in small clusters within the school. Connie wonders, "Where do all of these ideas come from?" "How do these changes reflect the needs of the students in our school?" "How can all this energy be harnessed into a coherent and collective voice?"

Finally, Connie found teachers who are struggling to survive. They are often the "new" teachers but not always. They are trying to find routines that work for them and their kids. They are searching for their identity. They strive to be good but are terrified of failing and often look at their own practice as flawed. Connie wonders, "How can I help them get on a positive path?" "What can I do to support them without just taking over or imposing my own views?"

As a program leader and reading specialist, you too will work with the same kinds of teachers as Connie. You will be expected to motivate and support them to change. Evaluation is a tool that you can use to effectively leverage change. We will use Connie's story to develop the ideas in this chapter. We will share scenarios throughout the chapter to enrich our descriptions of the ways in which evaluation can be used to support change. These illustrations are drawn both from our shared experiences and our individual experiences as classroom teachers, reading specialists, and teacher educators. We will also be sensitive to the realities of politics in education. "Mandates" for change have become part of the educational landscape in recent years. Many politicians believe that they have the answers

for educational reform, and the only ways to generate change in a "failing system" are to use the carrot ("There's more funding if you do what I say.") or the stick ("It's the law, stupid."). You cannot ignore or dismiss this reality. In fact, it is your role to help teachers and the school community to leverage these forces into positive reform efforts (e.g., see the recent conversations surrounding *No Child Left Behind* by the Commission on No Child Left Behind, 2007).

We organize the chapter around a set of 10 principles that we believe are important for you to consider as you engage in this kind of evaluation. Throughout the chapter we will try to connect the understandings and strategies that effective classroom teachers employ in assessment to your role in evaluation. We will offer frameworks and theories, but our focus is firmly set on the practical. We ground our discussion in the development of skills and strategies to work within a school to create a culture of change. These are ambitious goals. The literature on evaluation and educational change is extensive. We hope you will take this chapter as an invitation to read more deeply in this literature. We also encourage you to reflect back on the information in all of the previous chapters in this book as a source of inspiration and content.

DEVELOPING RELATIONSHIPS TO SUPPORT CHANGE

Principle 1: *Evaluation and change are highly personal. No claims of "objectivity" or "data-driven decision making" can circumvent this reality. People change first, then programs; and significant change is never easy. Anticipate emotional responses to evaluation and change. Take time to build relationships.*

Who really wants to be evaluated? Most of us are quick to judge others but terrified of being judged ourselves. We know what we like and are quick to share our views on just about everything from the personal to the professional to the political. "Where did she get that dress?" "You voted for that idiot!" "She doesn't know anything about teaching beginning reading." When we take on the voice of the "judge," intentionally or not, we assert our knowledge, power, and authority over others. But when the lens is turned on us we either do our best to escape notice or we strike back, resist, and even subvert. We live our lives in fear of having our shortcomings revealed to others. While few of us lay claim to perfection, we are terrified at the thought of having our insecurities exposed. It's human nature. We live in a culture where mistakes are a sign of weakness, not strength.

Evaluation in our professional lives is no different. All evaluation is personal. As a program leader and change facilitator, you cannot rush into or hurry evaluation. You have to take time to develop a positive relationship with the faculty who are part of the school community. Your initial efforts should focus on developing an intimate knowledge of the strengths that each teacher brings to the school community. You must take time to talk, to interact, to observe, to help, and to seek their advice. You have to find value in the differences and create opportunities for teachers to share with each other. This takes time. You work to build a personal relationship of trust and respect that rests not just on words but on knowledge and shared experiences. You might do some book clubs together around professional books. You might explore new children's literature together. You might go to a local or regional conference together and share. By valuing differences, you establish the understanding that program change is not about creating sameness. Rather, in program change you strive for responsive teaching that meets learners' needs in a context where learners are different and teachers are different.

Your relationship with teachers is crucial to your success, but your relationship with administration is critical as well. Sometimes this can be a challenge. An authoritarian principal (who must take charge of every decision) is not conducive to a culture of evaluation in a school. Administrators are rightfully concerned over the quality of their program. You must work to gain their confidence and assure them that shared decision making is the path to reform through evaluation. Later, we will address issues of "sustainable change" and how administrators play a critical role in supporting changes that make a difference.

Finally, as you consider relationships, don't forget the parents! Effective schools are linked to the community, and you will find the bridges you build to parents can become a strong support for change. Establish lines of communication through formal organizations and informal exchanges. Miniworkshops for parents (e.g., new children's books to enjoy or how writing instruction has changed) are appreciated. These kinds of experiences will build the relationships with parents that can be of importance.

Over time you will begin to identify a leadership team in the school that has a shared interest in the reading program. The structure even may be formally recognized as a committee or a team, but membership should always be open to others who are interested, and there must be ongoing communication from the team to the entire faculty. It should include an administrator and may include a parent representative. The leadership team cannot be viewed as something above or separate from the faculty. It is simply a group that shares an interest and who is willing to take on certain roles in the school program. In a sense, the team should emerge as the result of relationship-building activities within the school.

BUILDING CAPACITY FOR CHANGE

Principle 2: *The more those who are expected to change are involved in shaping the change process, the more sustainable the change effort will be. Evaluation that is controlled and managed from the outside is far less effective in supporting real change than evaluation that comes from within the system.*

There is a tension in the research literature on change that contrasts the benefits of top-down and bottom-up approaches. *Top-down* change tends to rely on mandates and is usually quite specific in terms of the kinds of changes to be made. These are the kinds of changes we see so often in schools today: For example, a school district adopts a commercial program, and all schools are expected to implement it; a school district wants to target specific changes in the reading curriculum to raise performance on state-mandated, high-stakes tests; a federal grant requires the use of certain materials and teaching strategies. *Bottom-up change* tends to focus on individual, small-group, or schoolwide initiatives that grow out of the immediate school context. For example, a group of teachers are working to introduce book clubs in their daily teaching routine; the school has committed to increasing the amount of time devoted to writing; parents and teachers are developing a plan for coordinating volunteer work in classrooms to support struggling readers. As a change facilitator, you will need to be responsive to both kinds of change efforts.

Bottom-up change efforts are capacity building. The teaching community is invested in the processes and develops a sense of ownership of the change effort. The bottom-up change efforts are effective because they reflect the needs and the strengths of the immediate context. Further, the teaching community also develops the capacity to take control over the top-down mandates and shape them in strategic ways to the needs of the school. The victimized mentality of "What do I have to do now?" or "Here we go again!" is replaced with an attitude of "How can we make this work for us?" Under these conditions the school community becomes self-renewing and independent.

Capacity building toward change is a process that requires patience and a view toward the long term. You may be convinced that the school, as a whole, needs to do much more work on comprehension using think-alouds and explicit strategy instruction. However, this is not a view shared by most teachers. You can spend your time trying to convince everyone that they should adopt your priorities ("Just look at our test scores!"), or you can start with something more modest as a goal that grows out of your listening to teachers as they talk about perceived needs (e.g., organize the leveled library in a way that is more convenient to teachers). You set some goals, establish a plan, work together, and you achieve a positive outcome. The capacity of the system to solve problems has grown. The next challenge you take on may not have been even considered possible prior to this time. You may not yet be ready to address the comprehension instruction issue, but you are a step closer. You are also in a much better place to deal strategically with the top-down mandates that can frustrate all of us.

Think back to your early days as a classroom teacher. Think of the small steps you had to take as a teacher to build your confidence that you could manage classroom tasks, take on an integrated curriculum, or create a portfolio evaluation scheme for your class. Think of your students and the steps you needed to take to build a learning community. You may have started with the "classroom jobs," but you moved forward to offer complex learning tasks that required collaboration among students with many different ability levels and interests. As a literacy specialist you are facilitating a community of learners to take control over and responsibility for teaching that goes beyond anything they may have experienced on their own.

SURVEYING THE READING PROGRAM

Principle 3: *You begin a program evaluation with a rich description of* what is, *not what should be. This program description is intended to serve as a "mirror" that reflects the reality.*

The best place to start a reading program evaluation is a survey description of the status quo. There is a rich tradition in reading education for program surveys as the first step for change reaching back to the early 1900s with William S. Gray (1933, 1960). The prevailing notion at that time was that experts should be brought in to assess and evaluate the effectiveness of a reading program in a school district. The experts would then make recommendations for change based on the ways they viewed the practices in the school in relation to research. By the 1960s this external and expert survey notion was being replaced with the idea that schools or districts should take responsibility for assessing internally and using the findings to guide change (Bush, 1962).

The literacy specialist facilitates the school survey. A leadership team should assist in organizing the survey, and the entire faculty should be invested in the process. A school survey might focus on the entire reading program in a school (expanded to include the other language arts), or it might focus on just a few grade levels, or it might focus on some specific component of the program. To illustrate some possible focusing points for a survey, consider that reading programs in the elementary grades address certain component areas and audiences

(Afflerbach, 2000; Hoffman & Condon, 1979). Traditionally called developmental programs, a core primary reading program (referred to as Tier 1 in Chapter 14) is the program designed to nurture basic reading skills (e.g., decoding, comprehension), and promote positive reading attitudes and habits for most students. This component is typically the responsibility of the classroom teacher.

The corrective reading program, or the Tier 2 program, is designed to support students who are experiencing modest difficulties in response to the developmental program. This component is typically directed by the classroom teacher with special support materials or the direct assistance of a reading specialist. The "accelerated" (Tier 3) program is designed to support students who might experience severe difficulties in response to the developmental program. This component may be offered directly to students through a pull-out program. Finally, the content area program is designed to support students in the use of learning materials (texts in particular) to support their learning in various subject areas.

A program survey may focus on one or more of these components. A survey seeks to describe the purposes, actions, students, and standards (PASS) within each of these components:

Purposes: What are the specific learning outcomes addressed in this component?
Actions: What are the teachers and students "doing" and "with what" that is designed to promote student progress toward the learning targets? What assessments are used to inform teaching?
Students: What are the students learning? What evidence of this learning is being gathered? How is this progress documented?
Standards: Do the goals, actions, and student assessments meet the expectations of the major stakeholders?

The processes for gathering the survey data will vary as a function of the area of focus. Certainly there will be surveys, self-reports, observations, artifact analysis, and assessments. We will illustrate some of the options available in the section that follows. For the sake of illustration, we are going to assume a limited focus for the survey on the Grades 1–3 developmental reading program.

Purposes

What are the purposes and goals that guide our developmental reading program? This description of purposes and goals is focused on uncovering the goals of the teachers not of the materials (e.g., the basal goals) or the district (the curriculum) or the state (the standards). The purposes may be stated in terms of broad learning outcomes, operationalized as performance standards, or some combination. Think of the identification of purposes as a process of consensus building. For example, you might begin with an open-ended survey of the teachers in the school, asking them to document what they believe to be the purposes of the school reading program. You might want to guide their thinking with a prompt such as, "Please list the purposes of your schoolwide reading program" and then leave them plenty of room to write. When these surveys are returned, it is not uncommon for teachers to list objectives or standards that guide their curriculum. We have seen teachers list such isolated skills as "Students will be able to read 60 words per minute by the end of the year" to broad goals such as "Students will choose to read over other activities by the end of the year." Both of these have a place in trying to determine what the broad purposes for the school are. In order to do this, you will want to look across the returned surveys, and incorporate a Delphi process (repeated administrations and iterations) that builds a consensus around purposes. You are ready to ask the teachers if and how those broad goals are supported by their classroom instruction.

You can do this in one of two ways. You might consider administering a second survey (as depicted in Figure 16.1) that invites affirmation, rejection, and modifications of the broad purposes. You might also consider conducting interviews with the teachers. The purposes may be organized by area or by levels.

To illustrate, you might have a general consensus around a broad word recognition purpose that, by the end of Grade 3, students should be automatic in their decoding of a core set of words. This purpose might be further operationalized in terms of some intermeditate benchmarks for Grades 1 and 2. You might develop similar goal statements around fluency (rate, accuracy, and prosody) and flexibility

Figure 16.1. Purposes for a Developmental Reading Program: Primary Grades

Which purposes do you regard as important for your classroom and our school reading program?	Yes	No	*Modify* (How would you change this goal statement?)
Students should reach automaticity in the decoding of high-frequency words by the end of third grade.			
Students should reach fluency targets (accuracy, rate, expression) for each grade level on benchmark texts.			
Students should develop flexible reading strategies in response to changes in purpose and text structures.			
Students should meet vocabulary targets for each grade level.			
Students should demonstrate effective and efficient use of comprehension strategies (e.g., inferencing, imaging) to support their learning in texts across content areas.			
Students should develop a critical stance in reading to judge the credibility, merits, and value of texts (including electronic texts).			
Students should demonstrate positive motivation and active response to texts based on their interests.			
Students should develop positive attitudes, appreciation, and reading habits both in school and out of school.			
Other goals you would suggest as important:			

(reading different kinds of texts for different purposes, including electronic texts). Vocabulary and comprehension might be broad goal areas with subcategories as well (for example, critical reading). Student attitudes, interests, and habits (including out-of-school reading) might fall into different goal areas.

The key in describing the program purposes is to have them emerge from what the teachers believe are important and serve to guide their instruction. The process itself will raise awareness of the complexity of reading, learning to read, and reading instruction. Avoid imposing your personal value system in describing the goals. Rely on "member checking" throughout the process, such as "Am I getting this right?" "Is this what we agree on as important?" "Is there anything missing?"

Actions

Now you can begin to envision the survey as a matrix that is taking shape. Once the goals are described it is time to move to the description of the actions that are taken to support the development in each area. This stage may involve another set of interviews, observations, and materials analysis. For example, what are we doing to support the development of fluency? Decoding? Flexibility? Comprehension? Attitudes? Out-of-school reading? What materials are used to support instruction? What assessments are we using to inform instruction in each of these areas? How are we using data to guide our instruction in this area? How are we using these data to evaluate our progress with learners?

Students

The focus of this next component is the students themselves. What are they doing? What performances can be observed. This area is one that we most often associate with evaluation. What are the students able to do in each of the critical learning areas? Where there are data available (e.g., student scores on state assessments and school assessments), you can gather and aggregate the data. You might have to conduct some data collection on all or a sample of the learners as part of the survey. You might even have to create or introduce some new assessments into the system. For example, are student attitudes toward reading currently assessed in the school? If not, then you may need to introduce an assessment tool and gather data on the students in the area of reading attitudes. There are many opportunities in a survey to introduce new assessments that focus attention on areas of reading not currently attended to in the school reading program.

Standards

Standards relate to the expectations for learning. Consider all of the different groups that might have standards. Are the teachers satisfied? Are the parents? Are the learners meeting district and state expectations? Are the goals aligned with the standards that professional organizations have set forth? Describing standards is not the same as evaluating the program. Standards are the basis for making judgments. They can and must be described first before they are applied.

The findings of the survey can be summarized in tables or a narrative document or some combination of the two. As you move through this summarization process, be sure to do member checking with the teachers and others. Is this what we believe? Is this what we do? Is this the best evidence we have to document student growth? Avoid language that is evaluative. The survey should focus on description.

ANALYZING SURVEY DATA

Principle 4: *Effective evaluation rests on the identification of coherence within the program as well as identification of the inconsistencies and contradictions within a program.*

A coherent program is one that has all of its Purposes, Actions, Students, and Standards fully aligned. A good survey should lead to the identification of aspects of the program (these might be levels or components) that are in full alignment. These may be regarded as the strengths of the program. A good survey should also lead to the identification of aspects of the program that are out of alignment. In other words, there are discrepancies revealed between particular goals, actions, products, or standards.

Discrepancy analysis is at the heart of most evaluation models (see Stake, 2000; Steinmetz, 2000). The program survey sets the stage for the process of looking at what *is* and shifting the focus to what *should be*. The PASS framework described above invites this kind of analysis. There are potential discontinuities at any juncture across the program matrix. In a perfect world, we would have a purpose identified for the development of decoding; we would have instructional actions, plans, materials, and assessments that nurture this goal; we would have students learning at the levels we have targeted; and our expectations would meet or exceed all of the standards. The reality is never so clean. We might find purposes (e.g., promote out-of-school reading or reading habits) that we have no actions to support and no data on how well the students are doing. We might discover levels of performance that are below standards. We might be measuring outcomes for areas for which we have no articulated goals. The possibilities are numerous.

The leadership team takes the initiative of identifying the significant incongruities. These are organized and presented for deliberation to the entire faculty. There should be no attempt to place blame on anyone or any particular thing in the program. The survey and the analysis provide the basis for thinking about next steps in program reform or change. The baseline is set. Now it is time to gain consensus on focus points for change. The group may decide to focus as a whole on one particular area and target that for the near future. There may be groups that take a few different focus points for change.

It is critical that the conversations around the program strengths and areas of need are grounded in the data that has been collected. It is often the case, in the early stages of analysis that there is a lack of evidence to support a position. Gather more data. These data are crucial in gaining a consensus on need. These data also become the basis for evaluating the impact of any changes that are put in motion.

BUILDING ON STRENGTHS

Principle 5: Innovations, especially early on, should strive to build on strengths.

Just as quality assessment will guide the teacher to modify instruction, good evaluation should guide program changes. It is important at this stage that the purposes be focused. The program evaluation process is designed to inform change that builds capacity in the school, not to solve all of the challenges at once. But, you have to start somewhere. As the literacy leader in the school, you may see attitudes or critical thinking as the primary need, but if the teachers see fluency as the target they want to address, you have to start there. Capacity will grow and the issues that used to seem beyond reach become more visible for the participants and more achievable. It is also important to try not to fall into a deficit model in program development, such as "Find the shortcomings. Fill in the needs." There is much to argue in program development for the idea of building on strength. Find what you do well and innovate to strengthen. You will build capacity with a focus on the positive, and you will also find ways to bridge your strengths to areas of concern.

Consider the case of a school that has done extremely well in promoting the use of trade literature in the classroom with thematic study within read-alouds, book clubs, and self-selected reading. But the survey data suggest that there are shortcomings in the area of comprehension. A useful innovation to strengthen the literature program might be to look for ways to add some work with think-alouds to model and teach specific comprehension strategies.

Avoid changes that rely on shopping around to buy a quick fix: "We have worked hard to identify our needs (e.g., fluency), so now let's go out and buy the best program we can find (research based, of course) that will fill the gap." The buying, implementation, and failure of programs to meet needs creates the opposite of a culture of change; it creates cynicism and what some call innovation fatigue: "Here comes another program. It will fail like all of the others."

Solutions have to come from within the program. The next stage in the development process must grow out of an evaluation. It should focus on what we can do to strengthen what we are already doing: "What can we learn from our program survey that can lead to our building capacity?" This is a deliberative process that takes time but in the process promotes a commitment to change. We are not on a search for a foolproof, "perfect" method to teach anything (Duffy & Hoffman, 1999). There is only "better," and the better has to do with the specific context for change.

SUPPORTING THE CHANGE PROCESS

Principle 6: You should plan for ways to systematically support the change process. You can use assessments to personalize the support you offer for change.

Innovations, as we will describe them in this chapter, are changes made to improve the quality of teaching and learning. Innovations can be simple and text driven (e.g., a new handwriting book for second grade) to complex, layered, and conceptual (e.g., team teaching). An innovation that enters a school as the result of a careful evaluation process has greater likelihood of impact than one that has been brought in simply by external fiat or mandate.

In this section we will rely heavily on the early work of Frances Fuller (1969) and subsequent research into the change process through the Concerns Based Adoption Model (CBAM). Our intention here is to be conceptual and not technical. You can inspect specific tools related to CBAM in a variety of publications (Hall, George, & Rutherford, 1986; Hall & Hord, 1987; Hall, Louckes, Rutherford, & Newlove, 1975; Heck, Stiegelbauer, Hall, & Loucks, 1975). The Southwest Educational Development Lab (2007) also offers extensive information on recent developments and applications of CBAM. Frances Fuller's pioneering work focused on teacher education and teacher development. She argued that teachers move through stages of concern as they move from preservice to inservice teaching. Concerns tend to center on the following:

- *Self*: How am I changing? What are the consequences for this change for me?

- *Task*: What do I have to do? How do I manage this process of teaching?
- *Impact*: Are the strategies I am developing the most effective ones for learners?

Fuller argued for the progression of concerns from self to task to impact. Concerns for self must be addressed before attention to task begins to rise, and finally attention to impact becomes strong only when the task level of concerns is addressed. Fuller focused on the affective side of change. Change is highly personal.

As the CBAM model developed, there was a shift from a tight focus on teacher education and teacher development to a consideration of any innovation. All educational change involves and reflects this progression from personal (self) to task to impact levels. Further, the CBAM model introduced the behavioral side to accompany the concerns (affective) side. In other words, adoption of a change progresses behaviorally from a vague awareness of the change that is coming, to its introduction, to mechanical use, to refinement of the innovation and beyond.

The CBAM model also introduced the concept of innovation configuration as a useful tool in monitoring the change process. The innovation configuration describes specifically the changes that are required on the part of the individual adopting the change. For the purposes of illustration, we will simplify several of the features of the CBAM model, and use a case study of change to illustrate the application of CBAM tools to plan for, monitor, support, and evaluate the change process in Progreso Elementary School.

Case Study:
Progreso Elementary School

At Progreso Elementary School, Connie has just guided the faculty through an evaluation of their developmental reading program at Grades 1 and 2, using the PASS framework. They identified their strengths in the areas of trade book use in support of learning. The teachers are energized by the use of literature, and they have experienced success in teaching skills and strategies with literature. After extensive analysis, they have decided to focus their efforts next year on promoting more positive atti-

tudes about reading as well as out-of-school reading. (They have some additional goals that relate to the development of fluency, vocabulary, and out-of-school reading.) These are all areas that the evaluation study suggested as needing attention. After extensive reading in the research and several visits to other schools, they are planning to initiate a schoolwide reading program in their school for the upcoming year. This schoolwide reading program will offer students the opportunity to engage in free-choice reading for a significant amount of time every day. The choice reading can be done with any books in the classrooms. The reading specialist has secured funding for the purchase of additional trade books for each of the classrooms to support the program. Data will be gathered to examine the impact of the program using this past year's evaluation study as the reference point.

The Innovation Configuration

How many times have you heard it said: "Oh yes, we do that program." Or "We do guided reading. We were trained." Or "We do language experience." Or "We do comprehension instruction." Or "We do the basal." Then you visit the school and observe teachers all doing different things—and none of them recognizable to you. One of the most important steps in effective change is the clear identification of the innovation that is being brought into classrooms.

At Progreso Elementary, the teachers have committed to a free-choice, schoolwide reading program for a significant amount of time every day. Can a teacher do this reading for just 15 minutes a day? Can the teacher limit the free-choice to books that are on the learner's instructional level? Does this count as doing the program? Can another teacher do the program for 45 minutes just once a week? Is it OK if another teacher plans on giving a test over every book that is read? Does this count as doing the program? How do you begin to evaluate the impact of a program innovation on student learning when everyone is doing something different?

There is an obvious tension here between providing *flexibility* for variation based on the context and meeting the need for *fidelity* to the program innovation. There is no simple answer. Each innovation must be considered carefully in terms of its critical components and acceptable variations within the components. Within the CBAM model, an innovation configuration is constructed to guide the change effort. The configuration is created to identify the critical elements (what everyone must do) and the variations that are acceptable (and not acceptable), as well as the optional components. To illustrate, consider the innovation configuration we have developed for the Progreso Elementary project. We envision this innovation configuration as a creation of the adopting group that is considerate of both the context for the program and the innovation as it was originally envisioned by the developer (Figure 16.2). There is no right or wrong here. It is a process that must be supported. The innovation configuration should be created through interaction and negotiation among the faculty. It is not predetermined and imposed from the outside. As you will see later, this innovation configuration may actually change as part of the adoption process.

Stages of Concern

Change, as we have noted, is a personal process. Progreso Elementary School is not different because the adoption of a new reading program was announced. Progreso Elementary School will change as the teachers change. For some of the teachers, the innovation may require minimum change to current practice. For others, there may be major shifts required. Consider the personal to task to impact progression in Fuller's work. How can you as a literacy leader support a teacher through this change process?

The first step is to assess. This can be done in a conversation or in written form. Start by asking, "When you think about implementing the schoolwide reading program in your classroom next year, what concerns you?" Keep the conversation focused on the specific innovation and the individual. Listen for words that reflect the personal, the task, or the impact issues. You cannot push a teacher into task or impact. Changes in concerns shift as the lower level concerns are resolved. You may need to work with teachers to resolve their personal concerns before you can focus on task or impact. For example, a teacher may be concerned about the evaluation of her teaching (perhaps an early career teacher without tenure). These concerns must be addressed first before any productive change can take place. A teacher concerned about the task may need support with materials, or perhaps a visit to another classroom, or perhaps a demonstration. Impact-level concerns may involve "permission" to vary the program to enhance it ("What if I let the kids check the books out to take home to read?").

We offer an example of a protocol that can be used to assess concerns in Figure 16.3. To illustrate some of the range in responses to the introduction of an innovation into a school, we give three examples of concerns expressed at Progreso Elementary School. Connie will look across the concerns to assess general trends. She understands that at the early stages of change you can expect personal concerns to be high. She knows she will have to work with teachers to lower these concerns to clear the path for positive changes. The assessment of concerns will also guide Connie in ways to differentiate support for individual teachers. Looking over the examples in Figure 16.3, what actions would you recommend for Connie? Remember, you cannot force teachers into higher levels of concern (for example, impact). You must resolve lower level concerns first.

Concerns can be particularly troubling in the case of top-down mandates that conflict with a teacher's personal philosophy. If the basis for change has been established through internal evaluation and the teacher has participated throughout, then concerns should be less of an issue.

Levels of Use

This is the behavioral side of the innovation. The level of use can be assessed using interviews and observations. The innovation configuration is crucial in assessing the level of use. Interview questions follow the configuration. Are you using schoolwide reading? Tell me about the time allotments you use? How are book choices offered? What kind of plan for sharing are you using? What data are you gathering on your students' reading in this program? These questions are tied directly to the program's critical features and the variation within their classroom.

In these interviews you are looking for the following groups of users:

Figure 16.2. Innovation Configuration for Schoolwide Reading Program at Progreso Elementary School

Components	Variations		
	Not Acceptable	*Acceptable*	*Optimal*
Required			
Student choice of reading materials	Teacher assigns books or restricts book choice by levels or topics.	Teachers provide a collection of materials for students to select from. There is a wide range of interests, genres, and difficulty levels represented.	Students have the option of selecting materials from the classroom or school libraries. They have the option of bringing reading materials from home.
Time for reading every day	Students have less than 30 minutes per day to devote to choice reading.	Students have between 30 and 60 minutes per day for choice reading.	Students have over 60 minutes per day for choice reading across subject areas.
Sharing expectations for response	There are no expectations for sharing of books after they are read.	Students are expected to share their reading of books through various response options. Students share a minimum of one book response per month.	Students are expected to share their reading of books through various response options. Students share a minimum of one book response per week.
Optional			
Book clubs as an option for reading	Students are required to read books individually.	Teacher accepts students who read books in pairs or small groups.	Teacher requires that students read at least some books in groups.
Vocabulary (word banks)	Students are not expected to do anything specific with vocabulary.	Students are expected to collect new words from their reading and create word banks.	Students are expected to collect new words from their reading and create word banks. Students are assessed on their knowledge of word meanings.
Home Reading Extension	Students cannot count books read at home toward this program.	Students are given the option of reading books at home.	Students are encouraged to read books at home and complete response activities at home as well.
Assessment	Students are not assessed in the program.	Teacher assesses students' comprehension, vocabulary, and fluency.	Teacher works with students to create a portfolio of comprehension, vocabulary, fluency, interests, and attitudes.

- *Nonusers*: not using all of the critical components in an acceptable variation
- *Mechanical users*: using all of the components but struggling to make it all work
- *Routine users*: using all of the components and not making any changes

- *Refinement users*: making changes to make the program more effective with their students

The goal of the use interview is to specifically target support for areas of need not to "catch" the individuals who are struggling. We offer an example

Figure 16.3. Assessing Concerns of Teachers at Progresso Elementary School

We have agreed, as a faculty, to implement a schoolwide reading program across our school. Our purposes are to promote skills in reading (vocabulary and fluency), a positive attitude toward reading, and increased out-of-school reading.

As you think about implementing this new program in your classroom, what are the concerns you have? Do not list the concerns that you think others might have. Focus specifically on the concerns that you have regarding making this change in your classroom. List the things that concern you the most.

Example 1

1. I really don't have the time to put into this program what is required. I'm still working on so many school committees.

2. How will I be evaluated by the principal on my use of this program? Is it required for everyone?

3. I really think we should be doing more work in phonics.

Example 2

1. I've been doing something like this in my classroom for a couple of years, but I just can't keep track of everyone.

2. I'm worried about the rest of the curriculum. How will I find the time to do everything?

Example 3

1. How can I encourage my kids to read broadly from different genres in their self-selected reading?

2. I want to assess inside of this program? What data should I gather and how can I use these data to inform my teaching?

3. I would like to encourage group reading (book club, literature circles) as part of this program. Is that OK? Can I join the groups in reading and talking about the books?

of a framework for this kind of interview in Figure 16.4. As with concerns, you can expect a general pattern of response to the innovation that leads from nonuse, to mechanical use, to routine use, and eventually to improving on the innovation. Connie uses this data to plan for support of the innovation. She also uses the responses from teachers to personalize the support. Consider the variation in teachers' use of the innovation in Figure 16.4. For those teachers who have not begun implementation, Connie might offer to help them begin with just one aspect and support them while they begin to feel comfortable with it. For those teachers who are beginning to implement, she would want to find something positive about what they are doing with their children (e.g., bringing in new books) and capitalize on that. She might create spaces where teachers such as Example 2 in Figure 16.4 have the opportunity to observe and interact with teachers who have implemented in a broader sense, such as Example 3.

Modification and Adaptation of the Innovation

There is a danger in using the innovation configuration as a fixed target. It is not. The effective change agent is open to modifications and adaptations of the innovation itself, based on the demands of the context. The importance of innovation adaptation was revealed vividly in the Rand change agent study (Berman & McLaughlin, 1978). These researchers examined innovations that were highly successful in one context and the conditions that surrounded and supported the successful transfer of this innovation to a new setting. One of their major findings suggested that when the innovation was transferred to a new setting with an emphasis on fidelity (do it in the new setting just the way it was done in the original setting), there was limited transfer of successful impact. In contrast, they found that when the innovation was adapted (changes made) in response to the new context, the impact was

Figure 16.4. Assessing Levels of Use at Progresso Elementary

We are gathering data on teachers' progress in implementing the schoolwide reading program. Please answer the questions in the way that reflects your use of the program in your classroom.

Question: Have you started the implementation of the schoolwide reading program in your classroom?

Example 1: No   **Example 2:** Yes   **Example 3:** Yes!

Question: If you have not started implementation of the schoolwide reading program, when do you plan on starting?

Example 1: After the winter break   **Example 2:** N/A   **Example 3:** N/A

Question: If you have started implementation of the schoolwide reading program, please describe how the program works in your classroom in relation to:

Student book choices	**Example 1:** N/A	**Example 2:** I bring 20 new books from the library each Monday to my classroom for my children to use during self-selected reading time.	**Example 3:** The students have books available to them all around the room. I try to store the books in ways that are organized (for example, there are tubs of books by author, topic, and theme), and I encourage the kids to bring their own books from home! I use books from the library and from my own collection.
Time for reading	**Example 1:** N/A	**Example 2:** 30 minutes each day, just after lunch	**Example 3:** 20 minutes at the very beginning of the day; 30 minutes just after lunch; and 20 minutes at the end of the day . . . and any other time we can get! ☺
Student sharing of responses	**Example 1:** N/A	**Example 2:** Each Friday, I have one child tell about one good book he read during the week.	**Example 3:** Organized sharing time once per week; informal as often as we can!

Question:What else are you doing with the schoolwide reading program in your classroom?

Book clubs?	**Example 1:** N/A	**Example 2:** No.	**Example 3:** We are just beginning. I introduced Book Clubs through a whole-group read-aloud and am trying to move the kids toward reading in small groups. This is challenging because they have not interacted with books and journals like this before.
Vocabulary?	**Example 1:** N/A	**Example 2:** The children ask me to help them when they find a difficult word.	**Example 3:** I try to find several new vocabulary words during each read-aloud. I would like to learn how to incorporate this more into the self-selected, individual reading time.
Home extensions?	**Example 1:** N/A	**Example 2:** Parents sign the reading log each night.	**Example 3:** I encourage the children to read at home each night.
Assessment?	**Example 1:** N/A	**Example 2:** No.	**Example 3:** Not yet. I need help with this one.
Other?	**Example 1:** N/A	**Example 2:** No	**Example 3:** No.

Question: What kinds of changes are you making in the program as you have worked toward implementation?

Example 1: N/A   **Example 2:** None.   **Example 3:** The children did not really know how to engage in independent self-selected reading for long periods of time when we started, so I started them out reading in smaller chunks of time and increased the time as they learned that reading like this could be fun.

replicated. The principle was referred to as *mutual adaptation*. The program changes, and the implementing site changes as well. The point to keep in mind here is that it's not just the teachers (adaptors) who can change. The innovation may need to be changed to make it more effective within your context. This is a negotiated process.

EVALUATING THE INNOVATION

Principle 7: *Effective evaluation requires the gathering, recording, and interpretation of data that focuses on both implementation and impact.*

The evaluation of the innovation should focus on two areas. First, was the program implemented as originally designed, and/or in what ways was it modified? The data for this area of program implementation draw on interviews and observations that focus on the innovation configuration and level of use.

Second, did the innovation have the desired outcome on the outcome measures that were targeted? The evaluation of impact on student learning will require careful planning. Existing measures may be used, or you may need to develop new measures specifically for the study. For example, in the case of the schoolwide reading innovation at Progreso Elementary, several measures were used that were already in place within the school to assess word recognition, fluency, vocabulary development, and comprehension. An interview protocol was developed to assess reading attitudes (see Figure 16.5). For assessing out-of-school reading, the following plan was developed: First, a reading log was created that the students complete at various points in the project to describe their out-of-school reading. Second, checkout records from the library were monitored. All measures used in this example were assessed at the start of the year, at midyear, and at the end of the year. Some of these measures are time-consuming and not part of the regular program of assessment. Therefore, a random sampling of the students was assessed to gauge program impact, especially that aspect that pertains to motivation and interest to read widely and outside of school.

Interpreting the Data

To address the question of program impact you will need to aggregate the scores across the implementing groups and compare students at the start and at the end. You can compare the progress of students from the baseline to the end. In most cases, you will not have a control or comparison group. Without a control group you are without information on how the students would have done without the program. This is a limitation of this kind of data analysis and your ability to argue for the direct link between your intervention and improvement. But you can make a good case if your data gathering is rich and trustworthy.

Managing data analysis can be a daunting process for those who are not experienced with statistics. We will present a rather straightforward plan for analysis, but we would encourage a literacy specialist to seek out support with this aspect of the evaluation, drawing on expertise within the system. An example of the data gathered by Connie on a sample of students at Progreso Elementary is presented in Tables 16.1 and 16.2. The data have been averaged across classes and broken down by grade levels and by measure. The statistical analysis of this data reflects the mean scores (averages) on various measures including the Normal Curve Equivalency (NCE) score, which is similar to percentile scores. The analysis of these data suggests that there has been a positive impact on most of the measures. There are more sophisticated statistical analyses that could be applied to these data. The data could also be further disaggregated by such factors as gender or ethnicity, if appropriate. The data on some of the measures could also be analyzed more deeply (e.g., by questions or clusters of questions on the student interview). Once again, we recommend caution because there is no control group to assess the relative impact of the innovation against traditional, normal, status-quo, or some alternative innovation. In Table 16.3 we offer a data display to show the progress of 25 teachers in their movement toward full implementation.

We urge you to consider the process of data analysis and interpretation as a collegial process with the teachers involved in the innovation. You do not want to take the data and go off and hide

Figure 16.5. Assessing Reading Attitudes

How do you feel about reading? What kind of reading do you like to do? Read the statements and put an X in the column that describes you. There are no right or wrong answers to these questions.	Not like me at all	Hardly ever	Some-times	This is like me most of the time	This is me all the time
1. In the evening and at night before bed, I like to read.					
2. I have a great chapter book at home that I am in the middle of reading.					
3. I like to go to the public library to check out books.					
4. I have several favorite authors that I like to read.					
5. There are some books that I have read several times.					
6. People who read a lot are usually very boring.					
7. I hate it when I get books as gifts.					
8. Someday I would like to write books.					
9. Sometimes I have two or more books that I am reading.					
10. I would rather read the book than see the movie that comes from a book.					
11. There are lots of books that I have started but never finished.					
12. I tend to choose books that are short, not long.					
13. I enjoy going to book stores to look around.					
14. Most of my friends read a lot of books.					
15. I find watching TV more fun than reading books.					
16. I like the time we have in class to choose our own books and read them.					
17. I like to choose and read books with my classmates.					
18. I like to share with my classmates about the books I am reading.					

(Item scores reversed for scoring: 6, 7, 11, 12, and 15)

away somewhere to do "secret stuff." You want to analyze and interpret (make sense of; make meaning with) the data that you have gathered. This collaboration not only enhances the quality of the interpretation; it also helps build ownership of the process and what comes next.

Resistance

We do not live in a perfect world. There will always be those who will resist change. What can you do? First, work to understand the source of the resistance. As Fullan (2005) points out, there is

Table 16.1. Student Progress in Reading: Progreso Elementary

Measures	First-Grade Students			Second-Grade Students		
	Early Fall (2004)	Early Spring (2005)	Late Spring (2005)	Early Fall (2004)	Early Spring (2005)	Late Spring (2005)
Accuracy on benchmark texts	88%	90%	89%	85%	87%	88%
Oral rate on benchmark texts	44 wpm	55 wpm	74 wpm	60 wpm	78 wpm	80 wpm
Silent rate on benchmark texts	51 wpm	58 wpm	60 wpm	62 wpm	85 wpm	94 wpm
Fluency rating on benchmark texts (5-point scale)	2.1	3.0	3.8	2.5	3.2	3.8
Standardized test: Comprehension (25% sample: 50 students, each grade): NCE score	40	45	52	44	49	51
Standardized test: Vocabulary (25% sample: 50 students, each grade): NCE score	38	43	51	41	49	58
Reading interest/ attitude survey (25% sample: 50 students, each grade)	3.0	3.4	3.8	2.5	2.9	3.3

Note. NCE score is the National Curve Equivalency score.

much to learn from those who resist. Keep yourself open to learning from them. Learn to redefine resistance into forces that are supportive of change by addressing legitimate concerns. Do not force anyone to participate. Keep everyone informed and invite input (even if they are reluctant to participate). Keep the door open to join at any time. And most important, engage in dialogue with those who resist; you might learn something in the process. I

(JH) once guided the implementation of a schoolwide, Joplin-plan grouping arrangement for reading instruction. A fifth-grade teacher refused to participate and chose to keep her own students for instruction. The principal of the school, supportive of the plan, was willing to require her to participate. I said, "No. Let's just leave room for her to join later." A year later, after the shortcomings of the Joplin-plan grouping became apparent to

Table 16.2. Cohort Comparison of Reading Scores from Years 2004 and 2005

Assessments	First Grade Late Spring (2004)	First Grade Late Spring (2005)	Second Grade Late Spring (2004)	Second Grade Late Spring (2005)
Accuracy on benchmark texts	86%	89%	88%	88%
Oral rate on benchmark texts	64 wpm	74 wpm	68 wpm	80 wpm
Silent rate on benchmark texts	58 wpm	60 wpm	78 wpm	94 wpm
Fluency rating on benchmark texts (5-point scale)	2.8	3.8	3.0	3.8
Standardized test: Comprehension (25% sample: 50 students, each grade): NCE score	46	52	44	51
Standardized test: Vocabulary (25% sample: 50 students, each grade): NCE score	42	51	48	58
Reading interest/ attitude survey (25% sample: 50 students, each grade)	2.9	3.8	2.5	3.3

Note. NCE score is the National Curve Equivalency score.

everyone, I started spending more time in her classroom. I learned about good teaching of reading in classrooms with mixed ability and skill levels. The next year was spent helping other teachers move to more flexible grouping in their own classrooms. I learned, and we all learned from the resistance.

Of course, not all resistance rests on a sense of a better idea. Some resistance is rooted in real personal concerns (e.g., time required, background knowledge, resources to implement). Here you must rely on the concerns model in guiding you to the right kind of support that will reduce low-level concerns and help teachers move forward.

NEGOTIATING BOTTOM-UP AND TOP-DOWN PRESSURES

Principle 8: *Program change must be strategic in the ways in which bottom-up and top-down pressures are negotiated.*

Table 16.3. Teacher Implementation of Schoolwide Reading Program: Progresso Elementary

Level of Implementation	Number of Teachers (Percentage of Teachers)		
	Early Fall, 2005	Early Spring, 2006	Late Spring, 2006
All of the critical components and some of the optional components at acceptable level or higher	3 (12%)	12 (48%)	16 (64%)
All of the critical components at acceptable level or higher with no optional components	2 (8%)	4 (16%)	6 (24%)
Some of the critical components at acceptable level or higher	14 (56%)	7 (28%)	2 (8%)
None of the critical components at acceptable level or higher	6 (24%)	2 (8%)	1 (4%)

There will always be mandates and prescriptions for change being placed on schools. Recent times have been particularly difficult, and we cannot expect things to change in the near future. We must learn to manage change within an outcomes and accountability climate. Connie faces this pressure at Progresso Elementary. She has to address the concerns over scores on state assessments, but she has to balance this pressure with the broader goal of an effective program for all learners. How can you help create a system that is empowered to take external mandates and make them work for the local system? As an example, let's envision a more extreme situation in Progreso Elementary School where the district has decided to mandate that all kindergarten and first-grade teachers spend at least 40 minutes per day with their students in phonemic awareness instruction. The district has offered some instructional materials and recommended some instructional strategies for teachers to meet this requirement. Many of the teachers feel that this is totally unnecessary for many of their students, does not take into consideration what they are al-

ready doing with phonemic awareness, and will displace many other activities that are central to the literacy instruction in their classrooms. How do you respond to this pressure? Resist? Protest? Conform? Or become strategically compliant?

While the first two might reflect the initial response to such a mandate, there is great potential in choosing the last option. First, you acknowledge the importance of phonemic awareness in reading development. Second, you read the research literature to determine the strategies that can be used most effectively to support the development of phonemic awareness. And finally, you devise a program plan and implementation schedule to meet the demands of the district (see Figure 16.6), ensuring that you and the teachers are meeting the instructional needs of students who do need instruction around phonemic awareness. You establish a plan for assessing concerns, collecting preassessment measures on students, monitoring and supporting the implementation of the program, and collecting postassessment measures. You might also include measures of word learning, spelling, and writing

Figure 16.6. Innovation Configuration for Phonemic Awareness Program

| | Variations | | |
Required Components	Not Acceptable	Acceptable	Optimal
Practice time in writing (relying on sound spelling).	Less than 3 times per week; or less than 20 minutes per session; or no explicit teacher scaffolding	At least 3 times per week for a minimum of 20 minutes with explicit teacher scaffolding	Daily, for a minimum of 20 minutes with explicit teacher scaffolding
Practice time in rhymes and word play.	Teacher-guided daily work with rhymes and in word work in poetry less than 3 times per week	Teacher-guided daily work with rhymes in poetry and word work at least 3 times per week	Teacher-guided daily work with rhymes in poetry and word work
Explicit instruction in phonemic awareness using Elkonin sound and letter boxes.	Teacher models to group and supports individuals through the application of letter and sound boxes less than 3 times per week	Teacher models to group and supports individuals through the application of letter and sound boxes at least 3 times per week	Teacher models to group and supports individuals through the application of letter and sound boxes on a daily basis
Optional Components			
Computer program XYZ	Students engage less than 3 times per week in software program XYZ to support the development of phonemic awareness	Students engage at least 3 times per week in software program XYZ to support the development of phonemic awareness	Students engage daily in software program XYZ to support the development of phonemic awareness

development. If you have built the capacity of the system from within, then mandated changes like these create opportunities to teach those higher up in the system about good literacy instruction.

SUSTAINING CHANGE

Principle 9: *No changes are important if they cannot be sustained.*

Good evaluation supports a cycle of growth. Teachers are empowered to shape their school. Teachers are encouraged to connect and not isolate themselves from one another. The literacy specialist has a crucial role to play in the process of supporting change. Of course, we have presented a somewhat idealized setting for change. Far too many schools suffer today from mandated changes that come from the latest fad or most popular guru. High-stakes testing has resulted in enormous pressure for

change that focuses only on certain outcomes. Yet we have seen literacy specialists who have found ways to encourage local autonomy and consensus building within their schools even with today's high pressures (see Au, 2001, 2005).

Sustainable change is not about supporting change to a point you stay at, but to always "stay changing" in ways that reflect growth. This is not change for change's sake. A faculty that has embraced change as the path for growth is taking control of the future. The power that comes with this control makes anything possible. Michael Fullan (2007) argues that the problem in schools today is not the absence of change (in fact, there are too many changes underway); rather, it is the lack of coherent change that is the problem.

Fullan (2005) has written extensively about change in schools and most recently about sustainable change. He advocates for the principle of "cultural change" in education. Cultural change includes attention to "moral purpose" and "social responsi-

Figure 16.7. Reflecting on Yourself in the Change Process: A Literacy Specialist's Guide

Guiding Principle	Self-Reflective Questions
1. Evaluation and change are highly personal. No claims of "objectivity" or "data-driven decision making" can circumvent this reality. People change first, then programs; and significant change is never easy. Anticipate emotional responses to evaluation and change. Take time to build relationships.	What is your relationship with the faculty, parents, and administration? Can you identify the strengths of all the teachers you work with in the school? In what ways have you actively reached out to build a community of learners that is willing to take risks?
2. The more those who are expected to change are involved in shaping the change process, the more sustainable the change effort will be. Evaluation that is controlled and managed from the outside is far less effective in supporting real change than evaluation that comes from within the system.	How involved are the faculty in the shaping of current change efforts? What are some of the ways you are attempting to bring some of those outside the process more inside the process? Is there a leadership team taking shape within your school?
3. You begin a program evaluation with a rich description of what is, not what should be. This program description is intended to serve as a "mirror" that reflects the reality.	What is the focus for change? Is it a level? A component? How is your description of the program informed and supported by empirical data?
4. Effective evaluation rests on the identification of coherence within the program as well as identification of the inconsistencies and contradictions within a program.	In what ways is your program tightly aligned? In what ways is your program out of alignment?
5. Innovations, especially early on, should strive to build on strengths.	What are the points of strength in your program that you can build on as you move to innovate?
6. You should plan for ways to systematically support the change process. You can use assessments to personalize the support you offer for change.	How will you gather data to describe the innovations? How will you assess concerns? Monitor implementation? Monitor impact on student learning?
7. Effective evaluation requires the gathering, recording, and interpretation of data that focus on both implementation and impact.	What existing data can we use to inform our program? What other data do we need to construct? Do the teachers and administrators at my school understand the importance of the systematic use of data to inform our decisions?
8. Program change must be strategic in the ways in which bottom-up and top-down pressures are negotiated.	What are the pressures from the outside that challenge your teachers? What are you doing to find a way to be strategic in addressing these pressures?
9. No changes are important if they cannot be sustained.	What provisions are being made for sustained changes in the program?
10. The literacy leader's work is never done because it is focused on the "cultural change" imperative, forming coherence and realizing a vision.	How comfortable are you in a leadership role? Is there a culture of change taking hold in your school? What evidence do you see of this? How can you continue to use evaluation as a tool to guide and support change in the reading program?

bility" in making significant changes in the lives of learners. This includes attention to changes, not just within a school, but changes that inform and lead to reform across a system (for example, a school district).

Effective change requires leadership. As a literacy specialist, you may find yourself in the role of change agent. You will be the one stirring the pot, reminding, and keeping everyone on track. The effective change agent finds the right balance between pressuring for change and supporting change (Fullan, 2007; Huberman & Miles, 1984; McLaughlin, 1987). You may find it helpful to involve someone from the "outside" to support the change process. This may be someone who brings expertise in evaluation or someone who brings expertise in the innovation itself. Outside experts offer perspective that can be lost as you are immersed in change. It is important that you not allow your role in leadership to be confused with ownership. The ownership of the program has to rest with those making the changes.

ACCEPTING THE MANDATE FOR CONTINUOUS IMPROVEMENT

Principle 10: *The literacy leader's work is never done because it is focused on the "cultural change" imperative, forming coherence, and realizing a vision.*

The "evaluator's life" represents a way of thinking about professional work in relation to improvement. You learn to puzzle through challenges and possibilities in a systematic way. You see your role as one of constantly linking within and to others outside your immediate setting (Hood, 1982). You are always in the frame of "We can do better." The next set of innovations is already taking shape while the current ones are just settling into place. You learn to enjoy the uncertainty of change, but you also enjoy the systematic, planful, and data-driven aspects of evaluation. You question yourself constantly about your role in the processes of evaluation and change (you become "meta" in reflecting on your own work). You are mindful of the importance of the moral imperative to meet the needs of

learners. You accept and promote issues of social responsibility. You are determined to make new changes fit into a coherent whole. A vision of what can be is at the forefront of your thinking.

CONCLUSION

We began this chapter with the story of Connie and the challenges she faces as a reading specialist at Progreso Elementary School. We have described an evaluation model and evaluation tools that can be used effectively to guide the change process in schools. Hopefully, we have been clear that effective evaluation for improvement is not something that outside "experts" come in and do to you, but rather is a process that we do as a learning community that serves learners. We have offered a set of 10 principles to consider in your role as a literacy specialist to guide the change process. We have emphasized throughout the chapter the notion that change is highly personal. As the program leader in a school, you will develop relationships that will enable you to guide effective change. You will become part of a process of community building that empowers a professional stance toward education. You will become a part of the support system that fulfills the notion that learning is a lifelong process.

How is this really different from your experience as a classroom teacher? Not that much, we would argue. Your experiences as a teacher who used reflection to guide your own professional development will be useful to you as you move from serving students to serving teachers. We close with a set of questions keyed to the 10 guiding principles (see Figure 16.7) that we would encourage you to use as you initiate and move through the processes of evaluation to support change.

REFERENCES

Afflerach, P. (2000). Part IV: Our Plans and Our Future. In J. V. Hoffman, J. F. Baumann, & P. Afflerbach (Eds.), *Balancing principles for elementary reading instruction.* Mahwah, NJ: Erlbaum.

Au, K. H. (2001). Elementary programs in the context of the standards movement. In S. B. Wepner, D. S. Strickland, & J. T. Feeley (Eds.), *Administration and supervision of reading programs* (2nd ed., pp. 42–58). New York: Teachers College Press.

Au, K. H. (2005). Negotiatiing the slippery slope: School change and literacy achievement. *Journal of Literacy Research, 37*(3), 267–288.

Berman, P., & McLaughlin, M. (1978). *Federal programs supporting educational change: Vol. 8. Implementing and sustaining innovations.* Santa Monica, CA: RAND Corporation.

Bush, C. L. (1962). School reading surveys. *The Reading Teacher, 15,* 351–355.

Commission on No Child Left Behind. (2007). *Beyond NCLB: Fulfilling the promise to our nation's children.* Washington, DC: The Aspen Institute.

Duffy, G. G., & Hoffman, J. V. (1999). In pursuit of an illusion: The flawed search for a perfect method. *The Reading Teacher, 53,* 10–16.

Fullan, M. (2005). *Leadership and sustainability: System thinkers in action.* Thousand Oaks, CA: Corwin Press.

Fullan, M. (2007). *The new meaning of educational change* (4th ed.). New York: Teachers College Press.

Fuller, F. F. (1969). Concerns of teachers: A developmental conceptualization. *American Educational Research Journal, 6*(2), 207–226.

Gray, W. S. (1933). *Improving instruction in reading: An experimental study.* Chicago: University of Chicago Press.

Gray, W. S. (1960). The teaching of reading. In C. W. Harris (Ed.), *Encylcopedia of Educational Research* (3rd ed., pp. 1535–1559). New York: Macmillan.

Hall, G. E., George, A. A., & Rutherford, W. L. (1986). *Measuring stages of concern about the innovation: A manual for use of the SOC questionnaire.* Austin, TX: Southwest Educational Development Laboratory.

Hall, G. E., & Hord, S. M. (1987). *Change in schools: Fa-*

cilitating the process. Albany: State University of New York Press.

Hall, G. E., Loucks, S. F., Rutherford, W. L., & Newlove, B. W. (1975). Levels of use of the innovation: a framework for analyzing innovation adoption. *Journal of Teacher Education, 26*(1), 52–56.

Heck, S., Stiegelbauer, S. M., Hall, G. E., & Loucks, S. F. (1975). *Measuring innovation configurations: Procedures and applications.* Austin, TX: Southwest Educational Development Laboratory.

Hoffman, J. V., & Condon, M. (1979). CORE: A Model for Comprehensive Reading Programs. *Journal of Reading, 22*(6), 506–511.

Hood, P. D. (1982). *The role of linking agents in school improvement: A review, analysis, and synthesis of recent major studies.* San Francisco: Far West Laboratory for Educational Research and Development.

Huberman, A. M., & Miles, M. B. (1984). *Innovation up close: How school improvement works.* New York: Plenum.

McLaughlin, M. W. (1987). Learning for experience: Lessons from policy implementation. *Educational Evaluation and Policy Analysis, 9*(2), 171–178.

Southwest Educational Development Lab. (2007). *Concerns Based Adoption Model.* Retrieved May 2007 from http://www.sedl.org/services/cbam.html

Stake, R. (2000). Program evaluation, particularly responsive evaluation. In D. Stufflebeam, G. Madaus, & T. Kellaghan (Eds.), *Evaluation models: Viewpoints on educational and human services evaluation* (2nd ed., pp. 344–362). Boston: Kluwer-Nijhoff.

Steinmetz, A. (2000). The discrepancy evaluation model. In D. Stufflebeam, G. Madaus, & T. Kellaghan (Eds.), *Evaluation Models: Viewpoints on educational and human services evaluation* (2nd ed., pp. 121–143). Boston: Kluwer-Nijhoff.

About the Contributors

Kathyrn H. Au, chief executive officer of SchoolRise, was the first person at the University of Hawaii to hold an endowed chair in education. She is best known for her research on culturally responsive teaching. She has published about 80 articles and chapters, three textbooks, and two edited volumes, including *Multicultural Issues and Literacy Achievement* (2006). Kathy has served as president of the National Reading Conference, vice president of the American Educational Research Association (AERA), and a member of the board of directors of the International Reading Association (IRA). She has won numerous awards, including being elected to IRA's Reading Hall of Fame

Rita M. Bean is a professor of education in the School of Education at the University of Pittsburgh. Current research focuses on the development and evaluation of early literacy reading programs and instruction for struggling readers. She has studied extensively the role of the reading specialist and literacy coach in providing support to teachers to improve classroom reading instruction. Her book, *The Reading Specialist: Leadership for the Classroom, School, and Community*, focuses on the multiple roles of reading specialists in improving reading performance of all students. She has served as a board member for the International Reading Association and as president of the College Reading Association.

Karen Bromley is a Distinguished Teaching Professor in the School of Education at Binghamton University, where she is Director of Graduate Studies and coordinator of the America Reads Program, and teaches literacy courses. Her research interests include classroom practices and strategies for improving reading and writing. She was a third-grade teacher and reading specialist in New York and Maryland, and has written articles for professional journals and several books for teachers on topics related to comprehension, writing, and vocabulary.

Mary Elizabeth Curran is an assistant professor in the Department of Learning and Teaching at the Graduate School of Education at Rutgers University. Her research interests focus on the intersections between language (ESL and world language) education and multicultural education and the need to prepare future teachers to be advocates for their linguistically and culturally diverse students. Some of her publications have appeared in the following journals: *Journal of Teacher Education, Teaching Into Practice*, and *TESOL Quarterly*.

Douglas Fisher is a professor of language and literacy education in the Department of Teacher Education at San Diego State University and a co-director for the Center for the Advancement of Reading at the California State University chancellor's office. He has received an International Reading Association Celebrate Literacy Award and a Christa McAuliffe award for excellence in teacher education. His books include *Creating Literacy-Rich Schools for Adolescents* (with Gay Ivey), *Improving Adolescent Literacy: Strategies at Work* (with Nancy Frey), and *Teaching English Language Learners: A Differentiated Approach* (with Carol Rothenberg). He is a former early intervention specialist, language development specialist, and high school teacher.

James Flood was a Distinguished Professor of Education at San Diego State University. He taught pre-K through secondary school, and was a language arts supervisor and vice principal. He was a Fulbright scholar and president of the National Reading Conference. He coauthored and edited many articles, columns, texts, handbooks, and children's materials, and he codeveloped with Diane Lapp *Content Area Reading and Learning* (2nd ed.)

and *The Handbook of Research on Teaching Literacy Through the Communicative and Visual Arts*. He was a member of California's and IRA's Hall of Fame. Dr. Flood was coeditor of *The California Reader*, and was on IRA's board of directors.

Jennifer L. Goeke began her professional career as an elementary inclusion teacher and received her Ph.D. from the State University of New York at Albany in educational psychology. She is currently an assistant professor of special education in the College of Education and Human Services at Montclair State University. Her research and publications are focused on the development of research-based teacher education pedagogy for inclusion and the development of special educators' instructional thought.

Bill Harp recently retired as professor of language arts and literacy at the University of Massachusetts–Lowell, where he taught courses in the master's and doctoral programs. When he taught the course Organization and Supervision of Reading and Language Programs (both online and in the classroom), he used previous editions of this book as the required text. Bill's teaching experiences range from Head Start through sixth grade, and he has been an elementary school principal and director of programs for the gifted and talented. His most recent publications include *The Informed Reading Teacher: Research-Based Practice* (coauthored with Jo Ann Brewer), and *The Handbook of Literacy Assessment and Evaluation* (3rd ed.).

James V. Hoffman is a professor of language and literacy studies at the University of Texas at Austin where he directs the undergraduate reading specialization program in elementary teacher education. He has served as president of the National Reading Conference and a member of the board of directors of the International Reading Association. He has also served as editor of the *Yearbook of the National Reading Conference* and *The Reading Research Quarterly*. His research interests focus on beginning reading and teacher education.

Barbara A. Kapinus is a senior policy analyst at the National Education Association where she works on policy and programs in literacy, standards, and curriculum. She worked for the Council of Chief State School Officers, the Maryland State Department of Education, and Prince George's County Public Schools as a teacher, reading specialist, and curriculum specialist. She directed the development of the current framework for the National Assessment of Educational Progress (NAEP) in Reading. She has helped to develop the NAEP in Writing for 2011. She served as president of her state reading council, and coedited the assessment column of *The Reading Teacher*.

Julie K. Kidd is an assistant professor in the College of Education and Human Development at George Mason University. She teaches courses in language and literacy development of diverse young learners and literacy assessment and instruction. Previously, she was a reading specialist, lead teacher, and classroom teacher in rural and urban settings. Her research and publications focus on the language, literacy, and cognitive development of young children and on preparing teachers to work with culturally, linguistically, and ability diverse young children and their families. She is currently the editor of *Reading News* and serves on the editorial boards of *Journal of Literacy Research* and *Reading Research and Instruction*.

Linda D. Labbo, professor of language and literacy education at the University of Georgia, researches computer-related early literacy development and preservice teacher preparation. Her work appears in journals such as *Reading Research Quarterly*, *Language Arts*, *Journal of Literacy Research*, and *The Reading Teacher*. Her coedited book, *Handbook of Literacy and Technology: Transformations in a Post-Typographic World* won an American Library Association Award and the Edward Fry Book Award. Other awards include the Technology in Literacy Education (TILE) Award from the International Reading Association's TILE Special Interest Group, Phi Delta Kappa Faculty Research Award, and Ira Aaron Award for Collegiality and Instruction

Diane Lapp is a Distinguished Professor of Education at San Diego State University, and has taught in elementary and middle schools. Her major areas of research are issues related to struggling readers and their families from urban settings. She continues to team teach in public school classrooms. Two of her many publications include *Teaching Reading to Every Child* (4th ed.) and *The Handbook of Research in Teaching the English Language Arts* (2nd ed.), both codeveloped with James Flood. Her many awards include California's and IRA's Hall of Fame and IRA's 1996 Outstanding Teacher Educator of the Year. She is a coeditor of *The California Reader*.

Michael C. McKenna is Thomas G. Jewell Professor of Reading at the University of Virginia. His books include *The Literacy Coach's Handbook* and *Differentiated Reading Instruction*, both coauthored with Sharon Walpole, as well as *Assessment for Reading Instruction*, *Help for Struggling Readers*, *Teaching through Text*, and *Issues and Trends in Literacy Education*. In addition to literacy coaching, his research interests include comprehension in content settings, reading attitudes, technology applications, needs-based instruction, and beginning reading.

Christine A. McKeon is a professor in the Division of Education at Walsh University in North Canton, Ohio, and teaches undergraduate and graduate courses in reading. She is a former elementary school teacher, Title I teacher, and high school reading teacher. She has published in a variety of literacy journals including *The Reading Teacher*, *Journal of Adolescent & Adult Literacy*, and *Reading Research and Instruction* and is coauthor of *Reading and Learning to Read* (5th and 6th eds.). She is also coeditor of *Ohio Reading Teacher*, a journal of the International Reading Association. Her interests include technology, adolescent and adult literacy, and preservice and in-service teacher education.

Kathleen C. Mooney is a doctoral student in literacy, language, and culture at the University of Illinois at Chicago. Her areas of research interest include school literacy reform, early literacy intervention, and literacy leadership in urban school settings. She has worked as a primary-grade teacher and an assistant principal in a large urban school district, and currently serves as a liaison for a school-university partnership focused on improving literacy instruction through professional development.

Maryann Mraz is an assistant professor in the Reading and Elementary Education Department at the University of North Carolina at Charlotte. She is the author of numerous articles, chapters, and instructional materials related to literacy education. Her professional interests include content area reading, the role of the literacy coach, and the professional development of teachers. She is a coauthor of two books: *Teaching Literacy in Sixth Grade* with Karen Wood and *Evidence-Based Instruction in*

Reading: A Professional Development Guide to Phonemic Awareness (in press) with Nancy Padak and Timothy Rasinski.

Diana J. Quatroche, an associate professor and chair of the Department of Elementary, Early, and Special Education in the College of Education at Indiana State University, teaches undergraduate and graduate courses in reading and language arts. In addition to teaching Grades 1 through 5, she has supervised school reading programs and coordinated Title I reading programs. Her research interests include the role of graduate programs in preparing reading specialists, school reading programs, and the effect of professional development on student learning. She has written articles that have appeared in *The Reading Teacher*, *Action in Teacher Education*, *Teaching and Change*, and *Educational Horizons*.

Ruth E. Quiroa is an assistant professor in the reading and language program at National-Louis University in Chicago where she teaches graduate and undergraduate courses in elementary literacy methods, muliticultural children's and adolescent literature, and literacy methods for linguistically diverse students. She completed her Ph.D. in the Department of Curriculum and Instruction at the University of Illinois, Urbana-Champaign. Her research interests include reader response of young Latino children to culturally familiar literature, the role of the teacher in mediating the cultural content of texts, and the trends and issues of Latino-themed children's books.

Taffy E. Raphael coordinates the literacy, language, and culture faculty at the University of Illinois at Chicago. Her research has focused on comprehension strategy instruction (e.g., Question-Answer Relationships), strategy instruction in writing, and frameworks for literacy curriculum and instruction (e.g., Book Club Plus). She has studied teacher learning, professional development, and school literacy reform. She directs Partnership READ, a school-university partnership to improve literacy instruction through professional development, recognized by AACTE's 2006 Best Practices Award for Effective Partnerships. She was selected for the IRA's Reading Hall of Fame in 2002.

Kristen D. Ritchey is an assistant professor of special education in the School of Education,

University of Delaware. She holds a Ph.D. from the University of Maryland. Her research interests include early identification and intervention of reading and writing disabilities and responsiveness to instruction as a model of identifying students with learning disabilities.

Misty Sailors is an assistant professor of literacy education in the Department of Interdisciplinary Learning and Teaching in the College of Education and Human Development at the University of Texas at San Antonio. She has worked in South Africa with classroom teachers for several years and is overseeing the development of supplementary reading and content area materials for elementary learners in conjunction with the Republic of South Africa Department of Education and several South African nongovernmental organizations. Her research interests focus on comprehension instruction, the professional development of teachers, and the importance of print-rich environments for literacy development.

Dorothy S. Strickland is the Samuel DeWitt Proctor Professor of Education at Rutgers University. A former classroom teacher and learning disabilities specialist, her research interests include children's early language and literacy development and intervention strategies for low-achieving students. She is a past president of both the International Reading Association and the Reading Hall of Fame. She is recipient of IRA's Outstanding Teacher Educator of Reading Award and the National Council of Teachers of English Award as Outstanding Educator in the Language Arts. Her most recent publications include *Bridging the Literacy Achievement Gap, Grades 4–12*, and *Improving Reading Achievement Through Professional Development*.

Liqing Tao is currently an associate professor of literacy education at the College of Staten Island in New York City, where he teaches literacy methods at both undergraduate and graduate levels and research seminars at graduate level. He has also been a member of the doctoral faculty at the Graduate Center of City University of New York. His main research interests are in technology application in literacy education, historical studies of literacy practices in ancient China, and orthographical and textual effects on Chinese language acquisition.

William H. Teale is professor of education at the University of Illinois at Chicago. Author of over one hundred publications, his work has focused on early literacy learning, the intersection of technology and literacy education, and children's and young adult literature. He has served as consultant to school districts, public libraries, and other education organizations in the United States, as well as internationally. He is a former editor of *Language Arts* and a member of the Reading Hall of Fame.

Jo Anne L. Vacca is a professor emeritus and former chair of the Department of Teaching, Leadership, and Curriculum Studies at Kent State University. She has coauthored two multiple-edition books in the field of literacy education. Her most recent publications include *Reading and Learning to Read* (6th ed.) with Richard T. Vacca, Mary Gove, Linda Burkey, Lisa Lenhart, and Chris McKeon and *Content Area Reading* (9th ed.) with Richard T. Vacca.

Richard T. Vacca is a professor emeritus from Kent State University. He currently works with school districts and universities throughout the United States on issues related to adolescent literacy and learning. He is the author of *Content Area Reading: Literacy and Learning Across the Curriculum*, first published in 1981 and currently in its 9th edition. He has been a member of the board of directors of both the College Reading Association and the International Reading Association, and has served as president of the International Reading Association.

Jean Payne Vintinner is a doctoral student and full-time instructor in the Department of Reading and Elementary Education at the University of North Carolina at Charlotte. A former high school English and reading teacher, her academic interests include adolescent literacy, content area reading, and motivating struggling readers.

Sharon Walpole, an associate professor at the University of Delaware, teaches undergraduate courses on language and literacy development in kindergarten and first grade, master's courses on content area reading instruction and on organization and supervision of the reading program, and doctoral seminars on literacy and educational policy. She has extensive school-based experience, including high school teaching and elementary school administration. She has also been involved in federally funded and homegrown schoolwide reform projects, and has been studying the design and effects of schoolwide reforms, particularly those involving literacy coaches. She is coauthor with Michael

McKenna of *The Literacy Coach's Handbook* and *Differentiated Reading Instruction: Strategies for the Primary Grades*.

Shelley B. Wepner is a professor and the dean at the School of Education of Manhattanville College. She was a reading teacher/specialist, Title I teacher, and K–8 curriculum supervisor. She has published over one hundred articles, book chapters, and books related to literacy and technology, connections between K–12 education and higher education, and leadership skills for effectively supporting teacher education and literacy development. She has also published award-winning educational software for literacy development. Her most recent book (co-edited with Linda Gambrell) is *Beating the Odds: Getting Published in the Field of Literacy*.

Junko Yokota is a professor of reading and language and director of the Center for Teaching through Children's Books at National-Louis University in Chicago. For 10 years, she was a classroom teacher and school librarian. Her publications include articles and review columns, the editing of *Kaleidoscope: A Multicultural Booklist for Grades K–8* (3rd ed.), and coauthoring of *Children's Books in Children's Hands* (3rd ed.). She served on the Caldecott and Newbery Award Committees, chaired the Batchelder Award Committee, and was president of the United States Board on Books for Young People. She received the Virginia Hamilton Award for Contribution to Multicultural Literature, and served on the 2006 IBBY Hans Christian Andersen Award Jury.

Index